TEACH
LIKE A
CHAMPION
2.0

TEACH
LIKE A
CHAMPION
2.0

62 Techniques that Put Students on the Path to College

DOUG LEMOV

Foreword by Norman Atkins

Uncommon Schools | Change History.

A Wiley Brand

Cover Design: Wiley
Cover Photographs: Jacob Krupnick
Author photo: Timothy Raab & Northern Photo

Published by Jossey-Bass
A Wiley Brand
One Montgomery Street, Suite 1200, San Francisco, CA 94104-4594 www.josseybass.com

Jossey-Bass books and products are available through most bookstores. To contact Jossey-Bass directly call our Customer Care Department within the U.S. at 800-956-7739, outside the U.S. at 317-572-3986, or fax 317-572-4002.

For more information about Wiley products, visit **www.wiley.com**.

Library of Congress Cataloging-in-Publication Data is on file.
ISBN 978-1-118-90185-4 (pbk.)
ISBN 978-1-118-89879-6 (ebk.)
ISBN 978-1-118-89862-8 (ebk.)

Printed in the United States of America
SECOND EDITION
PB Printing 10 9 8 7 6 5 4 3 2 1

Contents

PART 1   Check for Understanding

PART 3   Ratio

PART 4   Five Principles of Classroom Culture

Video Contents

For information on accessing the video clips, see How to Access the Video Contents near the end of the book.

Introduction

Clip	Technique		Description
48	Strategic Investment: From Procedure to Routine		**Paper Passing (Back in Ten):** Doug McCurry encourages students to pass in their papers faster and faster with Positive Framing.

Gathering Data on Student Mastery (Chapter 1)

Clip	Primary Technique	Additional Techniques	Description
1	Reject Self-Report	Culture of Error	**Spelling Words:** Amy Youngman collects data on student mastery by quickly scanning each student's answer to see whether it is correct.
2	Standardize the Format	Culture of Error, Tracking, Not Watching	**Disposition:** Meaghan Reuler immediately identifies student misunderstandings thanks to materials that make mistakes easy to find—and to some careful looking.

Clip	Primary Technique	Additional Techniques	Description
3	Show Me	Excavate Error	**Good Morning, Williams:** Bryan Belanger uses hand signals to gauge student mastery. He responds quickly in consideration of the extent of the errors.
4	Show Me	Culture of Error	**Go to IP:** Jon Bogard uses Show Me to identify and correct common errors. Some students review; some earn independent practice.
5	Affirmative Checking	Culture of Error, Name the Steps, 100% Cycle	**Here's the Deal:** Bob Zimmerli sets "checkpoints" where students must check their answers with him before proceeding to more difficult problems.
6	Affirmative Checking	Do It Again, Positive Framing	**Green Sticky Note:** Hilary Lewis uses a "ticket" system to check students' work before they move on to independent practice.

Acting on the Data and the Culture of Error (Chapter 2)

Clip	Primary Technique	Additional Techniques	Description
7	Culture of Error	Show Me	**Who Changed Their Mind:** Katie Bellucci normalizes error by encouraging students who corrected their work to raise their hands and "be proud!"
8	Culture of Error		**Intros:** Jason Armstrong tells students he "expects some disagreement" and doesn't care for now what the right answer is.

Setting High Academic Expectations (Chapter 3)

Clip	Primary Technique	Additional Techniques	Description
9	No Opt Out	Emotional Constancy	**Immigrant:** David Javsicas stays steady at the helm and sticks with a student who declines to answer a question.
10	No Opt Out		**Negative Five Halves:** Derek Pollak solicits help from the class when a student is very near to a correct answer.
11	No Opt Out	Cold Call, Do It Again	**Little Brown Insects:** Jamie Davidson gets a student to improve her expression in reading after another student models what it means to "snap."
12	No Opt Out	Targeted Questioning, Culture of Error	**Clever Fox:** Shadell Purefoy (Noel) asks a student to repeat a correct answer after she's unable to answer the first time.
13	Right Is Right		**Fabric:** Grace Ghazzawi holds out for an all-the-way-right answer.
14	Right Is Right		**Aunt Alexandra:** Maggie Johnson pushes students to use precise language to describe a particular scene.
15	Right Is Right	Positive Framing	**Volume:** Jason Armstrong holds out for a thorough definition of volume after students present formulas and partial definitions.
16	Stretch It		**Well Said:** Art Worrell stretches the original student and then begins stretching other students to build a rigorous classroom culture.
17	Format Matters		**"Gots to Be?":** Darryl Williams actively reinforces the language of opportunity by correcting informal phrases.
18	Format Matters		**Hither:** Beth Verrilli asks a student for more collegiate language.

Lesson Structure (Chapter 5)

Clip	Primary Technique	Additional Techniques	Description
19	Control the Game		**Control the Game:** Jessica Bracey keeps durations short and unpredictable, moving the reading around the room to involve lots of students.
20	Control the Game		**Eyes In:** Eric Snider balances student reading with his own modeling to build a culture of expressive reading.
21	Circulate		**Read and Annotate:** Domari Dickinson and Rue Ratray demonstrate the fundamentals of Circulate.

Pacing (Chapter 6)

Clip	Primary Technique	Additional Techniques	Description
22	Change the Pace	Show Me	**Talk to Me:** Erin Michels quickens classroom pace by shifting deftly among different styles of participation.
23	Change the Pace	Everybody Writes, Habits of Discussion	**Listen, Things Have Changed:** Jessica Bracey maintains a steady pace in her reading class by varying activities.
24	Brighten Lines		**Clean Start/Clean Finish Montage:** Seven teachers show examples of Brighten Lines by cleanly beginning and ending exercises.
25	All Hands		**Bright Hands:** Colleen Driggs shows her students how to raise their hands for a new question and lower them when someone else is called on.

Clip	Primary Technique	Additional Techniques	Description
26	Work the Clock		**You're My Brain:** Deena Bernett uses a stopwatch projection to allot specific amounts of time for certain activities.
27	Change the Pace	Brighten Lines	**Pencils Up:** Ashley Hinton puts together a number of pacing techniques to keep her class moving.

Building Ratio Through Questioning (Chapter 7)

Clip	Primary Technique	Additional Techniques	Description
28	Cold Call		**I Saw a Lot of Thought:** Gary Lauderdale's consistent Cold Calling keeps his students focused on the math.
29	Wait Time		**Wait Time Montage:** Maggie Johnson gives students think time, encouraging more reluctant scholars to participate.
30	Wait Time		**Continental Congress:** Boris Zarkhi narrates hands, and tells his students to put their hands down to make full use of the Wait Time he gives them
31	Wait Time		**Think Time:** Colleen Driggs encourages students to go back and look at their notes during think time.
32	Cold Call		**What Word:** Hannah Lofthus establishes a brisk rhythm with the way that she Cold Calls.

Clip	Primary Technique	Additional Techniques	Description
33	Cold Call		**Hot Call:** Colleen Driggs explains how she will "Hot Call," as an opportunity for students to show they are "on fire."
34	Cold Call		**In Your Mind:** Jon Bogard makes his Cold Calls predictable and positive, including calling on one student whose "hand was up in [her] mind."
35	Call and Response		**Birthdays:** Janelle Austin keeps her students' responses sharp.
36	Call and Response		**Read to Us:** Jennifer Trapp uses Call and Response to reinforce note-taking skills, grammar rules, and difficult pronunciations.
37	Pepper	Cold Call	**Amendments:** Art Worrell Peppers his classroom with questions about constitutional amendments.

Building Ratio Through Writing (Chapter 8)

Clip	Primary Technique	Additional Techniques	Description
38	Everybody Writes		**Troy:** Gillian Cartwright sets up rigorous student-driven discussions with eighteen minutes of pre-thinking in writing. Yes, eighteen minutes!
39	Everybody Writes		**Sophisticate It:** Rachel Coffin ups the ratio in her classroom by challenging students to complete a sentence that begins with a complex starter.

Clip	Primary Technique	Additional Techniques	Description
40	Everybody Writes		***Romeo and Juliet:*** Lauren Latto teaches her students to sustain their focus in writing for longer periods.
41	Show Call		**Beautiful Formula:** Paul Powell normalizes the process of "good to great" and sends a very clear message about accountability for written work by Show Calling exemplary work.
42	Show Call	Culture of Error	**Boxes:** Katie McNickle Show Calls a number of different students' work to show different approaches to solving the same problem.

Building Ratio Through Discussion (Chapter 9)

Clip	Primary Technique	Additional Techniques	Description
43	Habits of Discussion		**Master of the House:** Yasmin Vargas uses a series of questions and nonverbals to encourage productive discussion.
44	Turn and Talk		**Little Guy:** Rue Ratray uses a variety of methods to keep his Turn and Talks engaging for his students.
45	Turn and Talk		**Turn and Talk Montage:** Eric Snider uses a series of efficient prompts and follow-ups to keep his Turn and Talks accountable and efficient.
46	Turn and Talk		**Show Not Tell:** Laura Fern uses a number of different techniques to ensure efficiency, consistency, and rigor in her Turn and Talks.

Systems and Routines (Chapter 10)

Clip	Primary Technique	Additional Techniques	Description
47	Strategic Investment: From Procedure to Routine		**Thank You for Knowing What to Do:** Stephen Chiger delegates roles to create a culture of autonomy in his classroom.
48	Strategic Investment: From Procedure to Routine		**Paper Passing (Back in Ten):** Doug McCurry encourages students to pass in their papers faster and faster with Positive Framing.
49	Strategic Investment: From Procedure to Routine		**Before and After: "Group A" and "Stand Up":** Nikki Bowen works through procedures with her students until they become second nature and support student autonomy.
50	Strategic Investment: From Procedure to Routine		**Ben Franklin:** Lauren Moyle's class transitions from desks to the floor by singing a song about the continents.
51	Do It Again		**Faster:** Sarah Ott teaches her kindergarteners how to do classroom tasks such as coming together on her signal.

High Behavioral Expectations (Chapter 11)

Clip	Primary Technique	Additional Techniques	Description
52	This clip demonstrates what a culture of high behavioral expectations looks like at maturity.		**Perimeter:** Erin Michels demonstrates a number of high behavioral expectations in a lesson using "triangulous units."

Clip	Primary Technique	Additional Techniques	Description
53	100%, Part 1: Radar/Be Seen Looking		**Grab Bag:** Rachel King moves to Pastore's Perch and scans the room at the moment she wants to monitor her class more closely.
54	100%, Part 1: Radar/Be Seen Looking		**Crisp Sound of a Rip:** Patrick Pastore demonstrates effective use of Pastore's Perch.
55	100%, Part 1: Radar/Be Seen Looking	Pepper	**As a Decimal:** Michael Rubino scans consistently and uses some "moves" to intimate that he is looking carefully.
56	100%, Part 2: Make Compliance Visible	Show Me	**Show What You Know:** Amy Youngman makes compliance visible with visible commands like "pen caps on."
57	100%, Part 2: Make Compliance Visible		**Really Clever:** Ashley Hinton scans the classroom even while she works with individual students. Her vigilance pays off with a happy classroom.
58	100%, Part 3: Least Invasive Intervention		**Montage:** Ashley Hinton demonstrates a series of subtle nonverbal interventions used to keep her class focused.
59	100%, Part 3: Least Invasive Intervention		**I Need a Couple SLANTs:** Alexandra Bronson subtly resets her whole class via a positive group correction.
60	100%, Part 3: Least Invasive Intervention		**You Know Who You Are, and Puritans:** Bob Zimmerli and Laura Brandt demonstrate different takes on anonymous individual correction.
61	100%, Part 3: Least Invasive Intervention		**Eyes on the Speaker:** Jaimie Brillante demonstrates private individual correction by whispering to a student.

Clip	Primary Technique	Additional Techniques	Description
62	100%, Part 3: Least Invasive Intervention		**Don't Miss It:** Jason Armstrong uses a whisper correction to make public corrections feel private.
63	100%, Part 3: Least Invasive Intervention		**Nonverbals Montage:** Lucy Boyd uses a variety of different nonverbal interventions to keep her students hard at work during discussion.
64	100%, Part 4: Firm Calm Finesse		**Fix How You're Sitting:** Channa Comer demonstrates Firm Calm Finesse as her class gets restless.
65	100%, Part 5: Art of the Consequence		**Regular Polygon:** Ana O'Neil delivers two consequences with grace and calm, and encourages students to get back in the game.
66	100%, Part 5: Art of the Consequence	Culture of Error	**Examine:** Bridget McElduff demonstrates a number of techniques while giving a productive consequence.
67	Strong Voice		**Inappropriate Time:** Christy Lundy uses *do not engage* in a situation every teacher has seen some version of.
68	Strong Voice		**Draw My Line:** Jessica Merrill-Brown uses the *self-interrupt* to keep the full attention of her class even while she's sitting down.
69	Strong Voice		**Middle School:** Mike Taubman uses a series of *self-interrupts* to ensure student focus.

Building Character and Trust (Chapter 12)

Clip	Primary Technique	Additional Techniques	Description
70	Positive Framing		**Positive Framing Montage:** Janelle Austin demonstrates nearly a dozen ways to narrate the positive.
71	Precise Praise		**Symmetry:** Hilary Lewis gives positive reinforcement that provides students a model for success.
72	Precise Praise		**Looking Sharp:** David Javsicas privately and genuinely praises replicable student actions.
73	Precise Praise		**Kudos:** Stephen Chiger doubles back to help a student better see how and why she was successful.
74	Joy Factor		**Phantom of the Opera:** Roberto de Leòn makes the act of reading joyful.
75	Joy Factor		**Simón Bolívar:** Taylor Delhagen lightens the mood by getting in touch with the joyful side of Simón Bolívar.

For Mike and Penny Lemov,

my first teachers

Foreword

In 1983, a landmark US education commission famously declared that our "nation [is] at risk," that "a rising tide of mediocrity … threatens our very future," and that we should consider our woeful K–12 performance a self-imposed "act of war." With confidence in established educational institutions at an all-time low, various states invited teachers and fellow citizens to offer new ideas, new approaches, and new schools that might help rebuild a broken system. The charter schools that emerged, beginning in 1991, were to serve as a research-and-development arm of public education.

Over the past quarter century, a new generation of idealists has answered that trumpet blast for reform, mostly in cities where the country has ignored *millions* of children who live in poverty and attend ineffective, inhospitable, unhappy schools. To build schools and classrooms of their own making, these reformers scaled the walls of bureaucracy, and then struggled with the very challenges that plagued their forebears. But, as *pragmatic* idealists, they didn't chase educational equity in the abstract. They pursued it relentlessly as instructional problem-solvers in a mission-driven learning community.

Suddenly, classroom doors — for decades, sadly and oddly closed to outsiders and colleagues alike — flew open. Looking for models to learn from and copy, legions flocked to the classrooms of the most skillful teachers, whose students were joyfully engaged, academically focused, working together as teams, and generating jaw-dropping results.

Of those who studied outlier classrooms, one tall, unassuming teacher and leader — Doug Lemov — camped out longer than all the rest. He saw the significance of instructional brush strokes that most of us either missed or didn't appreciate: how teachers circulated, engaged all students, targeted their questions, framed the positive, worked the clock, waited strategically for, and then stretched out student answers.

Lemov had eyes to see the details of the well-delivered lesson, *and* a heart to love and celebrate teachers for their impact on students' life trajectories. He filled volumes of black notebooks with enthusiastic, illegible scrawls that slowly transmogrified into sticky phrases and ideas. Then, before anyone else, he sent cameras into classrooms to capture exemplary practices on video.

After watching the slow-motion replay of instructional moves, he converted his field notes into a taxonomy of effective teaching practices—initially for his private use, then for teachers across the network we founded, Uncommon Schools, and then as the basis for training thousands of teachers and principals nationwide. At a certain point—when he'd produced something like the 28th version—a bunch of us pressed him to publish; any hesitancy on Lemov's part was born of humility, a belief that his playbook was still *in process*.

So he was unprepared for what happened four years ago: hundreds of thousands of copies of his painstakingly assembled taxonomy, the first edition of this book, *flew* from bookstore warehouses with blazing speed, reaching about a quarter of America's teachers across all types of schools—public, independent, parochial, urban, suburban, rural. They found actionable, accessible guidance that they could use, not merely to set up their classrooms or plan their lessons, but *during* the act of teaching. Novice teachers adopted surefire routines to manage their classrooms, create a joyful culture, and build a productive platform for learning. More experienced teachers appreciated that Lemov "invented a new language of American teaching," as Elizabeth Green explains in *Building a Better Teacher*. His was *their* language, full of memorable catchphrases, and supplemented by pictures and video of real teachers, that helped them go from "good to great." In a subsequent volume, *Practice Perfect*, Lemov and his colleagues encouraged teachers to rehearse techniques and strategies before improvising in front of students.

Meanwhile, more than 18,000 principals and teachers have participated in Lemov's trainings through Uncommon Schools, and thousands more have learned his approach through Relay Graduate School of Education, which we founded, in part, to share elements of effective teaching that he codified. I've watched his work catch on in Brazil, India, and South Africa. The Queen of Jordan commissioned an Arabic translation, while teachers in China, Korea, Australia, Holland, England, and other countries have brought *Teaching Like a Champion (TLAC)* into their classrooms.

A funny thing happened on the way to *TLAC* becoming a global phenomenon. As teachers have learned from Lemov, he has learned from them. Over the past decade, he has probably visited 10,000 classrooms and watched 10,000 video clips. Since *TLAC*'s publication, he's observed countless teachers improve, adapt, and reshape the techniques he'd described. One of my favorite techniques is what Lemov named "the culture of error," in which teachers make it safe for students to show their mistakes, rather than hide them. By publishing the first edition when he did, Lemov gained four years of feedback that helped refine his thinking, his writing, and his taxonomy.

This culture, of course, leads ineluctably to a 2.0 edition, the one you now hold in your hands. Fans of the first edition will undoubtedly find in this one the same core techniques—in even sharper form. What's new, right at the start of the 2.0 version, is a much deeper, more specific treatment on how to "check for understanding." There's also new material on students' writing life, as well as on shifting the ratio of cognitive work from the teacher to students. In keeping with Common Core State Standards—a promising development that has raised the instructional bar across the land—Lemov's work, more than ever before, pushes teachers to ask *rigorous* questions and engage students in more *rigorous* learning.

For all of these reasons, I suspect that a broader set of teachers, with a wider range of styles, voices, and approaches, will see themselves in this book. They will discover new techniques they can employ in their classrooms, and encounter new language that will call them to be better still. At the same time, many will practice, adapt, and invent the next set of techniques that will emerge in the decades ahead. May the circle of champion teachers grow wider, may the community of practice enlarge, and may you be part of the generation of teachers who use and develop tools that will—as we say at Uncommon Schools—change history.

November, 2014   Norman Atkins

*Norman Atkins is Co-Founder
and President of Relay GSE and
Founder of Uncommon Schools*

Acknowledgments

My first thank you has to be to teachers, starting with my own, of whom there were many excellent ones who guided and shaped my thinking from kindergarten through graduate school. Ms. Cosgrove (Wood Acres Elementary) unlocked the door of math for me in third grade. In seventh grade, Mr. Lewis (Western Junior High School) taught me to write a thesis paragraph "the right way" — he was unapologetic on this point. Once mastered, this skill pretty much got me through college. In twelfth grade, I wisely determined that reading *Canterbury Tales* in history was unnecessary until Mr. Gilhool (Walt Whitman High School) sent me scrambling through the text to find out whether people in the Middle Ages were really and actually all that funny.

There were teachers I loved then — Ms. Cosby, whom I returned to visit for years after — and teachers like straitlaced, exacting Mr. Simmons, who could be a bit starchy, maybe, and had the temerity to think that English class should be text intensive, and interpretations precise. He did not offer the sorts of high jinks Young Lemov required of his favorites, alas, so I don't recall seeing or speaking with him again, though I have thought of him perhaps a hundred times since realizing that it was he, in the end, who taught me to read a piece of literature with focus and rigor.

But which teacher was it who handed me *The Old Man and the Sea*? Hemingway's novel was the first book that ever truly spoke to me. There was the night when my parents announced we were going out to dinner. I remember in which chair I was sitting when I said, no, I thought I'd stay home and read. I might have been eleven or twelve years old; the book was a challenge for me, but there had been a teacher whose expectations were high, and the book found its way into my hands, though ironically and altogether fittingly as a reflection on the work of teachers, I do not recall what teacher it was who thought to give me that book.

My job now, of course, is to learn from teachers — or, more precisely, to continue learning from teachers. The topics have shifted, but the principle is the same, and there are again so many teachers who in allowing me to observe their work have taught me deep and durable things, some of which I recognized in the moment and some that struck me only later — sometimes much later. The lessons they offered are the substance of this book, though inevitably there are many who go unnamed, so I will take this opportunity to thank all of the teachers I've had the honor to observe and study as a colleague and as a sometimes bothersome outsider. Sharing the things I learned from them is a huge responsibility. I hope I got at least part of it right. In any case, thank you.

When I talk about what "I've" learned, I am really talking about what "we've" learned, with the "we" referring to my colleagues on the Uncommon Schools Teach Like a Champion team: John Costello, Dan Cotton, Colleen Driggs, Joaquin Hernandez, Jen Kim, Tracey Koren, Rob Richard, and Erica Woolway. Their constant insights about teaching, not to mention their appreciation for and love of its craft, help me strive to do my job as well as they do theirs. Most of the better ideas are probably theirs, though you might not guess it — a merrier band there never was. A special shout-out for two members of the team in particular: Rob, who directs the Teach Like a Champion team's video work and who managed the preparation of the seventy-five videos in this book as a sort of side project amid the dizzying complexity of the rest of his work; and Joaquin "Jo Jo" Hernandez, who drafted and prepared materials for major portions of this book with wisdom and clarity. Rob and Joaquin have the inconceivable skill of being able to type in the car, so never, I am sure, has so much yeoman work been accomplished on the New York State Thruway.

Other colleagues at Uncommon Schools — our school leaders, my fellow managing directors, the organization's leadership from CEO Brett Peiser down, and the many folks who coordinate our work at the home office — have been an additional source of knowledge about teaching. This is true both in terms of their reflections on teaching and because they have built an organization that's full of great teaching and teachers, and this is so because, at its core, it's an organization *about* great teaching and teachers most of all. I'm proud to be a part of Uncommon, where my biggest anxiety is to make sure my work is worthy of my colleagues.

Writing can be a slow process, though I'm not sure that excuses just how slow I sometimes was with the manuscript for this book, so I'm grateful for the insight and patience of Kate Gagnon, my editor at Jossey-Bass, who first conceived of the book and unflappably saw it through to reality. She and the rest of the team at Wiley, including Debra Hunter and Lesley Iura, have been supportive of this book in a thousand ways and have constantly endeavored to see its potential to help teachers even if I didn't have time to put all of those ideas into action. I also note humbly that for all my excitement about the revised version of this book, there would be no volume in your hands without the constant guidance of development editor Nic Albert, whose support included the offering of nuanced insight about structure and phrasing as well as management of a dozen detailed tasks for which there was no space in my own brain.

It was only recently that I began to think of myself as a writer by profession, and this has come about thanks to the guiding influence of Rafe Sagalyn, who is more thought-partner than agent, and who helps me understand and contextualize my work and how to make it relevant and useful to people. I am grateful to have the guidance of someone so wise whose goal is to help me find my own vision of my writing and bring it to reality.

This book, and the larger teacher training project of which it is a part, would have been impossible without the generous support and guidance of the Carnegie Corporation of New York and the Kern Family Foundation.

Then there is Norman Atkins, who likes to start up audacious projects, founding Newark's North Star Academy, then Uncommon Schools, then Relay Graduate School of Education.

Norman wills projects into being when he believes they can help eliminate the gap between the achievement levels of poor and privileged students. And he got it into his head that one of those projects was the "taxonomy," the impromptu list I was making of what great teachers did in their classrooms. It should be a book, Norm advised. I said no, but Norman nagged me. For every excuse, he had a solution, and in the end I knew it would be easier to write the thing than to battle Norman's will, so it is fitting that I offer my sincere thanks and gratitude to Norman for his tenacity, faith, and support.

My three beloved children remind me daily of the commitment teachers and schools make to all parents when they set out to educate their children. They provide me with intense motivation to do my best work in my day job. If I ever tire, I only have to think of how much I cherish and genuinely enjoy my children's company in every moment we are together. This, I am aware, is a rare and true gift brought about by the very funny, thoughtful, independent spirit in each of them. I am proud of them and who they are—especially in light of my many gaffes and miscalculations, some of which (readers who are teachers will surely commiserate here) have been spectacularly public and all of which they have borne with grace. When I'm traveling, there is no hardship I will not endure if it allows me, come evening, to find myself beside them at the dinner table or at the very least bidding them a most adoring goodnight.

Finally, my biggest debt of all is to my wife, Lisa, with whom I share the responsibility for and joy in the most important work I will ever do: raising those children. She has for several years now done much of my "half" of the parenting and such so that I could write. That said, thanking Lisa for her help with this book is a bit like thanking the sun. Sure, there would be no book without light to write by, but it's hard to feel as if the thank you doesn't trivialize a gift of such magnitude. Still, you gotta try. So, Lisa, thank you for the hours squeezed out of Sunday mornings and Tuesday nights and all the extra work this meant for you. Thank you for talking ideas through with me while handing snacks and drinks into the backseat. And most of all, thank you for the sunshine.

The Author

Doug Lemov is a managing director of Uncommon Schools and leads its Teach Like a Champion team, designing and implementing teacher training based on the study of high-performing teachers. He was formerly the managing director for Uncommon's upstate New York schools. Before that he was vice president for accountability at the State University of New York Charter Schools Institute and was a founder, teacher, and principal of the Academy of the Pacific Rim charter school in Boston. He has taught English and history at the university, high school, and middle school levels. He holds a BA from Hamilton College, an MA from Indiana University, and an MBA from the Harvard Business School. Visit him at www.teachlikeachampion.com.

About Uncommon Schools

At Uncommon Schools, our mission is to start and manage outstanding urban public schools that close the achievement gap and prepare low-income scholars to graduate from college. For nearly twenty years, through trial, error, and adjustment, we have learned countless lessons about what works in classrooms. Not surprisingly, we have found that success in the classroom is closely linked to our ability to hire, develop, and retain great teachers and leaders. That has prompted us to invest heavily in training educators and building systems that help leaders to lead, teachers to teach, and students to learn. We are passionate about finding new ways for our scholars to learn more today than they did yesterday, and to do so, we work hard to ensure that every minute matters.

We know that many educators, schools, and school systems are interested in the same things we are interested in — practical solutions for classrooms and schools that work, that can be performed at scale, and that are accessible to anyone. We are fortunate to have had the opportunity to observe and learn from outstanding educators — both within our schools and from across the United States — who help all students achieve at high levels. Watching these educators at work has allowed us to identify, codify, and film concrete and practical findings about great instruction. We have been excited to share these findings in such books as *Teach Like a Champion* (and the companion *Field Guide*), *Practice Perfect*, *Driven by Data*, *Leverage Leadership*, and *Great Habits, Great Readers*.

Since the release of the original *Teach Like a Champion*, Doug Lemov and Uncommon's Teach Like a Champion (TLAC) team have continued to study educators who are generating remarkable results across Uncommon, at partner organizations, and at schools throughout the country. Through countless hours of observation and analysis,

Doug and the TLAC team have further refined and codified the tangible best practices that the most effective teachers have in common. *Teach Like a Champion 2.0* builds off the groundbreaking work of the original *Teach Like a Champion* book and shares it with teachers and leaders who are committed to changing the trajectory of students' lives.

We thank Doug and the entire TLAC team for their tireless and insightful efforts to support teachers everywhere. We hope our efforts to share what we have learned will help you, your scholars, and our collective communities.

Brett Peiser
Chief Executive Officer
Uncommon Schools

Uncommon Schools is a nonprofit network of 42 urban public charter schools that prepare more than twelve thousand low-income K–12 students in New York, New Jersey, and Massachusetts to graduate from college. A 2013 CREDO study found that for low-income students who attend Uncommon Schools, Uncommon "completely cancel[s] out the negative effect associated with being a student in poverty." Uncommon Schools was also named the winner of the national 2013 Broad Prize for Public Charter Schools for demonstrating "the most outstanding overall student performance and improvement in the nation in recent years while reducing achievement gaps for low-income students and students of color." To learn more about Uncommon Schools, please visit our website at http://www.uncommonschools.org. You can also follow us on Facebook at www.facebook.com/uncommonschools, and on Twitter and Instagram at @uncommonschools.

The Art of Teaching and Its Tools

Great teaching is an art. In the other arts — painting, sculpture, the writing of novels — great masters leverage a proficiency with basic tools to transform the rawest of materials (stone, paper, ink) into the most valued assets in society. This alchemy is all the more astounding because the tools often appear unremarkable to others. Who would look at a chisel, a mallet, and a file and imagine them producing Michelangelo's *David*?

Great art relies on the mastery and application of foundational skills, learned through diligent study — "craftsmanship," if you will. You learn to strike a chisel with a mallet and refine the skill with time, learning at what angle to strike the chisel and how tightly to hold it. Someday, perhaps years later, observers may assess the philosophy expressed by what you create, but far more important than any theory is your proficiency with the lowly chisel. True, not everyone who learns to drive a chisel will create a *David*, but neither can anyone who *fails* to master the tool do much more than make marks on rocks.

Every artist — teachers included — is an artisan whose task is to study a set of tools and unlock the secrets of their use. A chisel appears mundane, but the more you understand it, the more it guides you to see what is possible. Rounding a contour with unexpected smoothness, the chisel causes you to realize, suddenly, that you could bring added subtlety to a facial expression, more tension to the muscles of the figure you are sculpting, and this changes your vision for it. Mastery of tools does not just *allow* creation; it *informs* it. The process is often far from glamorous; an artist's life is a tradesman's life, really, characterized by calluses and stone dust, requiring diligence and humility, but its rewards are immense. It is a worthy life's work.

Traveling abroad during my junior year in college, I saw Picasso's school notebooks on display at the Picasso Museum in Barcelona. What I remember best are the sketches filling the margins of his pages. These weren't sketchbooks, mind you. These were notebooks like those every student keeps of notes from lectures. The tiny sketches memorialized a teacher's face or Picasso's own hand grasping a pencil, with perfect perspective, line, and shading. I had always thought Picasso's work was about abstraction, about a way of thinking that rendered the ability to draw accurately and realistically irrelevant. His sketches told another story, bearing witness to his mastery of fundamentals and constant drive to refine his skills. Even in the stray moments of his schooling, he was honing the building blocks of his technique. He was an artisan first and then an artist, as the fact that he filled, by one count, 178 sketchbooks in his life further attests.

This book is about the tools of the teaching craft. More specifically, it's about the tools necessary for success in the most important part of the field: teaching in public schools, primarily those in the inner city, that serve students born to poverty and, too often, to a rapidly closing window of opportunity. The price of failure there is high and the challenges immense. Teachers there often work in a crucible where our society's failures are paramount and self-evident, and sometimes seem nearly overwhelming. Still, every day in every neighborhood on the near or the far edge of hope, there are teachers who without much fanfare take the students who others say "can't"—can't read great literature, can't do algebra or calculus, can't and don't want to learn—and turn them into scholars who can. Impossibly, we often don't know who those teachers are, but they are everywhere—generally laboring unnoticed down the hall from one of the 50 percent of new hires in urban districts who leave teaching within their first three years. Think about that: It turns out that for those struggling new teachers, solutions to the challenges that will ultimately drive them out of the profession flourish just a few yards away. It turns out that for students, walking into the right classroom can pry the doors of opportunity back open. The problem is that we aren't serious enough about learning from the teachers who can provide these answers.

Consider Zenaida Tan, whom Jason Felch of the *Los Angeles Times* profiled in 2010 after data culled from the Los Angeles Unified School District revealed that over a seven-year period, Tan had been one of the top handful of teachers in the city, her students making dramatically larger gains than those of the average teacher year after year. "By the LAUSD's measure," Felch wrote, "Tan simply 'meets standard performance,' as virtually all district teachers do—evaluators' only other option is 'below standard performance.' On a recent evaluation, her principal . . . checked off all the appropriate boxes, Tan said—then noted that she had been late to pick up her students from recess three times. 'I threw it away because I got upset,' Tan said. 'Why don't you focus on my teaching?! Why don't you focus on where my students are?'"[1]

My goal was to find as many such teachers as I could and honor them by focusing on, and studying, their teaching. To write this book, I spent a lot of time standing in the back of classrooms and watching videotape of great teachers in action. I used Jim Collins's observation from *Built to Last* and *Good to Great* that what separates great from good matters more than what describes mere competence. I wanted to know not what made a teacher pretty good but what made her exceptional, able to beat the odds, what made certain teachers able to achieve what a thousand well-intentioned social programs could not. Were there consistent ideas that allowed them to more reliably transform lives? Were there words and actions the rest of us could copy and adapt? Were there general trends to provide a road map, principles behind the excellence? Or was their excellence idiosyncratic and unmappable?

What I found was that while each great teacher is unique, as a group their teaching held elements in common. I started to see both theme and variation, so I began to make a list of the things they did. I gave those actions names so I could remember them, and over time my list grew in both the number of topics and the level of specificity. Ideas coalesced into techniques. Not every teacher I observed used every technique I described. Like Felch, I found that great teachers came in every stripe and style: "They were quiet and animated, smiling and stern. Some stuck to the basics, while others veered far from the district's often-rigid curriculum." But in the aggregate, a story emerged. There *is* a tool box for closing achievement gaps, it turns out. The contents have been forged by ten thousand teachers working quietly and usually without recognition at the end of cracked-linoleum hallways. I am sure that some of my analysis of what they do is wrong. In fact, I have rewritten this book from the original to try to capture more of what they do with better accuracy. The pages that follow are my effort to describe and organize their tools and how they use them.

If you're a teacher near the beginning of your study of the craft of teaching, my aim is to help you become one of those teachers who, for a long and distinguished career, unlocks the latent talent and skill waiting in students, no matter how many previous efforts have been unsuccessful. If you commit yourself and your talents to this work, you deserve to be successful and to change lives. If you are successful, you will most likely be happy in the work, and when you are happy, in turn, you will do better work.

If you are a master teacher already, I hope a discussion of tools and their applications, the framing of a vocabulary for talking about the critical and sometimes overlooked moments of your day, will inspire you not only to refine your craft but also to love doing so and to feel the pleasure of committing (or recommitting) to the deepest possible mastery of the complex and worthy endeavor that is your life's work. I assume that in many cases this book may describe things you already know and do. That's great by me, and in that case, my goal is to help you get a little better at them, perhaps seeing useful applications and variations you haven't considered. Either way, your growth is at least as important as that of a novice teacher. Teaching is the best and most important work in our society. Those who do it deserve to experience constant growth and learning. That, after all, is what we wish for our students.

If you lead a school, I hope this book will help you in helping teachers do this challenging work as successfully as possible. In our field, the first obligation of an organization is to help its people succeed. When teachers end the day with a sense of accomplishment, when they feel they are both successful and growing more so, they stay in our schools for a long time, do outstanding work, work joyfully, and inspire others, and thus pay the organization back in spades.

Let me say, though, with a humility that is reinforced every time I observe a champion teacher at work, that I am no master. Far from it. My work has not been to invent the tools I describe here but to explain how others use them and what makes them effective. This has meant putting names on techniques in the interest of helping create a common vocabulary with which to analyze and discuss the classroom. The names may seem like a gimmick at first, but they are one of the most important parts. If there were no word *democracy*, it would be a thousand times harder to have and sustain a *thing* called "democracy." We would forever be bogged down in inefficiency—"You know that thing we talked about where everyone gets a say . . ."—at exactly the moment we needed to take action. Teachers and administrators must be able to talk quickly and efficiently with colleagues about a clearly defined and shared set of ideas in order to sustain their work. They need a shared vocabulary thorough enough to allow a comprehensive analysis of events that happen in a classroom. I believe that names matter and are worth using. Ideally, they will allow you to talk about your own teaching and that of your peers in efficient, specific language.

But I want to be clear. Despite the names, what appears here is neither mine, especially, nor a theory. It is a set of field notes from observations of the work of masters, some of whom you will meet in this book, and many others whom you will not, but whose diligence and skill informed and inspired this work.

WHAT IS 2.0?

What, you might ask, does the *2.0* in the title of this book signify? If you've read the original *Teach Like a Champion,* you might ask, why not just update the original and keep the name the same? The addition of the phrase 2.0 acknowledges that the book is so full of new ideas, within a different structure, that it is hard for me to think of it as the same book. Over the past four years, I have learned as much from watching great teachers in action as in the time it took me to write the original version of the book, if not more. In that time, I have been inspired by what talented and motivated teachers do with a useful idea when they find it.

True, they use it, of course, often to inspirational effect, but almost right away, great teachers start to adapt and adjust anything good; they make it fit their own unique style and approach, their setting and students. Most of all, it turns out, the best teachers find ways to take anything you give them and make it more rigorous. Almost as soon as I began to share the ideas I'd gleaned from teachers in the original version of this book, the guidance became obsolete. I began to see the ideas reflected back at me in the classrooms of teachers, but adapted, tweaked, and improved so that what I was seeing when teachers executed the techniques from the book was often better than what I described.

I came to call this process the Virtuous Cycle: give teachers a good thing, and they make it better, smarter, faster. They make you wonder how you didn't think of something so obviously good or nuanced the first time around. This to me is the most inspiring part of the profession, and why I am deeply optimistic about teaching. Nothing could make me happier than to be confronted by the obsolescence of the original ideas and to think about how soon this second version of the book will need further updating. For now, the new title reflects the depth of knowledge this cycle has generated.

As I will outline later, *Teach Like a Champion 2.0* also includes brand-new techniques. This is because great teachers are entrepreneurs, and teaching is full of what Deborah Ball, dean of the School of Education at the University of Michigan, calls "endemic problems." Endemic, in this case, is the opposite of "exotic"; it means problems that are entirely predictable — we know they're going to happen. Endemic questions include those such as, What do you do when a student gives up and simply won't try? How do you know what the student who hides silently in the corner is learning? How can you maximize the amount of work students are doing? And what do you do when you ask a student to sit down, and he smirks and tells *you* to sit down? As these examples suggest, the predictability of endemic problems does not imply that they are simple to solve. And it shouldn't take a dozen years of brutal trial and error, suffering, and fatigue for a teacher to figure out these problems. Further observation has helped me to see the many endemic problems for which teachers have derived brilliant solutions. The degree of these additions, too, argued for a book that was 2.0 — as much sequel as revision.

ON TEACHERS AND THE ADVICE THEY GET

Teachers are drowning in advice. Most of the time, they are tasked with executing ideas and directives that come from elsewhere — from people who don't actually teach every day. Perhaps as a result, many of those ideas and directives are disconnected from the challenges that shape a teacher's daily work. They are often developed for purposes other than mastering the mundane (to some) endemic challenges of teaching, and this tends to exacerbate the wide range of guidance teachers receive. It's worth asking then what advice *should* look like. I think of guidance as coming in three varieties: ideology driven, research driven, and data driven.

Ideology-driven guidance represents the most common form of advice teachers receive. From time immemorial, people have thought of things that could or should happen in classrooms and proceeded to tell teachers to do them. This kind of guidance tends to say, "This is what a classroom should be like," which is problematic *even if you agree with the idea in question*. A teacher might be told that a classroom should be democratic, for example, and perhaps given some parameters for what a democratized classroom should look like, but such a classroom is not assessed for whether student achievement rose but whether the teacher did what the democratizing guidance described. Assessment of the effectiveness of an ideology is usually self-reinforcing. Teachers in such cases are asked not to use and adapt ideas as they see fit to get to a few important outcomes — student achievement in a given subject, say — but rather to assess results by checking off a growing list of "musts": teachers must teach English, math, science, history, the arts, banking and financial literacy, environmental stewardship, entrepreneurship, and personal hygiene, in a technology-rich environment that builds self-esteem, seats students in pods, provides multiple solutions to every problem, avoids "teacher talk," and never exposes a student to a page of text that has more than five vocabulary words he or she doesn't know. Please don't forget the anti-drug unit. In other words, ideology-based guidance contributes to the development of schools where teachers are always trying to do lots of things that people are telling them to do, instead of using their insight, problem-solving abilities, and a wide array of tools to achieve specific goals. The result, often, is an administrator with a checklist.

Gradually, the guidance that teachers receive has begun to be more research driven. Research matters, so that's a step in the right direction, but there are still problems. Research needs to be distilled and digested for application. If research supports a particular action, does that mean you should always perform that action, to the exclusion of everything else, or should you combine it with other things? How often, in what settings, and with what other actions? And how do you meld them? Even if you nailed all those questions, the research might not prove effective until you'd figured out the details of implementing it in, say, forty-six minutes on Tuesday morning with thirty-one fourth graders of widely varying skill levels. Or it might not be of any value at all; there's a lot of research out there of varying quality, and even the useful parts are interpreted with a mix of good sense, cautious fidelity, outright distortion, and blind orthodoxy. This can result in "research" justifying poor teaching as easily as good. Research, in other words, works best when it is a tool, not a mandate—adapted and applied by professionals to achieve a specific goal and then assessed to determine whether and how it helps them meet that goal.

This brings up the third type of advice for teachers: data-driven guidance. Data-driven guidance is based not on what should happen but on what did happen when success was achieved. *How* were all the ideas and research knitted together and executed so as to survive their encounter with twenty-eight moderately skeptical seventh graders? *What else* had to happen to achieve that singular triumph? What were the themes and variations teachers employed across multiple successful lessons, considering their own personality, setting, and context? It's not simple, this data-driven guidance, and it has pitfalls of its own, but as you have probably guessed, this book is an effort to bring that kind of guidance to teachers, based on the work of those peers who successfully solve endemic problems.

To paraphrase a wise colleague, the only thing I know for sure about my effort at offering data-driven guidance is that I got some of it wrong. Surely, when one of the teachers I was watching did the thing that drove her results, I was looking in the other direction, misunderstanding what she'd done, confusing cause for effect, or seeing what I wanted to see at least some of the time. But one of the great things about data-driven guidance is that anyone can seek it out. Even if you disagree with my conclusions, whether you are a teacher or a leader in charge of a school, a school district, a state, or a nation, you can use a data-driven approach to take your best shot at measuring the outcome you think most valuable, finding its best practitioners, and inferring guidance from their work.

One major benefit of a data-driven approach is that it generates its knowledge from teachers: it's the process of showing teachers a picture of themselves at their very best. As a result, it considers teachers not just as recipients and implementers of the field's knowledge but as creators of it — problem solvers, entrepreneurs, generators of the professional insight. It makes teachers intellectuals. That, I think, really matters. It not only honors teachers and teaching but ideally also changes the perception of the field and the stature of the work.

We often talk about "the" achievement gap, but really there are many: the gap between rich and poor, true, but also the gap between what students think and what they can write; the gap between schools in our nation and the best school systems in the world; and the gap between what our schools offer and what they could be. One of the key messages of this book is that solutions to teaching's achievement gaps exist. There is no gap that has not been closed already by some teacher somewhere. We are not suffering from a lack of solutions so much as our failure to learn from teachers who have generated insight and put their ideas to work.

SPECIFIC, CONCRETE, ACTIONABLE TECHNIQUES

When I was a young teacher, I'd go to trainings and leave with lofty words ringing in my ears. They touched on everything that had made me want to teach. "Have high expectations for your students." "Expect the most from students every day." "Teach kids, not content." I'd be inspired, ready to improve — until I got to school the next day. I'd find myself asking, "Well, how do I do that? What's the action I should take at 8:25 a.m. to demonstrate those raised expectations?"

What ultimately helped me improve my teaching was when a peer told me something very concrete like, "When you want them to follow your directions, stand still. If you're walking around passing out papers, it looks like the directions are no more important than all of the other things you're doing. Show that your directions matter. Stand still." Over time, it was this sort of concrete, specific, actionable advice, far more than reminders that I must have high expectations that allowed me to raise expectations in my classroom.

My approach in this book reflects that experience. I have tried to describe the techniques of champion teachers in a concrete, specific, and actionable way that allows you to start using them tomorrow. I chose to call these tools "techniques" and not "strategies"—even though the teaching profession tends to use the latter term—because to me, a strategy is a generalized approach that informs decisions, whereas a technique is a thing you say or do in a particular way. If you are a sprinter, your strategy might be to get out of the blocks fast and run from the front; your technique would be to incline your body forward at about five degrees as you drive your legs up and out ahead of you. If you wanted to be a great sprinter, practicing and refining that technique would help you achieve more than refining your strategy. And because a technique is an action, the ✳ more you practiced it, the better you'd get. Mulling over your decision to run from the front a hundred times doesn't make you any better; practicing a hundred sprints with just the right body position does. This is why, I think, focusing on honing and improving specific techniques is the fastest route to success. My hope is that, with practice, you'll be able to walk to the front of any classroom and use *Cold Call* (technique 33 in Chapter Seven) and *No Opt Out* (technique 11 in Chapter Three) to hold your students accountable in a lesson with *Positive Framing* (technique 58 in Chapter Twelve) and a high ratio (Chapters Seven, Eight, and Nine). Mastering those techniques will be far more productive than being firm of convictions, committed to a strategy, and, in the end, beaten by the reality of what lies inside the classroom door in the toughest neighborhoods of our cities and towns.

It's also worth noting that this set of techniques is not a "system." For me, the benefit of considering individual techniques is that they are small, discrete units of inquiry. You can choose something that interests you and study it, improving quickly and seeing the results. And you can incorporate a new technique into what you already do without having to redesign your entire approach or buying in to everything in the book. As Chip and Dan Heath point out in their book *Switch,* how people encounter useful information has a lot to do with whether they are successful in using it to change and improve their *concrete* lives. Oftentimes what we conclude is resistance to change—by teachers, say—is in fact *ways* lack of clarity about what concrete thing to do next to begin the change: "OK, I get that I should be more rigorous, but how do I do that, or start to do that in a concrete, manageable way?" Giving people very small ideas to try might seem less efficient than giving them an overarching system that encompasses everything they do, but trying to ✳ do everything at once is a recipe for lack of action. Having a manageable focused idea to work on can help make change and improvement safe and easy to pursue, with the result that the technique becomes part of your life. We often achieve more change over the long run via small changes in the short run.

Another key observation from *Switch* is that we tend to assume that the size of a solution must match the size of the problem. You were observed; there were criticisms; it seems you have to make wholesale changes to everything you do. Or do you? Often, very small changes can have large and profound effects on big problems. I have a friend who struggled for years with his weight, wrestling to make huge changes in his lifestyle, with immense effort that drew his focus away from work and family. One day, he realized that an aching tooth had been keeping him from chewing food on one side of his mouth. He would push the food to the other side and gulp it down half chewed. He realized that this might be causing him to overeat. He had the tooth pulled and lost ten pounds in a few weeks. Teaching can be similar. Our mascot on the Uncommon Schools Teach Like a Champion team is Mighty Mouse. Little things, we like to remind ourselves, can have big muscles.

THE IRONY OF WHAT WORKS

Many of the techniques you will read about in this book may at first seem mundane, unremarkable, even disappointing. They are not always especially innovative. They are not always intellectually startling. They sometimes fail to march in step with educational theory. But they work. As a result, they yield an outcome that more than compensates for their occasionally humble appearance.

There's evidence of the effectiveness of these tools in the overwhelming success not only of the classrooms of the teachers from whom I learned them but in almost every urban school. In those schools, there are usually a few classrooms where the same students who moments before were unruly and surly suddenly take their seats, pull out their notebooks, and, as if by magic, think and work like scholars. In each of those classrooms stands one teacher—an artisan whose attention to technique and execution differentiates her from most of her peers.

One of the biggest ironies I hope you will take away from reading this book is that many of the tools likely to yield the strongest classroom results remain essentially beneath the notice of our theories and theorists of education. Consider one unmistakable driver of student achievement: carefully built and practiced routines for the distribution and collection of classroom materials. I often begin teacher trainings by showing a video clip of my colleague Doug McCurry, the founder of Amistad Academy in New Haven, Connecticut, and the Achievement First network of schools, both of which have a national reputation for excellence. In the clip, Doug teaches his students how to pass out papers on the first day or two of school. He takes a minute or so to explain the right way to do it (pass across rows, start on his command, only the person passing gets out of his or her seat if required, and so on). Then his students start to practice. Doug times them with a stopwatch: "Ten seconds. Pretty good. Let's see if we can get them back out in eight." The students, by the way, are happy as can be. They love to be challenged and love to see themselves improving. They are smiling.

See It in Action: Clip 48
Watch Doug McCurry encourage his students to pass in their papers faster and faster.

Inevitably there are skeptics when I show this clip. Some argue this isn't what teachers are supposed to be doing during classroom time. They think it's demeaning to ask students to practice banal tasks. The activity treats students like robots, they charge. It brainwashes them when it should be setting their minds free. Now, consider those objections in light of the following numbers. Assume that the average class of students passes papers and materials twenty times a day, and that it takes a typical class a minute and twenty seconds to do this. If Doug's students can accomplish this task in just twenty seconds, they will save twenty minutes a day (one minute each time). They can then allocate this time to studying the causes of the Civil War or how to add fractions with unlike denominators. Now, multiply that twenty minutes per day by 190 school days, and you find that Doug has just taught his students a routine that will net him thirty-eight hundred minutes of additional instruction over the course of a school year. That's more than sixty-three hours or almost eight additional days of instruction — time for whole units on Reconstruction or coordinate geometry! Assuming that Doug spends a total of an hour teaching and practicing this routine, his small investment will yield a return in learning time of roughly 6,000 percent, setting his students free to engage their minds several thousand times over.

Given that time is a school's most precious asset, you could put it another way: Doug has just increased his school's scarcest resource — the time it has already bought in the form of teacher salaries — by about 4 percent. He has performed a minor miracle. Then combine this manufacture of resources with the ancillary effects of having strong habits and routines: the self-fulfilling perception of orderliness it gives to the classroom; the routine's capacity to remind students over and over that in this classroom, it is always about doing things, even little things, right and then better. Now you have a potent technique, one that is common across almost every one of the highest-performing classrooms and schools I have seen. Unfortunately, this dizzyingly efficient technique—so efficient it is all but a moral imperative for teachers to use it—often remains beneath the notice of the avatars of educational theory. Few schools of education stoop to teach aspiring teachers how to train their students to pass out papers, even though it is one of the most valuable things they could possibly do.

To be fair to the teachers I've studied, not all, not even *most* of the techniques are so brass-tacks oriented. Many are about issues more common to discourse—boosting the amount of cognitive work students do, for example. But even then, what separates the champions are actions that are granular, specific, far beneath the level of philosophy, and knee-deep in the weeds. *Turn and Talk* is a great example. Done well, this technique is a powerful contributor to a rigorous classroom; done poorly, it is a boondoggle of wasted time and faux autonomy. The difference again lies in the mundane details of a design that builds on routines much like Doug McCurry's to ensure accountability alongside autonomy.

THE ART OF USING THE TECHNIQUES

In writing this book, I want to emphasize that the art is in the discretionary application of the techniques. I've tried to help artisans be artists, not because I think the work of teaching can be mechanized or made formulaic. There is a right and wrong time and place for all of the tools, and their effective application will always fall to the unique style and vision of great teachers. That, in a word, is artistry. Great teaching is no less great because the teacher systematically mastered specific skills than is *David* a lesser reflection of Michelangelo's genius because Michelangelo mastered the grammar of the chisel before he created the statue. I believe that given the tools here, teachers will make insightful, independent decisions about how and when to use the techniques of the craft as they go about becoming masters of the art of teaching.

You'll find that many of the descriptions of these techniques include "See It in Action" boxes. You can see the various techniques by viewing the video clips. These clips have the potential to help you drive practical and effective classroom results. I chose these for the book because they show great teachers using specific teaching techniques that differentiate the great from the merely good. To maximize the effectiveness of these clips, I suggest that you read the description of the technique, watch the video, and then reflect on your own practice and how you might use the technique.

WHO ARE THE CHAMPIONS?

The organization I work for, Uncommon Schools, is a nonprofit that runs charter schools—good ones, I am proud to say—and I observe that they are good for the reason most good schools are good: because they take teachers and teaching seriously and strive to focus every decision on serving teachers and increasing student achievement, two goals that are, if not synonymous, then at least deeply synergistic. But this is not a charter school book. This is a teaching book, a book about the actions inside the classroom rather than the policy decisions outside it. It is important to point out that the teachers from whom I learned the things I have written about here ply their trade in both charter and district schools. It would dishonor those teachers not to emphasize this point. As I sit at my desk, I can recall scrambling to write down the insights I learned in classrooms, district and charter, from New York to Nashville—not to mention Boston, Houston, and Oakland.

As you watch the videos, I hope you will be inspired by the teaching, but you may not always see the diversity of settings in which I learned the techniques those videos demonstrate. One reason for this is eminently practical. Observation is relatively easy. Walking into a classroom with a video camera and asking for the right to use the resulting video no matter what happens is another, and far easier to accomplish in some places than others. Further, video is an incredibly unforgiving medium. Buried in the recesses of our video archives are a thousand brilliant moments of teaching made unusable as teaching aids by a thunderous sneeze, the stumbling mispronunciation of a key term, or the ringing of the dismissal bell at exactly the wrong moment. The classrooms you see in this book offered the highest-quality demonstration of a technique I could find in a classroom with excellent results. In most cases, the amount we learned from the teachers was prodigious, but these classrooms may not be the only or the first ones where my team and I learned about the techniques.

The second reason may be more important. Many of the places I have shot most frequently are hubs of the Virtuous Cycle—places where teachers were deeply intentional about applying, adapting, and improving the techniques and willing to invest time in reflecting on that process. They are often places where, more than just having these conversations with me and my team, teachers engaged in conversations with each other, endeavoring to learn, via sustained conversation and dialogue, how to use and adapt the ideas. They tape themselves and each other constantly for inquiry and reflection, so it was easy to share. This often resulted not only in great 2.0 learning but in great video. Teaching, it turns out, is a team sport, where teachers make each other better fastest by building robust cultures where they study and share insights about their work. Our cameras practically exploded with amazing footage when we taped in such places. Many of them were the schools I am closest to personally, but they are by no means the only places where the techniques flourish, nor are they necessarily the places where they were first developed.

DEFINING WHAT WORKS

So how did I identify the teachers I studied and the schools I frequented? And what does it mean to say that they were successful in closing the achievement gap? My primary tool was a basic analysis of state test scores that controlled for poverty. I used this approach to look for "positive outliers," teachers whose students came from poverty and who dealt with the associated challenges such a demographic implied, yet still achieved results comparable to what was achieved by students of privilege. Consider Figure I.1.

The graph in the figure is of data showing performance on the 2011 sixth-grade math test in New York State. At the circled school, about 96 percent of its students are eligible for free and reduced-price lunch, the standard measure of poverty in the education sector. According to the data, schools with similar populations typically saw about 40 percent of their students pass the state test in 2011. The correlation between poverty and lower achievement is strong in the data, and also shows up in the results of schools without any students at all eligible for free meals: about 83 percent of their students passed the test. But at the circled school, even more passed the test. *Every* student passed the test. In fact, although it's not evident from this figure, 60 percent of students in the school scored advanced, an outcome that placed it in the top 5 percent of schools in the state, regardless of population.

Even more important, the trend continued over time. Sixth graders in the school in 2013 passed the sixth-grade test at a rate more than 130 percent of the statewide average, again despite dramatically higher poverty. And the initially strong results posted by sixth graders in 2011 were sustained. By 2013, this cohort of students passed the eighth-grade New York State math assessment at a rate of 74 percent. This sounds like a significant drop-off, but in fact the opposite is true. The 2013 scores were "post Common Core," coming after New York redesigned its exams to make them significantly more demanding. Overall, just 28 percent of students in New York State passed the math test that year. Students at our outlier school passed at a rate more than two-and-a-half times that of students statewide, despite a poverty rate more than double that of the state average. In short, the school, Troy Preparatory Charter School in Troy, New York (part of the

Figure I.1 2011 New York State Assessment Sixth-Grade Math Results

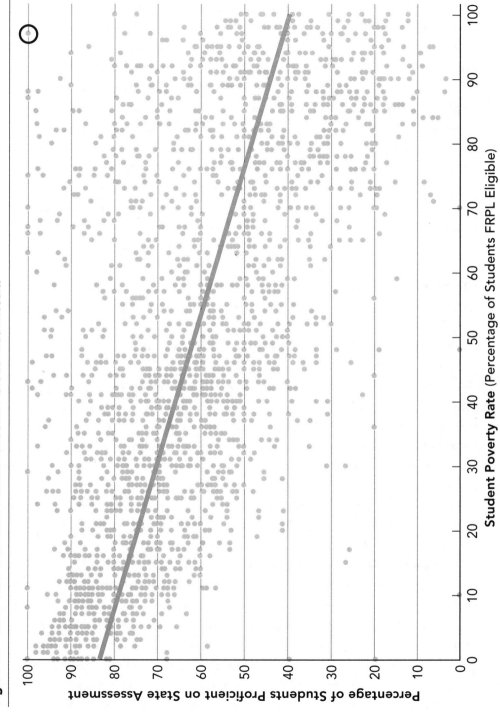

Uncommon Schools network), and its math teachers, Bryan Belanger, Katie Bellucci, Bridget McElduff, and Ana O'Neil (all of whom you can see in action in this book), deserve study and attention. How do they approach teaching, relationships, lesson planning, and the like? Surely there must be things each of us can take from their classrooms.

My goal was to turn up as many outliers like this as possible. Sometimes it was a single classroom—just the sixth grade, say—and sometimes it was an entire school. Whenever possible, I tried to use as much additional data as I could get and tried to look for signals that were durable over time—sustained results as opposed to one-time blips more likely to be the result of causes other than great teaching. When a school was successful for a long time, I also considered the principal's guidance and input in sourcing teachers. This sounds subjective, I suppose, but it's still useful. Although there are data to suggest that the average principal is only so-so at identifying the best teachers, very good principals are, of course, different from the average. One could argue that the reason they are successful is their ability to understand whose teaching is especially effective. And there are also data to support the idea that although it's hard to differentiate teachers around the middle of the performance curve by watching, the great ones are pretty reliably identifiable by effective administrators.

I used administrator input for several reasons. One, data are incredibly important, but they're not always simple to use. Consider the challenge of English language arts (ELA) results, which generally speaking take several years to show up. Is it plausible that somewhere an English teacher's breathtaking results were in fact caused by the work of the teacher (or teachers) who came before her, rather than the six months she spent with students in that year? Asking for a principal's input and securing other data were ways to ensure that decisions were more accurate—testing by confirming data points. Further, in many cases there are very few data about science, social studies, and the arts, so I observed teachers in those areas who were identified by school leaders whose track record of success in ELA and math was also outstanding. A bit of an extrapolation for sure, but better in the end than ignoring those fields entirely.

Because my primary measure was state test scores, it's worth addressing some misconceptions about their use, if only to underscore the exemplary quality of the work of the teachers who informed this book. State test results are necessary but not sufficient. Without doubt there are myriad skills and a broad knowledge base that students need to master to succeed in college, and many of these things are not measured on state assessments. But also, without doubt, there is a set of core skills that is also necessary and that many, even most, students not born to privilege have not mastered. They need to be able to read and discuss Shakespeare, but they also need to be able to read a passage they've never seen before and effectively make sense of its meaning, structure, and craft. They need to be able to write a short paragraph giving evidence to support a conclusion. They need to be able to solve for x. Most state tests do an effective job of measuring these skills, and although students who can demonstrate them are not yet fully prepared for college, there are no students who are prepared for college who cannot demonstrate them.

It's also worth noting that the teachers who are better at teaching the skills measured on state tests are most often also the teachers who are effective at teaching broader, higher-level skills. Within Uncommon Schools, when we study the success of our students on tougher internal assessments (essay writing assessments that are far more demanding than state tests, for example), there is a strong correlation between both the teachers and students whose results show the most growth and achievement on the two types. Furthermore, our teachers who achieve the strongest results from state assessments also have the strongest results in ensuring our students' entry into and success in college. In short, student success as measured by state assessments is predictive not just of their success in getting into college but of their succeeding there.

Finally, the correlation between success on even more straightforward assessments (nationally normed test scores) and ultimate academic success should be instructive to us. I often meet educators who take it as an article of faith that work on basic skills is in tension with higher-order thinking. That is, when you teach students to, say, memorize their multiplication tables, you are not only failing to foster more abstract and deeper knowledge but are actually interfering with it. This is illogical, and is one of the tenets of American education *not* shared by most of the educational systems of Asia, especially those that are the highest-performing public school systems in the world. Those nations are more likely to see that foundational skills like memorizing multiplication tables enable higher-order thinking and deeper insight because they free students from having to use up their cognitive processing capacity in more basic calculations. If you are to have the insight to observe that a more abstract principle is at work in a problem or that there is another way to solve it, you cannot be concentrating on the computation. That part has to happen with automaticity so that as much of your processing capacity as possible can remain free to reflect on what you're doing. The more proficient you are at "lower-order" skills, the more proficient you can become at higher-order skills.

With that I leave you to the champions and their work. Here's a brief map of what's in each chapter.

HOW TO USE THIS BOOK: CHAPTER ORGANIZATION

I've organized this collection of field notes from my observations of highly effective teachers as a how-to book and divided the techniques into four parts. The ideas behind these parts capture what I think are four core challenges of teaching: check for understanding, academic ethos, ratio, and behavior and culture.

Check for Understanding

In the first version of *Teach Like a Champion,* check for understanding (CFU) was a single technique described with good intentions and insufficient actionable, concrete, everyday guidance—the thing I care about most. In the first drafts of *2.0,* I quickly realized that CFU would need its own chapter. John Wooden, the UCLA basketball coach (who, as some people know, was first an English teacher, and continued to see himself as a teacher throughout his storied career as perhaps the greatest coach in the history of American sports), once said the most crucial task of teaching was to distinguish "I taught it" from "they learned it." If there is a better description of CFU, I don't know what it is. Agreeing with Wooden, I decided to make this topic the first chapter so as to capture its importance. However, because we'd learned so incredibly much about CFU in the ensuing years, a single chapter proved impossible. It took two and earned a section all its own. The ten techniques in these two chapters are entirely new to the second edition. I did not know they existed four years ago (though teachers did, of course). When I look back at footage of lessons I watched in writing the first version, I see that teachers were doing these things over and over. I just failed to see them.

Academic Ethos

Part Two of the book, Academic Ethos, is about the importance of seeking the maximum level of academic rigor. It comprises revised versions of four chapters from the first version of the book: "Setting High Academic Expectations," "Planning for Success," "Lesson Structure," and "Pacing." Of course, other key factors help determine the level of rigor in a lesson—the content you teach and how deep you go—but these four chapters examine concrete actions that build rigor in a variety of domains. If there were a theme to what has happened to the "Setting High Academic Expectations" techniques in the period after the publication of the first version of this book, it would be "toward greater rigor," and the resulting presentation is, I believe, much cleaner and easier to use. It much more clearly tracks, in a chronological way, the key tools and decisions you make in a lesson.

Ratio

Part Three of the book consists of three chapters on building *ratio*—getting students to do as much of the cognitive work as you can. In my brief introduction, I frame the three approaches—questioning, writing, and discussion; differentiate the two critical types of ratio that teachers seek—participation ratio and think ratio; and offer one of the most important reflections in the book in the section that I call "The Content Prerequisite." It argues that you cannot successfully cause students to do a great deal of rigorous thinking unless you are also serious about delivering and having students learn lots and lots of content knowledge. Knowledge is what you analyze and think about. Exercises where students try to "think deeply" about what they know when they in fact know very little may appear high ratio at first, but turn out to be vacuous. Investing directly and substantively in students' base of knowledge—what educators sometimes consider "mere" factual knowledge—allows them to do applied cognitive work of substance and rigor and independence; but try to do the same tasks without investing in a knowledge base, and you erode their value. Facts and rigor are not opposites as some educators continue to suggest, but synergistic partners; the necessity of facts and knowledge to thinking, I offer with the humility of retrospect, is the single biggest concept I overlooked or misunderstood in the first edition of this book. In short, please don't read the three chapters on ratio without reading "The Content Prerequisite" in Chapter Seven.

Behavior and Culture

Part Four of the book focuses on behavior and culture. This topic is one that teachers and school leaders who attend our workshops tell us is incredibly useful because positive culture makes such a difference in everything that happens in a classroom—not least of all academic achievement—yet there is so precious little guidance on how to build it. And the costs of poor culture are massive. If your classroom culture is not where you want it to be, assessing the effectiveness of discipline, control, management, engagement, and influence is a great first step.

I also have tried to frame more clearly in this version of the book two critical points teachers must understand in building classroom culture: first, that the purpose of order in the classroom is to promote academic learning; second, that there is a difference between the power of keeping things from going wrong (which is good) and the benefits of making our classroom a place where things go right—where culture and expectations are positive, joyful, productive, and caring. Put more succinctly, the two key framings are: (1) order is necessary but not sufficient to learning, and (2) great culture entails doing far more than just eliminating disruptions.

Of course, culture and behavior are not always about control and accountability. I close with Chapter Twelve, on the power of relationships—ending the book with *Joy Factor*. I hope to leave you thinking about the happiness that schooling can be—or should be—and about how powerful a force the joy of not just learning but *schooling* is.

The structure of the book—sixty-two core techniques spread out across twelve chapters—allows you to pick and choose techniques in order to improve and master specific aspects of your craft one at a time and in the order that best suits your teaching. At the same time, the full array of techniques operates in synergy; using one makes another better, and the whole is greater than the sum of the parts. So I hope you will also find time to read the book through end-to-end and push yourself to refine some of the techniques you might not initially choose to focus on. Alternatively, reading the book cover to cover might help you understand more clearly where you want to develop, either because you have talent and strong instincts for a group of techniques or because you wish you did.

As you consider how to use this book, I offer one preliminary reflection on developing people, including yourself. It's easy to slip into a "fixing what's wrong" mindset, with yourself and with others whom you're developing or managing. And although mitigating someone's weaknesses, including your own, can be an effective development strategy, it is also powerful to focus not on fixing what's wrong but on maximizing what's right. This also applies to the champion teachers I've observed in the course of my work: they too have weaknesses in their teaching, despite their results. What often makes them exceptionally successful are a core group of skills they are exceptionally good at. It's plausible that developing what you're already good at could improve your teaching just as much as working on your weaknesses, although even more likely is that a combination of the two would yield the best outcomes. Regardless, you might be tempted to skip a chapter because you already feel that you are effective at the topic it discusses, but I encourage you to study that chapter with special attentiveness specifically *because* you are good at those techniques. A bit of refinement could be something you quickly and intuitively apply and that could make you exceptional—or more exceptional. In other words, invest in your strengths, too.

HOW TO USE THIS BOOK: ADDITIONAL FEATURES

Beyond the organizational structure of the book, there are a handful of features that can help you get the most out of your time by highlighting and making more accessible certain techniques. They are:

Video clips: If you own the print book version of *Teach Like a Champion,* you'll find a DVD containing videos of champion teachers masterfully utilizing the techniques in their own classroom. For access to online videos for both print and eBooks, visit How to Access the Video Contents near the end of the book and see the instructions on creating an account using your unique PIN.

"See It in Action": Sometimes it's just better to see a teacher use a technique in a classroom than to try to picture it. Throughout the book, "See It in Action" boxes encourage you to learn from champion teachers during exemplary moments by coupling video with brief analysis.

"Want More?": Techniques, in practice, are about as varied as the teachers who use them. "Want More?" boxes try to eliminate some of the mystery by presenting different takes on a number of techniques.

Sidebars: Several ideas that were techniques in the first version of the book are still here, but are discussed in a sidebar and are not numbered as a technique. I did this to try to build more of an implicit hierarchy into the book. Throughout the book, I've used sidebars more extensively to (1) include additional guidance on existing techniques, (2) share brand-new ideas never discussed in version 1.0, or (3) repackage a 1.0 technique in a more stand-alone setting.

"Reflection and Practice": Part of our job as teachers is to be constantly learning. Reflection and Practice questions at the end of each chapter provide time and space to pause and examine your own teaching, as well as how you might effectively leverage champion techniques in your classroom.

Useful Tools: At the end of each chapter, you'll find artifacts to support your implementation of the techniques in your classroom and within your school. Many of the tools are located only on the companion website, www.teachlikeachampion .com, so please be sure to access the documents there. You'll be able to download and modify these tools to fit your particular needs. To access these, visit How to Access the Video Contents near the end of the book and see the instructions on creating an account using your unique PIN.

BEYOND THE BOOK

Beyond the book, there are more ways to engage with the global community of educators who are using this work in their daily lives. Please join the Teach Like a Champion community through our website, www.teachlikeachampion.com.

Website: The site serves as the main forum for continuing the conversations and sharing insights on all things Teach Like a Champion through my *Field Notes* blog. My team and I also share fantastic free resources on this site, ready to be downloaded and tailored to fit your needs. These include lesson materials, practice activities, student work samples, classroom snapshots, and mini training materials. You'll also find information about our workshops as well as our online training modules, called Plug and Plays.

Version 1.0 outtakes: One of the hardest parts of revising *Teach Like a Champion* was dropping things that were important and useful in order to make room for things that were more so. I realize that for some readers, those sections will be sorely missed. For this reason, the website will include a section where key content from the first version remains accessible. One of the sections I suspect readers will miss most is the series of chapters on reading. These I will continue to refine, update, and revise in anticipation of a separate book on the topic, *Reading Reconsidered*. In the meantime, the older versions of the reading material will live at www.teachlikeachampion.com. To access outtake material, simply sign in to Your Library at http://teachlikeachampion.com/yourlibrary/.

Social media: Here's where you can find the Teach Like a Champion team and me through the major social media channels:

www.facebook.com/TeachLikeAChampion

www.twitter.com/TeachLikeAChamp

www.twitter.com/Doug_Lemov

Part 1

Check for Understanding

INTRODUCTION: THE FOUR TASKS OF CHECK FOR UNDERSTANDING

Perhaps the most salient characteristic of a great teacher is her ability to recognize the difference between "I taught it" and "They learned it." She might have explained to her class the significance of the Stamp Act as a precursor to the American Revolution, but what matters, she knows, is whether her students understand it. As most teachers have learned through experience, a series of carefully planned and well-executed lessons may or may not always cause this to happen. The gaps that emerge between what was taught and what's been learned may even not be the teacher's "fault." Fault, in many ways, is irrelevant. To teach to student mastery is the job, and ensuring that it happens is our challenge as teachers.

The challenge of getting reliably to "They learned it" by reacting to misunderstandings as they emerge and then finding the best way forward is an immense one, but at least it has a name: *check for understanding* (CFU). Although I'd been familiar with that phrase for years, and included it as a technique in the first version of this book, it took me much longer to understand the full nature of the tasks implicit in CFU. The barrier to their successful execution is in pragmatic details more than philosophy; it's less that there are thousands of teachers who fail to say to themselves, "Gee, I really ought to be assessing what they're learning as I teach" than it is that there are thousands of teachers with three hundred other things to do at any given moment during a lesson. A sticky note on your dashboard with "Remember to really make sure they're learning!" written on it isn't likely to make you teach better. The champions of CFU win by making a habit of small intentional habits, some of which might seem trivial, but when applied consistently and in coordination, result in a reliable and trusty safety net for student learning.

My discussion of CFU in these chapters is limited to "real-time" actions—things teachers do "before the final bell rings"—that is, during the course of a single lesson. After students have filed out the doors, teachers have lots of great tools for determining how much their students have learned: tests, quizzes, essays, and homework, even *Exit Tickets* (technique 26). Most teachers use some or all of these. They're worthwhile, of course, so I encourage you to continue. But my focus here is on tools that teachers can use to figure things out sooner—before students leave the room and the lesson is over. This is important because misunderstandings don't merely linger but often snowball, becoming more entrenched and gathering further misconceptions. Recognizing and addressing them quickly keeps them from getting worse, and does so at a lower cost. A full lesson lost is a high price to pay in terms of missed learning. Ten minutes lost is easier to fix.

There's a decent analogy in driving. Good drivers, research says, check their mirrors every five seconds or so. They're seeking to identify and remedy misunderstandings on the road as quickly as possible—by switching lanes, say, or yielding to oncoming traffic. That's always better than making repairs after the fact, no matter how good the body shop.

Over time, the techniques of CFU have coalesced, for me, around three broader tasks. The first is *data gathering*. Here, efficiency is essential, especially given the time constraints of real-time teaching. If you had twenty minutes to gather data every time you wanted it (referring here to the twenty minutes), of course you could figure out how your students were doing. The key is being able to do it in two minutes. If you can't gather data quickly and simply, you're less likely to do it at all. There are two ways that teachers seek to gather data: via *questioning* and via *observation*. Chapter One discusses the tools necessary to do these efficiently and well.

Chapter Two looks at the next two tasks implicit in CFU after data has been gathered: acting on the data and building a *Culture of Error*. In many ways these tasks represent different *types* of challenges than those in the first chapter. Whereas the challenges of gathering data are logistical and pragmatic, the challenges of the second and third tasks are as much psychological as technical.

Acting on the data often involves immediately changing the course of the lesson to respond to lack of mastery. An array of factors creates the incentive for us to "bury the data"—to see evidence of struggle but ignore it. After examining strategies for combating these incentives, I'll take on another psychosocial challenge: making the CFU process a shared endeavor between teachers and students. In a classroom, where one of a teacher's primary tasks is to see and react to mistakes, the degree to which students readily expose those mistakes, rather than try to hide them, directly influences a teacher's success. To encourage students to more willingly expose their errors, great teachers make it safe to be wrong. They build a *Culture of Error* that respects, normalizes, and values learning from errors. These sections of Chapter Two describe an area of CFU that I didn't know existed when I wrote the first edition of this book. This isn't to say that the champion teachers whom I was watching didn't understand it. When I go back and look at the footage of their classrooms now, I see them clearly using the ideas I now understand. It's just that I didn't notice them then.

Although I discuss building this *Culture of Error* in the second chapter, many teachers will likely want to start implementing it even before they begin gathering data. Champions, I now see, start fostering a *Culture of Error* in the first hours their students spend in their classroom.

Gathering Data on Student Mastery

Technique 1: Reject Self-Report.   Replace functionally rhetorical questions with more objective forms of impromptu assessment.

Technique 2: Targeted Questioning.   Ask a quick series of carefully chosen, open-ended questions directed at a strategic sample of the class and executed in a short time period.

Technique 3: Standardize the Format.   Streamline observations by designing materials and space so that you're looking in the same, consistent place every time for the data you need.

Technique 4: Tracking, Not Watching.   Be intentional about how you scan your classroom. Decide specifically what you're looking for and remain disciplined about it in the face of distractions.

Technique 5: Show Me.   Flip the classroom dynamic in which the teacher gleans data from a passive group of students. Have students actively show evidence of their understanding.

Technique 6: Affirmative Checking.   Insert specific points into your lesson when students must get confirmation that their work is correct, productive, or sufficiently rigorous before moving on to the next stage.

Gathering Data on Student Mastery

There are two primary ways teachers can gather data on student mastery: through *questioning* and through *observation*. You teach something, and then you ask students questions, listening for the stream of data within their answers, often engineering your questions so the data stream is a little richer. Alternately, you assign students a task to complete on their own, and watch intentionally as they work, attending to what you observe and how to ensure that information about mastery is reliably visible. In either case, a few straightforward techniques can help you find and use data that come from your interactions with students.

The first step in increasing the data your questioning reveals is to avoid a common pitfall: using a yes-or-no question to ask students whether or not they understand. I don't know many teachers (myself included) who haven't said something like the following:

Teacher: OK, those are the basics of cellular structure. Everyone clear on the differences between plant and animal cells?

Or

Teacher: So, that's cellular structure and the differences between plant and animal cells. Got it, guys?

REJECT SELF-REPORT

Replace functionally rhetorical questions with more objective forms of impromptu assessment.

Such questions are usually greeted with silent assent or perhaps a muttered, "Um, yeah." Next, the teacher usually says something like this:

Teacher: Good. Let's push on to the role of chloroplasts.

Whether they're addressed to adults or kids, in a school, work, or athletic setting, questions like "Is everyone clear on . . .?" or "Everybody got it?" are functionally rhetorical—they're asked over and over, the answer is almost always a passive "yes," and it is almost never accurate.

Volumes of social science literature have established that self-report is highly unreliable. Questions that ask for binary (that is, yes-no) answers are particularly suspect. Throw in group dynamics in the classroom, and for the great majority of self-report questions, what we get back isn't really even an answer so much as a formality. Whether people understand or not, they almost always say they do, particularly in groups. The result is that we get little if any data at a moment when our instincts are telling us we should be assessing.

Let's go back to the earlier question, "So, that's cellular structure and the differences between plant and animal cells. Got it, guys?" Even if people thought the question was in earnest, most would be reticent to stop a group of twenty-five people and say, "Uh, no. Actually, I don't really understand what you mean by the rigid structure of plant cells." Even if they could, in that moment, (1) identify that there was something they didn't know, and (2) describe it quickly so that you could understand it, most people would be unlikely to do so in front of a group that size, out of embarrassment or fear that they would co-opt the better interests of the group. They'd assume they were the only one who didn't get it and that it wasn't fair to speak up.

Even more compelling than implicit social pressure is a deeper problem: often students don't know that they missed something because, well, they missed it. If they miss your description of the rigid structure of plant cells, they may not know they missed it. Similarly, students often think they understand when they don't, or they don't know how to reflect much on the question of whether they really understand something. When you ask, "Do you understand the differences between the structures of plant and animal cells?" what your students may be assenting to is, for all practical purposes, "Can you think of *something* you know about the difference between plant and animal cells?" The vague nature of most self-report questions exacerbates this. If our questions aren't directive, they have no reason to draw students' attention to the many things they should know; this encourages them not only to give us false positives but, possibly, to believe them themselves.

Finally, the *way* we often ask these questions — with a wait time of a fraction of a second; a willingness to accept silent assent without testing; a look of relief, even, when we get silent assent because we really just want the green light to move on — intimates very clearly that we're not expecting a response. Students know not to speak up. If they do, our response can also send the message that they weren't really supposed to answer. A teacher might offer a perfunctory recap in response to a student who says, "No, actually, I don't get it." "Well, David, do you remember their shape from when we looked at them under the microscope? They had a rectangular pattern. Did they pretty much all look the same? Got it now?" This isn't a message of "Thank you for that useful data; let's go back to that," so much as a message of "Here's what you missed, David." I'll discuss the cultural implications of the messaging around what it means to be in error to a greater extent in Chapter Two, but for now all David knows is that he was supposed to give his assent and didn't. He'll do better next time.

Champion teachers, then, strive to **Reject Self-Report** as often as they can. They strive to replace moments when they ask for it with a quick series of carefully chosen questions directed at a strategic sample of the class, intended to meaningfully demonstrate student understanding in a minute or less.

The Trouble with Asking, "Got It?"

You might be asking, "Does this mean I can never ask my students, 'Got it?' or 'Are you ready to go on?'" The answer is no; you will assuredly say it sometimes, and doing so is no sin. It's almost impossible to root out such familiar rhetorical habits from your interactions with people, and if you did, it would probably feel unnatural. However, it's powerful and important to recognize *how often* we use self-report and how often it is functionally rhetorical. When we ask self-report questions, it's in part because *we are acknowledging that we have reached a natural transition point. We have come to a spot where we should check in with students and find out how they are doing.* Ironically, asking rhetorically squanders that moment and can actually be counterproductive. Over time, if I ask questions that my students come to realize are not really genuine—if I ask and don't really want answers—the effect may be for students to generalize and assume that many of my questions are perfunctory. It's critical that students feel comfortable sharing their knowledge (or the gaps in it) in the classroom. Making a habit of asking questions that you don't really want people to answer can result in their disengaging at exactly the moment you need them to think deeply or take the risk of sharing an incipient thought.

A Look at Self-Monitoring

I've also watched teachers use a method of check for understanding (CFU) that at first glance may seem similar to self-report: self-monitoring. Unlike self-report, however, self-monitoring is very useful, so it's worth reviewing the differences between self-report and self-monitoring and exploring how (and maybe when) to encourage the latter.

Developing Self-Awareness Through Self-Monitoring

In a recent review of spelling words, Amy Youngman, of Aspire ERES Academy in Oakland, California, said to her students, "At the end we're going to vote on a scale of one to four about how confident we feel about taking our test tomorrow, so be thinking about that as you practice the words." You might ask, "Isn't this just a fancy version of self-report? One where you ask students to evaluate their own level of understanding?" Not quite. Amy, at the moment she says this, is also gathering objective data, quickly scanning and assessing her students' answers. She asks for their self-reflections not to assess their level of mastery—it's too unreliable for that—but to develop their own self-awareness, their skill, and their desire to think about whether they are approaching mastery. She advises them, "If you gave yourself a three or four, there's a sheet for extra practice you can take home." It's self-monitoring when students reflect intentionally on their own level of mastery. It's a good thing generally, and there are lots of ways to encourage it in the classroom—for example, asking them to reflect as you ask targeted questions, such as, "I'm going to ask you some questions now to get a sense of how ready you are to go on; if you're not getting all of these questions, it's a sign that you may need some extra practice. In that case, please come see me."

See It in Action: Clip 1.

Want to see Amy Youngman in action? Watch Amy as she collects data on student mastery by quickly scanning each student's answer.

Of course, deliberate self-monitoring can be worked into a lesson in other ways, building synergy with effective CFU. You could, for example, take self-report—a yes-or-no question asking students to subjectively evaluate their mastery—and replace it with a session in which you give students time to look back at work they've done and select areas where they have questions. In doing this, you'd probably want to use language that assumes there are questions (for example, "What questions do you have? I'll give you some time to go back and look over the last five problems." You might then even help them reflect by saying, "You should know what I mean by *anaerobic,* and if not, should be ready to ask about it.") You'd probably want to do this activity consistently over time to allow students to build proficiency.

Assess by Asking Objective Questions

After a round of guided practice and just before she released her students at Newark, New Jersey's North Star Academy to a period of independent practice, Katie McNickle asked students to identify problems they'd like to review. At first glance, this might not seem atypical in any way, and perhaps not much different from self-report, but how Katie approached the moment was critical. A sample of hands went into the air, and Katie called on several students. She did not rush. Her message: "I am making time for this, and I take it seriously. It is not perfunctory." A student named Youssef asked her to explain what distributing was. "Great question," Katie responded. She asked a student to define the term and then added her own clarification, giving an example. Youssef was still confused, however, so Katie chose an example from her packet for a classmate to "tell Youssef specifically how to do this problem." After the explanation, she responded to the student, "Do the second one for Youssef, and then Youssef is going to do the third."

Don't ask if they "got it" — be specific

In Katie's hands, then, self-monitoring involved students (1) identifying specific content they struggled with (rather than evaluating whether they "got it"); (2) having sufficient time to engage in reflection with the expectation that there *would* be questions; and (3) reviewing, practicing, and being accountable for answering correctly. Youssef ultimately had to show mastery, not just say he felt better about distributing.

This sort of self-monitoring, which ends with objective assessment and requires a significant investment in time, is highly valuable, but "expensive" from a time perspective. For that reason, it's important to make use of the next technique, *Targeted Questioning,* to replace self-report at a lower *transaction cost*—the amount of resources it takes to execute an exchange, be it economic, verbal, or otherwise. This allows you to save self-monitoring for times when it's most important and valuable.

TARGETED QUESTIONING

Ask a quick series of carefully chosen, open-ended questions directed at a strategic sample of the class and executed in a short time period.

If technique 1 focuses on "rejecting" self-report, you might ask, "What do I embrace instead?" One of the simplest and most valuable answers to that is **Targeted Questioning**—a quick series of carefully chosen, open-ended questions directed at a strategic sample of the class and executed in a short time period, often a minute or less. Using *Targeted Questioning* might mean replacing something like this:

Teacher: OK, now that we've reviewed cellular structure, is everyone clear on the differences between plant and animal cells?

With something like this:

ex →

Teacher: OK, so let's make sure we're clear on the differences between plant and animal cells. Jason, what does the presence of a cell wall tell me about the cell I'm looking at? . . . Good, and what else might tell me I was looking at a plant cell, Charlene? . . . And which cells have chloroplasts, Jose? . . . Yes, and why do they have them, Sasha? . . . Good; it sounds like we're ready to move on.

Ideally, you might choose a few key points of transition in your lesson — two or three maybe — and plan in advance to insert a round of questions at each one. Even though this might appear likely to add time to your lesson, it's usually faster in the long run — because getting it right before you move on is more efficient than circling back later.

It's important to note that the goal of your targeted questions isn't to be comprehensive. The goal is to take a small, brief data sample where previously no data existed, and ascertain something about the general level of knowledge in the room. There's a temptation for every teacher to take something that's "quick and dirty" and make it better. This is one case where you'll want to resist the temptation. It's better to be quick and bring data to multiple places in your lesson by making fast, frequent strategic guesses than to be comprehensive and exhaustive, but infrequent. The perfect is the enemy of the good. The following rules of thumb may be helpful.

Speed Counts

Delivering targeted questions should usually take less than a minute or two. The primary goal of *Targeted Questioning* is to gauge understanding accurately, of course, but speed is relevant because teachers who can gauge mastery quickly can frequently check for understanding *throughout* their lessons. Teachers who can ask targeted questions quickly and efficiently are able to incorporate them into lessons on a *consistent* basis, without breaking the flow of their instruction or dramatically changing their desired lesson plan. In other cases, you will of course use more thorough tools for checking for understanding, but in this case quick is what we want.

Plan Questions in Advance

For most teachers, asking questions with precision and efficiency requires thinking of them in advance. Planning questions not only makes them more precise measures of what you taught but also frees you from having to think of your next question on the spot. You can move through questions more quickly, listen more closely to student responses, and, in turn, track patterns or trends in student mastery, perhaps even tabulating them. Planning your questions in advance also allows for more precise word choice, which leads directly to better, more revealing questions. In addition, once the lesson is over, having these questions scripted into your plan makes it much easier to reflect on and sharpen your questioning skills (Did they work the way I asked them?), an advantage that can steepen your learning curve over time.

Scripting your questions in advance makes it easier to also script the answers you'd like to hear from your students. This clarifies what you're looking for in a correct answer and helps you anticipate and plan for likely errors. For the majority of teachers, there are few steps more useful than considering two questions: What are the mistakes I'm likely to get? and What could I do about it if I got them? Planning how to respond to potential mistakes makes it more likely that you'll take action should they occur.

Sample Strategically

When you ask targeted questions, you can maximize how much you learn by being intentional about choosing to whom you direct questions. Ideally, in asking five or six questions, you'd call on your best guess of a statistical sample of the students in the room. Two students who are usually around the middle. Two perhaps who tend to take a little longer to master the content. Perhaps one high flyer. Calling on a group of students who more broadly reflect the spectrum of skill in the class gives you a sense not only of what the students you called on know but also of what the students you *didn't* call on likely know. No sample will ever be perfect, but six students who represent a plausible cross section are more predictive of the rest of the class than your six most energetic and eager students.

Cold Call

You'll want to use technique 33, *Cold Call* (Chapter Seven), to get the most out of *Targeted Questioning*. Students who volunteer to answer a question are more likely to know the answer than those who don't. If you take only volunteers when you check for understanding, then your data will always tell you that the news is better than it really is. And because, obviously, the ideal statistical sample won't have their hands in the air exactly when you want them, you'll need to normalize the idea of choosing and calling on less-forthcoming individuals—*Cold Calling*—in order to see what they know. Be aware, though, that it's important not to limit your *Cold Call only* to when you check for understanding. You want to *Cold Call* long before that—and frequently—so that you normalize it, and students aren't surprised when you use *Cold Call* as part of your targeted questions. To truly check for understanding, you need the ability to call on anyone in your class at any time. And to do that, you need to make *Cold Call* part of the class's normal operating systems.

Track the Data

Sampling also offers the opportunity to see responses to your questions as a data set, rather than as isolated, individual answers. For example, when I used to ask my students questions in class, I would sometimes get a few wrong answers before a student provided the right one. "What's the protagonist afraid of here?" I might ask. The first answer wasn't really on target, typically, so I might say something like "Mmmm, not quite." The next answer might be closer, but still not really there. Then a student might repeat part of a previous answer without adding much. Then, finally, the fourth student I called on might give me a high-quality answer. "Right," I'd say and think to myself, "They finally got it." But, of course, *they* didn't get it. One out of four got it. I had imagined a story of progress in a data set that should have told me the opposite. Wrong, wrong, wrong, right is *not* good news, generally speaking. So instead, I want to think of the answers I get as a data set. What percentage of the group gave a correct or sufficient answer? Was it possible that students used their peers' answers to eliminate some possibilities and guess correctly?

Once you've replaced self-report with a sample set of targeted questions, you can make your CFU even stronger by ensuring that your questions (targeted and otherwise) possess two key characteristics: reliability and validity.

Reliability and Validity

When you use questioning to check for understanding, including *Targeted Questioning*, your questions must do a lot of important work in a short period of time. To get the most out of them, you'll want to think about a few topics in question design.

Reliability. The biggest danger in assessment is a *false positive*. You ask a student a question, and he gets the right answer. It appears to suggest mastery, but could it be an illusion? Your student might have gotten lucky and guessed correctly. Or maybe he got one right, but isn't likely to get most right. Still, you heard the right answer, concluded everything was fine, and checked him off your mental list. A false positive like this is dangerous because it's likely to go unaddressed. For that reason, you want to be as sure as you can that correct answers are also *reliable*—that they're repeatable and likely to reoccur. One of the best ways to do that is to ask "why" and "how" questions that give evidence of the quality of the thinking behind the answer. Another is to ask a question in multiple formats. You want to always ask yourself when you assess: What are the chances they'll get the next one right on this topic?

Validity. An assessment is valid if it measures what it claims to measure. In the classroom, validity means ensuring that the difficulty of your questions meets or exceeds the end goal *and* that you've included enough question variety to ensure that your students will be able to express their mastery no matter the format in which the question is asked. If students answer only multiple-choice questions when you check for understanding, for example, your assessment is not likely to be valid. Students are ultimately almost always responsible for open-response formats—usually on the test, and certainly in life. More subtly, if students almost always answer questions in the one or two formats that are most natural to you, they might not be prepared when they face questions from other sources.

It's perhaps obvious to point out that validity implies planning. What's the final standard? Do you derive it from a state test? From the SAT? In terms of college readiness? What's a plausible range of formats students might face?

Consider the following three questions about the Stamp Act of 1765. A teacher might check students' understanding by asking any sequence of these questions:

1. What was the Stamp Act? Why was it important?

2. Here is a line from a history textbook: "If this new tax were allowed to pass without resistance, the colonists reasoned, the door would be open for far more troublesome taxation in the future." What "tax" is it referring to? Was the tax "allowed to pass without resistance"? Explain.

3. What did the Stamp Act propose to do? What governing body passed it? How did the House of Burgesses react? Who led the reaction among the Burgesses? How did the governor of the Virginia Colony react?

The first question asks for a basic identification of the Stamp Act and a summary of its importance. Pretty good, but the teacher would have no idea how her students would fare if they were asked about the Stamp Act using a different format. The question might allow students to narrate what they know and avoid what they don't know, as some other questions might not. If the SAT asked the question differently, a correct answer to question 1 might not indicate how students were likely to do. Question 2, which asks them to recall the name of the historical event based on a description rather than vice versa, takes a different approach, and combining both in the course of an assessment would give you better validity. Question 3 looks at a broader scope of events and the connections among them. Balancing multiple formats helps you ensure that your students are prepared for uncertainty.

The demands of reliability and validity require asking a significant number and wide array of targeted questions to check for understanding—enough to establish that students aren't guessing, that they can tell you why, and that they can apply their knowledge in several formats. This need makes another strong argument for *Cold Call* (technique 33) and for asking small, quick batches of questions multiple times throughout a lesson. You can question students much more quickly when you don't have to wait for hands to go up. In many classes we've watched, teachers spend only a minority of their CFU time on actual questions and answers. Instead, they spend much more time than is necessary—and than they realize—waiting for students to raise their hands, and exhorting, cajoling, reassuring, and narrating it all back to them ("I'm seeing the same three hands," "I want to hear from more of you," or "This is going to be on the test tomorrow"). The result is a process that takes twice as long as it should.

Want More? Clip 12. Want to see more *Targeted Questioning*? Watch Shadell (Noel) in clip 12.

STANDARDIZE THE FORMAT

Streamline observations by designing materials and space so that you're looking in the same, consistent place every time for the data you need.

3

The second means of real-time data gathering in the classroom is through observation. One major benefit of observation is that it allows you to respond quickly to more complex ideas and formats of thinking than you can assess through questioning alone. Another benefit is that you can "parallel-process"—you can be checking for understanding while students are working, and this is highly efficient. You could, for example, quickly observe the quality of ideas and expression in your students' thesis paragraphs as they are writing them. That would be both efficient and revealing, and doing so suggests the final benefit of observation—that it allows you to check in on almost everybody in the class if you do it well.

Gathering data in the midst of instruction is almost always subject to significant time constraints. Say you assign independent work to students for five minutes. By the time you've given everyone a chance to get started and have checked to make sure they're under way, you might have two-and-a-half minutes to assess thirty students—five seconds per student. If you can gather information three times as fast with half as many distractions, you suddenly become able to gather data in situations where you weren't previously able to. In other words, if you reduce the transaction cost of data gathering, you will be able to use it consistently and intentionally without redesigning your lessons. And it allows you to better manage part of your lesson—independent student work—that often goes unmonitored.

Standardize the Format is one of the most powerful tools for streamlining data gathering and making your observation more efficient. It means designing materials and space so that you're looking in the same, consistent place every time for the data you need. You might ask for work to be shown in the margin of a specific page of your students' books, for example, or for students to mark up a page in a specific way. Or, at the beginning of class, you might give students a "packet" (see technique 19, *Double Plan*) in which to do key aspects of their work that day, and include clearly visible, preset places to write or take notes. In Dave Javsicas's packet from his study of *Lord of the Flies* with his seventh graders, for example, the first thing you'll notice is that Dave's students write a *ton* about really ambitious topics. But as they write, it's easy for Dave to assess them, because every paper looks the same. At a glance, he can scan for the key point. Using a packet like Dave's would mean that as you circulated around the room, you wouldn't have to spend time flipping through students' writing saying, "Hmmm, let's see where your paragraph about chapter 3 is" to find what you wanted. In addition to enabling you to find answers more quickly, *Standardize the Format* allows you to disrupt students less, as you won't be flipping through their work or asking them to help you find answers. Most important, though, is that instead of expending all that energy just finding answers, you can use your cognitive capacity to concentrate on identifying trends among your students' work. In essence, your reflections on their work are no longer interrupted by a series of scavenger hunts.

See It in Action: Clip 2

In clip 2, Meaghan Reuler of Leadership Prep Bedford Stuyvesant in Brooklyn systematically collects data on student understanding as she circulates, then uses what she learns to help them succeed. She begins her vocabulary lesson by prompting students to infer the meaning and "charge" (positive, neutral, or negative) of the word *disposition*. As soon as students begin, Meaghan combs each aisle, reading what her students have written. Because she *Standardized the Format* of every packet (see Useful Tools at the end of this chapter), Meaghan knows exactly where to look. Soon, Meaghan notices a trend and narrates, "I'm seeing a lot that are talking about [it] having good characteristics. This is actually a *neutral* word." To address the error, Meaghan instructs her students to mark the word as "neutral" and notes that "it's not always positive."

Soon after, Meaghan asks students to write a response to the question, "Why might someone who skips breakfast develop a cranky *disposition* by lunchtime?" Plenty of hands go up, but Meaghan gently waves them down and responds, "Guys, you can get started on your own." This frees her up to continue gathering data as she makes her "rounds" and encourages students to try to do the work on their own before they ask for help.

After taking a hand, Meaghan assigns another writing task: "How could you write a caption about this woman's *disposition*?" Again, she circulates, observes some good work, but then spots another misunderstanding: students are using the word incorrectly. She reteaches by scripting out an example to illustrate precisely *how* students should use the word, not just telling them it's wrong but describing—and making students practice—how to get it right.

You could take Meaghan's and Dave's idea and adapt it to different situations, too—asking students to place evidence or definitions on either side of a T-chart, for example—so you would be able not only to look in the same place for information but also to quickly and easily differentiate and compare the two ideas they were tracking. You'd have a standardized place where they made their comparison.

I recently tried this myself at a workshop on CFU. The topic was *Reject Self-Report,* and the activity was a series of case studies: six transcripts from classroom situations where a teacher had initially relied on student self-report to assess mastery. Teachers in the workshop were asked to rewrite cases, scripting their questions to better gather data about student mastery in lieu of self-report. Workshop participants were asked to complete several of the scenarios over the course of a few minutes. At the bottom was an additional section where people were asked to identify and rewrite a case from their own experience. The page I provided looked like Figure 1.1.

Figure 1.1   Reject Self-Report Mini Case Studies

Self-Report Statements	Rewritten to Reject Self-Report
Example 1: **Teacher:** A "regular polygon" is a two-dimensional shape with sides that are all equal and angles that are all equal. Got it? **Student:** Yes.	
Example 2: **Teacher:** To *glare* and to *gaze* are similar because they both mean that you are looking at someone or something—usually for a long time. They're different because when you glare, you're looking at someone angrily, and when you gaze, you're looking with great interest or wonder. *Glare* has a negative charge, whereas *gaze* has a positive charge. Get it? **Students:** Yes.	

As my team and I circulated, we were able to ascertain the following quickly and easily:

- How quickly people were working and how many scenarios they had completed. This allowed us to make a simple but fundamental decision: How much time should we allocate for the activity? Did people need more time?

- Which scenarios people chose to work on. It was clear at a glance which of the scenarios they'd chosen to rewrite. Each was in its own box of about a quarter page. I could glance over twenty shoulders and know which topics people had found interesting and would want to discuss during the postactivity discussion. It also helped us write scenarios for future workshops. If very few people chose example 5, say, we could replace it.

- What good ideas and common mistakes we could talk about during the debrief. It was easy for me to look for more evidence of something specific; for example, if I saw something intriguing in one participant's answer to example 3 and wanted to know if it was typical, it was ten times easier for me to track other people's responses to that example.

It was also easy to scan to the final question and differentiate those answers. That is, I wanted to look differently at the scenario of their own experience to get a quick sense of the sorts of settings they were finding applicable. This was easy to do because the answer I wanted to analyze more closely was located in the same place on every participant's paper. I could find it and tell it apart in an instant.

People worked for three or four minutes, and the room had about 120 people in it. But at the end of that time, I had a pretty good sense of what the strengths and gaps in understanding were, and it was mostly thanks to an apparently mundane design decision. Merely using *Standardize the Format* in a very simple way greatly leveraged my ability to understand what was happening in the room. But what if you're not using written material?

Standardize the (Visual) Field

Consider a video I sometimes use of an outstanding coach running a workshop for a group of fourteen-year-old soccer players on "preventing the turn." The coach explains how he wants players to line up defensively and how they should react to an opposing player with the ball. He models the drill to bring his explanation to life. Then he tells the girls to practice. In my estimation, most of the girls then proceed to do the exercise incorrectly. They practice getting it wrong and thus, you could argue, get better at getting it wrong. To my surprise, the coach continues, seemingly aware that mastery is imperfect, but not noticing the high rate of error. One reason for this, I believe, is the setup of the drill. The girls are working in pairs, but they're facing and moving in many different directions. (See Figure 1.2.)

so he can't tell

Figure 1.2   Standardizing the Field

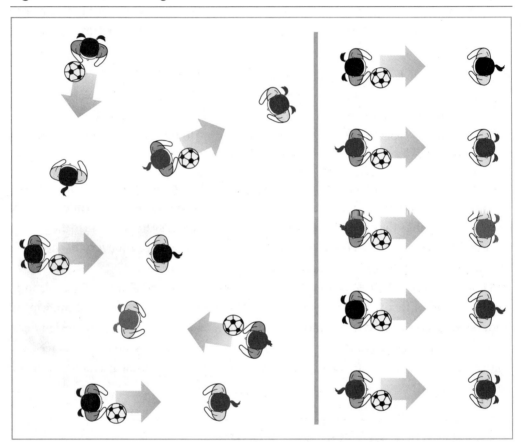

Viewing the group as a whole, it's impossible to track an individual amid the swirling movement (at left). Would the coach have seen the errors if the girls had lined up in a more predictable pattern (at right)? Could he have then scanned a simple and predictable place to see the event he was looking to evaluate? I suspect so.

Let's apply his on-field experience to the classroom. Think of some of the ways complex visual fields present barriers to data gathering in the classroom. Then think about some of the ways you might remedy them. One approach is to standardize the visual field: to arrange the classroom so that groups are in a predictable visual pattern. This allows you to scan and understand it at a glance. Another might be to add something observable to indicate engagement, setting the expectation that during group discussion you should see knee-to-knee conversations, eye contact, nodding, or other visual signs of engagement.

TRACKING, NOT WATCHING

Be intentional about how you scan your classroom. Decide specifically what you're looking for and remain disciplined about it in the face of distractions.

Another important tool in making yourself more efficient and effective at gathering information through observation is to add a healthy dose of intentionality to your looking. In fact, when your purpose for observation is the gathering of data, *tracking* is a better word for what you are seeking to do than *watching*. **Tracking, Not Watching** means deciding specifically what you're looking for and remaining disciplined about it in the face of a thousand distractions. It sounds mundane, but it's far from simple. By definition, few people are aware of what they don't notice—or that you can in fact "decide" what to notice. Moreover, we're inclined to think that noticing more things is better than noticing fewer things, but that's often not the case in the classroom.

In my first teaching job, for example, I knew to circulate around the room and observe when my students were doing independent work. I believed I was very observant as I did so. On my best days, I would circulate as though looking at a blank canvas, waiting to be struck by observations about students. There's a pastiche of quirks and color to observe in student writing, and it was truly fascinating. But what I noticed was often a random event. Therefore, what I gave students feedback on was also likely to be random. If on any given day there were ten really important things you could say about students' writing, I might notice something about number seven on the list. Or number nine. The cost was that I wasn't talking about topics one, two, and three consistently—and sometimes not at all. I wasn't giving students feedback on the most important things because I had not decided to look for them when I observed their work. I was looking rather than tracking, waiting to let chance decide what I saw rather than setting out to look for the most important things, even if it meant hunting them out through the thickets of my students' writing.

Great teachers are more likely to track—perhaps not every time they circulate the classroom, but more often, especially when they want to check for understanding. If those great teachers had been in my shoes, they'd have asked themselves what they wanted to see students doing. Whereas my internal narrative was often something like, "OK, Brandon is working hard. Good. And Sarah's working hard. Wes seems a little stuck, though." A better teacher's internal narrative might sound something like this: "OK, Sarah found her evidence, but she dropped in a full quotation without the partial paraphrase needed to weave it in, whereas Travis found the subtle evidence, and he's woven the quotation into his paragraph smoothly by paraphrasing part of it. Morgan's truncated the quotation she's cited for efficiency. Smart. No quotation marks for Walter. Red flag."

Whereas I was looking for signs that my students had completed the assignment, a better teacher would be looking for evidence that they were doing the things that would most help them master the skills they were working on.

Specific Errors and Success Points

Tracking, then, involves intentional observation: the active seeking of the most important indicators of learning. Those indicators fit into two categories: specific errors and success points. Tracking specific errors means asking *what* aren't they getting and *who* isn't getting it, and, ideally, quantifying those mistakes. Tracking success points, in contrast, means determining the most important things that distinguish *excellence* from *completion*, writing them down, and observing whether students do those things. Do you notice the significant similarity? Both specific errors and success points should be recorded or quantified, whether mentally or physically. Doing so provides a yardstick for reteaching. For example, you might put a hash mark by the name of every student in your class who, in citing evidence from the text, is still lifting that evidence in long sentences or chunks rather than using partial paraphrasing. And you may notice this because before your lesson, you took a few minutes to think through your students' most likely mistakes and plan your responses. In that case, your internal narrative may be something like this: "Just as I feared, I need to get them to digest those quotes in smaller chunks and more purposefully steer the argument. We'll have to circle back. I'll use that idea I worked out yesterday." This is much better than trying to think of an approach for reteaching on the spur of the moment. (Don't worry: if the concepts of specific errors, success points, and how to plan for them seem a bit unclear, I provide greater detail on all three in Chapter Two.)

Consider how Taryn Pritchard of Leadership Prep Bedford Stuyvesant applies this idea in her classroom. Many teachers use *Do Now* (technique 20) to start their class. One of the challenges of *Do Now* is that due to a lack of time, you often can't review every problem students did. But as Taryn circulates, she solves this problem by keeping tallies of which problems students are getting wrong. Each time she observes a student who's gotten a problem wrong, she puts a hash mark next to that question. Sometimes she writes the student's initials in as well so that she can call on him or her to review. Sometimes she notes what they did wrong or right ("didn't reduce"), paying particular attention to repeated errors and noting them with a "2x" or "3x." When she is done circulating, Taryn knows a lot of incredibly valuable information: Which of the questions should she review? Whom could she call on if she wanted to review a common error? Whom could she call on if she wanted an exemplar? What did they need to circle back to tomorrow? Simple and brilliant.

SHOW ME

Flip the classroom dynamic in which the teacher gleans data from a passive group of students. Have students actively show evidence of their understanding.

Another useful tool in making your observation of student work more effective and efficient involves flipping the common classroom dynamic, wherein the teacher actively seeks data from a passive group of students. In **Show Me,** students actively show the teacher evidence of their understanding, a reversal that also makes misunderstandings more evident. Students own the responsibility for facilitating the data gathering. There are two versions of *Show Me*: the first is *hand signals,* whereby students share data on their answers; the second is *slates,* whereby students show you their actual work.

Hand Signals

Although there are a variety of ways to employ hand signals, the key to the approach is that on a specific cue, students hold up digits in unison to represent their answer. Notice that it's their *actual answer,* not their perception of it. Asking for a thumbs up, down, or sideways to show "how well you understand this problem" is different, and has several problematic aspects: it's an example of a teacher using subjective and unreliable self-report when objective data would be far more accurate. (Asking for a thumbs-up for "agree" or thumbs-down for "disagree" serves a different purpose and is a technique called *Take a Stand,* which I highlighted in the first edition of this book. This technique involves pushing students to exercise their own judgment of their peers' answers. Doing so builds engagement, healthy skepticism, and confidence. For more information, please visit **www.teachlikeachampion.com/yourlibrary/**.)

See It in Action: Clip 3

In clip 3, Bryan Belanger, a math teacher at Troy Prep Middle School, uses hand signals to gauge student mastery of a multiple-choice question about percentage rates of change. Within seconds of the morning greeting, Bryan prompts students with the cue "rock, paper, scissors . . . one, two!" On "two," students pound their desks three times in unison before they raise their hands to reveal their response (one finger for answer choice A, two for B, and so forth). Evidently, Bryan has made the act of showing him their answers so habitual that this routine unwinds like clockwork.

Once students' hands are up, Bryan swivels his head from right to left, scanning the room and narrating what he's looking for ("making sure they're nice and high") as well as what he sees ("I see lots of twos, a couple of fours"). This draws students' attention to the fact that he's *Tracking, Not Watching* and that he cares about their answers. He then asks students to be ready to defend their answer. In doing so, he acknowledges that there are multiple responses, while also withholding which one is correct.

Instead of revealing the answer directly, Bryan calls on Blaize (who correctly selected B) to explain her answer and reasoning. He then affirms it, but not before calling on Elizabeth (who incorrectly chose D) to reiterate it. Bryan then asks students to "check or change" their work for that problem, saying, "Give yourself a check if you picked answer choice B. If you did not, circle that, and fix it now." By insisting that students *Own and Track* (technique 10), he ensures that they *all* internalize the answer and the reasoning behind it.

Slates

Slates is the second form of *Show Me*. With slates, students complete their work at their desk and then, at their teacher's signal, hold it up to show him. Often teachers use small erasable whiteboards to do this. (This is an approach you may think is the exclusive provenance of elementary or middle school teachers, but as clip 4 of Jon Bogard shows, the method is equally effective with high school students. More on that later.) In other cases, you might have students hold up their work in other ways: a graph on graph paper, or notebooks and the student pointing to a given place—say, to their sentence defining *verisimilitude*. Although your ability to scan might not be as fast and simple in those cases, the approach can still be revealing (and effective in stressing accountability).

Want More? Clip 22 and Clip 56. Want more *Show Me*? Watch Amy Youngman in clip 56 and Erin Michels in clip 22.

There's also a high-tech version of slates that, if you're lucky enough to have, involves students using handheld devices—"clickers"—to enter their response to a multiple-choice question during class, with the teacher gaining instant access to a full data set in seconds. It can result in instant understanding, can inform useful action (by, for example, identifying which wrong answer was most problematic), and has a certain "cool factor" that students love. If you have access to it, great. I would merely offer the caveat that it can be so appealing and efficient to use that it can drive out other forms of CFU, especially forms that have a wider range of formats—most important, open-ended rather than multiple-choice responses.

Among the various forms of hand signals and slates, some consistent themes emerge. In all of its versions, *Show Me* features students *showing their teacher objective data on their work in unison* so that the teacher can quickly assess it. Take a moment to consider several key elements of that definition:

- Objective data: teachers might be tempted to think they're doing *Show Me* when they ask for subjective data from students: "Hold up your fingers, one to four. One means 'I get it'; four means 'I'm lost.'" That tool may have other uses, but it's not good for CFU. Only objective data reports are included as part of *Show Me*.

- Shown *to* the teacher: the data in *Show Me* are actively presented by students in visual form—held up so you can see them and scan them quickly from where you're standing. No circulation is necessary. You probably circulate and observe what your students are doing all the time in class. That's a great practice, but it's different from *Show Me*.

- In unison: the data sharing from students usually works only if it happens in unison, so there's no piggybacking and changing answers by students in response to their peers. Everyone presents his or her data point on cue, and that's that.

See It in Action: Clip 4

Jon Bogard, a ninth-grade math teacher at Sci Academy in New Orleans, uses *Show Me* to collect and respond to data about student understanding in real time. To do this, he asks students to copy and then solve the following math problem on erasable whiteboards (that is, slates): "Find the inverse of f(x) = 3x − 9." He then asks students to raise their slates once they're done. This procedure is a powerful way to collect data without having to fish for it; instead, the data *come to him*. And because this *Show Me* requires *every* student to show his or her work, the data Jon collects are more reliable.

Initially, Jon notices that several students are struggling with his question, so he reframes it in clearer terms: "I want you thinking 'reverse your x and y's.'" As Jon continues scanning students' boards, he notices that some still need more help, so he continues breaking the problem down into smaller steps. First, he asks them to reverse their x's and y's in the equation y = 3x − 9. Next, he asks students to isolate y in the equation x = 3y − 9.

Once students begin raising their boards, Jon draws attention to the fact that he's closely examining their work. He occasionally points to boards, cranes his neck to read what they wrote, and responds with affirmatives like "good." In several cases, he notices that students are ready for more advanced problems and sends them off to independent practice with the phrase "Go to IP." With *Show Me*, Jon can catch errors before they snowball into bigger misunderstandings.

AFFIRMATIVE CHECKING

Insert specific points into your lesson when students must get confirmation that their work is correct, productive, or sufficiently rigorous before moving on to the next stage.

The last tool to help you use observation to check for understanding also involves students taking a more active role. In **Affirmative Checking**, you insert specific points into your lesson when students must get confirmation that their work is correct, productive, or sufficiently rigorous before moving on to the next stage — a new paragraph, a second draft, a harder set of problems, a new step in a lab. Watch Bob Zimmerli demonstrate in clip 5.

See It in Action: Clip 5

Bob Zimmerli, a former seventh-grade math teacher and current dean of curriculum and instruction at Rochester Prep's Brooks Campus, asks students to independently solve multistep equations. Because Bob knows that the content can be tricky, he instructs students to check in with him after every two problems. These checkpoints give him a way to collect data from every student, which in turn gives him a richer, more reliable snapshot of student understanding. This system of *Affirmative Checking* also holds students and teacher accountable to each other for achieving the same goal: mastery of the day's objective. By design, the process of spotting and fixing errors becomes a shared endeavor.

Bob circulates and carefully tracks students' papers. Because Bob *Standardized the Format*, carefully engineering the place where students record their work and answers, he's able to spend less time looking all over packets and more time processing and responding to student trends. Practically speaking, saving a few seconds from countless scans every day would enable Bob to add back several days (possibly even weeks) of instructional time to each school year.

After checking in with a few students, Bob begins to notice a trend: students keep forgetting to combine like terms. Initially, he responds by pointing to a poster at the front of the room that outlines the steps students should take to solve each problem. Although the poster helps, Bob soon realizes that it would be far more efficient to reteach everyone the skill of combining like terms. To do this, Bob selects a problem that no one started and begins working through it. This helps him makes sure that *everyone* (including high performers and early finishers) has something to learn from his mini-lesson.

There are many ways to include *Affirmative Checking* within an activity or lesson, but consider the following observations on implementation to help you ensure their effectiveness:

- The checkpoint(s) should ideally pass quickly. The rationale here is pretty clear—letting students wait around for you to check them off is a waste of instructional time and an opportunity to be off task. Arms folded, pencil down, or chatting with a neighbor, bolstered by "I'm waiting to get checked," is not the desired outcome. So move fast—have a rubric or an answer sheet ready even if the work appears pretty straightforward.

- Asynchronous checkoff is implicit here—the process from a student's perspective is that you get checked as soon as you're ready and don't wait for others to reach that point once you pass it. It's just on to the next step. Ideally the work would be challenging enough that students would tend to finish at different times, spreading out the checking naturally. I suspect that's why Bob Zimmerli gave students two problems to do before each check-off. The problems were similar in terms of the skills they required, so Bob could actually start affirming students as they complete the *first* of two problems. It bought him twice the time to check the room.

- It could be useful to make this approach more explicit by adding "bonus" work. In other words, you might, in Bob's situation, give students three problems in each stage of a problem set, but make the third an optional or extra (or extra credit) bonus they could do if they had time, and with the checking starting after they'd completed one or two. In other words, those who were waiting could always go on to the third bonus problem while you checked others' work. This might sound contradictory—the point here is to check before you go on. The difference is that the third problem is the same level of difficulty as the first two.

- If you incorporate the previous point, you want to make the signal for "I'm ready" the sort of cue that students can give while continuing to work. Keeping his or her hand in the air for three minutes makes it all but impossible for the student to go on to another problem.

- You could make your sign-off even faster by combining *Affirmative Checking* with *Show Me*, by having students hold up their work for you to sign off on. (Watch Jon Bogard in clip 4 do this with his ninth graders.)

See It in Action: Clip 6

Hilary Lewis, a first-grade teacher at Excellence Girls Charter School in Brooklyn, uses *Affirmative Checking* to gauge student mastery before independent work. At the outset, Hilary asks students to complete a math problem on a green sticky note or "ticket" and then to exchange that ticket for the opportunity to start independent practice (IP). She then continues to stoke interest and suspense by comparing this exchange to the experience of "going into a movie." By requiring students to "earn" the privilege of participating in IP, she turns it into a kind of reward. And because students must show correct work in order to move on to IP, they have no incentive to speed through it at the expense of accuracy. This sends an implicit message that Hilary values quality work over speed.

One by one, students complete the problem and patiently await Hilary's signal. She calls them up, and because all students were asked to show their work on a sticky note, Hilary knows immediately where to look. When students hand her work that's correct, she responds with a warm, positive, yet understated tone that seems to suggest: "Good. You got it right, just as I expected." When one student shows her work for the *wrong* problem, she responds with the same warm, supportive tone and comments, "OK. You did your own problem, which is great. I need you to do *that* problem [as she points to the board]." Her reaction signals to the student that "getting it wrong" is as normal as "getting it right."

Student-Driven *Affirmative Checking*

Affirmative Checking is a great tool: it enables you to be constantly aware of how your students are doing; it enables *them* to be constantly aware of how they are doing; and it ensures that their actions—going on or going back—inherently reflect the data on their success. That's a lot of upside. Its challenge is one of labor intensiveness. Twenty-five or thirty students are a lot to check. Despite all the pointers and tricks to make things go better, there's a risk that kids will be sitting around wasting time and becoming frustrated waiting for you.

Efficiency matters, and one way to increase it is to harness the labor of your students. The checking in *Affirmative Checking* doesn't necessarily have to be done by you. Students could self-check on a key you leave at strategic points around the room. Or they could be responsible for checking off one another's work. You could have partners working in pairs first confirm that they agree before either getting sign-off from you or checking the key, which would reduce the number of checks you needed to make. Or, on occasion, you could appoint a student to be a "checker." (If you do this, be careful to rotate the checker. It's important that what seems like a reward doesn't result in the student in question losing out on the chance to do more work and push his or her own skills in order to help you!)

One important fact to consider if you have students participate in *Affirmative Checking* is that there are two key purposes to the technique. One is to make sure that students are ensuring mastery before going on to more complex work; the other is for you to gather data on how your students are doing. Distributing the checking accomplishes the first with more efficiency, but risks reducing your access to the data: If students self-check, will you know how they did? I'm sure you will find a way to balance these goals—either by using student-centered checking sometimes and checking yourself other times, or by engineering ways to track the data during student-centered checking (or both). For example, if students self-checked against a rubric, they could check a box to show how they did so that you could track it later. It's just important to be aware of the challenge and the possible trade-off as you're out there adapting and designing new and better solutions.

CONCLUSION

Whether you utilize techniques of observation or of questioning, different teachers and different situations call for different means of collection. But once you've gathered all the relevant data surrounding student mastery, what do you do with them? In the next chapter, we'll look at some of the ways champion teachers both anticipate and remediate common errors, as well as the ways in which building a *Culture of Error* can increase a classroom's rates of risk-taking and learning, all toward the end of common mastery.

Reflection and Practice

1. To more effectively *Reject Self-Report,* write four or five targeted questions you could use to check for understanding in a lesson you are currently teaching, then practice with a colleague and see if you can deliver them in a minute or less.

2. How might you *Standardize the Format* in your classroom in terms of handouts and homework material? In terms of the visual field? What other ways might you standardize your classroom, and in what ways might they improve the overall efficiency of your lessons and your ability to assess student mastery?

3. Select one question from an upcoming lesson. Working with that question,

   a. Script a follow-up question for a correct response.

   b. Plan one anticipated wrong answer.

   c. Script the *first* question you'd ask to follow an incorrect response.

   d. Plan your cue and student hand signals.

USEFUL TOOLS

FIND THESE TOOLS AT WWW.TEACHLIKEACHAMPION.COM/YOURLIBRARY

Dave Javsicas's packet from *Lord of the Flies.* See how seventh-grade reading teacher David Javsicas designs packets that are both writing intensive and efficient for assessing student understanding.

Taryn Pritchard's *Do Now* markups. Check out the notes that sixth-grade math teacher Taryn Pritchard made for herself on a *Do Now* as she circulated to gather and respond to data on student understanding.

Meaghan Reuler's fifth-grade reading packet. Take a peek inside a fifth-grade vocabulary packet that reading teacher Meaghan Reuler carefully designed to make student errors easier to see and respond to.

Chapter 2

Acting on the Data and the Culture of Error

Technique 7: Plan for Error. Increase the likelihood that you'll recognize and respond to errors by planning for common mistakes in advance.

Technique 8: Culture of Error. Create an environment where your students feel safe making and discussing mistakes, so you can spend less time hunting for errors and more time fixing them.

Technique 9: Excavate Error. Dig into errors, studying them efficiently and effectively, to better understand where students struggle and how you can best address those points.

Technique 10: Own and Track. Have students correct or revise their own work, fostering an environment of accountability for the correct answer.

Acting on the Data and the Culture of Error

During a recent lesson, fifth-grade English teacher Meaghan Reuler was able to quickly scan for evidence of incomplete mastery and take action right away. Time and again, she stepped in quickly and seamlessly in response to data she'd quietly observed. During the lesson, which I described in Chapter One, Meaghan used *Standardize the Format* and *Tracking, Not Watching* to allow her to quickly recognize misunderstandings about the day's key vocabulary word, *disposition*. Each of her students assessed the "charge" (on a scale from strongly negative to strongly positive) in a cleverly designed box in the corner of their packet. By scanning the responses in the boxes, Meaghan was able to recognize the tendency on the part of many of her students to overgeneralize, within seconds of their doing so, and she stepped in immediately to fix it: "I'm seeing a lot [of answers] that are talking about [*disposition*] having good characteristics," she told the class. "It's actually a neutral word. It's [meaning is] positive *here*, but it's not *always* positive." Less than two minutes into this portion of her lesson, she was adjusting her teaching to address a misconception.

Minutes later, she was at it again. She'd asked students to use the word *disposition* to describe a painting of a woman. Again she *Standardized the Format,* having students all write their sentences in a dedicated box. Again she tracked carefully. And again she responded to the data, stopping her students to point out that a number of them had the meaning right, but were using the word incorrectly from a syntactical point of view. "I'm going to ask you to revise your sentences," she says. "I see a lot of good ideas about what her mood might be, but because this word is a noun, we should say, 'This woman has a *blank* disposition.'"

Want More? Clip 2.   Want more? You can see Meaghan responding quickly and seamlessly to data in clip 2.

It's an obvious but critical connection: strategic, intentional, efficient data gathering (the sort described in Chapter One) will result in increased achievement only if it consistently leads to a quick responsive action from the teacher, as it does in Meaghan's classroom. And responding to data is a much bigger challenge than we often acknowledge. Evidence that we fail to act on data, even when faced with evidence of gaps in student mastery, abounds. Who has not seen poor results emerge on a quiz or a test and recalled the lessons taught over the previous days, thinking, "I knew it!" (or at least, "I should have known it")?

Even when we're partially aware that what we're teaching isn't sinking in, it's easy to "bury the data" and explain them away or do nothing about them. The barriers to action in such situations are likely to be as much psychological as technical, which means that a different sort of approach is required to train oneself to act, and act right away. That process usually begins before the lesson starts, both with the planning process and with actions that build, over time, a classroom culture that makes errors visible, normal, safe, and even positive. When everyone in the room is comfortable with the idea of making mistakes, responding to them is easier.

PLAN FOR ERROR

Increase the likelihood that you'll recognize and respond to errors by planning for common mistakes in advance.

"Acting on the data" is risky. I mean that in the psychological sense. It can mean doing something new and possibly unanticipated, live, on the spur of the moment, sometimes in front of a room full of potentially skeptical adolescents. The data tell you something is wrong, so, as the students look on, you set out to devise an antidote, changing your lesson plan and instructional methods in unexpected ways that may not jibe with your ambitious lesson goals or fit within the ten minutes you have left in class, never mind the urgent pressure you feel to finish the unit on respiration by next Wednesday. All the while, a distant tick-tick-ticking reminds you of what happens when you fail for more than a few minutes to engage your students. When you adapt your lesson, you are not only boldly creating something new but also blowing something up—specifically, the lesson plan you labored over so as to arrange just the right sequence of events and maximize every instructional minute. There's potentially quite a bit of fear in doing so: fear of failing, of uncertainty, of changing course; fear of running out of time; fear of making more advanced students wait as others circle back. No wonder we sometimes bury the data. It makes you wonder, perhaps, who in their right mind would ever do anything else.

One of the best ways to reduce some of the anxiety and therefore make it more likely that you will take action is to **Plan for Error**. After all, although it's hard to predict exactly who will struggle with what, it's almost inevitable that errors will occur. It's just a matter of which ones and when. Predicting a single, specific error is difficult; predicting broadly is not. You know errors are coming, but foresight can help make them predictable and can allow you to respond with adaptations within your lesson rather than deviations from it. That's far easier to manage in the moment.

Troy Prep Middle School math teacher Bryan Belanger provided me with an impromptu clinic on this topic. A group of us were reviewing a series of his recent lesson packets. His packet for an eighth-grade lesson on the slope-intercept formula, I noticed, had more problems than his students could ever do in a class period—more than fifty! They ranged from simple to complex, roughly in sequence. "They're never going to do all of these problems in one class," I commented. "Not a chance," Bryan said with a smile. "I'm just planning for how things might go in [each of my] classes. If Homeroom Union is ready to jump ahead, I'll skip forward a few problems. If Homeroom Princeton is struggling, I'll loop back and do a few extra. I pick and choose what problems they need and how fast we go as the lesson happens."

In ordering problems roughly by complexity, Bryan can more easily navigate as he responds to data throughout the lesson. He compared it to a "Choose Your Own Adventure" novel, the sort you read in third grade, perhaps, where you flipped forward and back through the book as you made one decision or another. Light bulb! *There was no one, single path through Bryan's lesson*. His preparation assumed that he would need to be responsive to where his students' learning took him. In response to struggle or success, he could merely tell his students to flip back or ahead a few pages in the packet. I often advise teachers to choose a few key points in the lesson to intentionally check, but Bryan's lesson planning assumed that he would *always* be responding to data. He'd planned to ask himself every time his students finished a problem or two, "Should I loop back for more or push on a little? Or perhaps a lot?" Voilà—a response to error (or success) at almost no transaction cost and with almost no delay or on-the-spot rethinking required. It was all in the planning. (For a further discussion of the power of packet design, see technique 19, *Double Plan*, in Chapter Four.)

Reflecting on Bryan's lesson, I realized that many of the other top-performing teachers I knew did something similar, adapting the principle to different subject areas. For example, champion reading teacher Patrick Pastore's lessons often intersperse the text students are reading with segments in which students are asked to respond in writing or via discussion. You might find a three- or four-page section from a novel in one of his packets and then a pair of writing prompts, or perhaps a writing prompt and a discussion question, with space for note taking. His packets, I realized in looking again, usually contain more writing and/or discussion prompts than he would ever be able to use in a single lesson. Like Bryan's, Patrick's decisions in responding to his student's level of mastery then are simple: What questions do I choose to skip? Which types do I do more of? After a segment of text, do I choose the prompt that's more literal or the one that's figurative? In any case, the work they do is always of high quality because the questions are all planned in advance. If you don't plan in advance, you risk having less quality when you need it most—in the face of confusion.

Ways to Use *Plan for Error*

There are other ways to use the *Plan for Error* technique in your lessons, of course. Here are two.

Planning for Specific Errors

In Chapter One, I discussed the power of tracking specific errors—those that are both important and especially likely to occur. Once you've made this determination—that is, established that "these are the errors that are most likely to occur"—you know something profound and can plan in advance how you would react to them if, as you predict, they emerge.

In fact, just writing out the two or three things you think students are likely to struggle with is beneficial to your teaching, *whether or not students actually make the expected errors*. Even if you're wrong about what they get wrong, having anticipated likely errors reduces the "surprise" and "inconvenience" of it. In acknowledging to yourself that you know errors are sure to occur, you make it more likely that you will respond effectively to *any* error.

Anticipating errors and planning responses to them is one of the most productive training or planning exercises you can do as a teacher. If students make the mistakes you anticipate, you're likely to have a terrific solution; if you're wrong, you get to improve your level of insight about your students' thinking by reflecting on the dissonance between the errors you anticipated and the mistakes that actually occurred. And, when you have time to do it with focus and to be able to research alternatives, you're still getting practice thinking about how to clarify misunderstandings. Over time, such practice is likely to result in better spur-of-the-moment reactions as well. My colleague Julie Jackson, a world-class teacher, principal, and now a managing director of high-performing schools, uses the following activity with her teachers:

- List three to five of the most important questions you will ask in your lesson tomorrow.

- For each question, list two incorrect answers you think you're likely to get.

- Describe how you'd respond to each of the incorrect answers.

Making a habit of noting the two or three specific errors you think students are most likely to make and planning what you'll do if they occur allows you, like Bryan Belanger, to include tools for a potential reteach in your lesson materials in advance.

Planning Reteach Time

You can address another barrier to action—the pressure to "cover" your lesson—with a second element of planning: leaving time specifically to loop back to trouble spots (or to leap ahead if there are none). Planning time to review and circle back or push on for enrichment or challenge may not be viable in every lesson, but surely it is viable in some. If, say, you planned a minute to ask targeted questions followed by a five-minute "either-or" block of time, where you either circled back to review or tried something fun and tricky as the data indicated, you might combine your effective data gathering with taking action. As the idea of planning a section for review or extension suggests, checking for understanding can and should also mean responding when you do achieve success. In truth, that also is a form of acting on the data, though one we tend to reflect on less because good news seems less urgent. Nonetheless, it's still an opportunity. In such a case, you might include a focus on success points or planning "challenges" in your lesson.

CULTURE OF ERROR

Create an environment where your students feel safe making and discussing mistakes, so you can spend less time hunting for errors and more time fixing them.

In order to consistently identify misunderstandings, champion teachers create a classroom culture that embraces error. Over and over again, as my team and I examined videos of top teachers, we noticed that they made CFU a shared endeavor between themselves and their students. From the moment students arrived, the teachers worked to shape their perception of what it meant to make a mistake, pushing them to think of "wrong" as a first, positive, and often critical step toward getting it "right." They recognized that students could best learn from mistakes if they were willing to acknowledge and share them. There was immense value in the learning that came from error if they could make it feel safe to be wrong.

Once this **Culture of Error** is created, once it's safe to be wrong, students are as likely as not to *want* to expose their mistakes to their teacher. This shift from defensiveness or denial to openness is critical. If your goal is to find and address the mistakes your students make, your task is far more difficult if your students seek to hide their errors from you. If, in contrast, they willingly share their struggles, mistakes, and errors, you can spend less time and energy hunting for them and more time fixing and learning from them. Similarly, if the goal is for students to learn to self-correct—to find and address errors on their own — becoming comfortable acknowledging mistakes is a critical step forward.

My team and I observed this kind of *Culture of Error* in Katie McNickle's classroom at North Star Academy in Newark, New Jersey, during a recent lesson. After a series of challenging problems, Katie asked her students to nominate problems they would "like to review." Seven or eight hands calmly went up. A student asked for clarification on what it meant to distribute mathematically. "Great question," Katie responded, and explained the concept. The student remained confused, so Katie asked a classmate to model a problem and then another. Crucially, Katie's tone never wavered — calm, steady, nonjudgmental — implying "of course some of you are struggling with this." Also crucial: the student's classmates were supportive, not only providing explanations but also never denigrating a peer's struggle. None of this was accidental.

We asked Katie what sorts of things she did to make students so comfortable exposing their own errors and supporting their classmates. She told us that every day, students do a challenging set of problems, their "Excellence" problems. They track how many they get right, but their score doesn't count for their grade until Friday's lesson. Students are accountable for learning as much as they can for four days so that they succeed on the fifth day. The incentive is to ask as much as they can. Still, you could set up this structure and not have students engage as much and as positively as Katie's do. In terms of long-term investment in *Culture of Error,* Katie notes, "In the beginning of the year, I praise students who are brave enough to ask questions." In the lesson we watched, students reported their scores back to her as she tracked them on a clipboard. Katie's only comments were to quietly narrate growth: "You went up five points, Tiarra," she might say. "I shout out the students who show improvement from day to day as opposed to only complimenting the top scorers," she said. "I think I've also trained and encouraged students to be helpful to their peers, by really making a big deal of it when others eagerly volunteer to explain: 'Wow, great to see that so many of us are willing to share their expertise!' and I use a lot of language like, 'Who can help her out?' or 'Let's make sure he understands,' so the kids start to view their class as a team — working together toward the common goal of mastery."

Want More? Clip 42.   Want more? Watch Katie McNickle reinforcing her *Culture of Error* in clip 42.

See It in Action: Clip 7

In clip 7, Katie Bellucci reviews a distribution problem with her class. After collecting all student answers and working through the problem together as a class, Katie normalizes error by telling students who initially got the wrong answer but have since corrected themselves to hold up their hands high and "Be proud! You just figured it out!"—making it clear that getting it wrong is neither a negative nor a permanent state, but rather a positive step on the way to mastery.

Building a *Culture of Error*

A classroom is a culture established through the words and actions not only of the teacher but also of the students. A teacher alone cannot establish a culture in which it is safe to struggle and fail. If snickers greet a classmate who gets an answer wrong, for example, or if impatient hands wave in the air while another student is trying to answer, very little that a teacher does will result in students' willingly exposing their errors to the group.

Shaping how students respond to one another's struggles is therefore a must. It is a process that starts with teaching students the right way to handle common situations *before* they happen. Explain how you expect them to act when someone struggles with the rationale, practice those expected behaviors in hypothetical situations, and when a breech inevitably occurs, reset the culture firmly, but with understanding. You might say something like, "Just a minute. I want to be very clear about the respect we will all show one another when we are in this classroom. We will support each other and help one another. And we will never, ever undertake actions that tear down another person. Among other things, we know that person could just as well be us."

Want More? Clip 66. Watch Bridget McElduff reinforce expectations that students will not laugh at one another's errors in clip 66.

When you think about making it safe to struggle, it's important to consider that this is not about just eliminating potentially negative or corrosive behaviors among your students. Even better would be fostering a culture where students actively support one another as they struggle through the learning process. Collegiate Academies in

New Orleans does a great job of encouraging this culture. When someone is struggling to answer a question, peers (or teachers) "send love," making a subtle hand gesture that means, "I'm supporting you." When a student works hard to give an answer his or her peers appreciate, they show that appreciation with snapping—positive student-to-student feedback for quality work. This positive culture is one of the most remarkable and powerful things about a remarkable group of schools.

Lastly, let's not forget that it's not just students whose errors matter. You will of course make a mistake at some point in class, too. That much is inevitable. Most likely, your mistake will be public, with thirty or so students watching you make it. They will note whether you dismiss, deny, minimize, embrace, acknowledge, or even study it. How you communicate and depict mistakes—both students' and your own—in the classroom is very important.

That all said, a classroom culture that respects error, normalizes it, and values learning from it is one of the characteristics of a high-performing classroom. *Culture of Error* has four key parts: expecting error, withholding the answer, managing your tell, and praising risk-taking.

Expect Error

Take a moment to examine the language two champion teachers used to communicate to their students their expectations about making mistakes. Consider, first, Bob Zimmerli, who stopped his math class after observation revealed a consistent error (failing to combine like terms) among his students. "I'm so glad you made that mistake," Bob said to the class, calling them together. "It's going to help me to help you." Message: mistakes are normal, valuable in many ways, and a source of insight. Bob wasn't bothered by the mistake, but communicated that when they happened, he wanted to know about them. Then he proceeded to reteach combining like terms. Compare that to something more typical, along the lines of, "Guys, I should not be seeing people with –2x and +2x in the same equation. You know by now to combine like terms." In that case, students will quickly learn that if they are making mistakes, they are likely to be a source of disappointment to their teacher. As a result, students are likely to respond by trying to conceal their errors. That doesn't mean they combine like terms any better, just that when they struggle, the teacher won't find out about it.

By the way, I'm not saying here that you shouldn't have exacting standards and expect diligence from your students. You should. You don't have to jump up and down and say, "Hooray for your mistake! It's so valuable!" every time you get one. What you are looking to do is build a culture that, by seizing opportunities here and there over time, shows that errors are a normal part of learning — a positive part, often — and are most useful when they are out in the open. After a mistake occurs, our message should communicate that we are glad to know about it and, perhaps, that our first assumption is that the misunderstanding is likely to have some cause that is not anybody's "fault." It's easy to assume that confused students weren't paying attention or don't value the knowledge, and of course there are cases when that's true. However, it's far more productive to assume that students are confused because the material is complex the first time they see it, or because our explanations were somehow imperfect after all, or just because students are like you and me and sometimes need to go over it one more time.

Now, consider Roxbury Prep math teacher Jason Armstrong, who, in one recent lesson, began communicating his expectations even before he started teaching the problem he was reviewing with his class. Asking to hear the answers his students came up with, he didn't ask for someone who had the "right answer." His words were, "Let's hear people's answers for number 2. I suspect there's going to be some disagreement here, so I might hear a couple different people's answers." He then took *four* different answers from the class. Each time he asked for more, his words — "Are there any *other* answers out there?" — implied that the normal state of affairs is to see different answers among smart people doing challenging work. This also serves to teach that math is not just a matter of deciding between a right answer and a wrong one but, sometimes, a matter of deciding among a wide array of plausible answers. If the questions are hard, Jason's teaching intimated, of course people will disagree.

Withhold the Answer

In the same lesson as the one I just described, Jason Armstrong introduced a second problem to his students for discussion, and his choice of language was again striking:

Jason: OK, now for the four answers we have here, A, B, C and D, I don't want to start by asking which one you think is right, because I want to focus on the explanations that we have. So let me hear what people think of D. I don't care if you think it's right or wrong; I just want to hear what people think. Eddie, what did you say about it?

You've probably noticed that Jason's language emphasizes the importance of mathematical thinking (as opposed to just getting it right). That's valuable. Where many teachers say things like, "I want to focus on the explanation. How you think about this is as important as whether you got it right," what Jason does is different because *students don't know whether or not they are discussing a right answer*. He has asked them not to discuss how they got the answer *they* gave — and therefore think is right — but an answer that he chose.

We often begin reviewing a problem by revealing the right answer and then, suspense alleviated, talking about it. However, as soon as students know the right answer, the nature of their engagement tends to change. They shift to thinking about whether they got it right and how well they did. No matter how much they love the math for the math's sake (or the history or science or literature for its sake), part of them is thinking "Yes! I got it" or "Darn, I knew that" or "Darn, why do I keep messing up?" If Jason had said, "The answer here is B, but I want to look at D," some students would almost assuredly have thought, "Cool, I knew that," *and then stopped listening as closely because in their minds they had gotten it right and didn't need to listen.*

One of the simplest and easiest things you can do to begin building a *Culture of Error* is to delay revealing whether an answer is right or wrong until after you've discussed it, and perhaps an alternative. By *withholding the answer* until after you've discussed the question, you retain a bit of suspense, keep students productively engaged, and avoid the distraction of "Did I get it right?" for a few seconds. This can be very productive, not just as an intellectual exercise, but as a cultural one, in causing students to spend less energy evaluating their work ("I got it right. That's awesome! I'm awesome" or "I got it wrong. I am such an idiot") and more energy thinking about the underlying ideas ("I hadn't thought of doing it that way. I wonder if he'll get the answer I got").

The fact that Jason's question is a multiple-choice question makes it simple to withhold the answer, but it's also viable to do this with an open-ended question. If you were a history teacher and your question was, "How did the Treaty of Versailles affect Europe in the twenty years after the treaty?" you might put up an answer from a student, several answers from several students, or some bullet points "we might see in an answer" and ask: "So, what do you think?" Because knowing whether they are looking at right or wrong answers focuses students more on evaluating and less on analyzing, in many cases such an approach would be more productive than saying, "Here's Sally's answer. What'd she leave out?" or "Here's Sally's answer. Why is it right?"

See It in Action: Clip 8

In clip 8 we see Jason Armstrong, a fifth-grade math teacher from Boston's Roxbury Prep, initiate two different discussions during the same lesson. Jason creates an environment in which students are free to make and admit mistakes as they seek to understand every possible answer choice and facet of each problem.

Jason manages his body language and tone to support a strong *Culture of Error*. Notably, he responds to each student's contributions with "affective interest": leaning toward students as they share, glancing curiously at their papers, raising his eyebrows inquisitively, nodding his head in agreement, or showing he's deep in thought by placing his hand on his chin in a "thinking man" gesture. Jason also responds to *all* answers in the same neutral tone of voice and dutifully writes each of them on the board, which helps him avoid giving away the answer. Over the course of the lesson, we then see students mirror his affect, raising their hands to analyze answer choices that they initially eliminated or overlooked.

Manage the Tell

In poker circles, players have to watch their "tell"—the unintentional signals they give that reveal the status of their hand to savvy opponents. A good player can figure out that an opponent's habit of rubbing his eyes is a nervous tic revealing a poor hand. Having a tell puts you at such a disadvantage that some elite players wear sunglasses and hooded sweatshirts to ensure they don't reveal too much.

As teachers, we also have tells—unintentional cues that reveal what we're thinking, such as whether an answer was right or wrong or whether we valued what a student said. A tell causes us to communicate more than we realize, earlier than we realize it. It compromises our ability to withhold the answer. And it can often result in our unwittingly communicating disdain for errors.

One of my tells as a teacher was the word "interesting," offered in a benign but slightly patronizing tone of voice and usually with a "Hmmm" in front of it and a single long blink of both eyes. I would use it, without realizing it, in my English classes when a student gave an interpretation I thought was flimsy. I know this was my tell because one day after a student offered an interpretation of a chapter, I said, "Hmmm. Interesting." At which point, a student named Danielle said quite clearly from the back of the classroom, "Uh oh. Try again, Danny!" She knew what "interesting" meant: "Well, that was disappointing." Like most teachers, I was saying a lot more than I thought I was. My message to Danny was, "You probably should have kept that thought to yourself," and Danny and all my students knew that. So much for making it safe to be wrong. And of course I was tipping savvy students off in other ways. I could always count on Danielle to step in just when I wanted someone to debunk a poor idea. She was so reliable! In part, it turns out, because she'd been interpreting my tell all semester long and as a result got a steady stream of hints about how to express my own opinion back to me.

One of my most capable colleagues describes a different tell. When students gave an answer in her class, she would write it on the board if it was correct, but wouldn't bother if it was wrong. Sometimes she would call on a student and turn to the board, marker poised as if to write, only to turn back to the class upon hearing the answer, and recap the marker. Click. Message received.

We all have tells—several, probably—and because they are unintentional, we may send them over and over, communicating a message to students that undercuts what we might intend to say. Students figure out these tells surprisingly quickly, so it's important to seek them out in our own teaching and manage them. Of course, we'll never be perfect. Of course, it's fine to say, "Interesting" or even to explicitly say, "I think we can do better" or "No, I'm sorry that's not correct." You just want to be aware of and intentional about what you communicate and when. Think for a moment about what might be the most common teacher tell: "Does anyone have a *different* answer?" (When was the last time you said *that* when someone got it right?) In using this phrase without intentionality, you would first communicate that the answer was wrong and therefore risk disengaging students from thinking as deeply about it as they would if they didn't know. Second, you would implicitly say to the student who answered, "If that's all you've got, please don't speak again."

It's worth noting that the most persistent tells are usually in response to wrong answers, but we can also have tells for right answers—a big bright face or perhaps the inflection on the word "why" in a statement like, "And can you tell us *why* you think Wilbur is afraid?" Clearly, it's not a negative to show appreciation and enthusiasm for a great answer. But it *is* worth considering whether that enthusiasm sometimes gives away too much, too soon or, if it's used too often, what its absence communicates. Ideally, we'd all be alert to our tells and manage them—replacing them as often as possible with a consistent and balanced expression of appreciation that's not quite approval.

Praise Risk-Taking

The final aspect of creating a *Culture of Error* is to praise students for taking risks and facing down the challenge of a difficult subject. Katie McNickle talked about this when she reflected on how she built the *Culture of Error* in her classroom: "I praise students who are brave enough to ask questions." It's especially useful to encourage students to take risks when they're not sure. A statement such as, "This is a tough question. If you're struggling with it, that's a good sign. Now, who'll be bold and start us off?" reminds students that being a scholar means offering your thoughts when you're not sure, and sometimes *because* you're not sure. You can reinforce that positively by saying, for example, "I love the fact that this is a hard question and so many of you have your hands in the air," or you can shorthand that by simply referring to your students' "brave hands" when you see them raised (for example, "Who wants to take a shot at our challenge question? Beautiful. Love those brave hands ... Diallo, What do you think?"). If discussing a particularly difficult passage in a book, you could try acknowledging the difficulty by saying something like, "This is a question that people have debated for centuries, but you're really attacking this." In a *Culture of Error,* students should feel good about stepping out on a limb, whether they're right or wrong.

Want More? Clip 1, Clip 4, and Clip 5.   Want more? See if you can spot key elements of a *Culture of Error* in the classrooms of Amy Youngman in clip 1, Jon Bogard in clip 4, and Bob Zimmerli in clip 5.

9

EXCAVATE ERROR

Dig into errors, studying them efficiently and effectively, to better understand where students struggle and how you can best address those points.

Once you've made mistakes public, comfortable, natural, and a matter of course, the benefits of a *Culture of Error* really start to accrue. Teachers who use diagnostic assessments know that studying and analyzing error is one of the most valuable teaching tools there is. The great—and sometimes underutilized—benefit of such tools is the error analysis they enable you to conduct. You look at a question and assess not only who got it right but also who got it wrong, what they got wrong, and why. You notice that of the twelve who did not accurately describe the events in the passage, nine missed the sarcasm in the words one character spoke to another. You have a critical clue about how to remediate with those students, and perhaps about how to teach the story, or the next story, a little better next time around. Or you review the answers to a multiple-choice question and find that 60 percent of the students who got it wrong opted for choice D. Its logic was bright and shiny to students; it tied in to something they knew or thought they knew, and that made it seem right. If you can figure out that connection, you now understand how to approach the reteach and the presentation of similar material a little better next time around.

The process of looking at wrong answers and figuring out why people gave them is a powerful exercise for students as well. Making it safe to reveal errors encourages students to strive and struggle, which is important; but what is most valuable is unlocking the teaching value of errors as a classroom tool. When you **Excavate Error**, you dig into errors for that purpose.

There are probably limitless ways to do this, but to help make sense of them, I find it useful to organize them into three levels, based on the degree and type of error excavation they involve: assess and move, light excavation, and deep excavation. These correspond to three broad categories of action you can take in the face of error. To be clear, all of them are effective approaches, depending on the situation.

Assess and Move

Checking for understanding means regularly assessing the class and, when you see errors, deciding on a course of action, but that action need not necessarily entail doubling back to reteach a whole topic to the full class. There are times when you might, having observed an error, choose to keep moving and check in with the strugglers during independent work time, for example, perhaps pulling out copies of their erroneous work for study and analysis. I observed Bryan Belanger do this in a recent lesson. As students completed a problem set, Bryan circulated diligently, tracking errors as he went. Almost everyone in the class had a certain problem correct. Bryan therefore made a strategic decision not to address it with the whole class. Instead, he addressed it by stopping by one or two students' desks during his "rounds" and helping them through the problem.

If you watched him, you might assume that Bryan was not responding to error, but in fact he was. In a very quiet way, he assessed and then acted. He merely did so out of the public gaze, privately a few minutes later—the most *efficient* decision in this case. Obviously (and critically), this is different from gathering data, noting errors, and moving on without taking action. I mention it because every response to data need not imply addressing errors in the public eye and to the whole class—especially when a small number of students have made the error. Assessing and deciding on a more efficient alternative—assessing and (from the point of view of the class) moving on is still an important form of using data. Although it's a quieter method, it's one every teacher should use. It would be an unintended consequence of this section if teachers felt they had to make a public "teaching moment" out of every mistake they observed.

Light Excavation

If more than just a few students have made an error, or even if it's just one student but there's real value in the error, it's powerful to find opportunities to bring errors to the fore and discuss them as a class. When you do this quickly and in a way that's not necessarily planned into your lesson, it's called *light excavation*. It's error analysis in its daily dosage.

Let's say you're teaching Lois Lowry's novel *The Giver,* about a future society in which citizens can no longer experience a variety of sensations, including seeing colors. The book's protagonist, Jonas, begins to perceive them while tossing an apple with a friend, but the passage is tricky and ambiguous because, having never seen colors, Jonas doesn't understand what they are yet and so is unable to explain what he sees. Lowry reveals this with immense subtlety, and the passage provides as many questions as answers to most readers. So let's say you said to your students, "In the margin of your text, write a sentence explaining what this paragraph tells us Jonas could see that others could not." As you glance over their shoulders, you notice that many students have struggled, making vague statements like "It changed and then it changed back" or misinterpretations like "Jonas can see things moving." The subtlety of the passage and the skills needed to unlock its meaning make it worth further study; you'll want your students not just to realize that Jonas can see in color but to see how the book hinted at this fact—and how they missed it. The conclusions that led them awry are worth the time. The following are a few ways you might respond:

- **Ask for an alternative response.** After calling on a student to share his or her answer and discussing, you could, with or without revealing whether that reading was correct, ask for an alternative: "Who can share another interpretation of what the passage is telling us Jonas can see?"
- **Compare responses.** Instead of looking at alternative responses in sequence, you could compare them side by side. Perhaps by tracking during your observation you chose Darcy's and Kevin's answers: "Darcy says Jonas can see color; Kevin says

Jonas can see motion. Who can help us find evidence to support or rule out one of these answers?"

- **Analyze wrong choices.** Similarly, you might suggest a misreading, possibly deriving it from an actual student's reading, and ask something like "What in this paragraph might lead a scholar to say that Jonas could see motion, rather than color?"

- **Ask for a proposed response.** Instead of proposing a "common error" yourself, you might ask a student to do so: "Let's say I found this passage really difficult. What's something I might have guessed Jonas could see that I would have had a good reason for guessing, even if it was wrong?"

In each of these cases, you would be using common errors as teaching tools, drawing students' attention to the types of things that lead to misreadings, and the clues that might have helped them interpret correctly, all in a tone that's rigorous but judgment free.

The idea behind light excavation, then, is to seize opportunities to learn from mistakes by submitting them to brief impromptu study as they occur, ideally emphasizing both positives ("There's a lot of good thinking here") and learning opportunities ("but there's one especially important line right at the end that some of us could have read — or even reread — more closely").

Deep Excavation

There are times when you won't want to limit your study of student responses to a single "alternative" answer. You'll want to look at a variety of them, especially the errors, perhaps even trying to organize and analyze them systematically to make sense of what students did or didn't do. Jason Armstrong used this approach, which I call *deep excavation,* in a recent lesson. His topic was rounding, and he wanted to understand as much as he could about where his students stood and what kinds of mistakes they were making. So, asking them to round 246.718 to the nearest hundred, he asked students to answer in two parts. First he wanted them to identify the numbers they would consider rounding up to and down to and then to identify the number they chose between those two. He began by asking students for their pairs of numbers. The idea was to isolate the issue of choosing the right digit to round to from the issue of rounding up or down correctly.

The first student Jason called on, Jamilla, gave 246 or 247 as the numbers to choose between. "OK," Jason said. Although the answer was wrong, it was impossible to determine that from his demeanor. There was no "tell," and he withheld the answer deftly, adding, "Before we pick one of them, I just want to see if people picked different numbers than those two. Did anybody pick anything other than those two?"

A student named Cameron offered the choices 300 and 200. These were the correct choices, but again you couldn't tell from watching Jason's mannerisms. And even though he had the correct answers on the board (a fact that would have caused many teachers to stop taking answers and perhaps ask the class to decide which answer was right), Jason kept going. "Other answers?" he asked the class, with a student offering her answer: 246.71 and 246.72. Jason wrote them on the board. And still he kept gathering. "Anybody have any *different* answers than those?" he asked. "Cora, what'd you get?" As Cora answered, Jason wrote her suggested numbers on the board, just as he had all of the other pairs. There were now four pairs of numbers on the board.

Only then did Jason engage in a discussion that identified the correct pair. But even after that, Jason persisted in analyzing each pair of answers on the board. "Now let's classify the other ones here," he said, pointing to Jamilla's answer. "This is rounded to the nearest *something*; it's just not the nearest hundred because hundreds would be two hundred, three hundred, right? So what would this be? This is the nearest what?" A student offered the answer, "The ones," and Jason continued, "The nearest ones place, right. Now, we usually call this the nearest whole, because a whole number starts with the ones place." And so for each answer, he identified what was correct and what was incorrect.

Unlike light excavation, which tends to involve a comparison of two answers when students don't yet know which is right or a study of the right answer in comparison to a wrong answer, the core of deep excavation lies in looking at many errors systematically. Jason's goal was to unearth every answer he could get from his students and to present those answers back to the class for analysis and discussion. Over and again he asked for more answers, seeking to unearth as many as he could. This approach has several benefits. First, it addresses the errors in thinking of essentially every child in the class. It doesn't just apprise students of what the right answer should be, but analyzes what was wrong and what was right within their wrong answers—surely a way to build comfort with error. Second, it addresses "information asymmetry" by showing students just how many answers there were in the class. If you were struggling, you knew you weren't alone. I want to point out that Jason committed a significant amount of time to the problem, a commitment that could only be made occasionally. Trying to deeply excavate every problem would be a disaster from a time-management perspective. And if I were to spend a lot of time understanding the thinking behind the answer, I'd want it to be the most important time in my lesson. I rather like the idea of thinking, every other day perhaps, "What's the most important question I am asking today?" then anticipating the errors I'd be likely to see, and leaving a chunk of time to delve deeply into them. To me, it is a powerful occasional activity, done perhaps once a lesson at most, to unlock the usefulness of mistakes.

In looking at the types of error excavation, you might be tempted to infer a hierarchy: the deeper you go, the better, the more rigorous you are as a teacher. I would argue that this is not the case and that the best response is to constantly balance the different approaches.

OWN AND TRACK

Have students correct or revise their own work, fostering an environment of accountability for the correct answer.

10

One risk of all this error analysis is confusion on the part of students. In a lesser teacher's hands, the exercise Jason Armstrong conducted with his students could end with students unsure of which answer was correct, and walking away with the muddled and confused memory that there were lots of ways to be wrong, but, hmmm, which was right? In fact, there's research to suggest that discussing wrong answers can result in students, especially the weakest students, failing to differentiate correct answers from incorrect ideas and merely remembering even better the errors you describe. One study found that "incorrect examples supported students' negative knowledge more than correct examples." Error analysis benefited only students who had a strong working knowledge of how to arrive at the answer already, and students needed an "advanced" level of understanding before they were ready to benefit from analyzing errors. For other students, it actually made things worse![1] Now *that* is a note of caution!

Jason, however, took specific steps to defend against a confusion-of-right-and-wrong-answers outcome. First, he boxed the right answer to differentiate it from wrong and asked his students to make sure to correct their answer *and to make sure they had crossed out any wrong answers*. It's critical to ensure that after significant discussion, students write down a clear record of right answers and perhaps even, to take it to a level higher, a decent record of the errors. Jason did this as well. He labeled each pair of answers on the board according to what unit they rounded to. Essentially, he made an annotated table of answers to the problem. Ideally, he might ask his students to also be accountable for labeling the errors in their original work. These kinds of activities are typical of the final part of building and leveraging a *Culture of Error*: **Own and Track**.

With *Own and Track,* students correct and/or revise their work, becoming accountable for the correct answer. Once they have the right answer (or an answer of best quality), you want to make sure they all understand it and have it locked down. This is a critical time for circulation and *Tracking, Not Watching,* as you provide time for students to differentiate and explain the right answer, appropriately denote the wrong answer, and label their errors. By the way, you'll notice that just because answers get on the board during excavation doesn't mean they stay up there. The longer an answer is up there, the more likely that someone will remember it, even though it's incorrect. Because studying them would have risked more confusion, Jason subtly erased a pair of answers where there wasn't much logic to the error once it was clear they were not correct.

Some things you could say to help students *Own and Track* include

- "Give yourself a check for every one of these steps that you got correct. If you're missing one, make a note to yourself."

- "Circle answer B and write a margin note that explains that it uses the wrong operation."

- "Draw a line through the [insert grammar mistake] and rewrite it correctly in the space in the margin."

- "Make your paper look like mine."

- "Reread your response. Add at least one piece of evidence from our discussion to better support your answer."

- "I'm coming around to check that you've defined *fortuitous* in the margin and that your definition includes the word *lucky*."

It's often helpful to see how *Own and Track* might look all together, especially in a nonmath class, where answers aren't so cut and dried.

Let's say I was teaching Robert Frost's poem "The Road Not Taken" to my fourth graders, and I asked them to identify the theme of the poem. My definition of theme, in this case, would be "a claim that the text makes and that relates to other texts." I would also teach my students that if a theme is a claim, it therefore has to argue something and so cannot be a single word, but rather must be a phrase, usually with a verb in it. With that definition in hand, let's say I ask my scholars what they thought the theme of the poem was. I give them thirty seconds to write it down. Then I take four or five responses. I write all of them on the board carefully, managing my tell so as not to differentiate with my expression whether I agree or not at this point. I want to appear interested, probably indistinguishably interested, in all answers at this point. Let's say I write four on the board:

- "Independence"
- "Making choices"
- "Frost chooses a path"
- "Going your own way is better"

First, I might ask my students to write them down. Then I might ask them, "Well, let's start by asking which of these meets our definition of a theme." I'd expect my students to note right away that "independence" was just one word and thus couldn't be a theme. I might then erase it. If I wanted to focus a bit more on *Own and Track,* however, instead of erasing it I might label it "One word; can't be a theme," and ask my students to mark up their own copy, clearly denoting what was missing Maybe I'd frame it a bit more positively: "Start of a key idea, but one word can't be a theme. Develop!" Maybe I'd even ask my students to revise it so it met the criteria for a theme. Then I'd hope that a student might notice that it would be hard for most other texts to be about Robert Frost's choices, so I might mark up that choice with "Doesn't relate to other texts" and again ask my students to *Own and Track* the analysis by marking up their notes to show it and to correct the error. In this way, I am exposing multiple answers, discussing their value, and also seeking to track the thinking that this process reveals, in order to make sure the exercise is productive.

CONCLUSION

There are a number of ways to check for understanding and to act on data gleaned from our classroom, and each teacher will have his or her own flavor when it comes to developing a *Culture of Error.* In Part Two of this book, we'll look at additional tools you can apply and adapt in your own unique way, this time to build an academic ethos in your classroom.

Reflection and Practice

1. We all have indicators that tell students when an answer is right or wrong. Brainstorm all of the tells that teachers have, including your own (for example, nodding, smiling).

(continued)

(continued)

2. Brainstorm a list of responses you could give to a wrong answer that could help build a *Culture of Error* in your classroom. (Examples: "I expect there are a lot of different answers here." "That answer is going to be really helpful to us." "You did a lot of smart things to get that answer. Now there's one thing we need to change.")

3. If students are asked to round 246.74 to the nearest hundreds place, what errors are students apt to make? List as many possible student misunderstandings as you can. Plan for how you'd address those misunderstandings.

4. Pick one question in your lesson outline for which you anticipate the need for deep excavation.

   a. List the potential wrong answers that students might have.

   b. Discuss why students might give these answers and what correct thinking might lead to an incorrect answer.

USEFUL TOOLS   **FIND THESE TOOLS AT WWW.TEACHLIKEACHAMPION.COM/YOURLIBRARY**

Example phrases for building a *Culture of Error*. Draw from or adapt these classroom-tested phrases to build a culture where students feel safe revealing and learning from their mistakes.

***Own and Track* phrases.** Explore a variety of ways to prompt students to correct and/or revise their work.

Bank of common tells. Check out some of the most common ways teachers unintentionally signal whether or not they think an answer is right or wrong. I bet you'll recognize a few!

Exposing and analyzing error. Check out examples of what teachers say to encourage students to analyze their classmates' errors—and at different levels of depth.

A sample of Bryan Belanger's packet. Check out one of Bryan Belanger's exemplar lesson packets and see why Doug likens it to a "Choose Your Own Adventure" novel.

A sample of Patrick Pastore's packet. Take a look at how former reading teacher and current principal Patrick Pastore designs his packets to make sure that he always has something planned and can tailor each lesson to meet his students' evolving needs.

EXPECT ERROR

- "I'm really glad that you made that mistake. It's going to help me to help you."
- "Wrong answers are really helpful because we learn from the mistakes we make."
- "Which of these options do you think is my favorite wrong answer?"
- (After students point out a teacher's mistake) "Oooh, you all just caught the best mistake I've ever made! This is great!"
- "I suspect there's going to be some disagreement here."
- After scanning the room to check which answers students picked, say excitedly, "We have a lot of disagreement on this one!"

WITHHOLD THE ANSWER

- "For the four options to this question, I don't want to begin by asking which one you think is right because I want to focus on the explanations that we have."
- "I see that several students picked answer choice X and that a few picked answer choice Y. How can I defend my answer whether I picked answer choice X or Y?"
- "I heard some snaps and I heard some stomps. College discussion. Be ready to defend your answer."

PRAISE RISK-TAKING

- "I love the fact that this is a hard question and that I see so many brave hands in the air. Thank you for taking a risk."
- "People have debated this question for centuries. Who even knows if there's a right answer? What's important is that you're really grappling with it."
- "This is a tough question. If you're struggling with it, that's a good sign. Now, who will be bold and start us off?"
- "Romele has been brave enough to offer to share his work so that we can revise it, because he made a mistake that a lot of us made. So, give him two claps on two. One, two!"

Part  2

Academic Ethos

I WOULD BE LYING IF I TRIED TO TELL YOU THAT ALL CHAMPION CLASSROOMS function in the same way. There are a thousand ways to be a champion, and all champion classrooms are different: some great teachers are boisterous and some bookish; some are funny and some scholarly; and each emphasizes different techniques, in different ways, at different times, for different groups of students. That said, all champion classrooms share one overarching characteristic. Champion teachers are always pushing to create an environment in which the maximum level of academic rigor is expected, practiced, and valued. This pervasive and foundational academic ethos is one of the most important things separating champion classrooms from the rest.

But what contributes to the sort of common academic ethos, the sort of unrelenting rigor that underlies the type of work occurring in higher-performing classrooms? Lots of different factors come into play—from the content you choose to teach to the depth to which you choose to dive into it—but there are a series of concrete, actionable steps that teachers take to establish both an expectation of and a desire for academic excellence—both academic rigor and a seriousness of purpose.

The next four chapters take as a starting point something that I hope is obvious. It is very hard to have a rigorous lesson or a rigorous classroom without rigorous content. There's a big difference between reading *Narrative of the Life of Frederick Douglass* and reading, say, the *Diary of a Wimpy Kid*—sadly, one of the most read titles in sixth-grade classrooms according to data recently published by Renaissance Learning.[1] The sort of conversations that can happen in a classroom that is reading a memoir of a former slave turned eminent abolitionist, whose words have echoed through generations, just aren't the same as those that happen in classrooms flipping through pages of pandering, cartoonish preteen lamentations.

Similarly, students who add $\frac{1}{3}$ to $\frac{1}{2}$ may very well be working on the same "standard" as students who add $\frac{4}{11}$ and $\frac{2}{5}$ to $\frac{1}{2}$, but there is simply no comparison between the level of proficiency students in each group will have achieved when the lesson is over. Content matters, and no amount of planning or questioning or energetic engagement will compensate for insipid content. What you teach is as important as how you teach it, and the better your teaching craft, the greater the benefits resulting from a choice of rigorous content.

This next set of chapters, then, assumes that teachers are preparing to go beyond simplistic unit fractions and the tales of wimpy kids in favor of lessons made up of more complex compound fractions and the still-relevant words of great authors. Taking for granted the rigorous substance of your syllabus, I'll examine such questions as, How do the small iterative interactions you have with students as you together discuss topics of academic substance bring out the best in them? How do you plan your presentation of the content to be engaging, demanding, and productive? How does an effective lesson unfold, and what are its key elements? And how do you manage students' pacing and energy needed to bring out the best in Modigliani's sculptures, Langston Hughes's prose, or Mendel's pea plants? In the following chapters, we'll take a close look at the ways in which champion teachers engineer an academic ethos into the stuff of their lessons: making it not OK not to try, planning ahead of time, crafting an effective lesson structure, and keeping it moving in the right direction.

Chapter 3

Setting High Academic Expectations

Technique 11: No Opt Out.   Turn "I don't know" into success by ensuring that students who won't try or can't answer practice getting it right.

Technique 12: Right Is Right.   When you respond to answers in class, hold out for answers that are "all-the-way right" or all the way to your standards of rigor.

Technique 13: Stretch It.   Reward "right" answers with harder questions.

Technique 14: Format Matters.   Help your students practice responding in a format that communicates the worthiness of their ideas.

Technique 15: Without Apology.   Embrace—rather than apologize for—rigorous content, academic challenge, and the hard work necessary to scholarship.

Chapter 3

Setting High Academic Expectations

One consistent finding of academic research is that high expectations among teachers are the most reliable driver of high achievement among students, even students who do not have a history of strong achievement. Much of this research has been conducted to test the famous "Pygmalion" study in which teachers were told that randomly selected groups of students had been proven through testing to be on the brink of great academic gains. Those groups of students outperformed other randomly selected groups whose teachers had not been led to expect great things. Presumably the difference in expectations caused average students to learn at the rate of exceptional students.

One of the problems with findings about high expectations, however, is that they often include in the definition a wide array of actions, beliefs, and operational strategies. One study defined high expectations as including the decision to allocate and protect more time on task in academic subjects. Although that's certainly good school or district policy, it doesn't necessarily qualify as an action a teacher might take in his own room—or even frame actions that he might take.

So what are the concrete, actionable ways that teachers who get exceptional results demonstrate high expectations? In Chapter Two, we discussed how to build a *Culture of*

Error; in this chapter, the goal is to build a "culture of better" in which being pushed by your teacher to go a little further is normalized — is as commonplace in the schoolroom as a pencil. This chapter looks at five techniques derived from champion teachers — *No Opt Out, Right Is Right, Stretch It, Format Matters,* and *Without Apology* — that build such a culture, raise expectations, and differentiate great classrooms from good ones.

NO OPT OUT

Turn "I don't know" into success by ensuring that students who won't try or can't answer practice getting it right.

One consistency among champion teachers is their vigilance in maintaining the expectation that it's not OK not to try. Everybody learns in a high-performing classroom. One key step in the process is eliminating the option for students of "opting out": muttering "I don't know" or shrugging impassively when asked a question, and enforcing the message that they wish to be — that they will be — left alone by individuals who presume to teach them. **No Opt Out** can help ensure that all students, especially reluctant ones, take responsibility for learning. In the end, there's far less incentive to refuse to try if doing so doesn't save you any work, so *No Opt Out*'s attribute of causing students to answer a question they've attempted to avoid is a key lever.

No Opt Out is also effective in helping students who genuinely don't know the answer, because it rehearses success. Students hear themselves getting it right — and getting it right over and over again. Many students come to school expecting to fail because they've normalized failure. Teachers sometimes forget how powerful it can be to experience a simple success when good news in school is rare and elusive. We hardly notice an event that is a potential watershed to a child because it is so familiar to us.

Finally, *No Opt Out* honors and validates students who do know the answer by allowing them to help their peers in a positive and public way. With those benefits in mind, let's start by examining *No Opt Out* version 1.0.

No Opt Out Version 1.0: Getting It Right

Imagine this scenario: It's the first day of school, and you're reviewing multiplication facts with your fourth graders. You ask Charlie what three times eight is. Charlie mutters "I dunno" under his breath, then gives you a look full of sharp things, rolls his eyes, and turns away. It's a critical moment. Students all too commonly use this approach to push back on teachers when their unwillingness to try, lack of knowledge, or a combination of the two makes them unsure or resistant. Many teachers simply don't know how to respond and are forced to leave their Charlies impassively staring out the window instead of engaged in academic struggle. The result is a strong incentive for students to say, "I don't know." Those three words can save a student a lot of trouble. If Charlie establishes that he doesn't have to participate, it's going to be a long year of you gingerly (and weakly) stepping around him, of other students seeing that Charlie does what he wants, and of Charlie not learning—a lose-lose-lose situation.

If you used *No Opt Out,* you would turn to another student, Devon, and ask him that same question. Assuming that he correctly answered twenty-four, you'd now turn back to Charlie: "Now you tell me, Charlie, what's three times eight?" Charlie would have just found—without your stopping for a time-consuming and possibly ineffective lecture—that he had to do the work in your class after all. Later we'll look at more challenging contingencies that you may be wondering about: What if Charlie doesn't answer when you come back to him? What if Devon doesn't answer? For now, it's most important simply to understand the power and necessity of coming back to a student who won't try. The moment when you circle back and ask the student to answer the original question is the *No Opt Out.*

No Opt Out proves to be just as powerful in situations where students are trying. Here's an example from Darryl Williams's third-grade classroom in Albany, New York, in which a student, James, was unable to identify the subject of the sentence "My mother was not happy." He first tried to guess: "*Happy*?" he asked. Darryl persevered, asking "What's the subject?" again more slowly. However, James was still unable to answer, and Darryl asked the class, "When I am asking you for the subject, what am I asking for?" The student he called on now replied, "You're asking for who or what the sentence is about." Returning to James, Darryl repeated, "When I ask for the subject, I am asking for who or what the sentence is about. What's the subject?" James now answered correctly: "*Mother*." The sequence began with a student unable to answer and ended with him providing the answer. The second student's answer didn't replace the original student's; it supported it. James has seen himself succeed where just moments ago he was unable to. He has rehearsed success and practiced one of the fundamental processes of school: get it wrong, then get it right.

But let's examine what you might have done if things hadn't gone so well. What if James still couldn't answer the second time around, or, worse, what if he had shrugged his shoulders and refused, muttering "I don't know," looking straight at you as if to say, "I already told you that." Or if he actually looked right at you and said, "I already told you. I don't know." Darryl might respond by asking another student, "Well, what does that mean the subject is?" The student having answered, "The subject is *mother*," Darryl might then return to the original student, asking him, "OK, James, now you tell me: What's the subject of the sentence?" With only an answer to repeat, it's harder still for James to opt out and maintain the useful illusion that he can't answer. But in all likelihood, with any plausible gray area removed, he will answer. If he doesn't, it's a case of defiance that you can address with a consequence and an explanation: "James, you don't have to get the answers right in my class, but you will be expected to try. I'll see you here at recess," confident that you are not accidentally penalizing a student for not knowing.

Or you might use a firmer iteration of *No Opt Out* before returning to James: "Tell him again, David. What's the subject?" And then, "Let's try it again, James. What's the subject of the sentence?" Or you could repeat the answer yourself: "James, the subject of this sentence is *mother*. Now you tell me, what's the subject?" Regardless of which approach you take, the sequence ends with the original student repeating the correct answer: "The subject is *mother*."

Here's a last worry about using *No Opt Out* that you might have felt: What if in our math example Devon, called on to save the day, couldn't answer either or, worse, mimicked Charlie's impassivity and merely shrugged? In that case, you might give the answer yourself: "Class, three times eight is twenty-four. Devon, what is it? … Good. Now you, Charlie." If necessary, you might put a bow on the message: "As you know, I expect great things from all of you. Wrong is OK with me; failing to try is not." Then move on.

Oftentimes resistance is more subtle and nuanced. It's important to remember that students may push back a bit. What you're asking them to do—to give their best in public when they don't think they know and when their expectation may be failure—is scary at first. So responding to the resulting pushback with a bit of *Emotional Constancy* (technique 61) is key.

See It in Action: Clip 9

In clip 9, a student repeatedly declines to answer the question, "Who dreams the American dream?" asked by David Javsicas, a seventh-grade reading teacher at Troy Prep Middle School. When David first asks his student the question, she says she skipped the question (previously it had been asked in their writing class) because she "doesn't know" the answer. David responds in a warm and humorous tone ("You don't remember anything from writing class? You're going to make Ms. Catlett cry"), but his relentlessness is also evident. Notice the steps he takes:

- Providing context by reminding the student that she studied the concept in another class.

- Calling on a classmate to provide a cue. His cue, "Mexicans," is intended to refer to their previous discussion of various groups of immigrants who have come to the United States seeking opportunity. Note here that David asks the class to snap for the student who provided the hint to add positivity and to reinforce a culture in which students help each other.

- Returning to the original student, who then uses the hint to identify another group of immigrants: Chinese people.

- Prompting the class to answer. They note that both are examples of immigrant groups.

- Returning to the student to ask her to define *immigrants*.

Even though the student repeatedly tries to opt out, David remains purposefully calm and unperturbed. In doing so, he exudes *Emotional Constancy* (technique 61) and prevents a standoff. In sticking with the student, David also sends a powerful cultural message that there's no incentive not to try. His actions reinforce a culture of individual accountability.

Instances of resistance are pretty rare in most cases and diminish quickly once a teacher establishes a calm, thoughtful insistence about opting in. In fact, using *No Opt*

Out empowers you to help all students take the first step toward success. It reminds them that you believe in their ability to answer, and it results in students' hearing themselves get answers correct. This causes them to grow increasingly familiar with a successful outcome, normalizing the process for students who need it most.

Four Basic Formats of *No Opt Out*

There are four basic formats of *No Opt Out*. What's consistent across all four formats is that a sequence that begins with the student unable to answer ends with the student giving the right answer. This ensures that everyone comes along on the march to college.

Format 1

You provide the answer; the student repeats the answer.

Teacher: What's the subject, James?
James: *Happy.*
Teacher: James, the subject is *mother*. Now you tell me. What's the subject?
James: The subject is *mother*.
Teacher: Good, James. The subject is *mother*.

Format 2

Another student provides the answer; the initial student repeats the answer. (A variation on this method is to ask the whole class, rather than one individual student, to provide the correct answer and then have the initial student repeat.)

Teacher: What's the subject, James?
James: *Happy.*
Teacher: Who can tell James what the subject of the sentence is?
Student 2: *Mother.*
Teacher: Good. Now you, James. What's the subject?
James: The subject is *mother*.
Teacher: Good, James. The subject is *mother*.

Format 3

You provide a cue; your student uses it to find the answer.

Teacher: What's the subject, James?
James: *Happy.*

Teacher: James, when I ask you for the subject, I am asking for who or what the sentence is about. Now, James, see if that can help you find the subject.

James: Mother.

Teacher: Good, James. The subject is *mother*.

Format 4

Another student provides a cue; the initial student uses it to find the answer.

Teacher: What's the subject, James?

James: Happy.

Teacher: Who can tell James what I am asking for when I ask for the subject?

Student 2: You're asking for who or what the sentence is about.

Teacher: Yes, I am asking for who or what the sentence is about. Now, James, what's the subject?

James: Mother.

Teacher: Good, James. The subject is *mother*.

On Cues, Hints, and Questions

I use the word *cue* here to mean a prompt that offers additional useful information to the student in a way that pushes him or her to follow the correct thinking process. A hint, by contrast, could offer any related information. If I ask, "Can anyone give James a hint to help him find the subject?" a student might say, "It starts with the letter *m*." This would surely help James guess the answer, but it doesn't teach him anything that will help him next time.

Four cues are particularly useful for cueing students in a *No Opt Out*:

1. The place where the answer can be found

    "Who can tell James where he could find the answer?"

2. The next step in the process that's required at the moment

    "Who can tell James what the first thing he should do is?"

3. Another name for a term that's a problem

    "Who can tell James what *denominator* means?"

4. An identification of the mistake

    "Who can explain what James might have done wrong here?"

An alternative to cueing is to allow students to ask questions as part of a *No Opt Out*. I got this idea from Michael Towne, one of the winners of the 2014 Fishman Prize for Superlative Classroom Practice, a national award given by TNTP to the top teachers in the country. "If I ask them, 'What's the speed of the magnetic flux here?'" Michael told me, "I want them to be able to say, 'I'm actually not that clear on what you mean by magnetic flux.'" To Michael it's a sign of maturity to ask for clarification. So he explains that they always have this option and encourages his students to use it. But the sequence ends with a *No Opt Out*: "OK, now that we've clarified what magnetic flux is, what's its speed here?"

Although *No Opt Out* can be a powerful addition to your classroom, it's important to always strive to balance requiring a student to answer with the need to maintain momentum. As you do so, it may help to use this rule of thumb: the closer a question is to your objective, the more likely you would want to consider using *No Opt Out*.

No Opt Out Version 2.0: Toward Greater Rigor

No Opt Out 2.0 represents what my team and I have learned from watching teachers use the technique over the years since I originally described it. Mostly, that involved making it more rigorous. We noticed that champion teachers, leveraging initial success—a student answering correctly—often followed up right away to add challenge or extra practice. They added a second question for the student to answer, reinforcing the successful thinking right away, or added a more challenging follow-up, much as you'll read about in *Stretch It* (technique 13).

Consider this very basic interaction:

Teacher: What's three times five? Carson.
Carson: Eight!
Teacher: It's not eight. Who can tell Carson what operation he used?
Jalani: He used addition instead of multiplication.
Teacher: That's right. So, Carson, what's three times five?
Carson: Three times five is fifteen.
Teacher: Yes, good. And what's five times three?
Carson: It's fifteen also.
Teacher: Good. And four times five?
Carson: Twenty.
Teacher: Oh, you've got it now! I can't stump you.

This teacher not only gives Carson extra practice at a skill he struggled with but also subtly engineers the cultural experience: the sequence ends not just with Carson getting one right but showing that his success was no fluke. He answers several questions; his teacher acknowledges that she can't "stump" him. His success is palpable. Consider how this sort of interaction turns the tables after a "wrong" answer. Or consider how some small tweaks of this interaction could make it not only positive but more rigorous:

Teacher: What's three times five? Carson.

Carson: Eight!

Teacher: It's not eight. Who can tell Carson what operation he used?

Jalani: He used addition instead of multiplication.

Teacher: That's right. So, Carson, what's three times five?

Carson: Three times five is fifteen.

Teacher: Yes, good. And if I wasn't sure, what operation could I use to check that?

Carson: You could use division.

Teacher: Good. Tell us how.

Carson: Well, you'd divide fifteen by five and get three, and you'd know your multiplication was right.

Teacher: Thank you, Carson.

In this case, the teacher is focused on asking not another version of the same question but a related, different question. In both cases, she is using her follow-up to shape Carson's experience of success, as well as to push his skills.

In the following case studies, you can see how you might use the follow-up to build both rigor and a culture with more challenging material. Notice how these two teachers "stretch" their students after a successful *No Opt Out,* adding rigor and making a point of giving them a chance to show off how much they know.

Case Study 1

Ms. Klein: What's the definition of *vengeance*? Carla.

Carla: Um …

Ms. Klein: Shakani? *Vengeance*?

Shakani: Vengeance is violent revenge, getting back at someone who got you.

Ms. Klein: Thanks, Shakani. So what's vengeance, Carla?

(continued)

(continued)

Carla: Violent revenge.

Ms. Klein: So who seeks vengeance in *Romeo and Juliet*, Carla?

Carla: Tybalt, when he says, "This must be a Montague. Fetch me my sword."

Ms. Klein: Tybalt is doing what when he says that?

Carla: Looking for vengeance.

Ms. Klein: Yes, seeking vengeance. And would you agree that examples of people seeking vengeance are rare indeed in the play?

Carla: No. Pretty much everyone is seeking vengeance.

Ms. Klein: Nice, Carla. It does seem like just about everybody had vengeance on the brain.

Case Study 2

Mr. Vaca: What's the multiplicative inverse of negative three, Jason?

Jason: Three.

Mr. Vaca: But if I multiply negative three times three I get negative nine. Who can tell Jason what the multiplicative inverse of negative three is? Carlos?

Carlos: The multiplicative inverse of negative three is negative one-third.

Mr. Vaca: What is it, Jason?

Jason: Negative one-third.

Mr. Vaca: Good. Why, Jason?

Jason: Because negative three times negative one-third equals one.

Mr. Vaca: Good. So now tell me the multiplicative inverse of negative one-fifth.

Jason: It's negative five.

Mr. Vaca: And four?

Jason: One-fourth.

Mr. Vaca: (Smiling) Well, now you're just showing off.

Beyond the four basic formats for *No Opt Out,* there are a number of ways to think about following up on an initial *No Opt Out* sequence to get more out of it, to make *No Opt Out* a more positive experience, and especially to boost the rigor.

Add Another *At Bat*

Follow up a sequence of *No Opt Out* with another try at a similar problem. As in the case example of three times five, you could ask a series of questions that get increasingly harder, causing the initial student to do more cognitive work and offering her a chance to shine and feel like the success was real.

Add a Stretch

In the technique *Stretch It*, which you'll read about in a few pages, teachers respond to a correct answer with a range of harder and more challenging questions. Adding one of those forms of *Stretch It* questions — asking why or how, asking for evidence, asking a question that combines the skill under discussion with an additional skill — is often an ideal addition to a successful *No Opt Out.*

Add an Error Analysis

Consider again the example of Carson, who gave the answer of eight when asked to multiply three and five. It doesn't take much sleuthing to recognize that Carson added instead of multiplying. Another way that Carson's teacher might have made her *No Opt Out* more rigorous, then, might have been to ask Carson to explain that point: "And what did you do incorrectly the first time?" Or "What was the difference the second time around?" This allows Carson to narrate his thinking process — "The first time I added, and the second time I multiplied" — and demonstrate understanding of his own error.

Add a "Star"

At the end of Mr. Vaca's example in case study 2, he gives Jason a couple of chances to show how much he knows, and perhaps even how anomalous his initial mistake was. His last statement, "Now you're just showing off," offered with a smile, makes this point explicit. The moment of success offers a great opportunity to identify the place where the student used a successful action. See it as the equivalent of putting a star on a child's paper. By calling a student's attention to attributes like perseverance ("You really stuck with that") or to a bit of playful celebration ("You told me you couldn't, but when you used your notes, it turns out you could!"), strategic positive reinforcement can help underscore the success of a *No Opt Out* and leverage traits like grit and persistence so they happen more often.

How should you go about deciding which type of *No Opt Out* to use? As a rule of thumb, sequences in which students use cues to answer questions are more rigorous than those in which students merely repeat answers given by others. Similarly, sequences in which students do more of the narration and intellectual work are generally preferable. At the same time, there's no way to slow down enough to cue students on every question that stumps somebody. *No Opt Out* is most critical when you use it to establish far-reaching cultural norms in your classroom. If you're pretty sure a student is trying to establish his privilege of ignoring your questions when he sees fit, using *No Opt Out* to revise his expectations is quite possibly more important than any other objective.

No matter what balance you strike, students in your classroom should come to expect that when they answer incorrectly, say they can't answer, or decide not to try, there's a strong likelihood that they will conclude their interaction by demonstrating their responsibility and ability to identify the right answer.

Want More? Clip 10, Clip 11, and Clip 12. Want more examples of *No Opt Out*? Check out Derek Pollak in clip 10, Jamie Davidson in clip 11, and, in a clip provided by the authors of *Great Habits, Great Readers* from their Uncommon Schools' reading trainings, Shadell Purefoy (Noel) in clip 12.

RIGHT IS RIGHT

When you respond to answers in class, hold out for answers that are "all-the-way right" or all the way to your standards of rigor.

There's a real risk to calling "right" that which is not truly and completely right. The likelihood is strong that students will stop striving when they hear the word "right" (or, in the case of questions that have no objectively "right" answer, the word "yes" or some other phrase that indicates that they have met standard). **Right Is Right** is about the difference between partially right and all-the-way right—between pretty good and 100 percent.

Teachers are, in the end, the arbiters of quality—of what counts as right or what has answered a question fully and well. Although it seems obvious that we should set a high standard, we often drop those standards unintentionally. Fortunately, a few specific actions gleaned from the classrooms of peers can help us consistently hold out for academically rigorous answers. Of course, when I talk about right answers, I acknowledge that there are questions for which there is no right answer. Every champion teacher asks questions that are open to interpretation or require nuance, but even in such cases, there must be a rigorous standard for what constitutes a complete, high-quality response.

To better understand the need for all-the-way right, consider a common teacher habit that I refer to as "rounding up." Rounding up involves a teacher responding to a partially or nearly correct answer by affirming and repeating it, but then also adding critical detail (perhaps the most insightful or challenging detail) to make the answer fully correct. Imagine, for example, a student who's asked at the beginning of *Romeo and Juliet* how the Capulets and Montagues get along. "They don't like each other," the student might say, in an answer that most teachers would, I hope, consider at best partially correct. "Right," the teacher might reply. "They don't like each other, and they have been feuding for generations." There's the rounding up. Did you catch it? The student hadn't included "and they have been feuding for generations." That was the teacher's work, though she gave the student credit for it.

Sometimes a teacher will be even more explicit in giving a student credit for the rounding up, as in "Right, what Kiley said was that they don't like each other and have been feuding. Good work, Kiley." Either way, the teacher has set a low standard for correctness, and explicitly told the class that a partial answer was fully right when it wasn't. She has crowded out students' own thinking by doing cognitive work that students could—and should—do themselves. The student who answered thinks, "Good, I did it," when in fact she didn't. The teacher's crediting her has eliminated the opportunity for the student to recognize the gap between what she said and what would have constituted a top-quality answer. It flatters to deceive. The result, over time, is that students believe they're right, prepared, and up to standard, when in fact they're not.

Holding Out for All-the-Way Right

The most basic form of *Right Is Right* involves holding out for all-the-way right—the opposite of rounding up. It means using phrases that cause students to do more of the work and to recognize what fully correct looks like. A teacher might use one of the following phrases in response to Kiley's answer about *Romeo and Juliet*:

- "True. They don't like each other. But can you observe a bit more about their relationship?"

- "Good start, Kiley. Can you develop your answer?"

- "Can you elaborate on what you mean by 'don't like each other', Kiley?"

- "Good start, Kiley. Can you talk about the word Shakespeare uses to describe their relationship [that is, *feud*]?"

- "OK. Kiley said the Capulets and Montagues don't like each other. Can we put some more precise language to the task here?"

- "Thanks, Kiley. When you say they don't like each other, is that how they'd describe it?"

In holding out for all-the-way right, you set the expectation that answers truly matter. An answer, when arrived at in your classroom, is a substantive and honest thing. In time, your students will know that what you call correct is sufficient to be called correct in any other classroom or setting they encounter. Holding out for a high standard of right shows that you care about the difference between the facile and the scholarly, and that you believe your students are as capable of the latter as students anywhere else. This faith in the quality of a right answer sends a powerful message to your students that will guide them long after they've left your classroom.

The Power of Scripting "Right"

Many factors account for why we sometimes don't hold out for all-the-way right. The first is time. There's a time investment in pushing students to find the rest of the answer instead of simply providing it yourself, and we're always under pressure for time. "OK," we think, "I have ten minutes left, and I just might make it through everything I planned"; then we get an answer that's almost what we wanted. It's easy to jump at the quick fix. Another reason is that we want to be encouraging. It is the first time you can recall ever seeing Linda raise her hand. Her answer isn't perfect, but you want to be positive, make her feel successful, and encourage her to raise her hand again. So you avoid any implication of "not good enough."

It turns out that preparation is one of the keys to keeping standards high. As a teacher observed at a recent workshop, sometimes we haven't clearly defined a clear vision of "right" or "excellent" work beforehand, and it's hard to hold out for all-the-way right when you don't know what right is. If you're not sure of exactly what a great answer should contain, you won't be able to hold students to an exacting standard. Therefore, scripting not only your own questions but also model answers you hope students will provide to a few of the key questions in your lesson can help you do some of the "Is that good enough?" and "Is that all-the-way right?" thinking in advance. Of course this doesn't mean you can't override your initial model answer when you're surprised by an unexpected insight from a student; it just means you've started with a more concrete sense of the end goal, particularly for the most critical questions. The simple act of scripting correct answers ahead of time can help you better guide your students, as well as avoid filling in the blanks for them.

"Back-Pocket" Phrases

A final reason why we sometimes accept answers that are less than fully correct is that, as teachers, we are not neutral observers of our own classrooms. At the end of the day, we evaluate ourselves as professionals based in large part on how much we think our students learned. We have a vested interest in telling ourselves, "Yeah, they know that" or "I know what she meant to say." In a sense, if we give students credit for a correct answer, we give ourselves credit for a correct answer. Ironically, the very phrase "I know what she was trying to say," which is not uncommon among teachers, acknowledges the problem; the usually unsaid second half of the sentence is, "but she didn't actually say it." A lifetime of caring about students, of wanting to believe in them, puts us at risk of giving students credit for partial answers. This means that holding out for right can sometimes fight against some of our strongest impulses as educators.

To be effective, *Right Is Right* should take the challenges into account. If you're worried about sounding negative and making every response a chastising, "No, that's still not good enough," or if you want to find a way to express the belief that your students often do know more than they are able to express at first, rest easy. You can still tell students that they're almost there — that you like what they've done so far and that they're closing in on the right answer, that you think they know more than they said. To do so, it's worthwhile to come up with a few back-pocket phrases — planned ways of saying just what you want in common situations. Once you've come up with two or three simple back-pocket phrases that carefully express the positives *and* the need for more in a student answer, practice them outside the classroom so that you say them naturally. Then use them to simply and consistently enforce *Right Is Right* in your classroom and make rigorous answers a habit for your students.

Take, for example, a scene from Lauren Harris Vance's class several years ago at Roxbury Prep Charter School in Boston. Lauren asked a student for the slope of a line. The actual slope was negative four-fifths, but the student gave the slope as four-fifths. Where another teacher might have said, "Right, except you need a negative sign," Lauren said, "Hmm. I like *most* of that"—expressing in five short words both "You did some good work" and "You're still not all the way there." The positivity, honesty, and simplicity of Lauren's response provides a road map for *Right Is Right* responses. To be effective with *Right Is Right,* reply to "almost right" answers in a way that is

- Appreciative and often upbeat about what's been accomplished
- Clear and honest about the fact that more work is needed
- Fast enough to allow you and the student to quickly get back to the thinking
- Simple and familiar enough that you can use it with near-automaticity

Finally, it's important—and often difficult—to remember that *Right Is Right* is a technique you use when an answer is mostly right rather than when it's just plain wrong.

Want More? Clip 13 and Clip 14.   Want more *Right Is Right*? Check out Grace Ghazzawi in clip 13 and Maggie Johnson in clip 14.

Beyond Holding Out: More Versions of *Right Is Right*

Imagine yourself as a student for a moment. You're new to Lincoln High, and you find out you're in American History with Ms. Harlan. Right away you start to hear the stories about her classroom: all academic rigor, all the time; students called on out of the blue; no opting out of tough questions. The first two weeks are as tough as you'd feared, and you're working harder than you ever have. One day, you find yourself in a cold sweat. You were supposed to have read the Articles of Confederation, but with a big playoff game on TV last night, you really only skimmed them. Your nervousness is visible in the lunch room, so a seasoned veteran takes you aside.

"Kid," he says, "you're new here, so I'm gonna help you out. Consider it a gift." As you wonder what he could mean, he places a book in your hands: *Survive Like a Champion: 50 Student Techniques for Keeping Above Water When You're Not Keeping Up.* "Read this part," he says, with a nod, opening to a well-worn page with the corner folded down. "You can thank me later." You didn't know such a book even existed, but as you read it, everything starts to make sense:

Chapter 7: Techniques for Surviving When You Don't Know the Answer

Just because you aren't prepared for class is no reason to panic. If you get asked a tough question, try one of these time-honored techniques. Your teacher is sure to bite, and soon enough you'll be using these methods without even thinking about it.

- **The Kitchen Sink:** Don't know what the answer is? Just start talking. Say every true thing you can think of about the topic or the book or whatever. Eventually something like the right answer will come out, at which point your teacher will stop you and say, "Yes, that's right." She'll then quote back to you the part of your monologue that actually had the right answer in it. Just in case you want to know.

- **Bait and Switch:** You might have heard of something called "media strategy." It's for talking to people who make TV shows, websites, and something called newspapers. (I don't know either; apparently they used to be a big deal.) Anyway, the trick is to answer the question you *wished* you'd been asked instead of the one you *were* asked. So if someone asks you what Hamlet meant by "To be or not to be, that is the question," just go all "media strategy" on them and start in on how it must be very hard to be a prince, what with all the pressure and all, and how you sometimes think about what it would be like to be a prince yourself.

- **Heartfelt Topic:** If you don't know the answer or don't really even understand the question, just say something true and heartfelt about the world and try to make reference to our larger place in the universe. Look, I don't know what iambic pentameter is either, but trust me, if you start talking about justice and fairness in the poem, your teacher's going to forget all about it, whatever it is. If you're really in a pinch, just restate a few facts or a scene from the book and then sagely observe how that's "symbolic." That should get you some appreciative nods. You can leave it to others to decide what exactly is symbolic. And of what.

- **Vague Vagaries:** Abstraction is a blank canvas. You paint it with sweeping colors, and the teacher's job is to see the picture she wants in it. Why say "the protagonist" when you can say "the guy"? In fact, say

> "one guy" and "the other guy" when describing the key conflict. With "The scene where the one guy and the other guy are talking about that stuff," you're covered if you get your guys or your "stuff" confused. If it really matters, your teacher will explain it. She nails the details; you get credit for the big ideas. That's teamwork!

These "techniques" are offered tongue-in-cheek, of course. The great majority of students seek to learn and respond as earnestly as they can, even if they know their answers are not yet sufficient. Still, it's a playful reminder that intentionally or not, students figure out the rules of the game, the ways we tend to lose sight of rigor, often through our best instincts. If we allow the strategies in this mock student manual to be effective in evading responsibility for knowledge, we risk teaching students to be undisciplined. Fortunately, the situation is well under our control. We just have to be vigilant and remember that the "right" answer to any question other than the one we asked is wrong. Let's say you've asked for the setting of a scene in a story. If Daniella tries the Bait and Switch strategy and waxes poetic about how something like this happened to her grandmother once, you might respond with something like, "We'll talk about that in a few minutes, Daniella. Right now I want to know about the setting."

There are other reasons why students sometimes answer a question other than the one you asked. For example, they sometimes conflate different types of information about a topic. For example, you ask for a definition ("Who can tell me what a compound word is?"), and a student replies with an example ("Eyeball is a compound word!"); or you ask for the description of a concept ("When we refer to the area of a figure, what are we talking about? Who can tell me what area is?"), and a student replies with a formula to solve for it ("Length times width"). In the thick of the action, it's easy to miss that these are right answers to the wrong question. And as you begin to listen for them, you'll find these kinds of exchanges far more common than you might expect. If you ask students for a definition and get an example, try saying, "Kim, that's an example. I want the definition." After all, knowing the difference between an example and a definition matters.

Students sometimes want to show you how smart they are by getting ahead of your questions, but it's risky to accept answers out of sequence. Although it can be tempting to think that it's a good thing that the class is moving ahead quickly, the fact is that the *class* isn't. It's one student. Besides, teaching a replicable, repeatable process is more important than teaching the answer to one particular problem. Instead, consider responding with something like, "My question wasn't about the solution to the problem. It was about what we do next. What do we do next?"

Alternatively, if you are asking what motivates a character's actions at the beginning of a chapter, you might prepare to resist accepting or engaging an answer that discusses—even very insightfully—the more dramatic events that conclude the chapter, especially if the point of the discussion of the first part is to better understand the ending when you get there. By not jumping ahead to engage an exciting "right" answer at the wrong time, you protect the integrity of your lesson.

The last of the hypothetical student techniques I offered earlier, Vague Vagaries, requires a slightly different approach—asking for technical vocabulary or precise language. A student might indeed answer your question, but answer it like a horoscope—in such generalities that the answer could apply to any person or situation. Whereas *good* teachers get students to develop effective right answers using terms they are already comfortable with ("Volume is the amount of space something takes up"), *great* teachers get them to use precise technical vocabulary they're developing comfort with ("Volume refers to the cubic units of space an object occupies"). This response expands student vocabularies and builds comfort with the terms students will need when they compete in college. These teachers ask for specificity and follow up to reinforce.

To help you remember the scenarios in which we're most at risk of failing to set a high bar for right answers, I've tried to give them names:

- *Holding out for all-the-way right:* when we resist "rounding up" and saying that a student is right when he or she is only partially so

- *Answer my question:* when we insist that students are disciplined about answering the question we asked them

- *Right answer, right time:* when we resist giving a student credit when he or she rushes ahead of us

- *Specific vocabulary:* when we make students lock down the details in precise words and technical terminology

---

See It in Action: Clip 15

In clip 15, champion teacher Jason Armstrong demonstrates three examples of *Right Is Right*. Watch the video and see if you can identify each instance.

STRETCH IT

Reward "right" answers with harder questions.

One key differentiator of teachers with high academic expectations is that once students get the right answer, they're not done teaching. Instead, the learning process continues, and they **Stretch It**, making their classroom a place where the reward for right answers is harder questions. In addition to posing a challenge to a successful student, *Stretch It* can help you ensure the reliability of correct answers when you make your follow-up a "how" or "why" question. With consistency of application, *Stretch It* can help build a culture where students want, expect, and relish challenge, and where they perhaps embrace a growth mindset.

Stretch It involves doing three things:

- Making a habit of asking follow-up questions to successful answers
- Asking a diversity of types of questions
- Building a culture around those interactions that helps students embrace, and even welcome, the notion that learning is never done

The Reward for Right Answers Is Harder Questions

One of the best music teachers I know, John Burmeister, summed up the greatest effect of *Stretch It* on his classroom in a phrase he used with students directly and transparently: "The reward for right answers," he told them, "will be harder questions." His phrase captures not just the singular benefit of the added rigor of a good follow-up question but also the larger benefit of an emphasis on the growth mindset so powerful to long-term student achievement: I am never done learning, and when I overcome a challenge, I start looking forward to the next.

Asking follow-up questions in response to right answers yields two primary benefits. First, it lets you give students exciting ways to push ahead, applying their knowledge in new settings, thinking on their feet, and tackling harder questions. This keeps them engaged and sends the message that the reward for achievement is more knowledge. Second, *Stretch It* questions have a way of revealing more about the level of a student's mastery. This allows you to avoid false positives—moments when luck, coincidence, or partial mastery can lead you to believe that students have achieved fuller mastery than they really did.

Stretch It can also help you solve one of the thorniest classroom challenges: differentiating instruction for students of different skill levels. Asking frequent, targeted, rigorous questions of students as they demonstrate mastery is a powerful and much simpler tool for differentiating than breaking students into different instructional groups. By tailoring questions to individual students, you can meet them where they are and push them in a way that's directly responsive to what they've shown they can already do.

In the next sections, I describe six different categories of *Stretch It* questions. Although there's value in categories, it's also important not to get too hung up on them. The real value is that thinking intentionally about different ways to stretch students is likely to cause you to ask a broader variety of question types and thus reinforce a greater diversity of types of thinking. The categories, then, are tools to help you think about how to bring rigor and variety to the important task of challenging students in the moment of success.

Ask How or Why

The best test of whether students' answers are reliable—of whether they can get questions right consistently on a given topic—is whether they can explain how they arrived at the answer.

Teacher: How far is it from Durango to Pueblo?
Student: Six hundred miles.
Teacher: How'd you get that?
Student: By measuring three inches on the map and adding two hundred plus two hundred plus two hundred.
Teacher: How'd you know to use two hundred miles for each inch?
Student: I looked at the scale in the map key.

Ask for Another Way to Answer

Often there are multiple ways to answer a question. When students solve it one way, it's a great opportunity to make sure they can use all available methods.

Teacher: How far is it from Durango to Pueblo?

Student: Six hundred miles.

Teacher: How'd you get that?

Student: By measuring three inches on the map and adding two hundred plus two hundred plus two hundred.

Teacher: Is there a simpler way than adding three times?

Student: I could have multiplied two hundred times three.

Teacher: And when you do that, you'd get what?

Student: Six hundred.

Ask for a Better Word or More Precise Expression

Students often begin framing concepts in the simplest possible language. Offering them opportunities to use more specific words, as well as new words with which they are gaining familiarity, reinforces the crucial literacy goal of developing vocabulary.

Teacher: Why did Sophie gasp, Janice?

Student: She gasped because the water was cold when she jumped in.

Teacher: Can you use a word that shows *how cold* it was?

Student: Sophie gasped because the water was freezing.

Teacher: OK, how about using one of our vocabulary words?

Student: Sophie gasped because the water was frigid.

Ask for Evidence

By asking students to describe evidence that supports their conclusion, you emphasize the process of building and supporting sound arguments. In the larger world and in college, where right answers are not so clear and the cohesiveness of an argument is what matters, this will prove invaluable practice. You also help avoid reinforcing poor but subjective interpretations, a task that is often challenging for teachers. You don't have to say that an argument is poor; just ask for the proof.

Teacher: How would you describe Dr. Jones's personality? What traits is he showing?

Student: He's spiteful.

Teacher: And *spiteful* means?

Student: *Spiteful* means that he's bitter and wants to make other people unhappy.

Teacher: OK, so read me two sentences from the story that show us that Dr. Jones is spiteful.

Ask Students to Integrate a Related Skill ✓

In the real world, questions rarely isolate a skill precisely. To prepare students for that, try responding to mastery of one skill by asking students to integrate the skill with others recently mastered.

Teacher: Who can use the word *stride* in a sentence?
Student: "I stride down the street."
Teacher: Can you add some detail to show more about what *stride* means?
Student: "I stride down the street to buy some candy at the store."
Teacher: Can you add an adjective to modify *street*?
Student: "I stride down the wide street to buy some candy at the store."
Teacher: Good. Now can you add a compound subject to your sentence?
Student: "My brother and I stride down the wide street to buy some candy at the store."
Teacher: And can you put that in the past tense?
Student: "My brother and I strode down the wide street to buy some candy at the store."

Ask Students to Apply the Same Skill in a New Setting ✓

Once students have mastered a skill, consider asking them to apply it in a new or more challenging setting.

Teacher: So what's the setting of our story?
Student: The setting is in a town called Sangerville in the recent past.
Teacher: Good. I notice that you remembered both parts of setting. Can you remember the setting of *Fantastic Mr. Fox* then?
Student: It was on a farm in the recent past.
Teacher: How do you know it was the recent past?
Student: They had tractors.
Teacher: Good. But what about movies? Do movies have a setting?
Student: Yes.
Teacher: Great. I'll name a movie and you tell me the setting. Ready …

Stretch It Loves Objectives

Let's assume you asked a student to add three and five. After she correctly gave you an answer of eight, you decided to *Stretch It* a bit and reward correct work with harder questions. Here are a number of ways you might stretch her:

Good. What's 13 + 5?

Good. What's 30 + 50?

Good. What's 8 − 5?

Good. What's 5 + 3?

Good. What's 4 + 5?

Good. Can you write me a story problem modeling that equation?

Good. Can you show me how you know?

These are all fine follow-ups to the original problem, but which one do you choose? With so many options for stretching even a very simple question, how do you keep your stretching from becoming scattershot and haphazard? How do you keep your lessons from stretching all over the map?

Your being aware of a variety of types of questions can help you push yourself to be broad and diverse in the ways you challenge your students; at the same time, some strategic focus can help you ensure that your use of *Stretch It* accomplishes important, *objective-aligned goals* in your classroom.

Regardless of the type of question, it's always useful to remember lesson objectives. Although it's good to do some "lateral" stretching (that is, into new areas), and it's good to do some reinforcement stretching (that is, to keep skills students have mastered alive by circling back to them for occasional practice), reserve *most* of your *Stretch Its* for questions that align most closely to your objectives for that day or your current unit. This will help you keep the technique focused and productive.

Stretch It 2.0: Prompting

For the most part, the six types of *Stretch It* I've presented are directive: they guide students to think further *in a specific way* about something they've shown mastery of.

Questions like "Can you give me a better word?" "Can you tell me why?" and "How would the answer be different if the exponent was a zero?" shape the way students think about their original answer, and that's part of their strength. There are times, however, when it's also valuable to be nondirective. Prompting is a form of *Stretch It* that is nondirective, and the transaction costs are kept to an absolute minimum. Saying "Tell me more" or "Can you develop that?" doesn't tell a student how to think, merely to think further. There are benefits to being nondirective—allowing students to decide what they think is important to talk about or improve on develops their autonomy and independence—*but* there are also downsides.

Nondirective prompts clearly offer students more autonomy, and that can be a very good thing, but people often conflate autonomy and rigor. It's not necessarily true that prompting a student with "Say more" is more rigorous than asking, "How is Langston Hughes's vision of internalized anger different from that of another author we've read this semester?" Sometimes the most rigorous thing is for a student to elaborate on her own idea but often a specific probing question from a teacher will result in more rigorous thinking than a student merely adding what else was on her mind.

Prompting is often beneficial because it has such a low transaction cost. "Say more" comes faster and with less disruption to a student's train of thought than does a specific question about Hughes's vision. It's easier for a student to immediately pick it up and develop it. As the buzzing of our electronic devices constantly proves, even a few seconds' distraction is enough to break the spell of deep thinking. The absolute simplicity of prompting is critical, and many of the ways we see champion teachers prompting are about reducing transaction cost. However, answers that are left open to chance are, well, open to chance, which can mean high- or low-quality answers, answers that are relevant and useful for classmates to reflect on, and answers that are meandering or solipsistic.

The most common type of prompting is the verbal variety, whereby a teacher vocally indicates that a student should continue developing a particular idea. Some typical examples include

- "Say more."
- "Keep going."
- "Develop."

As teachers make prompting a habit, they can begin to remove the verbal portion of the prompt and replace it with a nonverbal prompt, which yields the ultimate in minimal transaction cost. It's also the least directive type of *Stretch It*. Effective nonverbal prompts include

- Making a rolling gesture with your hands, like the "traveling" signal in basketball
- A head nod
- Raised eyebrows or other distinctive facial gestures

Given the trade-offs between directive and nondirective forms of *Stretch It,* the best approach is probably to seek balance, in two ways: by using both directive and nondirective prompts and by combining the aspects of both approaches in semidirective prompts. A teacher might use the "Say more" prompt, for example, but direct it to a specific part of the answer that she thought was most worthy of follow-up.

Let's say I ask my students how Jonas is feeling during a section of *The Giver* where he is experiencing both horrible and pleasurable feelings for the first time. A student replies, "Jonas is confused and feeling scared. He never felt any of this before, and he feels isolated." One solution would be to say, "Tell me more about his confusion" or "Tell me more about why he feels isolated." Now I'm giving my student significant autonomy, but still helping her see where the most productive part of her observation might be. This would be a semidirective prompt.

As you're probably starting to recognize, you could put a variety of *Stretch Its* on a spectrum to reflect their degree of directness. Figure 3.1 arranges four different levels of prompting according to the degree of direction they offer.

It's important to see these possibilities as a spectrum, not a hierarchy. Sometimes the power of a champion teacher lies in his capacity to shape the answer and steer students to the most important ideas and concepts. In other situations, the most important factor is a low transaction cost or a student's decision about what's worthy of further comment. There's a place for both directive and nondirective forms of *Stretch It,* and

Figure 3.1 *Stretch It* Prompts: Degree of Directedness

Nonverbal	Prompt — Nondirective	Prompt—Partially directive	Follow-up question
"Traveling" gesture	"And?"	"Tell me more about the first part specifically."	"What evidence tells you that?"

teachers should seek to use all types in their classrooms. That said, where to strike the balance is a necessary question.

Part of finding that balance lies in recognizing the synergy between directive and nondirective versions of the technique. Asking lots of rigorous directive *Stretch It* questions is likely, over time, to teach students how to think more productively about developing their own answers. Then, when you stretch those students with less directive follow-ups, they're likely to do so, out of habit, in rigorous ways. This suggests that it may be worthwhile to invest time at the outset in directive questions, working in more nondirective prompts over time.

And although nondirective *Stretch It* prompts tend to come at a lower transaction cost, you only benefit from that when you are open to the directions a wider range of answer content takes you. If there is a specific topic you want to focus on, the balance probably shifts in favor of more directive prompts. In short, you'll want to match the decision you make about the balance you strike among *Stretch It* prompts to your objective. If you want students to understand how isolated Jonas feels, be more directive. If you want students to come up with adjectives to describe his character traits, be less directive.

Building a *Stretch It* Culture

Over the last few years, my colleagues and I have come to understand that *Stretch It* is a cultural phenomenon. The technique works best when it's practiced frequently. For a teacher to say "Develop" without further prompting, students must be listening to their peers. They must be practiced at reflecting on ideas as they hear them.

Explain *Stretch It*

A first step to building a *Stretch It* culture is to explain to students what's going to happen and how it's going to happen. Teach them what it means to give a good answer and what comments are likely to be interesting or helpful to other people. Teach students how to handle the difficult aspects—for example, what they should do if they're asked to develop an answer they didn't catch entirely, or one they don't understand.

Make *Stretch It* Fun and Transparent

Another step in creating a *Stretch It* culture is to make the challenge fun and transparent. Explain that you think the best part of learning is the challenge, and that if you respond to an answer with a tougher question, it's not because you don't like the answer—it's because you do. Relishing intellectual challenge is one of the most powerful outcomes that can result from school, and one of the most powerful determinants of success. This

growth mindset

intentional and purposeful type of classroom environment reflects what Stanford University professor Carol Dweck calls a "growth mindset."[1] You want students who don't think, "Oh, no, this is going to be a hard problem" but instead think, "Oh, yeah, this is going to be a hard problem." You can reinforce this by sprinkling in statements to help students embrace the growth mindset implicit in *Stretch It*: "I know if I keep at this, I'll eventually stump you" or "I know you love to push these ideas, so let me ask you this … " or "I know you want to keep going like this all day, but if you want to take it further, you can make it your paper topic."

Stretch Each Other

True cultures, of course, are built collectively, so the other key factor in building a *Stretch It* culture is the other students in the room. In the most robust classrooms, teachers find opportunities to have students stretch each other. Standing in such classrooms, you would likely observe

- Students having the opportunity to ask another student to expand on his or her original answer: "How do you know?"

- The teacher asking students to stretch one another: "Develop please, Jaquari" or "Who thinks they can stretch Jamilla's idea?"

Want More? Clip 16.   Want more *Stretch It*? Check out Art Worrell in clip 16. Notice how he both stretches the original student and then begins stretching other students to build a rigorous classroom culture.

TECHNIQUE

14

FORMAT MATTERS

Help your students practice responding in a format that communicates the worthiness of their ideas.

In school and in life, the medium is the message. To succeed, students must take their knowledge and express it clearly in formats that fit the demands and expectations of situations and society. If they don't, they risk having their ideas dismissed before they are fully heard.

Consider a former student of mine, the first in his family to go to college. In his first year at an elite college, he wrote a paper on Zora Neale Hurston. It was a good paper. Or might have been. It was plagued by tangled syntax and occasionally flawed subject-verb agreement. His professor's comments were, essentially, "Your writing has issues; please go to the writing lab." The professor made little effort to engage my former student's ideas about Hurston, and in the end, my student did not benefit from his professor's knowledge in the same way his peers did. The format of his arguments allowed people to dismiss them, and the simple fact is that, rightly or wrongly, people evaluate ideas based on the format they take. It's not just what students say that matters but how they communicate it.

If an idea, no matter how insightful, can get dismissed based on its format, then we serve our students well when we provide them with constant practice formatting their ideas in ways that ensure them the full attention of society: in complete sentences, spoken clearly and loudly, in grammatically correct format. The complete sentence is the battering ram that knocks down the door to college. The essays required to enter college (and every paper written once there) demand fluent syntax. Conversations with potential employers require subject-verb agreement. A muttered insight in a room full of peers disappears into the ether — suggesting perhaps that it's probably not worth hearing. **Format Matters** prepares your students to succeed by making complete sentences and proficient syntax the expectation in the classroom.

Grammar, Sentence, and Voice

Teachers who understand the importance of this technique rely on three basic format expectations: grammatical format, complete sentence format, and audible format.

Grammatical Format

Correcting slang, syntax, usage, and grammar in your classroom prepares students to succeed, even if you believe that divergences from "standard" are acceptable and normal, or even if you think there's no such thing as "standard." To gloss the vast sociological discourse on what's standard, champion teachers accept a much more limited but practical premise: that there is a *language of opportunity* — the code that signals preparedness and proficiency to the broadest possible audience. It's the code that shows facility with the forms of language in which work, scholarship, and business are conducted. In it, subjects and verbs agree, usage is traditional, and rules are studied and followed.

Still, many teachers worry that their corrections implicitly say, "You can't use that language because it's not good enough." They don't want to engage in such a conversation, nor appear negative or disparaging. You could address this concern by initiating a preliminary conversation that explains your intention, pointing out that everybody switches codes—most of us speak differently in different settings. You might say, "If you think that the way I speak in the classroom is the same as the way I speak when I'm out with friends, you're wrong. We all speak differently in different settings, but when we're in class, we'll all speak the language of college." Once that rationale is established, champion teachers reinforce the fact that *Format Matters*.

If students selectively choose to use the language of opportunity only in school settings, so be it. No matter what you tell your students about how they speak elsewhere, making the determination to prepare them to compete for jobs and seats in college by asking them to self-correct in class is one of the fastest ways to help them. Given the frequency of very real errors by students and the potential cost of allowing those errors to persist, your goal is to find simple techniques to identify and correct errors with minimum distraction. Two simple methods are especially helpful:

- *Identify the error*. When a student makes a grammatical error, merely repeat the error in an interrogative tone: "We was walking down the street?" Then allow the student to self-correct. If the student fails to self-correct, use the next method or quickly provide the correct syntax and ask him or her to repeat.

- *Begin the correction*. When a student makes a grammatical error, begin to rephrase the answer as it would sound if grammatically correct, then allow the student to complete it. In the example above, that would mean saying, "We were … " and leaving the student to provide the full correct answer.

See It in Action: Clip 17

In clip 17, Darryl Williams twice demonstrates *Format Matters*. In both cases, he actively reinforces the language of opportunity by correcting the phrases "It gots to be" and "It got a -*ed*." Williams uses two strategies to do so. In the first case, he identifies the error, repeating "It gots to be?" as a question and causing the student to self-correct. In the second case, he begins the correction: "It has … ," which the student completes. In both cases, Williams is effective in keeping his transaction cost low and maintaining a neutral and nonjudgmental tone.

Complete Sentence Format

Strive to give students the maximum amount of practice building complete sentences on the spur of the moment. To do this, try providing the first words of a complete sentence to show students how to begin sentences:

Teacher: James, how many tickets are there?
James: Six.
Teacher: There are …
James: There are six tickets in the basket.

Another method is to remind students before they start to answer:

Teacher: Who can tell me in a complete sentence what the setting of the story is?
Student: The setting is the city of Los Angeles in the year 2013.

A third approach is to remind students afterward with a quick and simple prompt using the lowest possible disruption:

Teacher: What was the year of Caesar's birth?
Student: 100 BC.
Teacher: Complete sentence.
Student: Julius Caesar was born in 100 BC.

Some teachers substitute a code phrase such as "like a scholar" to remind students to use complete sentences: "Who can tell me like a scholar?" ✓

Audible Format

There's not much point in discussing answers with thirty people if only a few can hear you. If it matters enough to say in class, then it matters that everyone can hear it. Underscore that students should be listening to their peers by insisting that their peers make themselves audible. Perhaps the most effective way to reinforce this expectation is with a quick, crisp reminder that creates the minimum distraction from the business of class.

Saying "voice" to students whose voice is inaudible, for example, is preferable to a longer disruption, in three ways. First, it is more efficient. In fact, a champion teacher can offer three or four reminders about "voice" in the time a less proficient teacher can remind one student. Second, merely stating "voice" as opposed to offering a long-winded explanation suggests that the rationale for speaking up in class should be understood. Third, by telling the student what to do as opposed to saying what he or she did wrong, the teacher avoids nagging, allowing her to remind often enough to make the expectation predictable and effective in changing behavior. Where "voice" positively reinforces an expectation, something like "louder" constantly emphasizes that expectations are not being met.

Format Matters 2.0: Collegiate Format

The thinking behind collegiate format has its roots in the research of Basil Bernstein, a British social scientist. In the 1970s, Bernstein developed a theory of language codes that describes two modes in which people communicate: *restricted code* and *elaborated code*. When people use restricted code, they assume that listeners share their own context and perspective. Restricted codes are often used among friends and families and other tightly knit groups.[2] When people use elaborated code, by contrast, they make a point of not assuming a shared perspective with the listener, even when there is good reason to assume there is one.

Bernstein observed class differences in the use of restricted code versus elaborated code. In one study, he showed a cartoon to two different groups of children, one made up of upper- and middle-class children and another that comprised lower- and working-class children. The cartoon consisted of two images portraying boys accidentally kicking a ball through a neighbor's window and the neighbor's angry reaction. There was no caption, and students had to describe to the experimenter what was happening in the cartoon. Children who were lower and working class described the cartoon in restricted code. Logically, they assumed that the person they were talking to was looking at the cartoon with them. "He's kicked it through there" they'd say, the "it" and "there" referring to a ball and a window, and assumed their listeners knew as much. "Now she's come out and she's mad," they'd continue, without bothering to provide any identifying characteristics of who "she" was. After all, the experimenter had given them the cartoon; he knew perfectly well what it showed.

This was very different from what the middle- and upper-class children said. They assumed their listeners knew far less about the cartoon. Nouns replaced pronouns. The children said things like, "Well, there are two boys kicking a ball, and one of them accidentally kicks it through his neighbor's window. Their neighbor comes to the window and shouts at them." This is the elaborated code, and Bernstein found a strong correlation between its use—between knowing you were supposed to use it—and things like class mobility and future success. In the most economically robust segments of British society—in universities and white-collar offices—people spoke differently and noticed when others failed to do so.

Here's why Bernstein's study of elaborated code matters to teachers: there's a version of it, let's call it collegiate code, that is expected in academic settings. Like elaborated code, it's not entirely logical, but is a key marker of expectations. Essentially, it's a language you have to speak—and know you have to speak—to participate in academic discourse and have the fullest opportunity for social mobility. Collegiate format involves pushing students not just to be grammatically correct but to use the sorts of discourse the classroom will require of them as they advance to college and beyond.

What does collegiate format sound like? When you discuss a novel in a classroom in college, you assume nothing of the audience—you talk about "Hurston's sense of self," even though everyone in the room knows who wrote the book. Similarly, when you write a paper, you write things like, "In Zora Neale Hurston's novel *Their Eyes Were Watching God,* we see the synergy of love and independence portrayed through the life and marriages of the protagonist, Janie Crawford," and you say those things even though, goodness knows, your professor already knows who Janie Crawford is and who wrote *Their Eyes Were Watching God*. You formalize your diction and provide full context, often couched in technical vocabulary, and this shows that you understand a certain body of domain-specific knowledge and that you are familiar with the professional discourse of a given discipline. You bring extra clarity to your ideas, and you show you belong in the conversation.

See It in Action: Clip 18

Watch in clip 18 how North Star Academy English teacher Beth Verrilli encourages her student to shift to more collegiate discourse in her response to a scene from *Macbeth*. The shift, for Beth's scholar, from "She gonna talk all this evil stuff in his ear" to "She's going to try to impose her negative beliefs onto Macbeth" not only mirrors the sort of discourse she'd use in college—slightly formal, with common and proper nouns replacing pronouns—but helps her to refine her idea. Same student, same basic content, but as the student revises her language, her words almost sing—their insight shines clearly, and they announce her, practically with trumpets, as a future college student.

One of the things I like best about Beth's clip is the way she frames her request for more collegiate language from her student. She asks for AP language and tells her student, "Now you're ready for college." These phrases are not only aspirational but also nonjudgmental.

One of the keys to collegiate format is the ability to push students, in a nonjudgmental way, to use collegiate discourse. Encourage students to practice articulating ideas as formally and elegantly as needed in a college class. Recognize that improving the clarity and quality of language actually improves the quality of answers. Collegiate format makes an idea better by putting it into better language. In fact, this is what all the *Format Matters* elements build up to: the ability to use language that not only gives credibility to ideas but also makes those ideas more refined and thoughtful.

WITHOUT APOLOGY

Embrace—rather than apologize for—rigorous content, academic challenge, and the hard work necessary to scholarship.

Sometimes, the way we talk about expectations inadvertently lowers them. If we're not on guard, we can unwittingly apologize for teaching worthy content, and even for the students themselves. You won't do this when you use **Without Apology**.

Apologies for Content

When I returned to campus after studying abroad my junior year, I found myself in Professor Patricia O'Neill's class on British romantic poets. I thought at first that there couldn't be any topic less interesting. I needed it for my major, however, and in this way was backed in to the single most engaging class I took in college. Professor O'Neill somehow convinced me that the well-being of the world urgently required me to stay up late reading William Wordsworth. She permanently changed the way I think and read. I suspect most readers have had a similar experience, finding that the subject that seemed least interesting became life changing in the hands of a gifted teacher.

There is no such thing as boring content. In the hands of a great teacher, the material students need to master is exciting, interesting, and inspiring, even if we sometimes momentarily doubt that we can make it so. This moment of doubt can put us at risk of apologizing for teaching it. There are three primary ways we are at risk of apologizing for what we teach.

Assuming Something Will Be Boring

Saying something like, "Guys, I know this is kind of dull. Let's just try to get through it" or even "You may not find this all that interesting" is apologizing. Think for a minute about the presumption that your students will find something boring, simply because it is uninteresting to you. Thousands of accountants love their job and find it fascinating, whether or not anyone else thinks he or she would like the work. Every year, thousands of students take pride and joy in diagramming sentences. A belief that content is boring is a self-fulfilling prophecy. There are teachers who make great and exciting and inspiring lessons out of every topic that some other teacher considers a grind. Our job is to find a way to make what we teach engaging and never to assume that students can't appreciate what's not instantly familiar or does not egregiously pander to them. Doing so suggests only a small faith in the power of education.

Blaming the Content

A teacher who assigns the responsibility for the appearance of content in her class to some outside entity—the administration, state officials, or some abstract "they"—starts with two strikes: she is undercutting the content's validity to students and eroding her own enthusiasm for teaching it. The blaming might sound like this: "This material is on the test, so we'll have to learn it" or "They say we have to read this, so … " The negativity here is a self-fulfilling prophecy and also a bit lacking in humility: if it's "on the test," it's also probably part of the school's curriculum or perhaps your state standards. You're never going to agree completely with anyone's judgment on what gets included in the curriculum and standards, but it's just possible that the (also smart) people who put it there had a good rationale for putting it there. Reflecting on that rationale can be a good place to start: "We're going to study this because it's an important building block for things you do throughout your life as a student."

Making the Content "Accessible"

Making material accessible is acceptable—preferable, even—when it means finding a way to connect kids to content at its full college prep rigor; it's not so great when it dilutes the content or standards. It's OK to use a contemporary song to introduce the idea of the sonnet. It's not OK to replace sonnets with contemporary songs in your study of poetry. Here are some alternatives to apology:

- "This material is great because it's really challenging!"
- "Lots of people don't understand this until they get to college, but you'll know it now. Cool."
- "This can really help you succeed."
- "This gets more and more exciting as you come to understand it better."
- "We're going to have some fun as we do it."
- "A lot of people are afraid of this stuff, so after you've mastered it, you'll know more than most adults."
- "There's a great story behind this!"

Content decisions are one of the places that teaching is most vulnerable to assumptions and stereotypes. What does it say, for example, if we assume that students won't be inspired by books written by authors of other races? Or by protagonists of different backgrounds than their own? More specifically, what does it say if we are more likely to assume those things about minority students? Do we think that great novels transcend boundaries only for some kids? That our students have a limited worldview because they grew up on a certain block? This doesn't mean that students—any students of any background—should not study content that is already accessible to their worldview (or what we *think* their worldview might be); it does mean that students should also study content that is entirely outside their frame of reference. This is one of the core benefits of education.

Apologies for Students

Assuming that something is too hard or technical for some students is a dangerous trap. At the first school I founded, the students we enrolled learned Mandarin Chinese as their foreign language. Not only did outsiders react with shock, but sometimes the students' parents did too. But millions of people, many of them far poorer and more isolated than our worst-off student, learn Chinese every year. In the end, every student did learn Chinese, much to their and their parents' enjoyment. There's a special pleasure in exploding expectations, and many of the black and Hispanic students in the school took special pleasure in using their Chinese exactly when people around them least expected it. At least one regularly went to Chinatown for lunch just for the enjoyment of seeing people's surprise when he ordered in Mandarin. This offers a reminder not to assume that there's a "they" who won't really "get" something—say, sonnets and other traditional forms of poetry—and that it's therefore better to teach them poetry through hip-hop lyrics instead. Kids respond to challenges; they require pandering only if people pander to them.

The skill of not apologizing for students is critical not only in the introduction and framing of material but also in reacting to responses to it. Sticking with kids, telling them you're sticking with them, and constantly delivering the message "But I know you can" raises a student's self-perception. Here are some alternatives to apologizing:

- "This is one of the things you're going to take real pride in knowing."
- "When you're in college, you can show off how much you know about … "
- "Don't be rattled by this. There are a few fancy words, but once you know them, you'll have this down."
- "This is really tricky. But I haven't seen much you couldn't do if you put your minds to it."
- "I know you can do this. So I'm going to stick with you on this question."
- "It's OK to be confused the first time through this, but we're going to get it, so let's take another try."

CONCLUSION

Creating an environment in which you couldn't imagine students not trying their best, in which semicorrect answers will be teased out until they are fully correct, in which correct answers will be met with rigorous follow-ups, and in which content and format will be held to unapologetically high standards creates a powerful ethos in champion classrooms. In Chapter Four, we'll look at how planning ahead of time can take some of the guesswork out of developing an academic ethos.

> ### Reflection and Practice
>
> 1. The chapter presented five techniques for raising academic expectations in your classroom: *No Opt Out, Right Is Right, Stretch It, Format Matters,*
>
> (continued)

(*continued*)

and *Without Apology*. Which of these will be the most intuitive for you to implement in your classroom? Which will be the toughest, and what will make it difficult?

2. One of the keys to responding effectively to "almost right" answers— reinforcing effort but holding out for top-quality answers— is having a list of phrases you think of in advance. Try to write four or five of your own.

3. Here's a list of questions you might hear asked in a classroom and the objective for the lesson in which they were asked:

   ○ 6 + 5 = ? *Objective:* Students will be able to master simple computations: addition, subtraction, multiplication, and division.

   ○ Who can use the word *achieve* in a sentence? *Objective:* Students will be able to increase their vocabulary through drills that explore the use of synonyms, antonyms, and different parts of speech.

   ○ What is one branch of the US government? *Objective:* Students will be able to understand the three branches of the US government and how they relate to each other and current events.

   Try to think of ten *Stretch It* questions you might ask for the one that's closest to what you teach. (This is a great activity to do with other teachers.)

4. Try to imagine the most "boring" content (to you) that you could teach. Now script the first five minutes of your class in which you find a way to make it exciting and engaging to students.

USEFUL TOOLS

FIND THESE TOOLS AT WWW.TEACHLIKEACHAMPION.COM/YOURLIBRARY

Rigor checklist. There's a lot to a rigorous lesson, but sometimes it's helpful to have a back-pocket tool kit for some things to listen for, particularly if you're helping teachers improve other aspects of their classroom. Use this checklist of concrete criteria to build more rigor into every lesson.

***No Opt Out* cueing kit.** How a teacher chooses to respond to a student's "I don't know" can be pivotal in the life of a classroom. Use this tool kit to get ideas for how to respond effectively.

RIGOR CHECKLIST

A RIGOROUS LESSON SHOULD INCLUDE SEVERAL OF THE FOLLOWING:

_____Students reading challenging text and answering text-dependent questions about it

_____Students processing academic ideas in writing that requires complete sentences

_____Students discussing ideas using technical vocabulary

_____The teacher consistently asking "why" and "how" questions and *Stretching It* so that the reward for right answers is harder questions

_____Students consistently giving evidence for their answers

_____The teacher consistently asking students to improve and develop their own and their classmates' initial answers

Chapter 4

Planning for Success

Technique 16: Begin with the End. Progress from unit planning to lesson planning. Define the objective, decide how you'll assess it, and then choose appropriate lesson activities.

Technique 17: 4 Ms. Use four criteria to write an effective lesson plan objective, making it manageable, measurable, made first, and most important.

Technique 18: Post It. Display your lesson objective where everyone can see it and identify your purpose.

Technique 19: Double Plan. As you plan a lesson, plan what students will be doing at each point in class.

Chapter 4

Planning for Success

The techniques in this chapter are different from the other techniques in this book in that they are designed to be implemented before you walk in the door of your classroom rather than executed during instruction, so few people will see you do them. To state the obvious, though, planning is critical to effective teaching—as critical as execution in many cases—so these techniques set the stage for your broader success in the classroom. In fact, references to planning and its role in executing the *Teach Like a Champion* techniques abound throughout this book—for example, how planning a right answer helps you hold out for all-the-way right, or how planning for emotional student responses helps you process them calmly. In many cases, the connection between a specific technique and certain planning tasks is so simple and direct that I've left the discussion of how to prepare in the relevant chapters. Still, I've tried to summarize many of those examples here so that you can reflect on them holistically as well. The theme is that planning is everywhere. In the end, it's almost impossible to execute at a high level if your planning isn't also thoughtful, consistent, and focused on the most important tasks.

I recognize as I write this that teachers are sometimes required to do significant amounts of planning that's of secondary value—they plan lessons in the format that serves their teaching, for example, only to translate it into another format in order to submit it to administration or upload it into a database (whereupon it may remain an open question whether anyone reads it). So I offer this side note to administrators: planning by teachers should be the expectation, but that planning can take many forms. Ideally a school would help teachers get better at key planning tasks; at a minimum, it should be careful not to crowd out high-value planning tasks with low-value ones.

It's worth noting that often when I have seen some brilliant teacher execute a stunning lesson or an inspiring new idea in class, he or she usually notes how critical it was to work through the idea in planning. She scripted just the right questions for the *Cold Call* or revised the writing prompt three or four times; he went over the directions in his car on the way to work until they had economy of language and he knew them almost by heart. Even what seems impromptu is driven by foresight. If, as Branch Rickey once put it, luck is the residue of design, then skill is the residue of planning.

TECHNIQUE

16

BEGIN WITH THE END

Progress from unit planning to lesson planning. Define the objective, decide how you'll assess it, and then choose appropriate lesson activities.

When I started teaching, I would ask myself while I planned, "What am I going to do tomorrow?" The question itself revealed the flaws in my planning method in at least two critical ways—even without accounting for my sometimes dubious answers.

The first flaw was that I was thinking about an *activity* for my classes on the following day, not an *objective*—what I wanted my students to know or be able to do by the end of the lesson. It's far better to start the other way around and **Begin with the End**—the objective. By framing an objective first, you substitute "What will my students be able to do by the end of my lesson?" for "In which activities will my students participate today?" The first of these questions is measurable in a meaningful way. The second is not. The success of an activity is not determined by whether or not you do it and students seem to want to do it, but by whether you achieved an objective that

132   Teach Like a Champion 2.0

can be assessed. Instead of thinking about an activity—perhaps, "We are reading *To Kill a Mockingbird*"—framing your objective forces you to ask what your students will get out of reading the book. Will they understand and describe the nature of courage as demonstrated in *To Kill a Mockingbird*? Will they understand and describe why injustice sometimes prevails, as demonstrated in *To Kill a Mockingbird*? Or perhaps they'll use *To Kill a Mockingbird* to describe how the author develops important characters through their words and actions.

In short, there are lots of worthwhile things you can do in class and lots of ways you can approach each of them. Your first job is to choose the rationale that is most productive: Why are you teaching the material you're teaching? What's the outcome you desire? How does this outcome relate to what you'll teach tomorrow and to what your students need in order to be ready for the fourth or eighth or tenth grade?

The second flaw my question revealed had to do with the fact that I was usually asking it the night before the class. Beyond the obvious procrastination that implies, it shows that I was planning my lessons singly. Each lesson was perhaps vaguely related to the previous one, but did not reflect an intentional progression in the purpose of my lessons. Of the two flaws, this was actually the more damning. I could cure the procrastination issue by planning all of my lessons the Friday before, say, but until I began to think of my lessons as parts of a larger unit, intentionally and incrementally developing ideas toward mastery of larger concepts, I was sure to be treading water. In fact, I would have been better off planning all of my objectives (only) for the trimester in advance and then procrastinating on the planning of each lesson than I would have been dutifully planning a batch of activity-driven lessons the week before.

Planning Units and Lessons

Great lessons begin with planning, and specifically with effective *unit* planning: planning a sequence of objectives, one or possibly two for each lesson, over an extended period of time (say, six weeks). Unit planning means methodically asking how one day's lesson builds off the previous day's, how it prepares for the next day's, and how these all fit into a larger sequence of objectives that lead to mastery. Logically, then, it also implies that if you know you've failed to achieve full mastery of one day's objective—an objective on which tomorrow's depends—you must go back and reteach the content to ensure full mastery before moving on. To be sure of mastery, great *Begin with the End* teachers often begin lessons by circling back to anything they're not sure the class mastered the day before.

The unit planning process is followed by lesson planning, which consists of

1. Refining and perfecting the current objective based on the degree to which the previous day's objective was mastered

2. Planning a short daily assessment that will effectively determine whether the objective was mastered

3. Planning the activity or sequence of activities that lead to mastery of the objective

Using this lesson planning sequence—objective, assessment, activity—disciplines your planning. It helps ensure that your criterion will not be "Is my lesson creative?" or "Does it employ enough of the right strategies?" but "Will it be the best and fastest way to help me reach the goal?"

Don't underestimate how critical this is. The prevalence of flawed lesson criteria is a major issue in teaching. Teachers care about earning the respect and admiration of their peers, and when teachers praise each other for their lessons, they are as likely as not to praise an artful, clever design or the loyal use of recommended methods such as group work, whether or not the lessons yield results. Having an effective lesson criterion ("Did this lesson accomplish the goal?") allows you to constantly evaluate and refine your strategy and technique, rather than fly blind.

To summarize, *Begin with the End* means

1. Progressing from unit planning to lesson planning

2. Using a well-framed objective to define the goal of each lesson

3. Determining how you'll assess effectiveness in reaching your goal

4. Deciding on your activity

Planning for Reading

In the schools I helped run, we used to plan reading lessons in almost the same way we planned lessons for all of our other subjects, beginning the process by developing unit plans, then dividing complex skills into a systematic sequence of manageable, measurable goals over a period of time—usually six weeks. In the case of reading, we adapted that process slightly by then choosing novels to read during our units, doing our best to use them to teach the standards we had planned. One novel might be used to teach three or four weeks on "character traits, perspective, and motivation," for example, another to teach "summary and main idea." A daily objective usually focused on some aspect of the skill we were focused on. It often didn't mention the book, or did so only as an afterthought: "To infer a character's traits from his or her words and actions."

Over time, with the help of a lot of really great teachers, I came to realize that we had it wrong. *Begin with the End* looks different in reading and literature classes than it does in most others.

Content-Based Objectives Versus Skills-Based Objectives

One primary reason for this difference is that good reading classes, in my opinion, must read first-rate literature, usually in book-length treatments, but novels and other great works of literature tend to be unwieldy, headstrong, unpredictable things. Sometimes teaching them went longer than we'd guessed. Other times, our daily objectives wanted one thing (character motivation!), but the novels went marching off in their own direction. Conflicts arose in our own hearts and minds as well. We kept trying to push our best novels to provide the perfect lens for teaching the day's objective rather than, say, telling the time-honored story of Scout and Jem. In reflecting on this conflict, we realized that being novel driven was often better from a teaching and mastery perspective than being explicitly and solely skill driven.

If things like understanding a character's motivation were "skills," they were only part of what led students to be able to read well, and, we came to realize, there were really two different types of skills we wanted students to practice. The first, portable skills (making inferences about a character, for example), could be practiced often and frequently throughout a novel. They tended to crop up everywhere and were best practiced in response to a situation in the text. Part of the skill, in fact, was learning to use it when a text demanded it. There were few enough portable skills that it was easy to cover them all in the course of a year if you let the novel guide when to practice them, so long as you tracked them to make sure you reinforced them constantly. We also realized that these skills weren't so much complex to understand as they were complex to execute. They were conducive more to a fast and simple explanation and repeated practice, time and again, in a variety of settings over the course of several months, than to a long explanation involving a mnemonic device and discrete practice for a few days in a row. It wasn't that kids didn't understand that they should use a character's words and actions to determine her traits; the problem was that they needed to do it a thousand times in a thousand different settings and with increasingly harder texts. We realized that being solely skills driven socialized us to be more formal than perhaps we should have been—planning a ninety-minute I/We/You lesson on character perspective when a ten-minute lesson and a lot of practice with a great novel would yield better results.

Sometimes, with portable skills, the more time we spent talking about them, the more time we wasted.

There were still nonportable skills, though: topics that didn't tend to come up in most texts. Understanding and defining characteristics of specific genres was a good example of that. We had to plan specific texts for our genre work because it was hard to talk about the characteristics of folk tales while reading *The Magician's Nephew*. We still needed a skills- or knowledge-based objective for that, but an exclusively skills-based approach to objectives had become a bit of a Frankenstein's monster. We found that it made more sense to start our planning by choosing great texts and then developing our objectives around the content of those texts, weaving in nonportable topics around them as it made sense.

Nonexclusivity

We also realized that we had to develop a nonexclusivity arrangement with our objectives—or at least to make that clear to our teachers. That is, even if our primary focus for a day was to study the development of Simon in chapter 3, we still wanted our teachers to ask students to reflect on other questions as a novel like *Lord of the Flies* raised them. A significant portion of the day's questions would be aligned to the objective in the lesson, but not all of them. You couldn't (and shouldn't) ignore other key moments in the novel if you wanted to get the most out of it and to understand enough to grasp why Simon's character was changing in the next chapter. The practical solution was to read to understand the novel and sprinkle character development questions, say, as often as you could in a given lesson when they were your objectives and as often as was sensible, even if the lesson had another objective, if understanding the novel required it. As students got older and more sophisticated, and were introduced to most of the types of questions we asked, we found that a typical lesson's balance began to shift, and more and more of what we were doing became deciding *which* of the skills students knew how to use applied in a given setting. There might still be a single objective, but much of the lesson was actually devoted to applying reading skills to interpret the text in a rigorous and intrinsic way.

In the case of reading, then, I'd suggest using a novel plan (or a book plan) instead of a unit plan, with part of the planning focused on tracking and ensuring lots of practice with the full array of portable skills and constant use of key literary terms. A novel plan should still address reading standards, but daily objectives should be driven by the content of the text more than the sequence in which a skill appears on the unit plan. Teachers still need to make sure to keep things in balance so that students are as able to paraphrase a very difficult piece of text as compare the perspectives of two characters, but the skills ideally become more of a means to an end—understanding an important and relevant story that students care about—and this makes them more compelling.

4 Ms

Use four criteria to write an effective lesson plan objective, making it manageable, measurable, made first, and most important.

17

Given the importance of objectives in bringing focus, discipline, and measurability to a lesson, it's worthwhile to think about what makes an objective useful and effective. My colleague Todd McKee artfully designed four criteria for effective objectives, the **4 Ms**, and if you're able to ensure that your objectives meet these criteria, your chances of starting with an effective one are high.

Manageable

An objective should be of a size and scope that can be taught in a single lesson. It's not that you don't want your students to master the important skill of adding or subtracting fractions with unlike denominators, for example, but setting the goal that students will learn to add fractions with unlike denominators in a single hour's practice is probably unrealistic. Firm mastery of such a skill in both simple and complex forms requires multiple lessons. You'd probably want to revisit that objective several times to build depth and context into your students' skill and to give them lots of practice.

Given the importance of adding or subtracting fractions with unlike denominators, a key part of the process is conceptualizing the steps necessary to achieve mastery. Perhaps you'd start by finding the least common denominator of two fractions, then try adding with simple unit fractions, moving on to increasingly complex fractions and then perhaps to word problems or adding more than two fractions with unlike denominators. In any case, it would be a mistake to use the same objective—adding fractions with unlike denominators—every day for two or three weeks while you "worked on" the skill. You would have a much greater chance of success if you built a series of day-by-day objectives that set achievable, daily goals. Not only would you make your work more strategic, but you'd also gain a better and better sense of what your students can accomplish in a day. Knowing how fast they can master information means knowing whether you need two or three weeks to master a basic skill. In addition, your students would learn a lot by understanding, through your objectives, how you conceived of complexity in math class. "Oh! Unit fractions are easier than most others."

Measurable

An objective should be written so that your success in achieving it can be measured, ideally by the end of the class period. This lets you better determine what worked in your implementation. The best teachers take this opportunity to the next logical step: they measure every lesson with a short activity, question, or set of questions that students must complete and turn in before leaving class (see technique 26, Exit Ticket). Setting an explicit, measurable goal beforehand helps you hold yourself accountable.

Setting measurable lesson objectives disciplines you in other ways. For example, it forces you to think through key assumptions. If your goal is to have students know something or understand something or think something, how will you know they have reached it? Thoughts are not measurable unless they are described or applied. Do your lessons rely on a balance of methods for describing or applying understanding?

If your goal is to have students feel, think, or believe something, how appropriate is that? Is it sufficient to read and understand poetry without enjoying, appreciating, or loving it? Are students accountable for accepting the judgments and tastes of others — or for learning skills that can help them make up their own minds?

I am a pretty fair case study of this. Although I have a master's degree in English literature, I do not enjoy reading poetry. In fact, I usually find it almost unreadable. I'm sorry to say (to all my fantastic professors and teachers) that I have almost never achieved the objective of loving a poem. Nevertheless, having learned to analyze and sustain arguments about poetry, and having had to critique those of others, has helped me to become a more effective thinker and writer and, occasionally (I hope), a more insightful person. So, in the end, I am truly glad to have studied and read poems in my literature classes. My point is that my best teachers held themselves accountable for what they could control (the quality of my thinking and the sustainability of my arguments), not what they couldn't (whether I liked reading the stuff). Even though their love for the things they taught me was probably their reason for doing the work, passing that love on to me fell into the realm of what they couldn't control. They eschewed loving poetry as an objective, even if it was their motivation—an irony, to be sure, but a useful one.

Made First

An objective should be designed to guide the activity, not to justify how a chosen activity meets one of several viable purposes. The objective comes first. Be aware, however, of just how many teachers who believe they are objective driven start with an activity ("We're playing Jeopardy today!" "We're reading *I Know Why the Caged Bird Sings* today") and retrofit an objective to it. You can often identify these teachers because their objectives look like learning standards (which are different and far broader) and are occasionally written on the board undigested from state documents: "3.L.6 Students will read a variety of texts for understanding." To risk beating a dead horse, you must digest the standard into a strategic series of daily objectives—component pieces—to ultimately achieve broader mastery.

Most Important

An objective should focus on what's most important on the path to college, and nothing else. It describes the next step straight up the mountain.

Assessing and Improving Objectives

The following objectives fail to meet at least one of the *4Ms* criteria:

- *Students will be able to add and subtract fractions with like and unlike denominators.* This objective isn't manageable. It contains at least four different objectives for four different days (and more likely four different weeks): adding fractions with like denominators, subtracting fractions with like denominators, adding fractions with unlike denominators, and subtracting fractions with unlike denominators. Realistically, this objective is in fact a standard, a huge one, and the topic of a unit plan.

- *Students will be able to appreciate various forms of poetry, including sonnets and lyric poetry.* What is appreciation? How will you know whether it happened? Can students understand T. S. Eliot and not like his writing, or do they have to pretend to assimilate your tastes as well? This objective isn't measurable. It's probably not manageable either.

- *Students will view scenes from the film version of* The Crucible. This is an activity, not an objective. Therefore, it's not made first. Showing the film version of Arthur Miller's play *The Crucible* could be a home run or a waste of time, depending on what its purpose is. Will students compare the film version of *The Crucible* to Elizabeth George Speare's *The Witch of Blackbird Pond*? If so, why? Will students better understand Speare's perspective on witchcraft by comparing it to another contemporary story? If so, that should be described in the objective: *To better understand the author's perspective on witchcraft in colonial America by comparing her portrayal to another contemporary portrayal.*

- *Students will construct a poster to celebrate Martin Luther King Jr. Day.* In addition to describing an activity, this objective isn't "most important." Skill at making posters won't help put students in a position to succeed through the content of their character. Understanding Dr. King's legacy certainly is deeply important, and that understanding might even be reflected in a poster, but a champion teacher would consider poster making useful only if it was the best way to reinforce that understanding. The objective should be about Dr. King.

POST IT

Display your lesson objective where everyone can see it and identify your purpose.

Once your objective is complete, **Post It** in a visible location in your room — the same location every day — so that everyone who walks into the room, your students as well as peers and administrators, can identify your purpose for teaching that day in as plain English as possible.

In the case of students, posting your objective is important because they should know what they're trying to do, which will help them work more intentionally toward the goal. In the example of *The Crucible,* students will watch better if they know what they're looking for. You can go a step further by making the objective part of the fabric of the classroom conversation. You can underscore its importance by asking students to discuss, review, copy, or read it, as a matter of habit, at the outset or at the conclusion of the lesson. You might even make a habit of asking your students to put the objective in context, to say why it matters, to connect it to what happened yesterday, and so on.

Draw the Map: Floors

Draw the Map isn't limited to wall space. Planning floor space is just as important. Many teachers seat their students in pods of desks that face each other because they believe that students should be socialized to interact in school. With the exception of realigning desks for tests, this classroom layout often doesn't change. If the teacher's goal is to be attended to for much of the lesson, she has created a strong disincentive for that. The classroom layout has made the primary lesson objective harder to accomplish in deference to philosophy.

What if, rather than asking whether students should interact in school or opining that they should, a teacher asked:

- *When* should students interact in school?
- *How* should students interact in school?
- *What* should the way students sit signal and incentivize about the various kinds of interactions?
- *Which kinds* of interactions support which kinds of lesson objectives?
- *What other* kinds of ways can students be socialized to interact appropriately without necessarily building the classroom around that one idea every day?

I am a big fan of rows as the default classroom structure—specifically, three paired columns of rows (see Figure 4.1), mostly because I see so many teachers use it. This layout socializes students to attend to the board and the teacher as their primary focus. It can of course be altered to match the lesson as your plan dictates, but if you're not sure what "default" layout to use as a starting point, I'd start there.

Figure 4.1

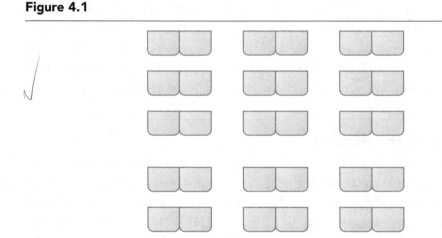

In addition, you have to be able to get anywhere in the room without a word—while you are teaching, in fact. Once you have to say "Excuse me," you are essentially asking permission. This limits your ability to hold students to high behavioral and academic standards. No matter what layout you choose, think as intentionally about aisles and alleys as about desks.

Beyond desks, aisles, and alleys, the floor itself can be helpful in terms of planning your own movements. A little piece of tape on the floor—not unlike the kind used to indicate stage directions during a theater performance—can help you move quickly and purposefully about the room. Another piece can help you get everyone moving and in line ("Class, everyone line up on the blue tape in three, two, one …).

Post It is important for visitors, your fellow teachers, and your supervisor, for example, because these people give you feedback, and feedback is more useful when the person giving it knows what you're trying to do—if he or she addresses not just whether your teaching was "good" in some abstract sense, but whether it appeared to be getting at your goal. A visitor who thinks you should be discussing more about how the characters are developed in *The Crucible* may or may not be right. Whether you should spend more time on the development of characters depends on what your ultimate purpose is. It's to your benefit to discipline those who offer help to focus on what best meets your objectives. Otherwise, their advice and evaluation of your lesson fall to idiosyncratic criteria—for example, your department chair observes you and says that you should be emphasizing character development more because that's what *she* does with *The Crucible*.

DOUBLE PLAN

As you plan a lesson, plan what students will be doing at each point in class.

It's natural for teachers to write lessons that focus on what *they* will be doing: which key points they will cover, questions they will ask, activities they will facilitate, work they will assign, and so forth. Still, the most effective teachers I know **Double Plan**, that is, they plan at least as carefully what *their* students will be doing each step of the way. You might imagine a sort of T-chart lesson plan in which the teacher details her actions on the left side and what students should be doing on the right, but it was in the course of reviewing lesson materials from top teachers that I realized that many of them *Double Plan* in a more specific format: lesson packets.

A lesson packet is a carefully designed handout that students work on during the lesson. It has space to write or take notes as well as background readings posted in it; it's a lesson plan from the student's perspective. (You can see examples of packets in the Useful Tools section at the end of this chapter. These packets can also be found on www.teachlikeachampion.com.)

Packet planning is an effective tool for *Double Planning* because it forces you to see the lesson through your students' eyes. Teachers who do this best design packets that satisfy six goals, which we'll explore in more depth in the next sections.

Goal 1: Everything in One Place

A well-designed packet gives both teacher and students everything they need for the lesson at their fingertips. Whether you're teaching students how to solve systems of equations or exploring the theme of the destruction of familial structure in *Night,* a packet can make sure that students have all of the lesson materials accessible in one place, minimizing the need to distribute additional materials, take out new documents, and move back and forth between activities, such as reading a text and writing about it. Great *Double Planners* embed it all: graphs, tables, maps, primary source documents, sometimes novel excerpts, places to write, and more. Further, having a copy of the packet yourself enables you to work from the same set of materials as your students, allowing you to manage the student experience—such as which activity to flip to or what passage you're reading—quickly and effectively.

Champion teachers also turn packets into a powerful *Double Plan* tool by making detailed margin notes. For instance, Colleen Driggs used the margins of her packets to carefully plan the pacing of each activity and section of her lesson. She noted everything from the length of her *Do Now* to the amount of time she would give students to read and then write for each independent practice question. Likewise, Taryn Pritchard, a middle school math teacher at Leadership Prep Bedford Stuyvesant in Brooklyn, uses this space to plan the format of the questions she will ask, as well as identify the students she will call on for each question. As we'll discuss later, in the section Synergy with Checking for Understanding" (goal 4), this level of planning enables teachers like Taryn to strategically collect data from students across a range of ability levels and frees them up to focus on other things, such as which follow-up questions they will ask or which topics they need to reteach. Meaghan Reuler, a fifth-grade reading teacher from the same campus, includes stage directions in her packets, or reminders to do things like "Put two scholars' work up on the document camera and evaluate which is better supported" or "Look for students to be marking up the question" as she circulates during independent work. By scripting in key teacher actions that might not ordinarily show up in a packet, Meaghan frees herself from having to rely on multiple planning documents. She keeps everything she needs in one place.

Strong *Double Planners* also work in the margins during instruction to keep a running record of any revisions and adjustments they want to make to the lesson. Jason Armstrong, a fifth-grade math teacher from Roxbury Prep in Boston, often jots observations about things that surprised him or that he wants to change for the next time he delivers this lesson. For example, during a lesson on classifying quadrilaterals, Jason noted that "some didn't realize that they should use the previous page for filling these out" or "some had trouble recognizing that sides could be parallel and congruent at the same time." He also flagged sections that students did not complete and added time stamps to indicate precisely when the majority of students reached specific points in the packet, so that he could improve his pacing for next time. Similarly, Bryan Belanger, an eighth-grade math teacher at Troy Preparatory Middle School in upstate New York, adds revision notes in the margins during the lesson so that he can make same-day changes to his lessons. This allows him to act on what he learned while his memories of the lesson are still fresh.

Draw the Map: Walls

You put a lot of time into planning out your curriculum, so why shouldn't the same kind of thought go into the way that content is delivered and received? To *Draw the Map* means making space planning part of your lesson planning. The first rule of thumb for effective wall space in the best classrooms is that walls should help, not harm. This means that they should avoid clutter and overstimulation. A few critical items should be up, and they should not distract students' attention from the primary instructional space by being too close to it. Posted items are best when they focus on useful tools: reminders of key steps in adding fractions; examples of common themes; seven types of conflict in a story; pictures representing recent vocabulary words; phrase starters for agreeing or disagreeing with a peer during discussion. Once you've taught a key skill, posting a tool quickly after helps students review it and use it frequently. (See Figure 4.2.)

This doesn't mean you shouldn't also post student work on the walls. You should, but be sure to post work that provides a model to other students. Can you make comments on posted work specific and aligned to learning goals? Can you replace writing "Great Job!" in the margin with "Great topic sentence—clearly previews the key issue in the paragraph"? If you can, it will help make success replicable for other students.

Lastly, some insightful teachers use wall space not only to remind students of key actions but also to remind themselves. One school asked teachers to work on economy of language and "bright face" (see technique 56, Strong Voice), so several teachers put signs on their own walls to remind themselves. Whenever they looked up, a bright and cheery sign reminded them to use the fewest words they could and to show their appreciation for their students in their visage. We can use the space in our classrooms and our schools to bring out our own best selves as much as our students'.

Figure 4.2 A more useful take on the Word Wall: vocabulary words with pictures to help scholars remember what they mean can better help them put the words to use.

Goal 2: Synergy with Pacing

A well-designed packet supports airtight pacing because it minimizes transaction costs involved with switching between tasks, formats, and activities. Embedding everything into students' packets allows you to skip pace-killing routines like distributing novels or collecting papers. Although it may seem trivial, saving minutes this way each day can help you add back days of lost instructional time to each school year.

Champion teachers often add visible markers to handouts so that it's easier to make sure everyone is on the same page. For instance, eighth-grade history teacher Ryan Miller of Williamsburg Collegiate in Brooklyn color-codes the pages so that lecture notes appear on red paper, readings on yellow, and so forth. Color-coding handouts also makes giving *What to Do* (technique 57) directions much easier. All Ryan has to say is "Flip to your notes on Social Security in yellow," or "Make sure the red one-pager is in your portfolio." This helps Ryan shave several seconds off each transition and makes his directions stickier for students.

As we discuss in the chapter on pacing, one way to draw attention to mileposts (see Chapter Six, "Pacing," for a definition of the term)—reference points inserted along the route of a journey to make the distance covered more visible to travelers—and to create the "illusion of speed" is to walk through the agenda for the lesson. Many teachers who *Double Plan* with packets already do this because their packets inherently provide students with a visual rundown of what's to come. They can embed new and intriguing activities, not to mention images and icons, into packets, building suspense and excitement and giving students something to look forward to.

Shortest Path

The goal in teaching is to take the *shortest path* from A (lack of knowledge and understanding) to B (durable long-term knowledge and understanding), so the primary criterion for evaluating a lesson should be "How quickly does it get me there?" Sometimes, alternative criteria—how clever, how artfully designed, how inclusive of various philosophies, even how enjoyable to teach a given lesson might be—can distract us from choosing the methods and lesson design that get students most quickly and effectively to the goal. So it's important to strive to keep in check the part of us that wants to evaluate lessons on how self-actualizing they were to teach or how well they demonstrated some theory (even one in this book!).

The shortest path almost always involves using a *variety* of teaching approaches, but it's also important to note the critical importance of the "I" portion of the lesson—that is, direct instruction. *A series of lessons that doesn't include at least some direct instruction is unlikely to lead to long-term mastery.*

For some readers, I have just committed the ultimate pedagogical sin by joining the words: "direct" and "instruction." But please note that I did not say that an entire lesson needs to be made up exclusively of direct instruction, merely part of it, and that I said this with the goal of pointing out that it plays a role in teaching that is often underacknowledged.

Critics of direct instruction often suggest that it inherently causes students to be passive. It consists of "teacher talk," which implies that students are not talking and are therefore inactive as learners. There are several problems with this argument. First, it's not necessarily true that teachers are always talking and students always listening during direct instruction. Perhaps this is so in an exaggerated version of it involving an uninterrupted monologue, but such a form of direct instruction is rare outside (1) certain very large or very technical classes at the university level and (2) the exaggerated straw-man arguments of those who set out to discredit direct instruction. Effective teachers often use direct instruction much differently—with questions and short discussion points and engagement strategies embedded within it, and generally for periods of time closer to ten or fifteen minutes, whereupon it gives way to guided and independent practice. Second, even if it were true that direct instruction was similar to "teacher talk," it could still be highly engaging—I note here that when you read or you watch a movie, you are technically a passive recipient of something a lot like direct instruction, but that doesn't mean your imagination and critical faculties are not highly active.

Finally, it's worth noting that even if there are occasional times when direct instruction lasts longer than ten to fifteen minutes *and* asks students to learn by listening, this may not be inherently bad. Certainly it would be if it were a daily offering, but it is probably a good thing for students to occasionally be able to absorb information by listening to someone more knowledgeable than themselves. They will have to do this in college classes, not to mention their graduate studies and professional lives should they choose to become doctors, say, or lawyers. An occasional lesson that requires engaged listening and diligent note taking, and that assumes that there might be power in great ideas shared to and noted by aspiring scholars, might not be the worst thing in the world.

Somehow, though, teachers have been convinced that "teacher talk" is the ultimate pejorative. Of course you can do too much of it, but you also can't do much without at least some of it. Daisy Christodoulou points out in her outstanding and important book *Seven Myths About Education* that highly non-teacher-centered activities (for example, projects and Socratic seminars and other forms of "active learning") are devoid of rigor unless first informed by extensive background knowledge. Direct instruction, when it provides facts, knowledge, and skills that are later practiced, applied, and reflected on, *builds the foundation that makes other forms of instruction possible*. And as Dylan Wiliam has astutely pointed out, more teacher words are not necessarily worse. In school systems of Japan and Hong Kong, for example, a greater proportion of the words in the average classroom are spoken by the teacher than in the United States. Let us respect the power of what a teacher can do enough to accept that a teacher talking to a class about content is not inherently bad.

So let me observe that effective teachers include direct instruction regularly in their lessons. Do they also pepper it with engagement strategies to involve students—brief questions to ensure involvement or to check for understanding, perhaps even a *Turn and Talk*? Yes. Do they use it for manageable periods of time before asking students to practice and apply what they've learned? Also yes. But they often use it frequently, and in my observation they use it more frequently as they progress in their teaching careers. They often start out believing it is wrong, using it only with trepidation, but with experience become more confident in accepting its balanced application. There is a fundamental difference between the fact that something poorly executed *can* result in passive and disengaged students and the assertion that it inherently does, and the solution to poor execution is better execution, not the dismissal of the method out of hand.

Goal 3: Engineered for Accountability

Double Planning with packets forces you to consider how you will at each step hold students accountable for the content and quality of their work. The teachers who do this best require students to constantly interact with their packets, and they engineer the physical space students need to do so. For example, Maggie Johnson, an eighth-grade teacher at Troy Preparatory Middle School, provides space for her students to write everything, from recording the objective to taking notes during a discussion (see Maggie's packet in the Useful Tools section for this chapter on the website, **www.teachlikeachampion.com**). She even includes a specific space labeled "Leave this space blank" for students to go back and rewrite their answers to writing prompts to make them stronger. Regardless of your approach, the key takeaway is that effective *Double Planning* involves constant written accountability—even for tasks that don't traditionally involve a lot of written work (for example, reviewing the lesson objective or tracking class discussions).

When you have a million things on your mind, it's easy to overlook an activity, forget a question, or neglect a topic that you intended to cover. Because *Double Plan* packets provide teachers with such a clear road map about what they and students should do at every step, teachers are less likely to let activities slip through the cracks or to short-change important content. If it's on the page, it's visible and therefore more likely to get covered. And if you still manage to skip something, students will often let you know.

On a similar note, when you script your questions into your packets, it also holds you accountable to ask them in the same form that you planned. This prevents you from unintentionally diluting the rigor of your planned questions or leading students astray with tangential prompts (for more information, see Chapter Nine). The same holds true for *What to Do* directions: the more clearly you script those into your packets, the easier it will be to ensure that students do what you planned, in the manner you intended.

Goal 4: Synergy with Checking for Understanding

Because *Double Planning* with packets inherently *Standardizes the Format* — enabling champion teachers to monitor the content and quality of student performance reliably and efficiently — these teachers often use them to collect and organize information on what students know and don't know. During their lessons, champion teachers gather data through observation as they circulate. Occasionally, they might stop to compare students' written work with the target responses that they've scripted into the margins of their packet. (For an example, see Taryn Pritchard's packet in the Useful Tools section for this chapter on the website, **www.teachlikeachampion.com**.) Planning target responses holds you accountable to sticking with the standard that you initially set. It's easy to accidentally miss errors or "round up" student responses, but it's much harder to do that when you can immediately compare students' work against a concrete exemplar. Scripting target responses also enables you to *experience* the lesson through their eyes, which can help you better anticipate error, gauge pacing more accurately, and draft clearer *What to Do* directions so that students can spend time grappling with content rather than the logistics.

Once champion teachers collect data, they use a variety of approaches to record and organize it in their packets. For instance, Taryn Pritchard of Leadership Preparatory Bedford Stuyvesant uses the margins to keep track of students who make common errors. Later, she intentionally *Cold Calls* these students (technique 33) so that she can address their common misunderstandings in front of the whole group. Taryn also jots the names of students who produced particularly stellar work so that she can *Cold Call* them to share their unique approach or insights with the class. In cases where students make isolated errors or need individual assistance, teachers like Ryan Miller of Williamsburg Collegiate also use their packets to keep a running log of the students they plan to check in with during independent work. This frees them up to devote their energy to collecting data and acting on it.

Goal 5: Success Oriented

The most effective *Double Planners* wire their packets to help as many students as possible meet or exceed a high standard of excellence. To do this, they view the lesson from the student's perspective and then systematically add supports or remove obstacles to success, without diluting rigor.

In one history class, for example, the teacher embedded the rubric she'd use to evaluate the quality of students' analysis of primary source documents. We've also seen teachers add supports like a "tip box," examples of correct work, standard-setting directions (for example, "Remember to include 4+ sentences"), and reminders about the resources students should refer to when tackling a question (for example, "Be sure to use your notes from yesterday's lecture on fascism"). Taken together, these additions set up students to practice success while also preparing them to self-monitor the quality of their work within and across subject areas.

Goal 6: Embedded Adaptability

Strong *Double Plan* teachers recognize that their lesson packets are living, breathing documents that should help them respond to the evolving needs of their students. As I've mentioned, Bryan Belanger regularly includes more questions in his packets than his students need so that he can strategically speed ahead or double back, depending on student mastery. Taryn Pritchard applies similar thinking to independent practice by dividing it up into sections by order of difficulty: "mild," "medium," and "spicy." Taryn asks all students to complete the "mild" independent practice first and then to get as far as they can through the final two sections for additional enrichment. This allows students to speed ahead at their own pace without having to disrupt other students by continually asking permission from the teacher before moving on. Other teachers have taken a slightly more binary approach by embedding their handouts with "Challenge" or "Deep Thinking" questions. Regardless of which format you choose, strive to design independent practice that ensures all students are able to challenge themselves at their own pace.

CONCLUSION

It seems obvious, but diligent planning—especially planning of the lesson through the student's eyes—is necessary to set the stage for productive class time. Even if things don't always go exactly according to what you have planned, simply having thought through activities, potential trouble spots, and ways to keep your lessons focused on specific objectives ahead of time can make responding in the moment feel more natural and less reactionary when the time comes. You may not have the time to *Double Plan* every lesson or to post everything just so before the bell rings each day. Still, the more you get in the habit of thoroughly preparing materials and responses ahead of time, the more meaningful you will make the already short time in your class. In Chapter Five, we'll look at ways champion teachers structure their time in class to make the largest, most efficient strides toward common mastery.

Reflection and Practice

The following activities should help you think about and practice the techniques in this chapter.

1. Choose an especially large learning standard from the state in which you teach. Before you analyze it, try to guess how many objectives you'd need to truly master it. Now break it up into a series of manageable, measurable objectives that flow in a logical sequence from introduction of the idea to full mastery. Next, try to increase or decrease the number of days you have available by 20 percent. How does this change your objectives?

2. Make a building tour of your school, visiting classrooms and writing down the objectives. Score them as to whether they meet *4 Ms* criteria. Fix the ones you can and then ask yourself where as a school you need to improve objective writing.

3. Think of a recent lesson you taught, and write out all of the actions from a student's perspective, starting in each case with an action verb— "Listened to" and "Wrote," for example. If you feel daring, ask your students whether they think your agenda is accurate. Even more daring is to ask your students to make a list of what they were doing during your class.

(continued)

(continued)

4. Make an action plan for your classroom setup:

   a. What should your default layout be, and what would the most common other layouts look like? Will you use them enough to justify having your students practice moving from one to another?

   b. What are the five most useful and important things you could put on the walls to help students do their work? Are they up?

   c. What things are on your walls that don't need to be? Nominate five to take down.

Maggie Johnson's *To Kill a Mockingbird* packet. Check out one of Maggie Johnson's reading packets for ideas on how you can hold students accountable for interacting with the content of every lesson from start to finish.

Ryan Miller's Double Planning. See how Ryan Miller color-codes students' packet materials to make it easier for them to find specific pages and activities.

Taryn Pritchard's marked-up packet. Take a closer look at how Taryn Pritchard marks up her packets as she circulates to keep track of what students know and don't know.

Meaghan Reuler's Word of the Day packet. Take a peek inside a fifth-grade vocabulary packet that reading teacher Meaghan Reuler carefully designed to make student errors easier to see and respond to.

Chapter 5

Lesson Structure

Technique 20: Do Now.   Use a short warm-up activity that students can complete without instruction or direction from you to start class every day. This lets the learning start even before you begin teaching.

Technique 21: Name the Steps.   Break down complex tasks into steps that form a path for student mastery.

Technique 22: Board = Paper.   Model and shape how students should take notes in order to capture information you present.

Technique 23: Control the Game.   Ask students to read aloud frequently, but manage the process to ensure expressiveness, accountability, and engagement.

Technique 24: Circulate.   Move strategically around the room during all parts of the lesson.

Technique 25: At Bats.   Because succeeding once or twice at a skill won't bring mastery, give your students lots and lots of practice mastering knowledge or skills.

Technique 26: Exit Ticket.   End each class with an explicit assessment of your objective that you can use to evaluate your (and your students') success.

Lesson Structure

A consistent progression of activities can be observed in the lessons of the teachers who informed this book. It's best described as "I/We/You." (Doug McCurry, founder of Achievement First, was the first person I heard use this phrase. Others use the terms *direct instruction, guided practice,* and *independent practice* to describe a similar idea.) This name refers to a lesson in which responsibility for knowing and doing is gradually transferred from teacher to student. "I" refers to beginning by delivering key information or modeling and explaining the process you want your students to learn. During "We," you gradually allow students to complete examples with less and less assistance on more and more of the task—from "I do; you help" to "You do; I help." Finally, in the "You" step, you provide students the opportunity to practice on their own, giving them multiple opportunities and situations of increasing difficulty. Put another way, I/We/You is actually closer to a five-step process:

Step	Lesson Segment	Who's Doing?	Typical Statement
1	I	I do.	"The first step to adding fractions with unlike denominators is to make the denominators equal."
2	We	I do; you help.	"OK, now let's try it. How did we say we were going to make our denominators equal, Martin?"
3	We	You do; I help.	"OK, Camilla, you take us through this. What's the first thing I should do?"
4	You	You do …	"Now that we've solved this example, try one on your own."
5	You	And do … and do … and do.	"Great; we're starting to get this. There are five more in your packet. Take six minutes and see how many you can get exactly right. Go!"

Note that the shift from one step to the next happens as soon as, but not before, students are ready to succeed given the additional independence. This process may sound obvious to some, but it doesn't happen this way in many classrooms. Often, students are released to independent work—to "You"—before they are ready to do so effectively, or asked to reflect on "big questions" before they know enough to do so productively. In other cases, students get very good at watching their teacher demonstrate mastery the "I"—without ever really learning to use a skill on their own. Students get to the point where they can complete a skill with an adult there to help them, but not on their own. Ensuring that students are ready—and challenged—to move toward mastery is essential.

I/We/You: An Overview

Thoughts About Good "I"

- Include both modeling (showing how to do something) and explanation (telling how to do something).

- Include student interaction even though you're leading. (You can still ask questions and engage in dialogue with students during "I.")

- Anticipate. "I knew I was becoming a teacher," champion teacher Kate Murray of Boston told me, "when I started being able to know in advance what my kids would do wrong, what the common mistakes would be. I realized I could plan for that. From then on, my planning process included a 'what could go wrong' conversation with myself. And I planned to preteach what I knew would be the pitfalls. I put that right into my lesson plans." Amen to that.

Thoughts About Good "We"

- The goal of "We" is to push more and more of the cognitive work out to students. Feigned ignorance—"Did I get that right, you guys?" "Wait a minute, I can't remember what's next!"—and unbundling—breaking one question up into several—can be especially useful.

- Use Two Stairways (see *Name the Steps* in this chapter) and make sure to ask process questions ("What should we do?") and execution questions ("Good. Can you show me how to do it?"). Prepare your students to understand and self-manage by asking what we are doing here (or what we just did there) and why.

Thoughts About Good "You"

- Repetition matters. Students need to practice over and over. Some of them learn the skill for good the third time they do it right; some of them learn it the tenth time. Very few of them learn it the first or second.

- Go until they can do it on their own. By the end of independent practice, students should be able to solve problems to the standard they'll be accountable for, entirely on their own.

- Use multiple variations and formats. Students should be able to solve questions in multiple formats and with a significant number of plausible variations and variables.

- Get more complex and challenging over time. Just be sure to use your CFU tools to make sure students continue to practice getting it right most of the time.

- Grab opportunities for enrichment; have challenge problems at hand for students who are ready for the next level.

The I/We/You recipe, I should note, is a "default"—a template to use much or most of the time because it's effective and easy to implement. Still, its being effective doesn't mean you can't ever deviate from it—or use variations of it. Most teachers vary I/We/You in some way or other on occasion, adapting it to the given situation.

For example, you might show students how to factor a very basic quadratic equation (I). Then you might try two together: "I do; you help," then "You do; I help." (We) Then, instead of giving students another problem to do on their own, you might circle back and, using harder problems, show students how their approach might change when the problems get more difficult (back to We), before releasing them for independent practice (You).

Alternatively, I often see something like I/We/You/I/We/You in reading lessons, especially if you think of reading in general as the "I" portion of your lesson where a story is told. The "We" tends to be discussion and development of interpretations, and the "You" is expressing an independent interpretation or analysis of a similar question or passage.

You might see that cycle repeat in 10- to 15-minute sequences over the course of a lesson, like this:

Read (I) 5 min
Discuss/Interpret (We) 5 min
Write (You) 5 min
Read (Control the Game) (I) 3 min
Discuss/Interpret (We) 6 min
Write (You) 4 min

Or it might look something like this (I/We/You/I/You):

Read (I) 5 min
Analyze/Discuss/Explicate (We) 5 min
Write ("Stop and Jot") (You) 3 min
Read (I) 3 min
Write ("Stop and Jot") (You) 4 min

Even with these variations, the principle is the same. There's a reading in which information is disseminated; the working together, during which I make sure you comprehend or can apply a skill (character analysis, say); then you doing it on your own: once, twice, three times. It's still I/We/You. The core idea is that most good lessons need doses of direct instruction, guided practice, *and* independent practice—often if not always in that exact order.

Even when teachers occasionally go completely out of order—starting with a "You," for example, and having students solve a problem on their own without any initial instruction—they are usually reliant on an overall structure of I/We/You. One school I admire, for example, generally uses I/We/You, but once or twice per week asks teachers to deliberately plan short rigorous lessons that start with "You." These involve the presentation of a very difficult problem or piece of text without explanation or a clear solution. Students are allowed to struggle to apply what they know to solve it. The teacher might say, "Here's a very difficult math problem [or section of text]. I won't tell you how to solve it [or what it is saying]. See how you do." These "You-first" lessons exist within a larger system of I/We/You. Students learn a range of skills efficiently and productively through I/We/You lessons and apply those skills in new ways and in a situation where they don't know which of their skills will apply. So the I/We/You is still the core tool for building skills that students then learn to apply in unexpected combinations. If teachers primarily used this You-first approach every day, their students would be sorely lacking in tools. I/We/You is the foundation that makes variations from it most effective.

DO NOW

Use a short warm-up activity that students can complete without instruction or direction from you to start class every day. This lets the learning start even before you begin teaching.

20

The first step in a great lesson is a **Do Now**—a short activity that you have written on the board or that, in printed form, is waiting for students as they enter. Either way, the *Do Now* starts working before you do. While you are greeting students at the door or finding that stack of copies or erasing the markups you made to your overhead from the last lesson, students should already be busy, via the *Do Now*, with scholarly work that prepares them to succeed. In fact, students entering your room should never have to ask themselves, "What am I supposed to be doing?" The answer, every day, should go without saying: "You should be doing the *Do Now*, because we always start with the *Do Now*."

An effective *Do Now* should conform to four critical criteria to ensure that it remains focused, efficient, and effective:

1. The *Do Now* should be in the same place every day so it becomes habit for all your students. You can write it on the board, post it on a piece of poster paper in advance, or put it in writing on a sheet of paper or the first page in a packet for the day's lesson—wherever you put it, keep it consistent.

2. Students should be able to complete the *Do Now* without any direction from you, without any discussion with their classmates, and in most cases without any other materials save what you provide. So if the *Do Now* is to write a sentence interpreting a primary source document that is a nineteenth-century *Punch* cartoon, that

cartoon should be posted somewhere easily visible to all, or copied into the *Do Now* materials. Some teachers misunderstand the purpose of the *Do Now* and start by explaining to their students what to do and how to do it (for example, "OK, class, the Do Now is on the board. You'll notice that it asks you to do X and then Y. Please get started"). This defeats the purpose of establishing a self-managed habit of productive work. If you have to give directions, it's not independent enough.

3. The activity should take three to five minutes to complete and should require putting a pencil to paper. That is, there should be a written product from it. This not only makes it more rigorous and more engaging but also enables you to better hold students accountable for doing it, because you can clearly see whether they are (and they can see that you can see). This allows you to check for understanding (see Part One) while they work, deciding, as Taryn Pritchard did in a recent lesson, which questions to review and possibly whom to call on for a quality answer or a common mistake (see "Secret Life of a *Do Now*").

4. The activity should generally (a) preview the day's lesson (you are reading *The Jacket,* and the *Do Now* asks students to write three sentences about what they'd do if they thought someone stole their little brother's favorite jacket) or (b) review a recent lesson (you want your students to practice all of the standards they've mastered recently so that they don't forget them).

The single most common downfall I observe with *Do Nows* is a teacher's losing track of time while reviewing answers. Fifteen minutes later, the *Do Now* has replaced the lesson that was originally planned—or at least has crowded out all of the crucial independent practice that was scheduled for the end. Just as important as the content of your *Do Now* is how you review it. You want to complete your review in the same amount of time you give students to work on it: three to five minutes. Thus the review portion requires the art of selective neglect. If you give your students eight problems to do, you won't be able to review all eight of them. You'll have to choose the two or three that are most important or where answers are most revealing. This makes the period when students are working critical from a CFU perspective—you'll want to track the data a bit to see which questions pose problems for students, as well as which students can provide correct answers or ones containing useful errors. Because you'll have just a few minutes to decide what parts to review, you'll probably want to draw on the principles of gathering data through observation (see Chapter One).

Secret Life of a *Do Now*

Figure 5.1 is a picture of Taryn Pritchard's *Do Now* from a recent math lesson. If you look closely, you'll notice that there are actually two layers of notation. The first layer consists of the notes Taryn made to herself before she started

Figure 5.1 Taryn Pritchard's *Do Now* Model

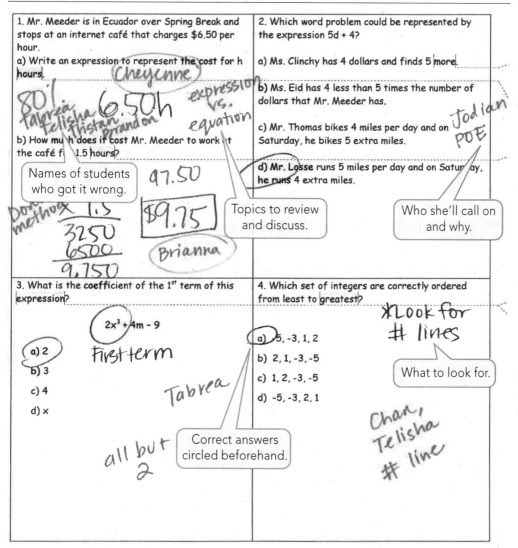

Figure 5.1 © copyright Uncommon Schools

class. They include the answers to the problems, the "shown" work for problem 1, and a note to herself to look for number lines on problem 4. You can also see in this image the notes she took as she circulated during her *Do Now*. She noted that 80 percent of students got number 1 right, but also the four students who didn't. She noted a student whom she wanted to call on for each problem (for example, Brianna for 1.b) as well as a key issue that emerged unexpectedly—the difference between *expression* and *equation*. Taryn has not only demonstrated fantastic CFU skills but also prepared herself to review her *Do Now* efficiently and with maximum value in five minutes or less by doing the most important things first. For even more examples of effective *Do Nows*, see the Useful Tools referenced at the end of the chapter and located on the website, www.teachlikeachampion.com.

Finally, some of the masters of the *Do Now* in my eyes are most effective because of the speed with which they transition from *Do Now* to review. They might count down the end of the *Do Now* with something like "OK, pencils down when you hear the beep, and we'll talk about some of these questions." When the timer starts to beep, they might immediately start in with a *Cold Call* (technique 33) or a *Show Call* (technique 39), stressing accountability for working hard during the *Do Now* and not wasting a second of time. What often comes between *Do Now* and review in other classrooms ("Good morning, guys. I'm so excited for our lesson today. We'll be looking at X and Y. Did everyone have a good morning?" and so on) happens after the *Do Now* has been reviewed in champion classrooms.

21

NAME THE STEPS

Break down complex tasks into steps that form a path for student mastery.

Why is it that the best coaches often rise from the ranks of the almost-great or not-so-great athletes, while the most gifted athletes rarely seem to make the best coaches? Why is it that brilliant and sophisticated actors can't help others do something similar and are so often at a loss to describe how they do what they do, while unheralded thespians manage to unlock world-class talent in others?

One cause may be this: superstars often don't have to pay meticulous attention to the what's-next and how-to of each step. The very thing that makes them brilliant, an intuitive and lightning-quick understanding of how to handle a given problem on the stage or the court or the field, keeps the most talented from recognizing how the rest of us, for whom the intuition does not come quickly, learn. The rest of us, who cannot see it once and then do it ourselves beginning to end, are more likely to take complex tasks and break them down into manageable steps. We move piecemeal toward mastery and need to remind ourselves over and over which step comes next. I call the technique based on this reality **Name the Steps**.

One of my soccer coaches had been an all-world superstar as a player. As coach, he'd stand on the sidelines and shout, "Defense, you guys! Defense!!" We were pretty aware that we were on defense, though, and also pretty aware that we weren't playing it especially well. He coached by offering pointers like "Don't tackle there, Doug!" When I started to play for another coach, I realized how a coach might also be a teacher. The second coach broke down defense into a series of steps: First, position yourself increasingly closer to your man as he gets closer to the player with the ball. Second, deny the ball if and only if you are certain you can intercept. Third, prevent your man from turning if he is facing away from the goal. Fourth, steer your man toward the sidelines if he has the ball and has turned. Fifth, tackle if you must. Sixth, otherwise keep position between him and the goal.

He focused his coaching (before the game, rather than during!) on reminding us what step came next. If my man got the ball, he would gently remind me, "Don't let him turn." If I let him turn (I usually did), he would say, "Take him wide." If, as was often the case, I found myself unsuccessful, he would say, "If you must ... ," a reminder that keeping my position between the player and the goal was more important than winning the ball. For years after I stopped playing for him, I'd recall his steps ("If you must ... ") while I played. Once I asked the second coach how he thought to teach the way he did. His reply was revealing: "That was the only way I could learn it."

If you are teaching in your area of skill and passion, you likely have more intuition (natural or learned) than your students do, and you can help them succeed by seizing opportunities to subdivide complex skills into component tasks and build knowledge up systematically. Champion teachers often traffic in recipes, then: the five steps to writing a short response to a question, the four parts of solving a system of equations, and so on. Their students learn the steps, refer to the map the steps provide as they are developing competence, and then leave the steps behind when they are familiar enough with the recipe to forget they are following it. With mastery, they add their own variations and flourishes. What starts as a recipe does not end up formulaic. Students write twenty-five STORY responses (discussed later in this chapter) and by the twenty-fifth are adapting and applying STORY in new ways. By number fifty, the scaffolding has all but disappeared.

Keep in the back of your mind the distinction between champion performers and champion teachers. Champion teachers help their students learn complex skills by breaking them down into manageable steps and, often, giving each step a name so that it can be easily recalled. This allows the process to take on a consistent, often storylike progression. There are not just five steps to combining sentences with the same subject, but the steps are named, given a catchy mnemonic to help students recall them in order, and posted in the classroom so they can be used and referred to over and over again.

The following are three key components that are often part of effectively *Naming the Steps*.

1. Identify the Steps

Teaching the process makes complex skills transparent to students. For example, Kelli Ragin doesn't just teach students to round whole numbers to a given place value; she teaches them the five steps for rounding whole numbers to a given place value:

1. Underline the digit in the place you are rounding to.
2. Circle the digit to the right of the underlined digit.
3. If the circled digit is four or less, the underlined digit stays the same; if the circled digit is five or more, the underlined digit gets one more.
4. All of the digits to the left of the underlined digit stay the same.
5. All of the digits to the right of the underlined digit become zeroes.

Kelli calls the portion of the lesson where she introduces these steps her "Rules and Tools." When she *Names the Steps*, she's careful about keeping to a limited number. Because people have a hard time remembering more than seven items in sequence, having more than seven steps is a recipe for confusion. If you have more steps than you can clearly and easily remember, you might as well have none at all. Kelli is also intentional about maintaining economy of language in her steps. As she teaches rounding, she adds wrinkles and complexity, but the part she wants her students to remember is intentionally focused and crisp.

A teacher who carefully examines a process like the one for rounding and puts it into sequential steps gives her students scaffolding. This scaffolding is powerful, and with it students can attack any similar problem. It essentially gives them a map to refer to if they get stuck, especially if they have written the steps down in their notes, as Kelli requires.

Finally, having clear and concrete steps lets you post them on the walls of your classroom as a reminder, and can also help you isolate problem steps. In a recent lesson, Bob Zimmerli was teaching students to solve multistep equations and had laid out four clear steps in a mnemonic: **Don't Cry; Bring It!** with, for example, the *D* standing for *distribute* and the *C* for *combine like terms*. As he circulated during independent work, he realized that students were failing to combine like terms. He referred several students to the chart and examples on the wall, but more errors emerged, so he stopped to reteach. Even as he did so, he walked students through the steps, saying, as he pointed to *Distribute* and then *Isolate the variable,* "You're pretty good at this and this. It's combining like terms that's tripping you up." This allowed him to simply and easily focus everyone in the room on the problem step during his reteach.

Want More? Clip 5. Want more *Name the Steps*? Watch clip 5 of Bob Zimmerli using his *Name the Steps* chart to help students.

---

2. Make Them "Sticky"

Once you've identified steps, name them. Naming steps makes them memorable, and they therefore stick in your students' minds. You may also go a step further in stickiness by creating a story or a mnemonic device around the names of your steps.

At North Star Academy's elementary schools, second graders use the acronym STORY to describe the five elements of a story. The name of course is easy to remember, and the five STORY elements, as described on a typical wall poster, include details that make the mnemonic sticky:

S — The **s**etting is where and when the story takes place.

T — **T**alking characters are who the story revolves around.

O — *Oops,* there's a problem. A problem is what a character wants but cannot have.

R—The attempts to **resolve** are when characters try to fix the problem and they fail.

Y—*Yes!* A solution!! A solution is when a problem is solved.

You'll notice that there are lots of elements here to make the mnemonic memorable—the acronym isn't a straight transliteration of the five story elements (setting, characters, problem, attempts to solve, solution). A strictly literal version would be something like SCPAS—a much less engaging alternative that's also a lot less fun to sing, for example. Moreover, the addition of "Oops" and "Yes!" helps students connect to the story on an emotional level.

Teachers use this kind of mnemonic as an analytical tool. For example, a teacher might ask students to "Explain the STORY you read today," as a writing prompt, reminding students of the five things they should discuss in order when summarizing. Of course, as students get older, they learn to diverge from the STORY template, but for a young scholar, the road map to summarizing a piece of fiction is certainly helpful—both in understanding it and in attending to important pieces—the first couple dozen times through.

3. Use Two Stairways

Once students know the steps, classrooms can have two parallel conversations going at once: how to get an answer to the current problem and how to answer any problem like this one. In other words, students can narrate the process or the problem, and the teacher can switch back and forth, as in this sequence from a lesson on multiplying fractions:

Teacher: What's the next step, Paul? [process]
Paul: Multiply the numerators.
Teacher: OK, what are the numerators? [problem]
Paul: The numerators are four and one.
Teacher: So the numerator in our solution is going to be? [problem]
Paul: It's going to be four.
Teacher: OK, good. So, Sasha, what do we need to do next? [process]
Sasha: We need to multiply the denominators.
Teacher: And the denominator is? [problem]
Sasha: The denominator should be two.
Teacher: So I'm done, right Conrad? [process]
Conrad: No, you have to reduce.
Teacher: Perfect. So what's our final answer? [problem]
Conrad: The answer is two.

You can often take advantage of this dynamic by adjusting roles, sometimes asking students to focus on explaining the process while they do the math, sometimes asking them to do the math while reminding them of the process, and sometimes doing both. Sometimes you can ask one student to concentrate on process, and another student to concentrate on the problem. Sometimes you can solve a problem and ask students to explain what you're doing and why. Sometimes you'll make mistakes and ask them where you went wrong or what a better way to solve would have been. In short, teaching the steps makes the process both legible and easily followed in a consistent way.

BOARD = PAPER

Model and shape how students should take notes in order to capture information you present.

22

Next time you observe a class at the high school or college level, take a minute to observe what students write in their notes. Do they systematically record the key ideas from the class? Do they leave the class with a record of the proceedings that allows them to revisit the ideas days, weeks, or even years later? Perhaps some do. I have a colleague who can still tell me what we said about each classroom we visited during a series of school visits in 2004. But many students will produce a haphazard series of scrawls scattered across the page. Their notes will be all but useless to them later. Unlike my colleague, I never learned (or, more important, practiced) an intentional system of note taking as a student. Teachers just assumed students knew how to take notes and would do a credible job. To this day, I find this enduring weakness to be one of the biggest drags on my productivity at work.

Students often have to learn how to be students as much as they need to learn content and skills, and the processes and practices of being a student must be assimilated by modeling. One of the most complex and critical aspects of being a student is learning to take notes and retain a record of one's knowledge. For the most part, however, if students learn this aspect of scholarship, they learn a suboptimal model by accident. To model good note taking more deliberately, expecting students to track what you are writing on the board and record it diligently in their notes is the right starting point (hence the name of this technique: **Board = Paper**). As students grow, they need to learn to make intentional decisions about what to include in their notes, but that process should wait until they can reliably get what matters down right as a matter of habit. The best way to start students on the path to autonomous note taking is to make your overhead a mirror image of the graphic organizer you give to students to take notes on. As you fill in a blank, they fill in a corresponding blank. You fill out the projected worksheet on the board and say, "Make your paper look like mine." Even as students earn more autonomy, having your overhead match the format in which they are taking notes allows you to model what note taking—one of the most important skills for any student—should look like.

Figure 5.2   Sample of Excellent Note Taking

The Muscular System

Your muscular system is made up of _muscles_ and _tendons._

Muscles _pull_ on your _bones_ to make you move.

There are two kinds of muscles in the Muscular System, _Voluntary_ and _involuntary_ muscles. You only get to choose when you move your _voluntary muscles._

Here are 3 examples of voluntary muscles:
Your arms
Your hands
Wiggling your nose

Here are 3 examples of involuntary muscles:
Your heart
Your eyes (blinking)
Your lungs (breathing)

There are _630_ muscles in a typical human body. Rounded to the nearest hundred that's about _600_ muscles.

Write a sentence below describing the most interesting fact about your muscular system:
When your heart beats. That's a muscle.

Re-write your sentence below adding one of the things your teacher asks you to add.
When your heart beats, it is an example of an involuntary muscle.

Figure 5.2 shows the overhead a third-grade science teacher used during her lesson on the muscular system. Her students filled out the exact same information in hard copy at their desks, allowing her to teach them not only about muscles but also about note taking and organizing information. By contrast, Figure 5.3 shows the notes a student took in another classroom where the teacher instructed students to "take careful notes on a separate sheet of paper."

Gradually, students should develop note-taking independence, filling out longer and longer passages of their graphic organizers on their own, ultimately taking notes on a separate sheet of paper as you write terms and definitions on the board exactly as you wish students to copy them down. As you introduce note-taking skills, guide students through the process, telling them what to title their papers, when to skip a line, how to make subheadings and headings. When they can do this reliably, you can gradually begin to divest yourself of responsibility for exact phrasing and let students own even that. But know that it may take years before students are ready to own full responsibility for such a critical piece of the process.

Figure 5.3 Sample of Poor Note Taking

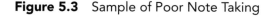

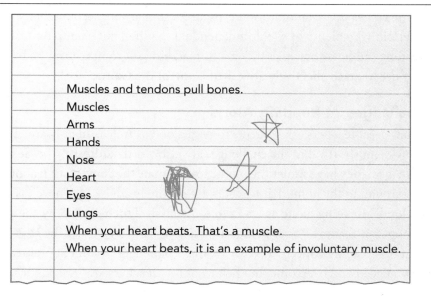

CONTROL THE GAME

Ask students to read aloud frequently, but manage the process to ensure expressiveness, accountability, and engagement.

Champion teachers integrate prodigious amounts of reading into their classes, and that, in my opinion, is one of the most salient characteristics. No matter what they teach, these teachers reinforce — with their actions as much as their words — that reading is indispensable to study and learning. They know we can't just say, "To be a scientist you must always read" or "When they are in doubt, historians go to the primary source to investigate." Teachers have to model the process of "reading to learn" in every discipline. If they don't, students won't believe us when we say it's at the core of learning.

Although silent, independent reading is a common and important part of champion classrooms, by itself it's insufficient if you seek to teach students to read diverse and rigorous types of text, monitor their progress, and ensure accountability. Yes, there should certainly be plenty of silent, independent reading, but champion teachers also make reading public — they ask students to read aloud — to maximize its benefit. The tools they use to do so effectively are called **Control the Game**.

The Challenges of Reading Aloud

The reasons great teachers ask students to read aloud as well as silently are many, and I will review them shortly. But the challenges are also worth addressing because, though easily managed, they have sometimes come to dominate the conversation about reading in the classroom, to the point that teachers are routinely advised to "never ask students to read aloud." Reading aloud is also often dismissively referred to by the pejorative phrase "popcorn reading," as if denigrating a simplistic straw man were grounds for ruling out oral reading entirely. There are surely challenges to student oral reading that must be managed and overcome, but believing that teachers are "not supposed" to ask students to read is counterproductive. Fortunately, it's advice that is routinely ignored by top teachers.

So why are teachers told not to read aloud? The reasons can be grouped in two primary buckets: leverage concerns and self-esteem concerns.

Leverage Concerns

Some teachers react to suggestions that they include more oral reading with a line of inquiry something like this: "Why would you allow a single student to read aloud during class time? What are the other kids doing?" The answer is that, in a great classroom, they are reading too. Having a lone student reading aloud to an otherwise passive classroom can indeed be a poor use of time, but why should the rest of the class be passive when they could be reading as well? I like to refer to how much work a teacher is getting out of the rest of the class when one student is reading as *leverage*. If one student is reading and twenty-seven students are staring into space or listening passively, the leverage is low. But if one student is reading actively and twenty-seven students are reading along with her, as actively engaged in the text as if they were reading independently, then the leverage is much higher. Although concern about the passivity of nonreaders is a legitimate one, it's a concern that's fairly easily managed by effective teacher actions.

Self-Esteem Concerns

Others have opined that students should not be asked to read aloud in class because they might struggle, and that would shame them or cause them to hate reading. Essentially, the argument here is that if students are weak readers, we should not ask them to read, withholding from them the best tool for learning to read because it might make them feel anxious. The argument further assumes that struggling is a bad thing and that classroom cultures are incapable of making it safe to struggle and take risks. Great classrooms give the lie to these fallacious and destructive assumptions. They manage the experience so that students gradually get better at reading by reading aloud. They replace fear of reading (if in fact there is fear, a big assumption) with the normality of it. When students are asked to read, they read aloud with expression and pleasure, capturing character traits and emotions in their voices and choosing important words to emphasize as they go.

Further, one sure ramification of not asking students to read aloud because it might shame some readers is that the reading ban is applied to *all students,* so no one gets to read aloud. The reading ban makes it far more difficult to expose readers, weak and strong alike, to a culture that relishes reading and communicates its joy and power through expressive oral reading by students. This might still be a sustainable argument if students were never required to read once they left school, but of course they are, so restricting students from oral reading because they are poor readers only ensures that they will remain poor readers.

So Why *Is* Oral Reading So Important?

One of the biggest reasons students don't read very well is that they don't read very much. If we want to help kids become great readers, we have to do more than just ask them to read. We have to ask them to read a lot. And then we have to make sure that they read when we ask them to.

These challenges are borne out in the methods that schools currently use to increase their number of "page miles." In one commonly used program, Drop Everything and Read (DEAR), for example, students are given quiet time in which they sit with books and are expected to read. It's a lovely idea, but if you observe students during this program, you will invariably see some of them sitting with books open but eyes drifting. Others practice reading poorly, reinscribing weak habits such as skipping words and dropping suffixes as they go. Often, there is an inverse correlation between quality of reading in such situations and the need for reading: the students reading least are often the ones who need to read the most.

Reading aloud neutralizes—or at least surfaces—many of these challenges, and it can be an excellent source of data. You hear not only whether your students are capable of reading a given text but also what they struggle with specifically, allowing you to give them constant practice and feedback. When a student misreads a word, you can immediately step in with something like "as they were *sitting* the table?" and cause him to practice reading correctly. This is especially important in the era of Common Core, which has rightly asked us to ensure that students read harder texts. Pushing kids to read above their comfort zone means that every student will sometimes need feedback and support.

Expressive Reading

There is something deeply powerful about a class in which students see one another reading and reading well. When students read silently, we don't know whether they are reading effectively and "getting it"; whether they are navigating the unique vocabulary, syntax, and narrative conventions of that discipline correctly; or whether they are following challenging text. We can gauge their overall sense of the text, but not the specific line-by-line mastery that's necessary to becoming an effective reader. So great teachers *teach* students to read the distinct forms of language used in each discipline by asking students to read it in a way that's accountable and that enables teachers to gather information and provide feedback: they ask them to read aloud.

Reading aloud also builds a culture of expressive reading. You'll notice in many of the videos in this book that students read with relish and verve. This is good for building and assessing comprehension skills. You can't read the first line of the Preamble to the US Constitution correctly unless you can understand it. But just as important, reading aloud causes students to bring books to life in their reading every day, to just slightly compete for who can read with the most flair, who can make their classmates hear the humor or anger in the prose. In other words, reading aloud makes reading what it is supposed to be: something shared, social, expressive, and dramatic. Seeing your peers reading joyfully and with relish sells the power of reading better than a thousand lectures on the topic.

How to *Control the Game*

How then do you unlock the benefits of student oral reading and mitigate its downsides? How do you ensure leverage and attentiveness? How do you prepare for strugglers? When you *Control the Game,* you ask students to read aloud, ideally with a bit of expression, occasionally asking for rereads to reinforce it when it's done well ("Ooh, can you read that sentence again, Milagros? I love the way you read that") or to ask for a bit more ("Good, Milagros. Now can you read it again and make Fern sound angry?"). As you have students read aloud, you can make it an immensely productive activity by executing the subtle changes described here.

Keep Durations Unpredictable

If you designate a student to read in class and say, "Read the next paragraph for me, Vivian," every other student in the class knows no one else will be asked to read until Vivian finishes the paragraph. *Stating the duration for which a student will read causes other students to follow along a little less.* Instead, when you ask a student to read aloud during class, don't specify how long you want her to read. Saying, "Start reading for me please, Vivian" or "Pick up please, Vivian" makes other students more likely to read along, as they don't know when a new reader will be asked to pick up.

In addition, keeping duration unpredictable allows you to address a struggling reader in a safe and noninvasive manner. If Vivian struggles with the paragraph you've assigned her, it's either a long, slow slog to the end, possibly exhausting for Vivian and reducing leverage with other students, or it's you suddenly cutting her short of what you promised: "OK, I'm going to stop you there, Vivian. Jalani, would you please read some?" which carries an implicit judgment. If you don't specify the length of the read initially, however, you can adapt in the interest of both the student who's reading and the rest of the class. Vivian can read two sentences really well and then stop before she struggles too much, making the experience positive, then you can move to a dynamic reader who will push the story along for the rest of the class. Or, if Vivian is doing well, you can let her keep going. All of this happens invisibly when you avoid telling students how long they'll read.

Keep Durations Short

Reading short segments can often allow students to invest energy in expressive reading and sustain the energy required for fluent, even dramatic reading. It's better to read really well for three or four sentences and stop than to read well for two and drone through six more. Short durations yield higher-quality oral reading and make the lesson more engaging. Moving quickly among primary readers can boost the energy level and can also keep the pacing lively by maximizing mileposts (see Chapter Six, "Pacing"). As a result, lessons feel quick and energetic rather than tedious and slow.

Knowing that segments tend to be short and may end at any time also reinforces for secondary readers that they will likely soon get a chance themselves to read, and this keeps them from tuning out.

A caveat: As students develop as readers, your definition of "short" will of course change. Maybe the average read is two or three sentences at first, but as students become more mature, as they get better as readers and become more socialized to attend carefully, as they come to love reading and lose themselves more in the text, you will naturally extend the average length of a read. Sometimes, as a class, you will lose yourself in a passage, and Vivian will just keep going. The key idea is that using shorter reads can bring engagement and energy to student oral reading—perhaps at the beginning of a passage, perhaps if things slow down, perhaps all the time. When and how often is up to you.

Finally, keeping durations short enables you to take better advantage of a crucial form of data: every time you switch readers, you gather data about your leverage. When you say, "Pick up please, Charles," and Charles jumps in with the next sentence without missing a beat, you know Charles was reading alongside the previous reader on his own. If not, you know otherwise. Ideally, you want this sort of seamless transition every time you switch readers, and frequent switching allows you to gather and manage transitions more often and more broadly. The more data you have, the more information and tools you will have to help you ensure leverage.

Keep the Identity of the Next Reader Unpredictable

If you move quickly from one primary reader to another, students focus more closely on following along. This is doubly true if they don't know who the next primary reader will be. A teacher who announces that she'll go around the room in a predictable fashion gives away this part of her leverage. Students can tune out until their turn is near. Retaining your ability to choose the next reader also allows you to match students to passages more effectively. Unpredictability makes for both better leverage and better reading, and when you call on students to read, make sure not to call exclusively on volunteers. A significant proportion of readers should be chosen regardless of who has raised his or her hand and should include those who haven't raised their hands. This will maximize leverage and normalize full and universal participation in reading. Of course you can occasionally call on an excited would-be reader who volunteers, so as to reinforce the fact that students who raise their hands are telling you they love reading and want to do more of it, but most of the time it's you who decides — after all, the message should be that reading is a pleasure and that a good teacher doesn't let just a few students hog all the fun.

Reduce Transaction Costs

When it comes to transitioning between readers, small differences in transaction costs can have a large effect, so it's critical to reduce them. (Again, *transaction cost* is the amount of resources it takes to execute an exchange, be it economic, verbal, or otherwise.) A transition from one reader to the next that takes much more than a second steals reading time and risks interrupting the continuity of what students are reading, thus affecting how well students follow and comprehend the text.

Make it your goal to transition from one primary reader to another quickly and with a minimum of words — ideally, in a consistent way. "Susan, pick up," is a much more efficient transition than, "Thank you, Stephen. Nicely read. Susan will you begin reading, please?" The first transaction is more than three times as fast as the second, maximizing the amount of time students spend reading. A couple seconds of difference may seem trivial, but if you transition fifty times per class, those seconds very quickly translate into minutes and hours of lost reading time over the course of the year. Just as important, reducing your transaction cost when switching readers causes less interruption to the text, allowing students to concentrate and keep the narrative thread vibrant, alive, and unbroken. If you make a habit of minimizing transaction cost, you can more easily switch at almost any natural pause in the text, giving you even more control over when to choose a new primary reader.

See It in Action: Clip 19

In clip 19, you can see Jessica Bracey of North Star Academy (Newark, New Jersey) executing a lesson with an effective segment of *Control the Game* reading embedded in it.

You'll notice how engaged Jessica's students are as she keeps durations short and unpredictable, moving the reading around the room to involve lots of students. You'll also notice that even though she calls on a number of students to read, every single one picks up on cue—solid evidence that they're all reading along with her.

You'll also notice a wide range of reading skills. There are outstanding readers who model expressive, engaged reading, and there are also some strugglers. Even so, the strugglers aren't afraid to read, even when it's tricky for them, and Jessica uses the resulting data stream to help them—asking them to recognize and embed meaning into their expression or to reread words they didn't get right. Finally, you'll notice the ultimate in unpredictable reader selection—the girl who is reading at the start of the clip gets called on again at the end. Just because you've read once doesn't mean the game is over in Jessica's class.

Use Bridging to Maintain Continuity

When teachers execute *Control the Game*, they are actually combining two types of reading—student oral reading and teacher oral reading. As the teacher, you are naturally the best reader in the room. In reading aloud, you model the sorts of expressive reading you want from students—joyful, scholarly, what have you. You may choose to step in yourself and read especially important or tricky passages—your reading of them can bring the nuance of the text to life and help expedite comprehension. You can also use segments when you read to resuscitate momentum after a particularly slow or struggling reader by stepping in for a few sentences, keeping the thread of the narrative alive and engaging for other students.

In bridging, a teacher takes a turn in the *Control the Game* rotation, reading a short segment of text—a bridge—between student readers. In a typical sequence of bridging, a teacher might ask Trayvon to read for a few sentences, then Martina and then Hilary, and then read for a stretch herself. She might have planned in advance a part she thought she should read, or she might read to model expressive reading and bring the story to life a bit. She might read because Hilary really struggled, and the teacher didn't want the slowing pace to cause other readers to disengage. She might step in more or less frequently.

Sometimes teachers will start the reading themselves to set the tone, occasionally even doing so transparently: "I'll start reading, then I'll ask some of you to pick up. Be ready!" Obviously, teacher reading needn't necessarily always bridge. When you do so is obviously discretionary, and part of the art of reading well. Harder texts often demand more bridging—to create more opportunities to model, and to balance the necessarily high rate of slower student readers.

Spot-Check, a.k.a. Oral Cloze

I learned Oral Cloze from watching Roberto de Leòn teach reading to third-grade boys at Excellence Charter School for Boys in Bedford Stuyvesant. In one example, Roberto kicked off his reading of *Phantom of the Opera* by leaving a word out at the end of his first sentence: "Carlotta had the … ," he read, signaling to students with his shift in tone of voice that they should fill in the blank. On the day in question, only a handful of his boys chimed in "leading role" exactly on cue. So Rob started over: "Ooh, some boys weren't quite with us. Let's try that again. 'Carlotta had the … ,'" and all his boys chimed in with "leading role," demonstrating that they were now following along. This quick device, which Roberto uses throughout his lessons, allows him to assess leverage quickly and simply.

Use a Placeholder

As champion teachers move between reading and questioning their students about what they read, they use quick and reliable prompts to ensure that students recognize the transition and react quickly. I call this prompt a *placeholder,* because it ensures that students retain their place in the text and enables a quick and immediate transition back to reading after discussion. "Hold your place. Track me," announces Patrick Pastore, modeling for his sixth graders how to point to the spot where they left off reading *Esperanza Rising,* close their books partway, and engage his eyes to show they are ready to discuss. After a brief discussion of why Esperanza and Miguel react differently to a train ride, he instructs, "Pick up reading please, Melanie." In less than two seconds, she and her classmates are back into the book at almost no transaction cost.

Similarly, Roberto de Leòn might intone, "Finger in your book; close your book," as he prepares his students to discuss *Phantom of the Opera*—and also prepares them to end that discussion and return to the book efficiently.

See It in Action: Clip 20

In clip 20, you can watch Eric Snider of Achievement First Bushwick Middle School in Brooklyn executing *Control the Game* with his sixth graders.

You'll notice that Eric begins with a long segment of bridging punctuated by several rounds of Oral Cloze. Given the challenging text he's asking his students to read (a 1950s-era science fiction tale imagining the future of space travel), he appears to have decided that a little engaged reading on his part can sell students on the story. He's also clearly modeling the kind of expression he wants his students to use when they read and, as you can hear later in the clip, that's what he gets—their reading voices show expression, comprehension, and even pleasure. What you're seeing is both the result of practice reading aloud over time and enthusiasm modeled by a teacher.

By the way, in this clip, Eric's class is reading a text by Ray Bradbury, perhaps the dean of early science fiction writers. Text quality matters. Not only is it a demanding text—matching Common Core expectations for more rigorous texts at all grade levels—but it's engaging, rigorous, even timeless. These qualities, as well as Eric's obvious passion for the book, matter too.

Hurdle Rate and Meaningful Reading

Imagine, for a moment, a hypothetical school. This school values reading above all other endeavors—to an exaggerated degree. It has recently decided that in addition to constant time on text in reading and English classes, it will ensure that students spend almost all their time in school reading. In science classes, they read chapters from articles and textbooks. In history class, they read primary and secondary source materials, often for the entire class period. In math, they supplement their problem sets with reading, and new concepts are often introduced in short descriptive texts. Students write too, but usually summaries and analyses of what they've read. Imagine also that teachers in the school are able to consistently ensure that all students, when asked to read, read effectively and with attentiveness. As a result, students in the school read for six or seven hours a day.

I offer this prospect as a hypothetical model, not as a proposal for an actual educational program. My goal is to reflect on what the results of such a school would be. If you could ensure that the reading was of reasonable quality, might reading for six or seven hours a day, 190 days a year, achieve better outcomes than those fostered by many schools today? The fact is that the answer could plausibly be yes, and that the question should be on our minds as teachers. If a teacher can ensure that her students read well, she can always, at any time, and for any duration, ensure that a high-value activity — the single most important skill of the educated citizen — will take place in her classroom. If she can do that, she can consistently invest her time at a reliable rate of return. She need never oversee a low-value activity again. She has a *hurdle rate*: a rate of return on an investment of her time that she must exceed to make it worthwhile.

The concept of hurdle rate comes from finance. If you know you can predictably earn 10 percent on every dollar you invest in a certain bond, for example, and you know that the bond is always available to you, you would naturally avoid any investment that returned less than 10 percent; you could always do better with your bond. The question you'd ask in assessing any potential investment, then, is not "Will it make me money?" but "Will it beat my hurdle rate?" — Will any investment yield a stronger return than the best alternative investment you know you could make?

Businesses ask this kind of question all the time, and it results in their choosing not to pursue activities, even if they are likely to have a positive return — when there is a better way to invest the resources. Although we also manage finite resources as teachers — in this case, time — we rarely think this way. We ask whether our actions will result in learning, but this is an incomplete question. The right question is whether our actions yield a learning return that exceeds our hurdle rate — that is, more learning per minute than the most reliable alternative use of class time. In the classrooms of the many teachers who informed this book, *meaningful reading* — accountable, expressive oral reading with occasional questions or explanations mixed in — provides an exceptionally strong and reliable hurdle rate. It's a high-quality activity (when done efficiently) that can be carried out in any classroom, at any time, and with limited additional preparation or expense required.

You can always invest any stretch of time, short or long, in meaningful reading, and reap a strong and predictable return. Furthermore, if you know you could always be doing meaningful reading — in any class, at any time — you can examine your other investments of time critically: Do they exceed the value of meaningful reading? Are they potentially higher return, but riskier, and should they therefore be balanced with something more reliable? As you ask these questions, you may well find that reading crowds out some of the other ways you invest your time. Some of them probably do not exceed your hurdle rate (that is, they are not reliably more productive than meaningful reading), and it would be smarter to have students read meaningfully instead.

Accountable Independent Reading

Of course oral reading, supported by *Control the Game,* isn't the only form of reading featured in a great classroom. There's still plenty of independent reading, but given concerns about accountability and comprehension that teachers are wise to harbor—Who's reading? Who's understanding? What aren't they understanding?—a few tools can make independent reading more productive, ensuring that it remains a viable classroom activity at any time and in any subject. That's important: teachers who don't perceive themselves to be literacy specialists often worry about how to do reading well; they are even concerned that, as one teacher put it, "If we're just reading, I'm not teaching"—and this keeps them from reading. The general principle of *accountable independent reading* is to gradually increase the duration and complexity of independent reading, assessing as you go.

When you choose to assign independent reading, you are always making a decision—"I think they can read this text successfully"—but inferring a student's "reading level" is really guesswork and generalization. More accurately, students probably have multiple reading levels: varying degrees to which they can master a text, depending on a number of factors. Whether a given student can read and comprehend a given passage at a level sufficient to support classroom work depends not only on her general reading skills but also on her familiarity with that topic. Each student's background knowledge, vocabulary, and comfort with various forms of discourse is a stew, and the unique elements lurking beneath the surface are all but invisible in each case.

Because the degree to which any passage is at a student's level is at best a guess, it is wise to test as you go. Gauging the degree to which students are ready to fly on their own sends a message of accountability: "We read independently and rigorously and methodically as we read in a group. When we read independently, we are reading to learn."

Many teachers often assign independent reading like this: "Read chapter 3 on your own, and we'll discuss tomorrow" or "Read the rest of the chapter on your own and answer the questions for homework."

Using accountable independent reading would mean assigning independent reading through a progression of prompts that gradually increase the amount of text students read on their own, as well as broaden the scope of the questions. This ensures that the teacher can confidently give larger and larger doses of independent reading to his students, knowing that they can and will read them well. All told, a sequence of accountable independent reading might look something like this:

1. Read the next paragraph on your own and paraphrase what the author means in the last sentence. Circle the part that's an allusion and try to make a main note telling what he is making an allusion to. Then we'll pick up reading together.

2. Read to the top of page 92 on your own and underline the part that reveals what happened to the mouse. In the margin, make a note summarizing this part. If you find an allusion in the passage, circle it and explain it.

3. Read to the end of the chapter on your own and be prepared to compare how the two characters are both similar and different, according to the author, and why he keeps using the phrase "freedom from want and fear."

CIRCULATE

Move strategically around the room during all parts of the lesson.

Circulate is a technique for moving strategically around your room during all parts of your lesson. Teachers frequently talk about "proximity"—getting near students to stress accountability and eliminate behavioral problems—but we often expect proximity to magically work of its own accord. Teachers know to move toward trouble, but don't always know how to maximize the benefits of proximity, or what to do when they get there if proximity by itself proves insufficient. There's more to know about moving around your classroom than ensuring proximity.

Break the Plane

The "plane" of your classroom is the imaginary line that runs the length of the room, parallel to and about five feet in front of the board, usually about where the first student desks start. Some teachers are hesitant or slow to "break the plane"—to move past this imaginary barrier and out among the desks and rows. Doing so adds energy to your teaching and allows you to observe what students are doing. You can subtly raise your eyebrows at one student as you ask an intriguing question or place a warm and gentle hand on the shoulder of another as you progress around the room.

It's important to break the plane within the first five minutes of every class. You want to make it clear to students that you own the room—that it is normal for you to go anywhere you want in the classroom at any time. The longer you wait to break the plane, the less natural and normal it's likely to seem to students, and the more daunting the idea of wandering as you teach will seem to you.

It's also important to break the plane early because getting near to students plays such a critical role in managing behavioral situations and especially in making those interactions more private (see, for example, the discussion of the private individual correction in Chapter Eleven). If, in contrast, you move out into the classroom to establish proximity only when you need to (to address a behavioral situation), this action will be highly visible. In essence, you tell students that things aren't going well and that they've got you off your game. It also calls heightened attention to your actions when you do break the plane, making it almost impossible to exercise the subtlety necessary to make corrections that don't interrupt instruction (for example, via proximity). If instead you're constantly out and about, you'll be able to correct inconspicuously as you teach—breaking the plane is just a normal part of the routine.

Full Access Required

Not only must you be able to break the plane, but you must have full access to the entire room. You must be able to simply and naturally stand next to any student in your room at any time, and be able to easily get anywhere in your room without interrupting your teaching. If you can't, students will quickly establish a "no-fly zone" that they know to be safely insulated from your influence.

If getting between any two points requires the shuffling and dragging aside of backpacks or the moving of multiple chairs, you have already ceded ownership. If you have to say "excuse me" to get around chairs and backpacks and desks to reach the back corner, you are asking for student permission to stand in that space. This means that they own it, not you, and it's a price no teacher can pay. Keep your passageways wide and clear;

find a better place for backpacks than on the back of chairs; and seat your students in pairs so that you can stand directly next to anyone at any time.

Engage When You *Circulate*

It's not enough to just stand there; you've got to work the room a bit. If you're teaching actively (in the "I" or "We" portion of your lesson), make frequent verbal and nonverbal interventions (a smile; a hand subtly on Steven's shoulder; "Check your spelling" to Pamela as you gaze at her notes).

It might be useful to try to mix and match these types of interactions as you *Circulate*:

Simple walk-by. You walk by a student's desk slowly enough to show that you are monitoring what she's doing but without engaging more extensively.

Touch/nonverbal. You have a brief, unspoken interaction, perhaps just touching a student's desk as if to show you are glancing a bit more closely at his work, say, or perhaps using a quick nonverbal—a thumbs-up for good progress, a traveling gesture for "c'mon, keep going."

Basic read/review. You stop and make a point of reading or reviewing what a student in working on. You might comment on what a student has written, but you don't necessarily have to. Reading a student's work, alone, is a powerful message.

Pick-up read. You stop and pick up a student's paper and read what she is working on, intimating an even greater level of interest in or scrutiny of her work.

These last two are especially important. Reading, assessing, and responding to student work in "real time" are indispensable to checking for understanding, showing your interest in students' work, and setting a tone of accountability—all functions that are critical to your ability to provide academic support and rigor ("Try that one again, Charles"; "Just right, Jamel"; "You haven't shown me the third step").

Dot Round

Recently, I had the pleasure of observing classes in one of our schools with visitors from the Netherlands—four leaders of a school as well as a teacher trainer and school adviser whom I admire, Carla van Doornen. At the end of the day, Carla gave me some ideas that we might try at our schools. One of them was Dot Round. I loved the idea, but before then, I had never heard of it.

The idea is simple: you assign students independent work, and as they are working, you *Circulate* to observe their work. If their work contains an error, you put a dot on their paper. It is very subtle, and it's not a permanent "wrong" mark—just a reminder that there's something that needs checking. The best part is that that's *all* you do. No verbal commentary. No directions to check again. The idea is that the dot reminds students, subtly, to find their own mistake and, in time, encourages self-reflection and self-correction. You could then even ask students to discuss—Who got a dot and found their mistakes? Who got a dot and didn't?

Although this technique didn't originate in the classrooms of the champions, several tried it and are happy with the results. Champion teacher Rue Ratray of Edward Brooke Charter School in East Boston took the idea of Dot Round and moved it a step further. Instead of using one general dot to indicate a wrong answer, Rue used three colors—green, yellow, and red—to indicate different degrees of accuracy. After *Circulating* for ten minutes or so and marking thesis statements, he would then say, "Green, read your thesis statements," followed by "Yellow, read your thesis statements." This allowed students to hear the difference between an answer that was good and one that was "almost there." For the students receiving red dots (who now knew they weren't on the right track), it helped them to hear models of successful theses. According to Rue, this kind of Dot Round "made a huge difference in their writing right away."

Move Systematically

As you move around the room, your goal is to be systematic—to cover all parts of the room and be aware of what's happening everywhere, and to show that your movements and any interactions when you *Circulate* are for the most part "normal" and natural. You are likely to engage anyone at any time by checking his work, nodding at him, or sharing a smile.

Recently my team and I noticed how some top teachers tended to "walk the circuit" when approaching students they needed to correct. Let's say in this case it's Alphonse, who's off task and distracting the student next to him. If you march too directly toward Alphonse, you intimate to him that you are worried that he will not comply. This is counterproductive long term. Moving too directly can also cause other students to watch your interaction with Alphonse. Taking a bit of a circuitous route to Alphonse won't make him feel as though he can control you, and it just might buy you a few seconds to chose your words a bit more carefully before you arrive.

Be aware, finally, that systematic is not the same as predictable. If you always follow a predictable order of interactions as you *Circulate,* students will know when you'll be likely to get to them, and will react accordingly. Avoid using the same pattern every time (left to right; clockwise around the room). Vary your pattern, skip interacting with some students, and invest heavily in time spent with others unpredictably as you *Circulate.*

Position for Power

As you *Circulate,* your goal should be to remain facing as much of the class as possible. That way, you can see what's going on around you at a glance and with minimal transaction cost. You can lift your eyes quickly from a student's paper and then return to reading in a fraction of a second. Turning your back, by contrast, invites opportunistic behavior.

First, think of yourself as the Earth: it turns on two axes at the same time, both revolving (moving around the sun) and rotating (changing the way it faces). This may require you to consider what side of students you stand on as you *Circulate,* and to lift a student's paper off his desk and reorient yourself as you read. Second, leverage student blind spots. The most powerful position to be in with another person is one where you can see him, he knows you can see him, and he can't see you. Standing just over a student's shoulder as you peruse his work or standing at the back of the classroom as a class discusses a topic builds subtle but pervasive control of the classroom environment in order to focus it on learning.

See It in Action: Clip 21

For a great tutorial on the fundamentals of *Circulate,* watch clip 21 and look for the similarities between Rue Ratray and Domari Dickinson. You'll notice not only steady, unhurried progress around the room in both cases but also that both teachers make a point of positioning for power and engaging (nonverbally!)—picking up a paper and silently reading it in Domari's case; putting a finger on a student's work as if deep in reflection in Rue's—to stress both interest in and accountability for student work.

AT BATS

Because succeeding once or twice at a skill won't bring mastery, give your students lots and lots of practice mastering knowledge or skills.

25

Many years ago, at a school where I used to teach, I was assigned to coach baseball, a sport I'd played only casually and felt unqualified to coach. A friend of a friend was a master baseball coach, however, and I got an hour of his time over coffee to figure out how to organize my practices. His most helpful piece of advice was both simple and enduring, and it's key to the **At Bats** technique: "Teach them the basics of how to hit, and then get them as many at bats as you can. Practice after practice, swing after swing after swing: maximize the number of at bats. Let them do it over and over again until they can swing quick and level in their sleep. That's the key. Don't change it. Don't get too fancy. Give them at bats." At bats, it turned out, were the key to hitting.

Sometimes the obvious truths are the best ones. In fact, this truth is reaffirmed by data in just about every field and situation. Want to know what single factor best predicts the quality of a surgeon? It's not her reputation, not the place where she went to medical school, not even how smart she is. The best predictor is how many surgeries of a particular type she's done. It's muscle memory. It's repetition. It's *At Bats*—for complex surgery, hitting baseballs, solving math problems, or writing sentences. Repetition is the key for a surgeon, not just because it means she'll be smoothest when things go as expected, but because she'll have the most brainpower left over to engage in problem solving in the moment if things go wrong. With her clamping and cutting skills refined to automaticity, she'll calmly have all her faculties available to focus on how to respond to the critical and unexpected event.

Nothing else inscribes and refines a skill like *At Bats,* so great lessons should have plenty of them. And if it's true that people master a new skill on the tenth or twentieth or one thousandth time they do it, it's important to factor that into your lessons. Once your students are doing independent work—once they get to "You"—they need lots and lots of practice: ten or twenty repetitions instead of two or three. This is especially important to remember because, on a busy day, repetition is the first thing to go. We teach all the way to the part where students can ingrain the skill, we run out of time, and we stop. They try it once, and we say, "Good, you've got it!" or worse, "We're running out of time. Try it at home, and make sure you've got it!"

Although a lesson should often begin with a few *At Bats* on previous material ("cumulative review"), it should end with students getting *At Bat* after *At Bat* after *At Bat*. Here are the key points to remember (you may notice their resemblance to the keys to good "You"):

1. **Go until they can do it on their own.** By the end of independent practice, students should be able to solve problems to the standard they'll be accountable for, and entirely on their own.

2. **Use multiple variations and formats.** Students should be able to solve questions in multiple formats and with a significant number of plausible variations and variables.

3. **Grab opportunities for enrichment and differentiation.** As some students demonstrate mastery faster than others, be sure to have bonus problems ready, to push them to the next level.

3-30-30

Doug McCurry, CEO of Achievement First, together with top school leaders designed a tool to help guide teachers through managing times when students are working independently in the classroom: the *3-30-30* rule. In a nutshell, at the start of independent work, a teacher should spend the first three minutes setting expectations for work product, process, and behavior and then stand sentry (in other words, not *Circulating* actively) where he or she can see 100 percent of the students and ensure that everyone is on task. Once an orderly and productive work environment is established, the teacher should *Circulate* intentionally: checking in, doing individual conferencing, holding students accountable for their work, providing guidance, and so on in thirty-second bursts (30i), followed by thirty seconds of group-oriented accountability (30g): standing up, scanning the room, using proximity, and correcting. The goal is to ensure accountability among the larger class and limit the opportunity of a single student to "draw the teacher in" at the expense of the rest of the class.

Here are a few ways to make the most of 3-30-30:

How to 3

- Give clear directions.
- Check to see that students understand the task.
- Use nonverbal signals like a shake of the head to disengage from students who ask for your time.
- Make it transparent to students that the first three minutes are about getting started.

How to 30i

- Use a stopwatch to remind yourself when thirty seconds have elapsed!
- Try to ensure that at least half of your 30i interactions are initiated by you.

- Rather than engage in direct teaching, give direction and support that prompt the student to return to independent work.
- Speak softly and/or try to lower your posture (that is, squat down) as much as possible.

How to 30g

- Walk away.
- Say "Keep working."
- Make occasional statements that emphasize visible actions: "I should see everyone's pencil moving. Just like Miranda's."
- Use nonverbal gestures or *very* brief verbal comments to acknowledge industrious work.

EXIT TICKET

26

End each class with an explicit assessment of your objective that you can use to evaluate your (and your students') success.

End your lesson with a short sequence of questions that reflects the core of your objective. When you collect this from students before they leave, and cull the data, it's called an **Exit Ticket**. Use of *Exit Tickets* will not only establish a productive expectation about daily completed work for students but also ensure that you always end the lesson with an objective check for understanding that you can take with you, analyze, and even bring back and reteach the next day if necessary.

After reviewing the results of an *Exit Ticket,* you hope to know: What percentage of your students correctly answered a key question measuring the objective? What mistake did those who got it wrong make? Why did they make that mistake? You can start to reflect on whether your "gut" sense of how well the lesson went was correct, and why. You'll know how to refine the next lesson, and you'll no longer be flying blind. You'll know how effective your lesson was, as measured by how well they learned it, not how well you thought you taught it.

Characteristics of Effective *Exit Tickets*

Not all *Exit Tickets* are created equal. Some of the more effective ones tend to share some characteristics in common, including the following:

They're quick: one to three questions. Honestly, that's it. It's not a unit quiz. You want to get a good idea of how your kids did on the core part of your objective with ten minutes of analysis afterward.

They're designed to yield data. Think about asking each question (or part of a question) to focus on one key part of the objective. That way, if students get it wrong, you'll know why. Also remember to vary formats—one multiple choice and one open response, say. You need to know that students can solve both ways.

They make great Do Nows. After you have looked at the data, let your students do the same. Start the next day's lesson by analyzing and reteaching the *Exit Ticket* when students struggle.

Exit Ticket Advice from Teachers

Because *Exit Ticket* is one of the most commonly used and deeply trusted techniques in the book, I recently asked some teachers for their advice, and the results were pretty amazing. The insights came from the United States and the United Kingdom; they came from district school teachers, charter school teachers, and private school teachers. They came from teachers whose lessons I'd watched and admired, and teachers I'd never met. Here are a few gems.

Review Data Efficiently

One of the key themes was reviewing the data. Teachers advised looking at the data quickly and using a standard, low-transaction-cost way of processing to make it easy to take action. Leanne Riordan of Baltimore suggests looking at the *Exit Tickets* as soon as you can, right after the lesson if possible, and sorting them into three piles: Yes, Some, and No, based on the responses. After looking for reasons that students missed a concept entirely or grasped it partially, make quick notes right on the *Exit Ticket*. You can then use these piles to differentiate small groups the next day or to create a *Do Now* for the whole class if needed.

As an added tip, keep the No pile on the top as a reminder to check in with those students more frequently the next day. Alternately, tracking the number of students who get a certain score—5, 4, 3, 2, 1, or 0—and adding notes to sum up misconceptions can help you stay accountable for grading nightly and give you a glimpse of how the lesson went.

Hand in hand with reviewing results quickly is creating a format that makes it super easy to do. For example, Janice Smith, from Durham, North Carolina, uses sticky notes, having students write their name on the front and their answer on the back. On the way out of the classroom, students stick the notes to the door, allowing Janice to quickly flip through them between classes and easily enter data in a spreadsheet later in the day. Regardless of whether you use handouts or even just have students write their answers on something as simple as a sticky note, ensuring consistent placement (a variety of *Standardize the Format*) makes reviewing answers far more efficient.

Have a Clear Purpose

Another common theme surrounds the purpose of *Exit Tickets*. One teacher in the United Kingdom talked about the importance of having a "clear sense of why you are using *Exit Tickets*." If *Exit Tickets* show poor understanding across the class, then reteach; if *Exit Tickets* show just a few students to be struggling, then that small group may need a separate intervention; if the class kind of gets it, but is a bit unsure, then focus on weak spots for homework or during regular ten-minute slots for a few weeks; if *Exit Tickets* reveal the class to be very secure about a certain topic, then schedule a refresher in a week or two, but don't give this topic too much time, as there will be better things to use it for. In short, responding to *Exit Tickets* is often about being entrepreneurial with time.

Alexa Miller, a fourth-grade teacher in New York, addressed that theme as well, saying that she leaves *Exit Tickets* in student mailboxes to be corrected the next morning. This works well for elementary, because students can fix mistakes during breakfast while the teacher *Circulates* to assist and recheck. This extra step in the screening process for remediation helps keep groups small.

Finally, there was a great piece of planning advice from a champion teacher whose lessons I'd watched multiple times. Heather Snodgrass of Nashville advised: "[I] write the exit ticket first, before planning out any other parts of the lesson. This helps me focus in on the key points that are essential to conveying the most important content, and occasionally helps me refine the objective so I'm homing in on a manageable and appropriately rigorous skill." She added, "I also like having a consistent routine for students who frequently finish their *Exit Tickets* very quickly. One I've used for math is having students write their own problems about the skill we've learned that day. Students also like this if they get an opportunity to solve each other's problems."

CONCLUSION

There is something comforting about the format of a late-night talk show: after the opening credits, the band plays and the host delivers the monologue. After a few minutes of jokes, there are probably some interviews, maybe some hip new band plays a couple fresh cuts of their new record. Then the host offers some parting words, the house band plays out the credits, and the screen fades to black.

Beyond comfort, having something of a standard format to the way that content is presented lowers the cognitive load placed on viewers. Because you and I more or less know the script, the parts of our brains that might otherwise have been tasked with figuring out the sequence of events are freed to engage more fully with the content of the program, allowing us to catch subtle jokes and references.

None of this is to say that your lesson plan should resemble late-night television, but it is to say that having a solid and relatively predictable lesson structure can free up some of the cognitive capacity of your students to engage more deeply with the material you're teaching. Although it may seem as though frequently changing things up would be beneficial in terms of increasing student engagement, if they have to learn the rules of a new game every day, that leaves only so much time left to actually practice and play it.

Now that we've built a framework for the structure of your lessons, Chapter Six looks at a number of ways that you can present material so that students experience the lesson as speedy and exciting or slow and reflective—depending on your goals.

Reflection and Practice

The following activities should help you think about and practice the techniques in this chapter:

1. Choose one of the following deliberately informal topics and sketch out a lesson plan that follows an I/We/You structure. In fact, you can go one step further by planning a five-step process: I do; I do, you help; you do, I help; you do; and you do and do and do. You don't have to assume you'll be teaching your actual students.

    Students will be able to shoot an accurate foul shot.

    Students will be able to write the name of their school in cursive.

    Students will be able to make a peanut-butter-and-jelly sandwich.

    Students will understand and apply the correct procedure for doing laundry in your household.

    Students will be able to change a tire.

2. Now take your lesson and design a three- to five-minute hook that engages students and sets up the lesson.

3. Be sure to name the steps in the "I" portion of your lesson. Review them and find four or five ways to make them stickier.

4. Design an *Exit Ticket* that will allow you to accurately assess student knowledge at the end of the lesson.

USEFUL TOOLS **FIND THESE TOOLS AT WWW.TEACHLIKEACHAMPION.COM/YOURLIBRARY**

Four sample *Do Nows*. These *Do Nows* are great models, and in these four you'll find (1) a good example of a teacher using the *Do Now* to reinforce a wide array of skills the class has mastered over the course of the year; (2) a more straightforward *Do Now* that emphasizes critical thinking and student writing; (3) a forward-looking *Do Now* that's designed to anticipate the discussion in the coming lesson and build context and insight; and (4) an example that makes sure students have done the reading in preparation for class. Draw on the strengths that you see in these *Do Nows* to make the first step in your lesson a great one.

Two sample *Exit Tickets*. Browse this gallery of exemplar *Exit Tickets* to learn from the different ways that teachers check for understanding at the end of each lesson.

Pacing

Technique 27: Change the Pace.   Establish a productive pace in your classroom. Create "fast" or "slow" moments in a lesson by shifting activity types or formats.

Technique 28: Brighten Lines.   Ensure that changes in activities and other mileposts are perceived clearly by making beginnings and endings of activities visible and crisp.

Technique 29: All Hands.   Leverage hand raising to positively impact pacing. Manage and vary the ways that students raise their hands, as well as the methods you use to call on them.

Technique 30: Work the Clock.   Measure time—your greatest resource as a teacher— intentionally, strategically, and often visibly to shape both your and your students' experience in the classroom.

Technique 31: Every Minute Matters.   Respect students' time by spending every minute productively.

Chapter 6

Pacing

When my son was five years old, we flew as a family to visit my parents for Thanksgiving. As the jet was about to touch down on the runway, he turned to me and asked, "Daddy, does the plane go faster when it's landing?" His question was an observant misperception; he was "right" in being "wrong." The plane did feel as though it was speeding up at exactly the moment it was slowing down, so I asked him why he thought so.

"When we're landing," he said, "I can see the buildings and the trees going by. I see that they're going past us fast, and I know that we're going fast, too." Passing things made speed more evident, and in many ways was more important in shaping his perception than our actual speed. I thought for a moment about the classroom, where the experience of a student can be similar. In the classroom, the coming and going of *mileposts*—reference points that make the rate of progress visible—also shape perception. Could a teacher manage mileposts to make slower feel faster to students? My son's question had given me insight into the principles and paradoxes of one of the most nebulous concepts in teaching: pacing.

Teachers frequently use the term *pacing*, but the underlying idea is surprisingly hard to pin down. It has something to do with speed, but pacing can't just be a synonym for how fast you go through content. Sometimes you're moving through material slowly (working on problem after problem determining the slope of a line, or deep-reading as a whole class just a few paragraphs of *To Kill a Mockingbird*), but there's energy crackling in the air. The work of teaching and learning can feel fast when you're moving slowly—and it can feel slow when you're moving fast. You review three chapters on the American Revolution (that's moving fast), but the minutes tick slowly away, and students stare blankly. We sometimes assume that a plodding lesson results from our overall choice of methodology: "You shouldn't lead the review; you should let them review!" But the desperate slowing of the classroom clock can just as likely happen in a less traditional setting. Who hasn't found themselves fanning barely smoldering interest during a "student-led discussion" or a few minutes into a "special" lesson they had assumed would excite students?

So pacing is different from speed. It's more like your students' perception of speed as you teach, or the illusion of speed. You manage actions and decisions to create a perception of rapid progress when you *want* your students to feel as though they are "moving." And you balance that with times when you'd prefer a pace that, while it still maximizes engagement and focus, feels slower and more reflective. Mastering pacing can help you accomplish that.

In this chapter, I'll discuss some ways of switching activities to create mileposts and give students a sense of the new. Because you sometimes need to stick with an activity for a longer period of time, I'll also describe some tools to frame activities (slow or fast) so that you can be more effective at helping students get lost in rigorous work (and lose track of the passage of time), regardless of how long you actually spend on an activity.

PACING SKILLS

The skills implicit in pacing can be broken into two groups. The first involves varying the *types* of activities your students engage in during a lesson, the goal being to cause dynamic changes in student thinking and participation. The second set of skills involves managing activities and the *transitions* between them to ensure crisp, decisive, and noticeable shifts—the illusion of speed.

Many of the tools for managing the illusion of speed deal in perception—for example, by maximizing mileposts and making beginnings and endings visible and energetic so that students are more aware of the changes around them.

Generally, speed is exciting and change is interesting. As a student, it's engaging to feel as though you're moving, to see evidence of rapid progress, and to think that something new is just about to happen. Students feel as though they're moving when they see mileposts passing. Perhaps that's why TEAM Academy's Ryan Hill advises, "Nothing for more than ten minutes": frequently changing activities creates more mileposts and the perception of speed.

It's useful also to think of the limits of speed, however. Imagine my son on a plane flying five times as fast as the jet we were traveling in. He would likely grip the armrests tightly and perhaps close his eyes. It would be thrilling, but he'd be unlikely to reflect deeply on the nature of motion. Too much "illusion of speed" would distract him from observation. My colleague Chi Tschang once mentioned that too much passivity wasn't the only way students could get distracted. "If there are two (or three) highly active kinesthetic activities in a row, the class's energy level can shoot off the charts, and kids can lose focus." Too much speed can be as problematic as not enough. The goal is balance. And the good news is that the tools of pacing can often make what you choose to do feel dynamic and engaging, even when at its core, it's reflective, deliberate, and even slow.

CHANGE THE PACE

Establish a productive pace in your classroom. Create "fast" or "slow" moments in a lesson by shifting activity types or formats.

27

As many teachers know firsthand, doing the same thing for too long can be a recipe for trouble. A patch of independent writing that started out with a soundtrack of scratching pencils and the hum of productive reflection can give way to a dirge of muted grumbling with pencils seemingly stuck in mud. The momentum created by your engaging *Call and Response* (technique 34) can evaporate before your eyes, as participation grows tired and superficial. One cause is likely to be that you've stayed with the same activity for too long.

Achieving the right balance of energy in your classroom requires a technique I call **Change the Pace**—the ability to shift between "fast" or "slow" moments in a lesson by changing activity types (for example, transitioning from independent practice to discussion) or activity formats (for example, staying with discussion but changing its dynamics from, say, a pair activity to a whole-class discussion). Over the course of these next few pages, we'll dig deeper into how teachers do that.

See It in Action: Clip 22

In a recent lesson, Erin Michels of North Star Academy Vailsburg quickened classroom pace by staying laser focused on the objective of adding fractions while shifting deftly among different styles of participation. The series of tangible shifts among activities ensured that the pace felt energetic and kept the lesson intellectually engaging without diluting the focus.

During the study of a single problem, 2/5 + 3/8, Erin used the following activities:

- First, Erin asked students to solve the problem on their own, working independently on eight-by-twelve whiteboards at their desks.

- As they finished, Erin asked students to show their answers to her. She then held up the whiteboard showing the work of a student she had selected a moment or two earlier and asked the class to reflect on their peer's thinking. "Talk to me," she said, and students raised their hands to discuss.

- When it became clear that students had observed errors in the model, Erin noted, "I'm seeing people disagree. Turn and talk to your partner and explain why you disagree."

- After giving students a minute or so to discuss, she brought the group back together and asked one student to begin analyzing the problem. Quickly, she called on others to follow up, engaging in rapid guided questioning (for example, "Good. So how would I find the least common denominator … ") that engaged multiple students.

By most measures, Erin was moving slowly here—spending almost ten minutes on a single problem!—but the pacing felt dynamic and fast because Erin shifted among different types of activities—some reflective, some more active. I counted in those ten minutes not only three different activities, but three different types of thinking. Students completed independent work, discussed with a peer, and participated in teacher-driven guided questioning in rapid succession. That was the lesson I took from Erin's class: shift the type of thinking students do, and keep the topic consistently focused on a single objective.

Changing Activity Types: The Five Major "Muscle Groups"

At the risk of oversimplifying a complex topic, I'm going to propose that there are generally five types of activities we can ask students to participate in. Each requires students to think and engage in a different way. They are

- Assimilating knowledge directly from sources such as the teacher or a text
- Participating in guided practice or guided questioning structured by the teacher
- Executing skills without teacher support, as in independent practice
- Reflecting on an idea — thinking quietly and deeply
- Discussing and developing ideas with classmates

Because all five activity types are important, and because students should develop skill with all of them through constant practice, my team and I call them "muscle groups." It's important that teachers work all of them regularly to ensure that students get a well-rounded mental workout. Fortunately, shifting among the five muscle groups creates not only balanced intellects but also a sense of engaging change — in other words, good pacing.

A caveat: it would be easy to take a list like this and see it as a hierarchy. It's not; all five types are important, and if one is most important, it's just possibly the one you're not doing as much of (therefore the one you think is least important)! The list also isn't a formula suggesting the same approach every time. Each lesson will require something different; each teacher's style and approach will shape the progression.

Finally, the list is not a rubric. It doesn't describe five things you *must* include in *every* lesson. Of course, it's good to work multiple muscle groups during a given lesson — and to eventually work them all at various points during a unit — but the idea is to adapt activity types to the content of the lesson, your students' needs, and your own style as a teacher. It's better to do two or three types of thinking really well than a superficial job of all five. That said, let's look at the five muscle groups in more detail.

1. Knowledge Assimilation (KA)

When students are presented with new information while they listen, read, or take notes (including when they ask or answer basic questions), they are engaged in KA. This could involve a class reading a text (silently or aloud, by teacher or students) or a teacher lecturing, modeling a problem, or sharing a presentation (with or without occasional Q and A from students). Some examples:

- A teacher explains what juxtaposition is and why an author might use it. Students take notes in a section of literary devices. "Is that what Steinbeck is doing with Lenny and George?" a student asks. "Good example," the teacher replies.

- A teacher presents a PowerPoint slide show with pictures and text on daily life in America in the eighteenth century. She offers additional detail as she narrates, asking and answering a few student questions with the purpose of increasing their knowledge of facts about daily life in the eighteenth century.

- A teacher asks students to join her in reading a chapter of *To Kill a Mockingbird*, partially aloud and partially independently.

- A teacher models how to solve for rate of change in a variety of situations.

2. Guided Practice/Guided Questioning (GPGQ)

When students engage in activities that involve more extensive back-and-forth with the teacher, practicing the use or application of knowledge, they are engaged in GPGQ. Guided practice might involve executing the steps in solving a problem, with the teacher asking questions to remind students what step to take next, or it might involve explication of a text passage with the teacher consistently providing new and more targeted questions to unlock understanding. It is usually used before students have independent mastery. Some examples:

- A teacher asks a group of students a series of questions to see how well they understood her presentation on daily life in America in the eighteenth century, making additional inferences about eighteenth-century life:

Teacher: What were some of the key ways their daily lives were different from ours?

Student: They worked harder.

Teacher: Can you tell me one way they would have had to work harder?

Student: Well, making meals. They would have had to light a fire every time they wanted to cook.

Teacher: Yes, and what work would they have had to do to be able to light a fire?

- A teacher tells students, "Let's examine some passages from the novel and see if we can find examples of juxtaposition together. What's our definition of juxtaposition? … Okay, so where are some places where contrasting ideas or people appeared in direct proximity? … Okay, and is there any evidence that this might have been a deliberate decision? … So, what's the purpose of the juxtaposition?"
- A class solves a system of equations together, with the teacher asking various students to explain the steps or share an answer for each step.

3. Independent Practice (IP)

When students complete work that they know how to do on their own, they are engaged in IP. IP is usually done without significant support from the teacher; it's often done silently, but just because work is silent and independent does not make it IP. For example, silent reading is often KA, and reflecting on or brainstorming solutions to questions students don't know how to solve is reflection and idea generation, the next topic in this section. By way of distinguishing, IP implies autonomous execution of a skill or application of a knowledge base that students are in the final stages of mastering. Some examples:

- Telling students, "Now that we've learned what an adverb is, look at the next five sentences and see if you can find all the adverbs. There are seven of them. Go."
- Students apply what they've learned about "showing, not telling" by writing three sentences about the experience of a character named Jonas as he rides a roller coaster (without ever saying he rode a roller coaster).
- Students independently solve a problem set with various problems involving systems of equations.
- Students examine additional sections of a novel "on their own" to find and analyze further examples of juxtaposition.
- Students write a summary of the important ways daily life in eighteenth-century America was different from now.

4. Reflection and Idea Generation (RIG)

Reflection is usually solo work, but even though it often looks like IP, it serves a different purpose. In IP, students execute work they know how to do on their own. In reflection, students are given time to try to make sense of things they are in the midst of learning or do not yet understand. Reflection is often silent, and frequently involves writing.

When the task involves brainstorming potential solutions, it is idea generation. Some examples:

- A teacher asks students to reflect in writing on how differences in daily life in the eighteenth century might have caused people to understand the role of family differently from how we do today.

- A teacher asks students to reflect on why an author might use juxtaposition, or to think of examples of juxtaposition they could use in their own autobiographies and what purpose it might serve.

- A teacher asks students to think about what steps are hardest for them in solving systems of equations and make notes to themselves on how to be successful.

- A teacher gives students a very challenging math problem and asks them to list the skills they've mastered that might be helpful in solving it.

5. Discussion (Disc)

Activities in which students develop ideas and answers by talking directly to one another, in small groups, or as a class are Disc. They often make use of *Habits of Discussion* (technique 42, discussed in Chapter Nine) designed to make discussions productive and efficient while preserving student autonomy. In some cases, you might insert batches of discussion during GPGQ to ensure that students *Batch Process* (technique 44)—that is, make a certain number of comments without mediation from you. We call this "playing volleyball, not tennis." Some examples:

- A teacher asks students to debate the ethics of genetically modifying food and organisms.

- A teacher asks students to participate in a whole-class Socratic seminar and discuss the impact of corruption on American politics in the 1890s.

- A teacher asks students to *Turn and Talk* (technique 43) to a partner to identify where a peer made a mistake in adding two fractions with unlike denominators.

Establishing perfect distinctions between activity types won't always be a possibility. Although I have tried to establish boundaries by outlining general characteristics and providing some examples, it's notable that some activities will blur the bounds between one type and another and that at some point the categorization becomes more trouble than it's worth. Don't know exactly what type of activity it is? Not to worry. If in the pursuit of a single objective you are making regular shifts in the types of work you ask students to do, even if you can't categorize them all, you're probably doing fine!

See It in Action: Clip 23

Now, let's take a closer look at how the different activity types can come together in a lesson—in this case, one taught by Jessica Bracey, a fifth-grade reading teacher at North Star Academy Vailsburg Middle School (clip 23). Here is an outline of the activities Jessica shifts between, and the amount of time she allots for each:

Activity Description	Activity Type	Time Spent	What It Sounds Like
Review where class left off in the novel	GPGQ	1 min, 20 sec	"Yesterday we left off at a really juicy point in the story. Who can remind us what was going on?"
Control the Game reading	KA	1 min, 10 sec	"So we're going to read to find out what happens now that Mattie and Tony are thinking two different things. Your books need to be open to page 87. I need some strong readers for chapter 10. Micah, start us off today … Continue, Ramani … "
Everybody Writes	RIG	2 min, 45 sec	"Pause there. Tent your books. First question. You should be focusing on question 87 in your reading response journals. You have evidence in the text; make sure you find it and write it. Please get to work."
Whole-class discussion	Disc	1 min, 35 sec	"Pencils down. Hands up! What is the plan? Why? And what does this reveal about Tony? Let's start off with Omar … "
Control the Game reading	KA	3 min, 50 sec	"That was a really strong discussion. Let's keep this up. Taijon, please pick up starting with, 'Listen, things have changed … '"

As class begins, Jessica asks her students to summarize what happened in the previous chapter of the novel they are reading. As her students comment, she steps in to ask for clarification or steer the next question to a given student: "Yes, Angel's bracelet was stolen. What else is going on?" This is guided questioning. Jessica's students spend about two minutes engaging in it.

We often try to do "new" things with students to keep class interesting and make things feel more engaging, but what makes Jessica's class interesting is doing *familiar* activities that students know how to do well. By shifting between familiar activities, she allows her students to do and do and do with very little unproductive time. They shift from reading to writing in their reading response journals in a matter of seconds, because they've done it so many times. Stopping to explain a new activity they hadn't done before—for example, "We're going to do a new kind of writing today; let me explain how it works … "—would result in a lot of downtime while she explained all the details and while her students struggled to internalize the process. Even though it might seem as though this activity would be more interesting, it would be as likely to have the opposite effect. (You can read more about the power of academic systems and routines in Chapter Ten.)

After a minute or two of discussion, Jessica's students go back to reading. In fact, Jessica repeats the same cycle again: students read, *Control the Game* style; write in their reflection journals; and discuss throughout the class, with the cycles getting longer and the questions getting harder over time.

At a recent workshop, teachers shared that the shorter recurring cycle of read-write-discuss was different from what they tended to do in their classes. They did the same three activities, but in long, "nonrecurring" chunks. For example, in a typical class, they might read for fifteen to twenty minutes, write for five to ten minutes, and discuss for another ten to fifteen minutes before tackling an *Exit Ticket* and wrapping up. As Jessica shows in the "See It in Action" clip, you can bring energy and engagement to your class merely by breaking those chunks into shorter cycles of the same activities.

Further, the writing in the sequence ensures that students get a mental workout that is not only engaging but rigorous. Asking students to write *before* they discuss prevents students from freeloading insights from discussion rather than making their own based on reading the text. Reading before writing forces students to do the hardest cognitive work independently, and arms students with ideas that they can draw on to elevate the quality of discussion. (For more about writing before discussion, see technique 41, *Front the Writing*.)

A final point about how my own understanding of the relationship between the five activity types has evolved over time: the more I watch champion teachers, the more I see evidence of Daisy Christodoulou's assertion that rigorous and independent work, such as discussion, is most effective when it's informed beforehand by assimilation of deep knowledge. There's a direct synergy between a robust and disciplined investment in KA and success with the other four activity types.

Changing Formats

Of course, you can't always change activities every few minutes. Sometimes it just won't work that way. Still, you can bring energy—the "feeling of fast"—to a lesson or to a section of a lesson that needs some mojo, even if you stay with the same activity. Changing formats *within* an activity is one way to do that. By changing formats, I mean changing how you interact with your students or how students interact with each other. You're not changing the essential nature of the task, just how students experience it. Maybe you stay with discussion, but go from pairs to whole group. Or perhaps you continue with reading, but alternate between accountable independent reading (see Chapter Five), *Control the Game* (technique 23), and teacher oral reading. Such shifts create a sense of engaging change while providing students all the focus they require on a given activity. It's especially important to change formats when you need more time than usual in one muscle group, or if you sense the energy waning while you're in a muscle group.

I learned a lot about how to shift formats from watching Bridget McElduff's fifth-grade math lesson at Troy Prep Middle School in upstate New York recently. During her lesson, Bridget had to cover what might at times be a dreaded lesson topic: measurement conversions. Moving back and forth between metric and standard, cups and gallons, can be tedious, but it must be done; a lifetime of confusion on word problems—not to mention basic life tasks—awaits if not.

To keep students engaged, Bridget divided into groups the set of conversion problems she gave her students. In reviewing, Bridget first called on a single student to report his answers to three or four questions in rapid-fire fashion. Next, she *Cold Called* (technique 33) a wide range of students on a section of further problems, asking them to share their answers, one per student, moving around the room widely and quickly. Finally, for yet another section, and with momentum and energy high, she allowed students to begin raising their hands to volunteer answers, which made it feel like a whole different activity. Turns out a few quick shifts in format were all that stood between the doldrums and a fresh breeze.

Here are a few ways that my team has observed teachers change formats. We're sure you'll come up with many other ways, but these might serve to get you thinking:

- Use a combination of accountable independent reading, *Control the Game,* and teacher oral reading to read extended blocks of text.

- Break a whole-class discussion by telling students, for example, "Darius just made a very interesting argument. Turn and talk [see technique 43] with your partner to discuss how accurate it is."

- Alternate between prompting students to reveal their answers to a question using hand signals (for example, A = 1 finger, B = 2 fingers, C = 3 fingers, D = 4 fingers) and have them record their answers on whiteboards before holding them up. (See Chapter One on CFU for more on these techniques.)

Managing the Illusion of Speed

As we move on to the next section, I hope you'll forgive another short digression on the topic of travel. My family takes an annual summer vacation to Vermont. For my littlest one, passing the sign that we are entering Vermont is a critical moment, one that makes her feel as though we are "getting there." Of course, we call out the sign and occasionally count down the miles to it. Our goal here is to make the passing of that critical line more visible to her. A milepost isn't much good, after all, if passengers don't notice it.

Once in Vermont, we pass a simple baseball diamond nestled in a cornfield in a tiny crossroads town. We stop there every year. A few short minutes of catch or kickball are all it takes. When we get back in the car, everything is different. We are on vacation. This, too, is a milepost, but we mark its passage in an active and collective way. Seeing everyone else marking the passage into vacation makes it real.

In both the countdown to the border and the ritual at the baseball diamond, we are making mileposts more visible and influential. In the classroom, the situation is not entirely dissimilar. Mileposts are more effective if students are more aware of them, if they are clearly observed by the rest of the class, and if they can be invested with meaning. The next section of this chapter describes ways you can get the most out of mileposts—whether you are speeding up or slowing down. Visible transitions influence not only the perception of speed but also more subtle aspects of student participation, such as helping to more clearly cue students to shift their mode of thinking.

BRIGHTEN LINES

Ensure that changes in activities and other mileposts are perceived clearly by making beginnings and endings of activities visible and crisp.

28

When you take steps to make the beginnings and endings of your lesson activities more visible and crisp, you **Brighten Lines**. By calling attention to shifts in activities or formats, you ensure that your students can perceive mileposts clearly, and make it hard for them not to notice that something new is occurring. There are three key ideas implicit in *Brighten Lines*: a clean start, a clean finish, and interactive lines.

Clean Start

The first way to *Brighten Lines* is with the *clean start*—shifting from one activity to another on a cue. Starting everyone at the same time with a statement such as, "Okay, scholars. You have three minutes to write a response to this question. Ready? Go!" has several advantages.

First, making the beginning of an activity "pop" makes the activity itself feel a bit like a special event. It suggests that, as with a footrace, you are not allowed to start until the teacher tells you to; otherwise, you might be tempted to race ahead and sneak in some extra writing. Not only does this implicitly frame the forthcoming activity positively, but it also causes everyone in the class to start exactly on cue. That half-second delay causes students to work more industriously once they are "allowed" to. Plus, students see all of their peers snap to it—normalizing the idea of snapping to it and making productive use of time.

In addition, you build a strong disincentive against malingering—gazing around the classroom and then, gradually, getting out a pencil and paper. If it's unclear whether everyone else has actually started something, there's an incentive to take your time so as to avoid being the outlier (the first to start), or to make the optimum decision from a social standpoint: experimenting with answers to the age-old question, "What rate and degree of action will communicate maximum status to the cute girls/boys sitting next to me?" If everyone begins on cue, there are no grounds for strategically managing the optimum starting point. Everyone else just started. Better catch up!

Previously, I mentioned that you can use pacing tools to make "slower" work more reflective and engaging; some simple adaptations to the clean start can help. You might, for example, encourage deeper, more reflective thinking by prompting students with a slower, quieter cadence, "Ah, a fascinating question: Just who *is* the hero of this book? [Pause] You have three minutes to reflect in writing. [Pause] Who is the hero, and how do you know?" Now perhaps you've dropped your voice to a whisper. "*Begin* ... " This approach still socializes efficient use of time by getting students started right away and as a group, but your slower and quieter pacing can communicate something about the tone of reflection you expect. Even using the cue "Begin" as compared to the cue "Go!" suggests less a race and more of a journey. This way, you get the benefits of everyone starting on cue and making good use of time, as well as clear and efficient communication of the key idea: "I want you to think deeply here; I am looking for thoughtfulness as much as productivity."

Clean Finish

Being able to end an activity reliably on cue is also a critical skill for several reasons—the most obvious being time management. How many meetings have you been in where the person running it was unable to say, "Okay, we're done with that; now we're moving on to this," as it became increasingly obvious that the meeting would run over time or that other topics would be truncated? Time use in the classroom can be done a similar disservice when a teacher can't reliably bring students back to attention.

There's more value in making activities end crisply and clearly—a skill I call the *clean finish*—than just time management. Ending on cue establishes a clear and discernible transition point from one activity to the next. When the transition is obvious, students are more likely to make sure they join in with the change, right on time. Ensuring that all students switch activities on cue is especially important if the next activity draws on the preceding one—doubly so if it draws on it in a public way. Consider the example in the previous paragraph. You've said to your students, "You have three minutes to reflect in writing: Who is the hero, and how do you know?" If you're going to transition from writing to discussion or guided questioning, you don't want to allow a third of the students to continue writing—or to pretend to still be writing so they don't have to listen to their peers or risk being called on. You want the writing to end on cue, in a single moment, so that you can immediately start looking forward to your next step.

As the three allocated minutes of writing come to a close, you might provide a preliminary reminder that you will be enforcing a "hard stop": something like "I'll need pencils down in twenty seconds. Try to finish that last thought." When you get to the end of the allocated time, ideally there'd be a signal. The timer would go off and you'd say, "I hear the timer, and that means pencils down and eyes up, please." Or perhaps you'd have established that three hand claps is a call to attention and means to end writing or peer discussions and come to order. Whatever the signal, every student can see every other student transitioning right on cue, making it far less plausible to continue doing something else under the guise of lack of clarity.

Another reason for a clean finish is speed. If your transition from writing to discussion is fast—a few seconds at most—then the ideas that students had before the transition are more likely to cross over to the second activity. What students wrote will show up in the discussion if it begins without stray verbiage about how the time for writing is over, or reminders about the importance of joining the group because education is a collective endeavor. For those who were ready all along, stray thoughts introduce themselves in the tedious interregnum. Fast, unnarrated, and universal—that's the transition you want. The icing on the cake is that sharp, visible transitions also affect pacing. The milepost is bright and clear, and students can see it passing.

See It in Action: Clip 24

To show you some especially crisp clean starts and finishes, my colleagues on the Uncommon Schools Teach Like a Champion team put together a montage of various teachers using these tools in their classrooms. Watch for the different cues they use to tell students to start or stop an activity, as well as how they vary their cadence.

Interactive Lines

My brief story about my family's annual drive to Vermont recalls one final aspect of *Brighten Lines*: the idea that when passing mileposts is an interactive experience, those mileposts are more engaging and noticeable. On the Uncommon Schools Teach Like a Champion team, we call this *interactive lines*. Ana O'Neil uses these in her math lessons. Prepping students to start their timed practice, she counts, "Ready, set … " and students respond, "Go!" thus participating in marking the line between activities. At the end of an activity, John King of Brooklyn often counts down "Three, two, one … ," to which his students respond "Done!" again marking the line between activities more clearly through their participation. We've also seen teachers create energy by counting down the last three seconds of an activity—"Three, two, one, and … ," whereupon students slap their pencil on their desk (lightly) and raise their hands.

It's fascinating to note how teachers often engineer these interactive aspects of class to tacitly suggest positive, productive activities. Joining in the fun of slapping your pencil down at the end of a bout of writing, for example, requires you to have your pencil in your hand, and is thus an incentive to write all the way to the end (instead of putting your pencil down with thirty seconds to go). Letting students slap their desk and then raise their hands (a "loud hand" as the teachers who use it call it) is fun and tactile, and results in students with their hands in the air ready to be called on—some of whom might not otherwise be so inclined.

A final note to observe here: the same tools used to speed up pacing, lightly adapted, can slow things down as well. For example, you might say to your class, quietly and with a slow and reflective tempo: "In thirty seconds, your journal writing session will come to an end. At the beep, please close your journals and give me your eyes." Then you might let the timer beep for a few seconds or leave a silent pause of a few seconds and add, "Good. Now we're ready to discuss." It's still a clean finish with interactive lines, but it establishes a slower pace and quieter tone. In fact, you could argue that *Brighten Lines* is *most* useful for this kind of slower, more thoughtful task, where stepping in to be more directive is also more disruptive to the quiet, reflective mood of the room. Crisp transitions are often most useful at exactly the time you would least expect them to be, and where their use is least intuitive.

ALL HANDS

Leverage hand raising to positively impact pacing. Manage and vary the ways that students raise their hands, as well as the methods you use to call on them.

To raise your hand is a critical act that deserves some reflection, even if at first it seems obvious. In a micro sense, every time students raise their hands, a milepost passes—an important one. To raise your hand is to mark the passage of an event worthy of action. You say, both to others and to yourself, "Hey, there was a question there, and I want to answer it." **All Hands** is the technique used to manage student hand raising.

Consider a student in the third row of your classroom who raises his hand to answer a question. In fact, his hand is raised to answer during each of your first three questions. At least you think so. It's hard to say for sure, as his hand has been up the whole time: while you were asking, while another student was answering the first question, and while you were asking a follow-up. All that time, his hand sways back and forth as if in a light breeze, languidly persisting in announcing his desire to answer. Surely you have seen this child, right? You've had him in your class many times. He's a bit of an archetype.

You're probably also familiar with what happens if you respond to his semaphore. Maybe he exhales audibly when you finally call on him. Maybe then he pauses. Perhaps the anguish of keeping his big idea inside has caused him to lose track of it entirely. "Um, I forgot what I was going to say," he notes in exasperation. But maybe he remembers and begins "What I wanted to say was … " If so, his comment is likely to demonstrate the difference between a discussion, in which people listen to one another and collaborate to mutually develop ideas, and a series of disconnected comments strung together in a vaguely related sequence—a state of affairs that isn't actually a discussion. The fact that it's very hard to listen carefully to what others say while you have your own hand in the air means it's likely that he wants to talk about something that was said several minutes ago or something unrelated to the conversation.

Socializing students that it's fine to make comments that literally or figuratively begin with the words, "What I was going to say was … " is not only bad for your class but bad for students. Do you really want to tell students that when they get to college or enter the workplace, they should interact with a group by making comments that are of keen interest only to them, when everyone else has gone on to another topic?

Now consider this alternative: When you ask your first question, a student in the fourth row raises her hand to answer, but doesn't get called on. As you call on another student to answer, she puts her hand down. Then, on your second question, her hand is up again. Again, someone else answers and her hand goes down, but on your third question she raises her hand again. Her comment, should you now call on her, is likely to be more productive than the first student's, because each time she put her hand down, she acknowledged to herself that the opportunity to answer a specific question had passed—that her role was now to listen to what her peers said.

Just as important, her comment is likely to be valuable because she's engaged differently in class. Each time she raised her hand anew, she acknowledged and considered a *different* question, which, in each case, she has decided to try to answer. Where the first student sees only one event—a period during class when you ask questions and he seeks to say something—the second student sees that there are multiple events. For the second student, the discussion is made up of specific questions rapidly evolving based on the comments offered by her classmates. She underscores the differentiation of questions within her mind by choosing to raise her hand selectively in response to each one independently. The process of putting her hand down to consider each new comment has caused her to engage more deeply. Mileposts have proliferated in her mind and given rise to a qualitatively different form of participation. For this student, a distinctive and engaging series of events, each one unique and interesting, replaces the muddy, self-interested muddle the first student perceives.

Perceiving questions as different events teaches students to notice the differences between questions. In fact, a person who's truly engaged in a discussion is often engaged *because* he or she attends to the differences among questions and becomes increasingly interested in those differences. A discussion, to that person, is not one event, but a series of fascinating events that come up in unpredictable order. To raise and lower your hand at each question is an acknowledgment that the questions are important and distinct; doing so also communicates respect for your peers because, as the first student demonstrated, you can't really listen and have your hand up at the same time. A classroom where hands are up while someone is speaking is a classroom where people are saying, essentially, "What you're saying doesn't matter much to me; it won't change what I want to say."

All Hands, then, is an important technique to master. Although the strategies by which you regulate hand raising and calling on students may appear mundane, they shape in profound ways your students' perception of what's happening in the classroom.

Mix Modes

Needless to say, you want lots of hands in the air most of the time. Seeing peers choosing to participate causes others to make the same choice, so hands in the air are self-perpetuating. Asking great questions and planning them (as well as ideal answers) in advance are critical, but mixing modes can keep the process of hand raising fresh. Briefly restricting participation rights—"Only boys on this one … Okay, now the girls," or "Wow, the left side of the room is on fire. I'm gonna give someone on the right the chance to step up!"—can make things seem new. It can also introduce a bit of scarcity — you don't get the chance to answer every question — and scarcity increases value.

Bright Hands

Once lots of hands go up in response to your questions, you want to *Brighten Lines* between each question and answer by ensuring that hands go down while someone is answering, and back up for a new question. This is pretty simply an "academic routine" and therefore something you

Explicitly introduce and explain. For example, "We're going to have a lot of great discussions this year, and one thing we need to learn to do that well is to put our hands down when others are speaking. This is a gesture of mutual respect and a great way to show we're listening to one another."

Model and practice. For example, "Let's practice that now. I'm going to ask you a question: What was the single most important event in history you studied last year? I'm going to let you reflect and write for one minute and then I'll ask three or four of you to share. As we do that, let's make sure to practice putting our hands down while others are speaking."

Reinforce constantly. For example, "Just a second, Margretta, I just want to let everyone check to make sure they're showing full respect … [if no compliance] … by putting their hands down … [if still no compliance] … Jeremy, if you would. Thank you."

See It in Action: Clip 25

Watch Colleen Driggs in clip 25 teaching her students bright hands: how to raise their hands for a new question and lower them when someone else is called on. You'll notice that Colleen is teaching a variety of productive classroom behaviors here—tracking the speaker, not monopolizing the floor when you're called on, raising your hand energetically—but she's most intentional about the idea of raising your hand brightly to answer and then putting it down for someone else's turn. Colleen is using a very simple lesson on one of the first days of school as much as a vehicle for teaching academic systems as a means of teaching content or skills. This use of a sort of semilesson early in the year as a way to practice key routines is common among champion teachers.

Unbundle and Scatter

Because each new participant adds a milepost to the activity of discussing, you can increase the number of mileposts and the apparent speed of your lessons by unbundling your questions, breaking them into a series of smaller questions, and spreading them around quickly to more students.

For example, if you've recently discussed three causes of the Civil War, you might replace, "Who can tell me the causes of the Civil War?" with "Who can tell me one cause of the Civil War?" and then "Great; who can tell me another?" and then "So what's the last cause we discussed?" Not only do three students get to participate instead of just one, but those students have to listen carefully to the answers their peers have provided so as not to be redundant. You might emphasize the listening-to-one-another aspect by adding a bit of follow-on to your unbundling—for example, by saying, "Tell me more about what that 'differences between the Northern and Southern economies' means." Listening better to peers socializes strong engagement, as well as maximizes the number of mileposts. My single question with a long answer is now a series of four different questions moving rapidly around the room—the creation of an engaging illusion of speed.

A hint for effective unbundling: frame your expectation in your question so that students know that you are asking for a limited part of the answer. For example, "Who can tell me one cause of the Civil War?" (possibly with one finger held up for emphasis if you think students might not fully attend to the expectation) is clearer than "What caused the Civil War?" or even "What caused the Civil War? Tell me one reason … "

Follow-on

Another critical tool in fostering peer-to-peer listening is to make your questions refer to or be contingent on a previous answer. So if your first question is "What's the setting of the novel?" and a student answers that it's in a small town a long time ago, your second question might be, "Well, who can be more specific? How long ago?" or perhaps, "Well, how do we know it was a long time ago; who can provide some evidence for Todd's claim?" or perhaps "Do you agree with Todd, Christina?" or "Can you develop Todd's answer, Christina?" All of these will have the effect of forcing students to listen better to one another and not just to the teacher. In the long run, this will cause students to listen more carefully to questions and answers, as well as notice the mileposts implicit in each question and answer.

Cut Off Rally Killers

One of the most common ways pacing is destroyed in classrooms is by a long-winded, meandering student comment at the wrong time. You ask for the third and final cause of the Civil War as brief review and activation of prior knowledge in the lead-up to today's reading of a primary text; the student you call on begins telling you about her trip to a Civil War battlefield with her family and how the guide thought X and how her father didn't agree and … Two-and-a-half meandering minutes later, the prior knowledge activation is distant; the mojo has fled the room; and you've lost 5 percent of your remaining time and have to think about scrapping an activity.

Don't get me wrong. I love long and insightful student comments—when they come at the right time. A long and tangentially related comment at the wrong time is a killer. I officially give you permission to cut such comments off, guilt free!

Stock phrases such as "freeze" or "pause" can help; then remind students of the original question or tell them they've given you enough to discuss already. In short, keep it positive, as in "Ooh. Pause there. Your comment that the Southern states didn't call it the Civil War at all should remind us of the third and final cause of the Civil War!" or even "Ooh. Pause. Interesting. If the Southern states didn't call it the Civil War, who can tell us what they did call it and why that matters?" Keeping it positive but unapologetic when you break in makes it easy on both your students and you. If you don't feel bad about doing it and you can do it quickly and easily, you'll be more likely to do it when it's warranted. It's true that students will occasionally use deliberately off-task stories and comments to keep class from going to activities they'd prefer not to get to. (I know this because I chronically engaged in it as a middle school student: "Just keep asking her earnest-sounding questions about what it was like to perform Shakespeare and what roles she played, and maybe we won't have time for the quiz!"). Although some unexpected student comments are worth their weight in gold, some are not, and it's the job of the teacher to make sure she controls how time is allocated in the classroom.

You can also focus rally killers by redirecting them to the most productive part of their answer: "Pause. Go back to that phrase, 'the War between the States.' Let's focus on that for a minute." This is a way of cutting them off while still extracting value from their answer and, you hope, helping them see what was valuable in it for next time.

WORK THE CLOCK

Measure time—your greatest resource as a teacher—intentionally, strategically, and often visibly to shape both your and your students' experience in the classroom.

We measure things because they matter. Because time is the greatest resource you as a classroom teacher must manage, measuring that time intentionally, strategically, and often visibly is a critical skill in shaping both your and your students' experience in the classroom. There are several ways to **Work the Clock**.

Show the Clock

First, *show the clock*—that is, make time visible to students. Showing how you allocate time—indicating how much you allow for certain activities and that you track its passage during a lesson—will help students understand that you value its wise and careful allocation, and will ultimately teach them to be attentive to it as well.

Showing the clock also has the added benefit of helping you discipline yourself. What teacher hasn't planned five minutes for an activity, for example, but unintentionally spent fifteen on it? What teacher hasn't told her students, "You have ten minutes to work on this," only to lose track of time and give students twice—or half—that? The result can often be a lesson that ends incompletely; you don't get to the end of the story or the experiment, or you end with only guided practice rather than independent practice.

When you send students off to try a problem for a few minutes, make your best guess as to how long it should take and say, "Okay, try one of these on your own. I'll give you three minutes." Then start your stopwatch or, better, start an overhead stopwatch—one of those LCD clocks you can project on the overhead or on the wall. If students can see the clock, they can self-manage—learning, for example, to pace their time for a short-answer response.

Some might protest that they don't want to be locked in to a specific time allocation for an activity when they don't really know how long it will take, but it's important to remember that you're not actually locked in by giving an initial time allocation. If the time you allocated wasn't enough, you can always extend it ("Okay, we've been working hard, and it looks like another two minutes might help") or shorten it ("Wow, your answers are too interesting and too good to wait the full three minutes, so we'll check in at two minutes").

Showing the clock gives rise to a time-sensitive culture. Although I would love to tell you that classrooms should be timeless places where we take as long as we need and follow every digression, we all know that's not the reality of our 42- or 55- or 75-minute daily periods. The fact is that you are more likely to be able to occasionally meander timelessly if you manage the rest of your time very well.

Showing time also allows you to narrate time less. Projecting a clock as it counts down the minutes or seconds on an activity requires no additional narration once your students have learned to respect the primacy of the clock (that is, they know that you're going to enforce it and that zero means the end). You just say, "Okay, let's go," start the clock, and let it run, perhaps offering an occasional reminder ("You'll hear the beep in just under a minute," for example). Then say, "Okay, let's see how we did" when the timer has finally wound down.

Several years of applying the tools of master teachers has led my Uncommon Schools Teach Like a Champion team to use this at our workshops. During independent work (or breaks!) we often project an Internet stopwatch so that participants know where they stand on time. Generally we find that they much prefer self-management to being constantly managed by us—particularly at lunch breaks.

You can encourage students to embrace time management and develop time management skills by setting up opportunities for them to complete multiple tasks during a block of independent time. "I'm putting twenty minutes on the clock. In that time, you need to edit your paragraph and complete your self-assessment."

Use Specific, Odd Increments

Whether you are showing the clock or are the only one who can see it, it's valuable to *use specific times and odd increments* when you discuss time allocations with your class. Consider this mundane case study. If I was leading a professional development session for teachers and said, "Okay, let's take a short break and pick up again in ten minutes," I would probably not have people return ready to work in ten minutes. The time allocation I used—ten minutes—sounds like an estimate. Round numbers often contain an implicit "about" in them, as in "Let's pick up again in about ten minutes." Ironically, I'd get people back and ready to work much more quickly if I gave them a longer time increment for their break, *as long as it was specific*. In a race between "Okay, let's take a short break and pick up again in ten minutes" and "Okay, let's take a short break and pick up again in twelve minutes," I am betting on the second group every time.

In your classroom, be specific about exactly how long students have for an activity, and vary your allocations. Four minutes of group work is usually better than five minutes of group work (and three minutes is better than two minutes, which also sounds like an estimate), but better than both is an initial round of solo writing for two-and-a-half minutes and then a group discussion for three. The variation in allocations for different activities or different iterations of the same activity communicates your intentionality about time. You care about and are precise about time, and this makes others respect it as well. Having established such a track record, you're actually likely to get a pretty good response from folks if you do occasionally use "two minutes" and the like.

Want More? Clip 26. Want more *Work the Clock*? Check out Deena Bernett in clip 26. Notice how she uses different amounts of time for different kinds of work—three minutes for developing notes with your partner; two minutes for doing three problems on your own—but in both cases, the increments are specifically planned (and measured).

Set Goals

Because you have implicit goals for the use of time in your classroom—for example, to get really nice first drafts of thesis paragraphs done in the forty minutes remaining in Friday's lesson—it's useful to let students participate constructively in setting and achieving goals for time use. When you *set goals,* you ask students to try to accomplish things with the greatest efficiency they can. Essentially, you make time management a team sport. The "things" in question can be procedural ("Let's see if we can be ready to go in twenty seconds") or content based ("Let's try to get ten problems done carefully and well in eight minutes. Go!"). The word I am using to describe the goals you seek, however, is important—it's *efficiency* (getting the highest value in the least time), not speed (doing it the fastest). You want quality, not rushing. Saying, "Let's try for high-quality first drafts in twenty minutes" is better than saying, "Let's see if we can get our drafts done in fifteen minutes."

Using Countdowns Effectively

A *countdown* is a statement of a desire to get something done within an explicit time frame—one that's shorter than it might otherwise be. On the basis of observations of champion teachers, I encourage the judicious use of countdowns in most classrooms, especially when they follow some important dos and don'ts:

DO

- Use countdowns for simple tasks, wrap-ups, or transitions. Be aware that you will disrupt a certain percentage of work in the room. For this reason, many champion teachers tend to transition, over time, to less narrated countdowns, advising students to be "ready for the [timer] beeps in ten seconds" or merely counting selected digits (for example, "Ten, nine [pause for a few seconds], five, four [pause], two, and one.")

- Use the lowest countdown possible. Beware of giving students too much time to do a simple task. Putting pencils down shouldn't take ten seconds, so don't use a countdown from ten. Try three. The idea behind a countdown is to give students just enough time to do something well. Don't rush students by setting an unreasonable goal, but do be constantly pushing students to manage their time efficiently during transitions and other mundane tasks and to be attentive to efficiency in academic tasks.

- Narrate compliance *during* a countdown. If I narrate during countdown, for example, "I'll need your eyes up here in five, four, Nick is ready to go, two, Sarah's ready," I am describing students who exceeded expectations. In other words, call students' attention to exemplars *during a time when they can all still meet your expectations for them.*

DON'T

- "Stretch" a countdown—that is, don't slow it down to match student behavior. If you do, it means that the students own the countdown, which defeats the whole purpose. It's much better to end on time and respond appropriately with a consequence or a clear and powerful message, "We have to be faster. We have a lot of work to do."

- Use excessively short or excessively long countdowns.

- Narrate compliance *after* a countdown has finished. In doing so, you are describing a student who has merely done what you asked, and you risk making it sound as though you are pleading for compliance ("Won't you please try to be like the kids who've done what I asked?"). This can undercut expectations as effectively as it can reinforce them.

- Overnarrate compliance. A few quick acknowledgments of those who are ready is great. Too many, and it sounds as though you're worried you won't get compliance.

EVERY MINUTE MATTERS

Respect students' time by spending every minute productively.

I observed one of my favorite moments in teaching—simple, humble, and powerful—early in my Teach Like a Champion process when I saw Annette Riffle of North Star Academy in Newark working with her fifth-grade math students. The moment started with an utterly typical scene. Students had solved a problem on the coordinate plane independently at their desks. They'd had to plot certain points to show the outlines of a hypothetical stadium. Annette ended the independent work with a crisp, pace-accentuating clean finish—a series of claps that she gives and that students echo to bring them to attention. Then she said, "Someone come give us a stadium," handing the marker to a girl named Kadheisha, who excitedly approached the front of the room to model her work on the overhead.

A million teachers have, from time immemorial, called a hundred million students up to the board to "show their work," and not much usually happens while one student puts said work up on the board. Twenty-nine students sit and wait for thirty seconds or a minute while the student in question completes the work they will soon review. Perhaps in some classes, three or four students put problems up on the board at once. But the rest of the group does precious little, even if told to "pay attention to what they're writing." Twenty-nine students wasting thirty seconds are the same as one student wasting almost fifteen minutes, except that, in addition, precious amounts of momentum is also squandered reenergizing students who've lost the task.

What came next in Annette's class, though, was quietly brilliant.

While Kadheisha did her work at the board, Annette did a quick review of key terms and ideas with the rest of her students. "What quadrant are we in? Fatimah? And what do we call that line along the bottom? Sean? And which direction does the x-axis run, Shatavia?" The result was not only a productive use of time and the reinforcement of key facts during what would otherwise be downtime but also an exercise that increased the likelihood that students would use key vocabulary to analyze and describe Kadheisha's work.

Time, I was reminded in watching Annette's class, is water in the desert. It is a teacher's most precious resource—it is to be husbanded, guarded, and conserved. Every minute of it matters. Yet, in a variety of situations, we risk letting the minutes slip by, often without realizing it. We fritter away the seconds while Kadheisha works at the board, without even knowing we could be putting them to productive use. We blithely give away the last few minutes of class, saying, "We don't have time to start anything new" or "We worked hard, so I'm giving you guys a few minutes to relax."

Let's say this kind of thinking applies to just the last four minutes of class. That adds up to roughly twelve-and-a-half hours of "last few minutes" during each of perhaps six classes in each school year. If you did that every day, you'd give away seventy-five hours of instruction—several weeks of school. Or think of it this way: if you had a student whose success was absolutely critical and you were entrusted with her progress, you would never dream of spending an hourlong tutoring session doing nothing. But there's not much difference between that wasted hour and the wasted hour in an unutilized "last two minutes of class" except that it is spread across thirty students whose success is absolutely critical and with whose progress you've been entrusted. Don't let the diffusion across multiple classes and students fool you—the same amount of time has been wasted.

Mastering **Every Minute Matters** means spending time with the greatest possible productivity by attending to the everyday moments when time is often squandered. It means assuming that events will forever create new and unanticipated opportunities for downtime to occur, and therefore being prepared with "back-pocket" activities: a high-energy review of what your students have learned, or a challenge problem. It means keeping a series of short learning activities ready so that you're prepared when downtime threatens: at the end of class, when you're stuck in a hallway, while children are waiting for buses. Time spent waiting outside the cafeteria or by the flagpole during a fire drill is a perfect time for a vocabulary review. Packing up backpacks at the end of the day is a great opportunity for reading aloud from an inspiring novel. There's no better way to keep kids engaged while lining up for the next class than by peppering them with multiplication problems and mental math. You can, in short, always be teaching.

Every Minute Matters ... **Even in the Hallway**

Every few months, I reinspire myself by watching one of the very first videos we shot in what became the Teach Like a Champion project, long before there was such a name. It's a short video of history teacher Jamey Verilli managing his minutes one afternoon at North Star Academy. Waiting with a group of his students outside his classroom for the rest of the class to arrive, he begins quizzing students on their vocabulary:

- "What does it mean to be 'bound' to do something?"
- "Can you use it in a sentence, John?"
- "Who would have been bound to the land in a Middle Ages town?"
- "What are you bound to be doing right now?"

The students are standing in a line in the hallway just outside his classroom. Class has not even started yet. Not in the classroom, not during class time, and Jamey doesn't care: there's learning to be done. Meanwhile, his students are excited, smiling, happy to be engaged, and showing off their knowledge.

Squandered time kills momentum. It's not just the lost time; the perception it creates—of lack of progress, of valueless time—is devastating to a classroom. Fortunately, as Jamey shows, the opposite is also true. By valuing every minute and, over time, communicating his commitment to each minute's immense potential value, a teacher like Jamey—or you—creates a sense of meaning and productivity that pervades the room.

The first step in *Every Minute Matters* is a psychological one: recalibrating your expectations so that you think not "Well, it's just thirty seconds" but rather "Good gosh, thirty seconds—that's too much to waste." There's a quiet confidence implicit in such a shift. The well-it's-just-thirty-seconds teacher tacitly assumes that he could not do much with thirty seconds, so why bother? The second knows, believes in, and embraces how much he might accomplish even in a short period of time. After all, almost everything we've ever learned, we learned in the end, in a minute. There was an extra minute of reflection, practice, explanation, or discussion that pushed us over the top and perfected our skill or knowledge. There's no reason to believe that the profundity of the learning has to correlate to the glamour, predictability, and formality of the setting. The critical moment can just as easily come at 2:59 on Friday afternoon as the buses start to fill the circle in front of school as it can in the middle of your lesson on Wednesday morning.

Once you've embraced that notion, you'll start seeing downtime everywhere, where once, it seems, none had existed. A bit of occasional advance planning will help you do battle with it. Keeping at the ready — in your "back pocket" — some activities and groups of thematic questions aligned to what you're teaching can make the difference.

Back-Pocket Questions

If you work in a school, you are alert to the constant potential for the unexpected. Schools are complex organizations where the perfect flow of scheduled events is sometimes disrupted. So it's useful to be ready for the unexpected by having a portfolio of quick and useful back-pocket questions ready to go. They can live in a real pocket (on a set of note cards) or a metaphorical one. Plan the questions both periodically (every three weeks or so) and in advance, so that they are aligned to key objectives for your current unit. I also know champion teachers who keep a mental list of good topics for Q and A among mastered skills, enabling them to strategically spiral in practice and ensure retention of mastered content. You can always review key vocabulary, just as you can always ask students to put historical events in chronological order or put events from a novel in sequence.

You can also always ask students to identify the speaker and characters in a passage from a text your class has read, or to explain the context of that passage, for example. All you'd need would be a copy of the novel, a chapter printed, or something similar. All the better if you have a dozen passages highlighted in advance.

Without any props at all, you can always ask "math chains" — sequential math problems such as "Three times six. Now doubled. Take that number's square root. Subtract seventeen and take the absolute value. Add 104. Your answer is?" My colleague Paul Powell, a math teacher turned principal, did this daily when he started a school — Troy Prep in Troy, New York — in a building whose layout had students regularly waiting for others to clear tiny landings and passageways before they could move between classes. There on the landings and stairs, with Paul calling problems to students a dozen stairs above or a dozen below, his students mastered hours of math—ultimately resulting in some of the highest math scores in New York State.

Back-Pocket Activities

There will also be a time during your meticulously planned lesson when the whole class waits on some unexpected hiccup to be resolved—you forgot to put the overhead on the projector. Alas, you used it last period as well, and the answers are written on it in purple marker. It's important to be able to buy yourself needed time for mop-ups with high-value activities that students can complete autonomously.

With just a little preparation, you can ask students to read and write and to work independently on high-value activities. The idea that reading is always an incredibly high value activity if you can cause all students to participate or attend to someone else's reading carefully is a key benefit of *Control the Game* (technique 23). Once you've familiarized your students with it, you can always read, and you never have to do anything less valuable in your classroom. This gives you a great, productive *Every Minute Matters* question: Not only "Am I using every second?" but "Is my use of every second better than having them read, which they could be doing in an instant?"

The result of asking this question is that sometimes, perhaps rarely (or perhaps with more frequency than you first think), you'll be doing an activity and realize that it's a bit less valuable than you thought. It's just not coming off as you planned it. At that point, the *Every Minute Matters* question becomes, "How fast can I switch to something more valuable?" Try to have at least one or two high-value activities that you can always run and that are familiar enough that students can transition at a moment's notice with little direction from you. Practice these key activities regularly to keep students "in shape." Then, when the lesson comes unexpectedly crashing down—either during class or when the copy machine breaks just before—you're ready to deliver your best.

Look Forward

In a recent lesson on *To Kill a Mockingbird* with her eighth-grade students, Troy Prep reading teacher Maggie Johnson prepped her students with an intriguing question: "Whom does Atticus compare himself to at the end of this chapter? Thoughts? I bet you have 'em, but you have to write about it first!" she said, before releasing students to write their response for several minutes. It was a clever move, causing students to think about the coming discussion and to raise their hands to say, "I want to participate," then delaying their gratification and vesting them deeply in their writing (which they undertook vigorously). Afterwards, they were dying to talk about it. Even mild suspense creates tension, excitement, and anticipation. You can harvest that energy in your classroom and make your pacing feel more vibrant by using *look forward*. If you put an agenda on the board for a lesson or the morning, you can start students looking forward. If you add a catchy name to some of the topics on your agenda, they seem all the more intriguing. If you call one "Mystery Activity" and refer to it occasionally, you can make the anticipation even more intense: "We're almost there. Charles thinks he knows what it is, but … oh, no. He has no idea."

Bob Zimmerli once entranced a class of fifth graders during a lesson on place value by writing a number with twelve digits on the board and announcing, "At the end of class today, somebody's going to stand up and read this number correctly to the class. Everyone's going to be able to, but one of you is going to get to represent! You're going to march up here and show us how. Be ready. It might be you."

Here are a few other ways to refer to the future:

- "Later we'll be making this really tricky, so stay with me now, even if it seems easy [or hard]."

- "By the end of class you'll be able to [or you'll know the true story behind] … "

- "This is the first step in a skill that you'll want to show off to all your friends."

Consider upgrading some of your everyday statements to include a bit of suspense, turning "Take some time to answer the questions in front of you" into "Take exactly three minutes to answer the questions in front of you. Then we'll begin discussing the story" or "You've got three-and-a-half minutes to answer these questions; then we'll discuss who the true hero of the story is. Go!" Similarly, listen for the difference between "If we have time, we'll try to read a few lines of the Declaration" and "Later, if you're good [wink], you'll get to read one of the most famous passages in democratic society."

PUTTING IT ALL TOGETHER

Because great pacing is about the sum as much as the parts, we'll end with an analysis of what it looks like when these tools and techniques coalesce into a single lesson—in this case, one taught by fourth-grade teacher Ashley Hinton of North Star Academy Vailsburg Elementary.

Over the course of a writing lesson whose objective was to have students practice "showing" instead of "telling" in their writing, Ashley employed a variety of the techniques I've described. For starters, she *Changed the Pace* to give students a rigorous and well-balanced mental workout. During one particularly well-paced fifteen-minute chunk of her lesson, Ashley created a sense of engaging change by moving between four muscle groups:

- **Disc.** Students participated in a quick small-group discussion to brainstorm ideas for a writing prompt.

- **RIG.** Students recorded the ideas they gained through discussion with their partners.

- **GPGQ.** Ashley called on students to share the ideas they brainstormed with their partners.

- **IP.** Ashley's students then drafted a response to the following writing prompt: "Imagine that a character named John rode a roller coaster. Write three sentences using juicy details to help readers picture John's experience in their minds (without ever saying that he rode a roller coaster). You may use some of the details you brainstormed with your partner(s)."

Want More? Clip 27. Want to see Ashley Hinton put it all together? Watch her in clip 27.

To enhance her pacing, Ashley also leveraged four of the tools we described earlier:

- **Look forward.** Before releasing students to discuss, she built suspense and a sense of anticipation by saying, "I'm going to be looking for examples to share with the class, so make sure *they are juicy* …"

- **Clean start.** Ashley sent students off to discuss with a quick, efficient, and punchy cue: "Pencils up … go to work!" She also transitioned students into their writing task with a similar cue: "Go to work!" Although her clean start was crisp, it was not rushed. You can hear how she dropped her voice to a hush and slowed her cadence to model the reflectiveness she wanted from students during their writing activity. Because Ashley is so consistent about using this cue to prompt students to transition into activities, they were able to jump into them quickly, efficiently, and without hesitation. Her clean start also established a clean break between the prior activity and the next, which in turn *Brightened Lines* and helped the lesson content continue to "feel fast."

- **Work the clock.** Note that Ashley used a timer and kept the amount of *Turn and Talk* (technique 43) and writing time tight so that the lesson didn't drag. Most of her countdowns were limited to three seconds—no more or less time than students needed to follow her directions.

- *Every Minute Matters.* Ashley used marks to reward students who came up with especially juicy ideas during independent work. Once they'd finished, she prompted those whose papers she had highlighted to stand and share their ideas with the class. Because she had already "precalled" these students, she reduced the transaction costs involved with switching between students. This enabled her to hear from a number of students in a short period of time. Note that the quick succession of students adds mileposts, which also builds the illusion of speed.

CONCLUSION

In this chapter, we looked at the various ways champion teachers present or frame material to create mileposts—points in a lesson that have the effect of either increasing or decreasing the perception of speed within a classroom. Skillful pacing—together with high academic expectations, a strong plan of attack, and a stable and sturdy lesson structure—makes for a productive classroom experience and enables the creation of a rigorous academic ethos.

Ultimately, one of the many goals of teaching is to encourage and support students in the act of thinking for themselves. In Part Three, we'll look at a variety of ways champion teachers work to shift the balance of classroom work from themselves to their students.

Reflection and Practice

1. Go through a lesson plan you're likely to use in the next week, and if you don't do this already, assign the amount of time you think each activity is

(continued)

(continued)

likely to take. Now that you have general parameters, go through and find every direction you'll give to your students during the lesson, and designate an amount of time you will allot to each activity. Write a short script for each that makes the amount of time available clear and gives a beginning and end prompt to *Brighten Lines*.

2. Take the biggest single block of activity in your lesson (as measured in minutes) and try to break it into two or three activities with the same objective but with slightly different presentations. For example, if you had a section of problems for a math lesson on rounding, you might divide it in half, with a clear line between numerical and word problems. Then, between the two sections to make them seem like three, you might insert a brief reflection on what rounding is and why we do it.

USEFUL TOOLS | **FIND THESE TOOLS AT WWW.TEACHLIKEACHAMPION.COM/YOURLIBRARY**

Pacing case studies. A great exercise! Evaluate classroom examples of economy of language, *Brighten Lines*, and *Work the Clock*. Note what each teacher does that's successful as well as his or her possible areas for improvement. Review the example analysis.

Part

Ratio

IN THE FIRST EDITION OF *TEACH LIKE A CHAMPION*, I INCLUDED RATIO AS A single technique in the chapter "Lesson Structure." "One of our most important goals as teachers," I wrote, "is to cause students to do as much of the cognitive work—the writing, the thinking, the analyzing, the talking—as possible." This definition of ratio as the proportion of the cognitive work students do was coined by David Levin, cofounder of the highly-lauded KIPP schools and a uniquely insightful and effective teacher as well.

Ratio, in its first version, glossed one of the key ideas in teaching. I'd seen—and taught—more than a few lessons where the teacher got a great intellectual workout while the students blithely observed. So the concept was useful and important, but my treatment of it in that first version was insufficient. There was clearly more to it than I'd described. If nothing else, it was a huge idea, and there had to be a way of thinking about how it could be applied differently in varying settings and in situations with different purposes.

At the same time, ratio was one of the most requested topics for trainings, and the combination of these factors—that my work on it was insufficient, but educators always seemed to want help with it—led me to action. Knowing there weren't many knots that my incredible team of Teach Like a Champion analysts at Uncommon Schools couldn't unwind, I set off on a full year's study of ratio. We started over and took our time, with the goal of figuring out ratio once and for all.

The result is a big step forward (I know better than to think anything in teaching is "once and for all"), with the original single technique transformed into three chapters encompassing fifteen techniques, some that existed previously and some completely new. Ratio has become something more than a technique, something more like a guiding concept. For clarity's sake, then, here's an overview of the concept and the content of the next three chapters.

THINK RATIO VERSUS PARTICIPATION RATIO

I'll start by differentiating two types of ratio: participation ratio and think ratio. *Participation ratio* is a measure of who participates and how often. Maximizing it means getting all students involved in speaking, responding to questions, thinking actively, participating on cue, and processing ideas in writing, as often as possible. *Think ratio* refers to the level of rigor in the engagement you foster. What's the quality and depth of thinking students are engaged in? Do they revise and improve their thoughts, or leave them in draft version once they've initially thought them through? If participation ratio is a synonym for engagement, think ratio is a synonym for rigor. Champion teachers maximize both.

Next, I'll reflect on the role of knowledge in the applied-thinking activities characteristic of ratio. Thinking actively and learning facts are chicken-and-eggish. They require one another. So before delving more deeply into how to ratchet up the degree of thinking students do, I will make the case for the need for periods of instruction that instill facts and knowledge as a means of maximizing ratio over the long run.

After digging deeper into this point, we'll examine three paths teachers can take to increase ratio: questioning, writing, and discussion, each in their own full chapter, with explanations of techniques that are effective in increasing ratio in each of these areas.

Pathway 1: Building Ratio Through Questioning

In Chapter Seven, I'll discuss techniques for increasing ratio through questioning: *Wait Time, Cold Call, Call and Response, Break It Down,* and *Pepper,* often updating and upgrading discussions you may have seen to make them more focused on ratio.

Pathway 2: Building Ratio Through Writing

In Chapter Eight, I'll look at techniques for increasing ratio through writing. To me, this is the most rigorous and often the least appreciated way to maximize both types of ratio. It includes material from the first-edition technique *Everybody Writes,* but looks at writing's role in the classroom more broadly.

Pathway 3: Building Ratio Through Discussion

In Chapter Nine, I'll look at techniques for increasing ratio through discussion. These will comprise three new techniques — *Habits of Discussion, Turn and Talk,* and *Batch Process* — and other key ideas, such as question delegation.

Chapter 7

Building Ratio Through Questioning

Technique 32: Wait Time. Allow students time to think before answering. If they aren't productive with that time, narrate them toward being more productive.

Technique 33: Cold Call. Call on students regardless of whether they've raised their hands.

Technique 34: Call and Response. Ask your class to answer questions in unison from time to time to build energetic, positive engagement.

Technique 35: Break It Down. When a student makes an error, provide just enough help to allow her to "solve" as much of the original problem as she can.

Technique 36: Pepper. Use *Pepper* as a fast-paced, vocal review to build energy and actively engage your class.

Chapter 7

Building Ratio Through Questioning

We've all seen the lesson where the teacher gets a keen workout at the front of the room. She explains why the chapter is so critical to the novel, and some ways you might interpret it. She takes a few passages and explicates them. Meanwhile, students' primary activity is to "listen"—something they're not very active in doing and not very accountable for. By contrast, in a lesson with *ratio,* the workout belongs to students: they are constantly on their toes answering questions, drawing on their knowledge base, reflecting, and refining their ideas.

Ideally, every time you ask a question, every student tries to answer, and you ask a lot of questions. Still, it's important to recognize that you could have a lesson with lots of engaged and active student participation, but not much rigor. Your lesson could have fifty interactions that engage students actively but superficially:

Teacher: OK, scholars, today we're going to be adding fractions! What are we going to be adding, class?

Class (in unison): Fractions!

Teacher:	Yes, fractions. And who can tell me what the two parts of a fraction are? Everyone take ten seconds to get both parts in their head. OK, David, what's the top part of a fraction?
David:	The numerator.
Teacher:	Yes, we call that the numerator; we call that the …
Class:	Numerator!
Teacher:	And what's the other part of a fraction, Kylah?
Kylah:	The denominator.
Teacher:	Yes, the bottom half is called the denominator. What's the bottom half of a fraction called, class?
Class:	The denominator!
Teacher:	Yes, so a fraction has two numbers; on the top, it has a … ?
Class:	Numerator!
Teacher:	And on the bottom, it has a … ?
Class:	Denominator!

If it's not obvious, I have deliberately exaggerated this example to show that although participation is necessary, it is insufficient by itself. Participation must be rigorous, too.

The phrase "necessary, but insufficient" also applies to deeper, more rigorous participation. For example, I could have a deep and demanding discussion of the role of class and caste in *To Kill a Mockingbird* with a handful of engaged, insightful students, while the rest of the class essentially watched passively. My lesson would have a very high think ratio, but not much participation ratio. Of course, you need both: full and energetic participation from everyone, and work that is rigorous and demanding. You might imagine two axes on a grid, then. When you seek ratio, you ultimately seek to be high on both axes—somewhere like point A (see Figure 7.1). However, in some lessons you might need to build participation ratio first, drawing students in and then boosting the level of thinking. In other words, your curve might work its way to point A, looking like the line in Figure 7.1, with your lesson first gathering speed and then increasing in rigor, so you have all students involved as the think ratio grows. Not always, of course; every lesson is different. The end goal is to achieve both types of ratio, but you may have to emphasize one or the other differently at times to get there.

Figure 7.1 Think Ratio Versus Participation Ratio

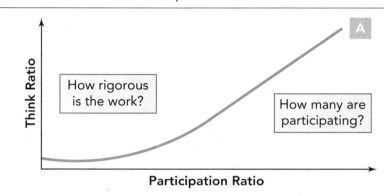

See It in Action: Clip 22

You can also use Figure 7.1 to reflect on other teachers' lessons. For example, I find it helpful to watch two of the videos in this book, clip 28 of Gary Lauderdale at West Briar Middle School in Houston and clip 22 of Erin Michels at North Star Academy in Newark, and reflect on their ratio. To my mind, both Gary and Erin demonstrate outstanding teaching, and there is clear evidence of both participation ratio and think ratio in both classrooms. Still, they are different in their relative emphasis on each. Try taking a moment now to watch them both and score them on this grid. How would you compare them?

Perhaps Gary's lesson emphasizes participation ratio a bit more; he's trying to build a culture of effort in math, and you can hear him talking about that at the beginning. His *Cold Call,* as we'll study later in this chapter, is very systematic. If you're sitting in Gary's classroom, you *know* that you're likely to get called on with a question of substance and that after you answer, it's just as likely you'll get a follow-up question or be called on to follow up on your classmate's answer, so you know you have to listen carefully and stay in the game. That said, the tone is so positive, you'd probably want to stay in the game anyway.

Erin's class also engages the whole group pretty consistently, though she provides a bit more optionality to it: she *Cold Calls* with less frequency.

There's more autonomy to the *Turn and Talk*—"Talk to me" [implicitly about what your classmate did right or wrong] is a less directive question.

One classroom isn't better than the other. Both, I think, are exemplary. They show different emphases at specific times. Once you've been in a classroom like Gary's for weeks, have been socialized to always participate, and have begun to do so successfully and to have found that in fact you are not afraid of math as maybe some people had told you (you had been, but now you rather like it), maybe then you are more willing and able to operate with greater autonomy on some tasks. Or the dynamics of school that day (for example, a slow day in February) or the needs of the lesson might be slightly different. So my goal would be to observe and analyze differences in emphasis in their ratio and the methods they use to build it, rather than to try to judge one lesson against the other.

THE CONTENT PREREQUISITE

One thing both Gary's and Erin's classes have in common is that students are able to think deeply because they know a lot. Imagine, by contrast, a class in which the teacher asks her students to discuss in pairs why the sky is blue. It's an interesting question, and the participation ratio might be high, but with insufficient factual knowledge to support their analysis, students would devolve into discussions of empty ideas and the trading of unfounded speculation. They'd be guessing without knowing what to guess. You can talk about the sky all day long, but if you don't have a strong base of facts, you're not likely to be thinking about the relevant factors and forces, and are just as likely to be wasting your time.

In fact, you need to know a lot about pretty much anything to think deeply about it. This is one of the most undervalued truths about learning. Rigorous activities with a high think ratio rely on knowledge — often shared knowledge among students — and the deeper and broader the knowledge, the more rigorous the application. You can't have "applied" learning, as valuable as it is, without something factual in your memory to apply. This is because active cognitive processing capacity is finite. Knowledge stored in your long-term memory can be accessed without using active capacity, but knowledge that isn't in your long-term memory has to crowd out deeper thinking from your active mental capacity. If you want to think deeply about a math problem (Why do we do it this way? Is there another way I could do it? What does the answer tell me?), you need to be automatic on the calculations. Similarly, if you want to hear the echoes of history in a contemporary speech, your long-term memory needs to have stored knowledge of those events—Lincoln's words at Gettysburg, Wellington's bold pronouncements at Waterloo—to catch the allusions, references, even unintended repetition of hubris and flawed arguments. Ranging through history for analogies and comparison points has to happen fast or it won't happen at all, so it relies on knowledge *learned in advance*. So too does realizing how a narrative voice plays with or riffs off of conventional forms of narration.[1] You can only make connections, comparisons, and analogies to what you already know.

Educators often think in either-or terms on this topic: "thinking skills" or "facts and knowledge." Although I'm sure the answer involves some form of both, I'd been struggling for some time with the question of how to think about balancing them until I read Daisy Christodoulou's outstanding book *Seven Myths About Education*. Referring to high-ratio activities in which students work on their own to apply understanding and problem-solve, Christodoulou writes, "This kind of activity is meaningful if you already have knowledge ... But if [students] have always been taught via this method, it is unlikely they will have extensive knowledge of the topic. Pupils will be caught in a chicken-and-egg scenario: unable to work independently because they do not have necessary background knowledge, but unable to gain that background knowledge because they spend all of their time working independently."[2]

Christodoulou's observation was an epiphany, as it advocated the approach I see so many top teachers take: making consistent investments in knowledge transmission—the direct teaching of facts—as a necessary prerequisite and companion to independent and applied work, taught with the understanding that there are deep synergies between facts and "deeper" applications, the former of limited value without the latter, and the latter all but impossible to sustain without the former.

The power of knowledge, further, comes from its breadth. The date of the battle of Waterloo is probably not that useful if it's all you know about European history. But if you know that Waterloo marked the demise of Napoleon's final effort to rule Europe and that it represented the coordination of multinational troops and resulted in one of the longest periods of peace in modern European history, you are likely to see its echoes in a thousand other events. If you grasp the thirty most important events in European history and can link them in a chronology of actions and reactions, you can reflect on and "apply" the meaning of those events, their connections, their antecedents, and their causes much more deeply. You can't know in advance that you will see a connection to previous events in history in the account you read this morning. Contrary to myth, you can't "look it up on the Internet" if you don't know why you would do so in the first place; and even if you did, if you had to absorb its facts in the moment, your active processing capacity would be taxed, and you would have nothing left over to see the broader connections.

Fortunately, knowledge dissemination — teaching facts — can also be made relatively more high ratio through effective teaching. But it's important to remember that it is also necessary to keeping your think ratio strong.

We spend a great deal of time in our classrooms questioning. If we are doing our jobs right, we are constantly asking students questions and then responding to their answers with further questions. Techniques that can help you make those bouts of questioning effective are among the most critical you can master. We'll start with one of the simplest and most underrated techniques: *Wait Time*.

WAIT TIME

Allow students time to think before answering. If they aren't productive with that time, narrate them toward being more productive.

After asking a question of his class, the typical teacher waits about a second before taking an answer, and the challenges and limitations posed by such a habit are significant. The answers the teacher can expect to get after less than a second's reflection are unlikely to be the richest, the most reflective, or the most developed his students can generate. And taking answers after just a second has the effect of systematically encouraging students to raise their hands with the first answer, rather than the best one they can think of. If they wait any longer, someone else will have answered. What's more, a lack of **Wait Time** makes it more likely that the teacher will waste time processing a poor answer before he gets to discuss a good one. *Wait Time* can often save you time in the end, as it ensures that you start with higher-quality initial answers. Under ideal circumstances, what happens during *Wait Time* is thinking. And, of course, affording students significant periods to think after each question you ask increases think ratio.

Benefits of waiting a few seconds between question and answer include

- Allowing more hands to go up
- Enabling a wider range of scholars to raise their hands
- Supporting better, more rigorous answers
- Prompting more cognitive work during the "wait"
- Decreasing the number of failures to respond (those who say, "I don't know")
- Increasing use of evidence in answers

See It in Action: Clip 29

You can see a great example of *Wait Time* in clip 29 of Maggie Johnson's eighth-grade reading class. The class is discussing *To Kill a Mockingbird*, and the clip begins as Maggie follows up on some writing she's asked her students to do. "As I walked around, [I noticed] many of you were able to tell me what the difference in opinion is between Aunt Alexandra and Atticus on Calpurnia," Maggie says. "The question is, why?"

After about a second (the amount of time a typical teacher waits), there's just one hand in the air. After three seconds or so, perhaps eight more students have raised their hands. Just a second or two to reflect, and a spate of students energetically offer to participate, having realized they have some insight on the matter. In another few seconds a few more hands go up, these a bit more tentative. This is especially interesting: the students who've raised their hands seem as though they aren't sure they want to risk it, but they decide to after all. In many ways, these are exactly the kids you want raising their hands, and it's exciting to see the courage a few seconds will cause to take hold.

In the end, Maggie gives, by my count, eight seconds of *Wait Time* before she calls on Jaya to answer. As a result, she has better choices for her discussion: a dozen kids who've thought through an answer if the first student's answer needs developing; more thoughtful answers than the answer of the student whose hand went up as soon as Maggie stopped talking; some hesitant students taking the risk of weighing in.

For her next question, Maggie gives almost thirteen seconds of *Wait Time*. Again, you can see students starting to raise their hands, slowly, thoughtfully.

Note the girl in the front row right who starts to raise her hand, puts it down, and then slowly raises it again. She's wrestling, apparently, with whether to try to join in or not, and the extra time allows her to opt in. Several students are using the time to scan the book for useful insights, a fact made evident by Maggie's narration.

A similar process plays out again in the seven seconds of *Wait Time* Maggie offers in response to her third question: "What does Atticus say about mockingbirds again?" What's striking is the high levels of participation, enthusiasm, and reflection among Maggie's students. They love the book, are invested in it, and are learning to think deeply.

Implementing *Wait Time* can be challenging. It is hard to discipline yourself to allow time to pass after a question, and it takes a bit of practice. Making a habit of silently counting to three in your head or narrating your intention to wait (for example, "I'll give you a few seconds … OK, let's see what you have to say") can help.

Even so, there's no guarantee that students will use *Wait Time* to think. To confound the issue, it's hard to assess what students do with the time you give. It may not necessarily be apparent to students how they should respond to your waiting. There are several steps necessary to teach, remind, and acculturate your students to use *Wait Time* effectively and to help make *Wait Time* as productive as it can be.

Step 1: Narrate Hands

Wait Time is productive only if students are likely to engage in the material after the *Wait Time* is over. In a rigorous classroom with a robust academic culture, students strive to answer questions as a matter of habit, assuming and expecting that their classmates will do the same. Under these circumstances, where they expect to use the ideas they generate, students are likely to put *Wait Time* to good use. However, there are a great many classrooms where it is unusual to see hands in the air and students do not participate as a matter of course. In those classrooms, the expectation that they won't use the time they spent thinking to engage with the teacher and peers about content renders *Wait Time* far less effective.

One useful thing to do during *Wait Time* is address potential motivational issues (students who don't want to raise their hands) and build a culture that normalizes participation by *narrating hands*. Let's say you ask, "What exactly was the purpose of the first Continental Congress?" Maybe one or two students raise their hands. Others stare vacantly. Most students, probably, are engaged in a subtle and silent calculus: Is the teacher really expecting a forest of hands on a question like that? Your first goal is to show them that, in fact, you do. "One hand," you say out loud. "Two hands. Now three," you say, building momentum and calling students' attention to the number of hands that are up. Perhaps you incentivize another fence-sitter or two. "Four hands," you say. "Five. I want to see ten hands on this question."

Perhaps some students are a bit more resistant. If so, you might tell your students to put their hands down. "I want you all to take fifteen seconds and go back to the text and find the answer. I want to see everyone rereading, and I'll tell you when you can raise your hands." After fifteen or twenty seconds, you might say, "OK, now, hands!" Over time, by narrating hands—by pushing students and reinforcing your expectation that most students will raise their hands on an interesting question—you can begin to shift the culture.

Step 2: Prompt Thinking Skills

Once you've normalized and reinforced the expectation of hand raising, it's time to *prompt thinking skills*. This is a step by which champion teachers tacitly teach their students what to do with *Wait Time*—how to turn it into think time—by providing students with guidance about what they should be doing with their three or five or twelve seconds to be most productive. For example:

- "I'm seeing people thinking deeply and jotting down thoughts. I'll give everyone a few more seconds to do that."

- "I'm seeing people going back to the chapter to see if they can find the scene. That seems like a great idea."

- "I'm waiting for someone who can connect this scene to another play, ideally *Macbeth*."

- "I'm going to give everyone lots of time because this question is tricky. Your first answer may not be the best."

In each of these cases, the teacher is prompting students what to do with their *Wait Time*. It turns out that you use it to check your notes or glance back through the text or double-check your first thought. That's what it means to think.

Step 3: Give Real Think Time

The third step is simple: stop talking. This is critical because the first two steps require you to interrupt student thinking. It's important to give students *real think time*. It's simple, but critical, and because it requires inaction, it can be hard to do. Counting silently to yourself can help you build the necessary habit of self-discipline. You might also walk around your room as you wait, with the goal of waiting until you reach a specific spot on the other side of the room before you call on someone. Or you might use the clock to your advantage, saying, "I'll call on someone in ten seconds" and then forcing yourself to wait until the second hand releases you. After the socializing of hand raising and the praising, remember that this is the most important part: there has to be some time when no one is talking, when students are thinking. By your silence, you are intimating that this is as important as anything they will do all day.

Step 4: Make *Wait Time* Transparent

Let's say I'm a student in your class and you ask a rigorous question. Perhaps it's something like, "What forces pulled the border states toward the Confederacy, and how did Lincoln respond to those forces?" Then you give the class some think time, and as your student I start to reflect. After about five seconds, I've come up with a few nascent ideas. If you called on me, I could say something credible, so I begin to wind down my thinking. But let's say you were hoping for something a little more robust—you were hoping I'd be ready to cite a few specific incidents and describe how they connect, and you'd decided to give the class twenty or thirty seconds of think time to make sure we thought deeply. I'd be more likely to meet those expectations if you made your intentions transparent to me by saying something like, "This is a hard question. It requires some thinking and the use of specific examples. I'll give you thirty seconds or so." If you did that, I could gauge my thinking accordingly. In other words, I would start off understanding that this was no throwaway moment, because you'd told me about how much think time to expect. It's a simple but useful idea: when you intend to give students more than a handful of seconds of *Wait Time*, make that information explicit to them so that they can manage their time accordingly.

See It in Action: Clip 30

You can see the balance of the steps of *Wait Time* managed effectively by Boris Zarkhi in clip 30. He really does ask his students, "What exactly was the purpose of the first Continental Congress?" He narrates hands with lots of positive energy, then adds, "I love all the people looking back in the text, trying to find that answer," a clear example of prompting thinking skills.

After a few seconds of silent *Wait Time*, he tells his students, "Take ten seconds, go back into the text, and find it." Being transparent about *Wait*

Time, telling students roughly how long they'll have as Boris does here, is incredibly productive. If I give students thirty seconds of *Wait Time* but don't tell them they'll get that long, they may rush to get the task done in just a few seconds.

While some students do go back to the text as Boris suggests, several just sit with their hands up, assuming their original answer was perfectly good. Boris waves them off and tells them to put their hands down, go back to the text, and use their *Wait Time* productively, too. Early hand raisers often need additional discipline as much as students who don't raise their hands. At the end of a batch of real think time, Boris calls "Hands up!" and narrates hands again. This time there are almost twenty students who think they have the answer.

Want More? Clip 31. Want more *Wait Time*? Check out Colleen Driggs in clip 31.

TECHNIQUE

COLD CALL

Call on students regardless of whether they've raised their hands.

33

If I was working with a group of teachers and had to help them make the greatest possible improvements in the rigor, ratio, and level of expectations in their classroom with one technique, the technique I'd choose might well be **Cold Call**, the practice of calling on students regardless of whether they raise their hands.

The Four Purposes of *Cold Call*

There are four reasons why this simple change has such a transformative effect on a classroom.

1. Checking for Understanding

Knowing whether you taught it is easy, but knowing whether they learned it is hard and requires you to be able to ask questions of any (and every) student at any (and every) time during your lesson to assess who knows what. If you are limited to assessing only those students who raise their hands when you ask a question, you will never be able to assess all the members of your class, and, what's more, you will think you've achieved more mastery than you have. (Students who volunteer to tell you they think they understand something are more likely to know it than the students who don't.)

2. Creating a Culture of Engaged Accountability

When students see you calling on members of the class who don't have their hands raised, they will come to understand that raising their hands is an opportunity to signal that they have something worthwhile to say, but *not* a tool they can use to control whether or not they participate in class. They come to expect and prepare for the possibility that they might be asked to offer their opinion or answer a question or solve a problem or read something at any time.

3. Pacing

Picture this scene from a classroom near you. Mr. K is reviewing a problem set from last night's homework. He says, "OK, who'd like to tell us how they answered number 2 on last night's homework?" Pause. Crickets. Finally, after five or six seconds, Natalie raises her hand. Unfortunately, she just answered the previous question, so Mr. K tries another approach. "I'm seeing the same two or three hands," he says, scanning slowly and awkwardly. "Do I need to remind you that participation is graded in my class?" Teachers like Mr. K routinely waste a great deal of time — ten or fifteen seconds per question, perhaps, but hours and hours over the long run, pleading for someone to answer their questions. What's worse, watching a teacher desperately plead for someone to participate slows the perceptive clock to a crawl. It would have been a lot simpler, a lot faster, and a lot less painful for everyone for Mr. K to say, "OK, let's take a look at the second problem. How'd you answer that one, Mamadou?"

4. Backstopping Your Ratio

By itself, *Cold Call* is an excellent tool for ensuring a high participation ratio. It causes all students to be engaged and ready to answer. But it also helps boost think ratio by backstopping other techniques that are cognitively demanding. Let's say I give my students thirty transparent seconds of *Wait Time* to reflect on a challenging question about the novel *The Giver*. Having asked my students to think deeply and independently, my telling students I intend to use *Cold Call* on the back end of the activity (or merely making a habit of it) makes my most rigorous activities less discretionary and more accountable. If students know that the two minutes during which they are to write in reflection are likely to end with "OK, so a tough question. Let's hear what some people reflected on. We'll start with you, Jabari. What did you observe here?" they will engage more fully, and they are more likely to do their best work.

See It in Action: Clip 32

Watch clip 32 of Hannah Lofthus. You'll notice that her *Cold Calling* follows a distinctive rhythm. And although the lesson she's doing—sight words—is particularly well suited to an especially brisk pace, you can still establish a rhythm (albeit slightly slower) in the rate at which you ask questions. The benefit is that, as a former student of mine put it, "When you start a rhythm, people join you. Even without your telling them to." Hannah, for example, never says, "Let's review these words as fast as we can." Her kids just respond to her pace, and she manages to ask a lot of questions in a short amount of time, checking in with every student in the group. It's much easier to establish a rhythm when you're *Cold Calling* and don't have to worry about who raises their hands and how fast.

Four Keys to Effective *Cold Call*

As with any powerful tool, it's important to use *Cold Call* effectively. Poor implementation can do as much harm as good. There are four keys to effective *Cold Call*.

1. Keep *Cold Call* Predictable

Cold Call works in building a culture of engaged accountability—in part because students know a *Cold Call* is a possibility. The fact that it might be coming causes anticipation, and the more plausible it is that students could be *Cold Called*, the more they will anticipate and the more engaged they will be. If you *Cold Call* reliably for a few minutes of your class almost every day, students will come to expect it and change their behavior in advance; they will prepare to be asked questions.

If your *Cold Calls* surprise students, they may learn a lesson ("Darn, I should have been ready!"), but one too late to help them. They may also feel ambushed, caught off guard, and therefore more likely to be thinking about the past ("Why'd she do that?") than about the future ("I'm going to be ready!"). If *Cold Calls* are predictable and students begin to anticipate them, the effect will be universal.

See It in Action: Clip 33

The ultimate from of predictability is transparency: explaining to students, the first time you use *Cold Call*, exactly what you'll do, why you'll do it, how often you'll do it, and how they should react. We call this a *rollout speech*. Scripting some brief remarks to explain the what and the why makes the exercise rational, systematic, predictable, and, with a little skill, inspiring.

You can watch in clip 33 the rollout speech that champion teacher Colleen Driggs gave her fifth graders at Rochester Prep. Colleen quickly tells her students how to act during *Cold Call*, explains why she uses this technique, and, you'll surely notice, frames the activity in a positive way: it's a chance to shine and show that you're on fire.

Many teachers assume that *Cold Calls* have to be stressful for students—that they'll be forced to participate when they don't want to. But your expectations of students' interest are often a self-fulfilling prophecy. As you watch Colleen, make a list of the things she says that you could borrow or adapt if you gave a rollout speech to explain *Cold Call* to your students.

2. Make *Cold Call* Systematic

Teachers who use *Cold Call* take pains to make it clear that *Cold Calls* are universal (they come, without fail, to everyone) and not an effort to single out students for lack of attentiveness, in response to specific behaviors, or according to some other hidden calculus. *Cold Call* is about expectations—"This is how we do it here"—and that means asking *Cold Call* questions in a calm, even tone, perhaps with a bit of a smile or a look of sincere interest. Most champions I've observed are careful to *Cold Call* in batches so that it couldn't appear as though one person was "in the teacher's sights." They *Cold Call* all types of students—not just those whose attention might be questioned, say—and sprinkle their questions to all corners of the room, not just that certain group of desks in the back. Some of them even track their *Cold Calls*—or plan them in advance—to keep themselves accountable for getting to everyone with reasonable consistency. I've even seen Julie Jackson keep a chart on the wall during her reading groups for this purpose.

It had the ancillary benefit of reminding students that her *Cold Calls* came to everyone in the end.

Be cautious of tying your *Cold Calls* to specific behaviors when you're not sure students are eager to be called on. If you say, "Hmm, I see you hiding over there, Caitlin," you not only risk making Caitlin self-conscious but also cause students to think about whether they look as though they are hiding and how they should look if they do (or don't) want to be *Cold Called*. Besides, a *Cold Call* is not a punishment; as teacher Colleen Driggs put it, it's "a chance to shine."

3. Keep *Cold Call* Positive

The purpose of *Cold Call* is to foster positive engagement in the rigorous work of your class. One of its benefits is that students occasionally surprise themselves with their own capabilities. They don't volunteer, because they don't think they can answer, but when they are forced to try, they are happily surprised to find themselves succeeding. In other cases, students suspect they know the answer, but are hesitant to volunteer for a variety of social reasons. Such students benefit from answering, sometimes surprising themselves at their own success and always knowing that you thought they were capable of answering the question. A *Cold Call* is a good thing, an opportunity you give your students.

When you *Cold Call,* you want students to get the answer right. In your heart, you have to be rooting for success. If you're not, your *Cold Call* could be a "gotcha"—calling on a student when you know he was tuned out, in order to chasten him. ("What did I just say, John?" or "Isn't that right, John?"). I recommend against this. *Cold Call* is an academic technique. It's designed to engage all students in the academic discourse of your classroom. You don't want to confuse an invitation to participate with a consequence or a correction.

You can ensure positivity by using an even, slightly upbeat tone, suggesting that you couldn't imagine a world in which a student would *not* want to participate. If you're worried that a student might be anxious, start with a very simple question ("Did you try problem 2, David?") to establish a bit of comfort, then ask a more substantive one ("Good. Tell us what you got").

In addition, consider the power of explaining to students in advance what to do if (1) they don't know the answer ("Smile. Say, 'I'm not sure' and then add 'but' and give me your best guess") or (2) their classmate can't answer ("Be supportive. Smile warmly and track them. Don't raise your hand until they're done trying, and remember that all of us will be there at some point").

One final aspect of *Cold Call* that leads to a positive tone can occasionally elude some teachers when they aren't prepared: both the question and the ideal answer should be clear. Every teacher has had the experience of asking a student a question that, in retrospect, wasn't clear. It's doubly important to avoid this kind of question when *Cold Calling*. Many teachers address this challenge by planning their exact questions and answers word for word as part of their lesson planning process.

4. Unbundle Your *Cold Call*

One way to maximize the participation ratio of *Cold Call* is to "unbundle" questions: to break up larger questions into a series of smaller questions, ideally with contingent answers, and distribute them to multiple students. This can give you fast, energetic pacing if you want it, and a culture of peer-to-peer accountability.

To help visualize what unbundling might look like in practice, consider, first, a teacher who *Cold Calls* a student, D'Juan, and asks him how to find the volume of a cylinder. The class listens while D'Juan ably describes the necessary calculations, but they become increasingly passive participants to the exchange. The longer it continues, the more they (rightly) suspect that they won't play any role in answering. It's easy to tune out a bit.

Now, compare that sequence to this one, which also uses *Cold Call,* but unbundles the question:

Teacher:	How many variables and constants do we have to consider in finding the volume of a cylinder? D'Juan?
D'Juan:	Three of them.
Teacher:	Good tell me one, Janella.
Janella:	Radius.
Teacher:	OK, and D'Juan, is that a variable or a constant?
D'Juan:	Um, radius is a variable?
Teacher:	OK, so what's the other variable, Carl?
Carl:	Height is the other variable.
Teacher:	Good. So what's the constant we need, Kat?
Kat:	Pi.
Teacher:	And how do we know it's a constant, Jameer?
Jameer:	Well, because it never changes.
Teacher:	Good. So Taylor, when I multiply my constant and my two variables, I get my volume, right?
Taylor:	Well no, you need to square your radius.
Teacher:	Ah, yes. Thank you, Taylor. Well done.

By breaking up a single question into several *Cold Calls,* the teacher in this scenario keeps the pacing fast and all students on their toes; in making questions contingent on one another, she forces students to attend even more closely. Not only were six students engaged actively where only one had been before, but all students were likely thinking through the answers silently, given the plausibility of being called on. And because the students are all working together toward answering a question, unbundling tends to build a positive cohesive culture. It makes school a team sport.

Another simple but useful way to make unbundling work is to add a bit of scaffolding—to start very simple to give students an early taste of positivity. You might, for example, begin a sequence of *Cold Calls* by asking a student to read the question. This allows you to engage the student successfully (the answer is right in front of her) and signals to the rest of the class to be on their toes. Plus, it allows you to be conversational and positive in your follow-up: "Thanks, Marta. And what did you put for your answer?" Or you might start by asking a simple yes-or-no question ("Were you able to come up with an answer to number 6, Shawn?"), which you can use to diffuse any anxiety before you follow up ("Great. Let's hear what you said" or "OK, tell us how far you got").

Of course, a sequence that begins with simple questions should progress to more rigorous follow-up questions—ones that build think ratio as much as participation ratio. Starting simple doesn't mean ending that way, but it does tend to engage and motivate students and cause them to be inspired by the building level of rigor and challenge.

Cold Call Variations

Great teachers use most techniques in a variety of successful ways, depending on the situation, their lesson goals, and their own style and approach. In the case of *Cold Call,* there is an especially wide variety of what you might call "right-or-right choices": options for implementation whereby both approaches can be right depending on the context.

Hands Up/Hands Down

When you *Cold Call,* you can still allow students who wish to participate to raise their hands. You can take some hands and also make some *Cold Calls,* striking whatever balance you wish. I call this "hands-up" *Cold Calling.* In contrast, you could tell students, "No hands right now; I'm *Cold Calling.*" Both approaches are effective, though they emphasize different aspects of your classroom. Champion teachers often use both at different times. The two tables here note some of the trade-offs to consider:

Hands-Up *Cold Calling*

Advantages	Limitations
• It provides an important data source: raised hands tell you how many students think they know the answer to your question. • It enables you to continue to provide an incentive for students to raise their hands and signal their desire to participate. • It often leads more students to get engaged and want to raise their hands. • It allows you to engage in balanced *Cold Call*, deliberately moving back and forth between taking hands and hands-down *Cold Call* (see next table). • It enables you to continue encouraging and rewarding students who ask to participate by letting them have a turn.	• Raising hands can often tacitly encourage students to "call out" answers. • It can cause your *Cold Call* to be less apparent and transparent to some students: they might not realize you're *Cold Calling* when they see hands, and they may not always realize that the classmate who just answered was *Cold Called* too. This can make the technique seem less systematic.

Hands Down *Cold Calling*

Advantages	Limitations
• It's the ultimate in predictability. It explicitly tells students to be ready because the *Cold Call* is coming. • It's faster and can have a stronger effect on pacing because you don't have to spend time navigating and narrating the raising of hands. • It sends a very clear message about your firm control of the classroom and students' accountability for remaining attentive. • It's ideal for reviewing material before a test, say. • It can be effective for checking for understanding because it reduces the likelihood of students' calling out answers in eagerness. • Students who do want to answer are rendered less visible (they don't have their hands up), so your decision to target your questions to more reticent students is less visible to others and therefore seems a bit more systematic.	• It can discourage this key classroom behavior if not balanced with lots of other times when students can raise their hands. • It's harder to combine with moments when you choose to call on a hand amid *Cold Calling*.

Follow On/Follow Up

In the section on unbundling, I pointed out how *Cold Call* can support a peer-to-peer culture in which students listen to their classmates as carefully as they listen to their teacher. The follow-on especially enhances that element and emphasizes how much a teacher values students' contributions to class.

Patrick Pastore uses this approach. He decides on a few consistent, simple prompts that he can use to *Cold Call* students to develop a classmate's idea. Although he varies his terminology occasionally, he most often uses the word "develop" as his *Cold Call* prompt. In a typical sequence, a student might make an observation about a text, such as this one about Ambrose Bierce's *Occurrence at Owl Creek Bridge*:

Brandon: I think [the author] feels some sympathy towards the Confederacy.
Patrick: Develop, Christina.
Christina: Well, Farquhar, he's a Southerner, but the author just seems to like him.
Patrick: Develop, Alyssha.
Alyssha: Well, he goes on and on about how "no service was too humble for him to perform." He keeps saying how brave he is.

Patrick uses the follow-on "develop" not just to cause students to expand on one another's ideas but to cause them to listen to one another and engage intellectually with their ideas.

Follow-up involves revisiting previous comments later in discussion. For example, Patrick might ask, via *Cold Call,* "Earlier, Alyssha, you told us that you thought the author was sympathetic to the protagonist. Now that you've seen how the story ends, what can you say about *why* the author might have been trying to make us feel sympathy toward him?" Using *Cold Call* to follow up on Alyssha's previous comment underscores how much Patrick valued it. He shows that he still remembers it twenty or so minutes later and that he still thinks it's relevant. It also establishes accountability for and ownership for ideas. To make an observation in Patrick's class is to then have to reflect on its relevance and connection to subsequent developments in the discussion.

Timing the Name

When you *Cold Call,* you can vary when you say the name of the student you're calling on. The most common and often the most effective approach is to ask the question, pause, and then name a student — for example, "What's three times nine [pause], James?" Using the sequence *question, pause, name* ensures that every student hears the question and begins preparing an answer during the pause. Because students know a *Cold Call* is likely, but not who will receive it, every student is likely to answer the question, with one student merely called on to give their answer aloud. In the example, it means that every student in the class has done the multiplication during the pause between question and name. If you say the name first, as in "Jairo, what's three times nine?" far fewer students practice because they know they're not getting called on. The difference in leverage between this scenario (twenty-five students answering a question and one saying it aloud) and the alternative (one student answering a question and twenty-four watching) is significant, so the default approach for most *Cold Calling* should be question, pause, name.

In some cases, however, calling a student's name first can be beneficial. It can prepare a student to attend, and increases the likelihood of success. This can be especially effective with students who may not have been *Cold Called* before, students who have language processing difficulties, or students whose knowledge of English is still developing. You might "precall" a student before class ("OK, Jamal, I'm going to ask you to go over the last problem from the homework today. Be ready!") or while *Circulating* and looking at independent work ("Love this idea, Jermaine. Be ready in case I ask you to share it"). Finally, using the name first can help establish clarity after a chorus of *Call and Response* (technique 34) so that students know before they hear your questions that you're not asking them to call out answers.

Cold Call 2.0

The Uncommon Schools Teach Like a Champion team and I have learned a lot from watching great teachers use *Cold Call* in the past few years. This section describes some of our key insights.

Manage the Pause (a.k.a. Slow Call)

Watching Troy Prep math teacher Katie Bellucci one morning, I was struck by something distinctive about her use of *Cold Call*. "What's 40 percent of fifty?" she asked. Then, before she called on a student, she tapped her head and paused; "Get it in your head," she whispered to remind students to use the time to solve the problem. Then she waited, stretching her pause out for four or five extra seconds to make sure all her students had time to work the whole problem. In the default sequence of *Cold Call*—question, pause, name—the pause is the most important part, I realized; it's when the thinking takes place, and Katie was making sure to maximize the thinking that was supposed to happen there by stretching it out and guiding students to use it actively. Informed by Katie's approach, I started to notice slower versions of *Cold Call* in one classroom after another. Although I had initially conceived of *Cold Call* as a way to speed things up (and speed can be a benefit of *Cold Call*) slow *Cold Call*—Slow Call, if you will—turns out to be just as powerful.

Let's say you're reading Lois Lowry's *The Giver* and you say, "I want each of you to come up with one way that something intended to be utopian has turned out to be dystopian instead. It's a hard question, so I'm going to give you thirty seconds of think time and then I'm going to *Cold Call* a couple of you to share your thinking." The result would be a significant block of time for deep, steady thinking with a gentle accountability loop on the back end. Using this slower, more thoughtful version of *Cold Call* also makes it easier to apply the technique to more reflective and open-ended questions, especially the sort you might ask when introducing new material, rather than merely during review.

Evan Stoudt of Collegiate Academies in New Orleans riffed on this idea recently. Working on slope-intercept format, he presented his students with the coordinates of two points on a line and asked them to solve using "mental math." Asking, "Is the slope positive or negative? Remember, when I say 'mental math,' it means I will be *Cold Calling*." After a block of solid think time, he added, "Thumbs up when you have it." This was interesting: it allowed him to ensure that he gave his scholars sufficient think time, and gave them the opportunity to affirm that they were ready. It was also a subtle form of intellectual accountability. Evan's students were accountable for saying they'd thought the question through and were ready to answer.

In addition to using *Wait Time* to extend the pause in your *Cold Call*, you could just as easily turn the pause into an opportunity for students to write. The question about dystopian elements in *The Giver* is a good example: "I'm going to give you thirty seconds to write at least one complete sentence explaining how something intended to be utopian has turned out to be dystopian instead. Then I'll *Cold Call* a few of you to share what you wrote about." Or you could focus on discussion and make your thirty seconds a *Turn and Talk* (technique 43). "I'm going to give you thirty seconds to discuss with your partner how something intended to be utopian has turned out to be dystopian instead. Be ready to share what you or your partner said. I'll be *Cold Calling*."

I recently watched Amy Parsons of Leadership Prep Bedford Stuyvesant Middle Academy do this in her seventh-grade reading class. Students were reading *Of Mice and Men,* and Amy asked her students, "How does George react, and how do we see that he's conflicted? How do we see that he has at least two different reactions to this? I want to give you thirty seconds to reread pages 97 and 98" (a great example of predictable

Wait Time), advising them, "Skim through looking for how George is conflicted." After a full thirty seconds of think time, Amy said, "I want you to tell your partner what you found. Turn and talk." Coming out of it, Amy used a *Cold Call*, "We'll start with Roslyn and then we'll go to Jalen. What's one of the ways you thought George was conflicted?" The discussion made for more polished contributions to the discussion that followed. And the *Cold Call* at the end made sure that everyone made the most of the opportunity to reflect. It got the most out of all the teaching tools Amy used.

A final thought on Slow Call: as you ask the question on which you intend to *Cold Call,* you can use the pace and tone of your own voice to signal the level of rigor and reflection you want. Just by slowing down your own words and making your voice sound reflective, you can signal that you are anticipating students to engage your question with depth and consideration: "Hmmm. Very challenging thought. [pause] Let's all take a few seconds. Are there elements of Utopia here? [pause] What are they? [pause and then the *Cold Call*] David?"

Data-Driven and Data-Driving *Cold Call*

Only with *Cold Call* can teachers truly understand the state of mastery in their classroom. Champion teachers not only use *Cold Call* to gather data but also use data to decide whom, how, and when to *Cold Call.*

Consider, for example, Meaghan Reuler's lesson plan. When planning her lessons, Meaghan works with a copy of the packet she hands out to students each day, and uses the Comment function in Microsoft Word to make notes to herself. On the day in question, students were reading Christopher Paul Curtis's *The Watsons Go to Birmingham, 1963.* One of her comments read:

Shared Reading

Throughout lesson, add quotes and inferences to three-column chart on board.

Read p. 118

COLD CALL L: What contrast is shown in the dialogue between mom and dad?

Jot: note about Kenny's perspective of the news.

COLD CALL M: Why does he feel this way?

Underline what actions reveal that Byron has a different perspective.

COLD CALL H: What does this evidence reveal about Byron's perspective?

Jot: note about mom's perspective of the decision.

COLD CALL M: What specific evidence within the dialogue reveals that mom is fed up?

COLD CALL H: How does the author write to convey mom's feelings of frustration and irritation? BID [*Break It Down*]: What do you notice about the sentences?

Read p. 119

Turn and Talk: How is Momma's tone in this paragraph different from her earlier tone?

COLD CALL M: What evidence shows this?

COLD CALL H: Why did mom change her tone? What is she trying to do?

COLD CALL L: Repeat reason.

I am starting to notice some setting contrasts as well. Right after Momma says it's different from Flint, she begins listing the differences in Birmingham. Look back and see if you can number at least three differences.

You'll notice that Meaghan's planned eight *Cold Calls* and scripted the exact questions she intends to ask. You'll also notice that all of her questions are focused on the same skill—inferring a character's perspective and supporting with evidence. She's also planned to make sure she asks just the right *Cold Call* questions to ensure mastery of the most important skill. Finally, you'll notice her notations *L, M,* and *H.* This is her reminder to herself to choose a student whose mastery is likely to be on the low, medium, or high end, so that she can get the most predictive statistical sample of the room she possibly can.

When *Cold Call* is data driven, it is informed in intentional ways by data about student mastery. *Cold Call* is ideal for this duty because it's the tool that best allows a teacher to target any question to any student at any time. Thus it opens up a series of strategic choices about who, what, and when that wouldn't otherwise be available. For example, a teacher might use assessment data from a quiz, an *Exit Ticket,* or the previous night's homework to choose specific students to *Cold Call* the next day in class with specific questions based on their skill deficits, replacing the L, M, or H in Meaghan's lesson, for example, with the initials of a student who most needs to practice inferring character perspectives.

Or a teacher might identify a skill the whole class needs to work on (or a skill they'd mastered that she wanted to make sure they retained) and plan a round of fast *Cold Calling* into her lesson as a high-energy change of pace.

Or she might, as Troy Prep kindergarten teacher Jamie O'Brien did, make "Ask Me" stickers for her students. The stickers are individualized according to specific topics each student is working on (for example, "Ask me to skip-count by threes!"), and they allow adults anywhere in the building (the lunch room, the library, and so on) to ask kids to show off their skills in a positive way.

Finally, one of the most powerful forms of data-driven *Cold Call* is also one of the most straightforward, as one of the best principals I know, Hannah Solomon, recently reminded me. "Our teachers also definitely preread answers to a quick write or a *Do Now* question and then call on kids who they know will have different or interesting or useful answers to facilitate discussion." *Cold Call* is also ideal for gathering data; you can refer to the fuller discussion in Chapter One of how it can provide critical data on real-time student mastery.

Want More? Clip 34. Want more *Cold Call*? Check out Jon Bogard in clip 34.

34

CALL AND RESPONSE

Ask your class to answer questions in unison from time to time to build energetic, positive engagement.

The basic elements of **Call and Response** are a teacher asking a question and the whole class responding aloud in unison with the answer. Effectively used, *Call and Response* can be useful in engaging students and making lessons feel energetic and positive.

For such a simple technique, *Call and Response* can accomplish a lot:

- *Academic review and reinforcement.* Having students respond as a group ensures that everyone gets to give the answer. Of course, there are limitations to the kind of work that can be reinforced this way, but in some areas — reinforcing definitions or pronunciation of key vocabulary — it can have a powerful effect.

- *High-energy fun.* People like cheering in crowds and going to exercise classes because being part of a coordinated group can be energizing and exciting — loud, even. *Call and Response* can invigorate your class and make key moments boisterously fun.

- *Behavioral reinforcement.* There's a hidden benefit to *Call and Response*: students respond to a prompt as a group, exactly on cue, over and over again. Everyone sees everyone else doing just what the teacher asked, usually with spirit and happiness. You ask; they do — over and over again. Students don't see *Call and Response* as behavioral reinforcement, but it makes crisp, active, timely compliance a habit, committing it to muscle memory.

Five Types of *Call and Response*

Call and Response is a fairly straightforward technique, so it's easy to overemphasize its most simplistic forms: asking students to repeat aphorisms and chants, for example. In fact, there are five types of *Call and Response* sequences you can use, listed here roughly in order of intellectual rigor, from least to greatest:

1. *Repeat.* In these sequences, students repeat what their teacher has said or complete a familiar phrase that he or she starts. "Those who don't learn history are ... ? [doomed to repeat it!]"

2. *Report.* Students who complete problems or answer questions on their own are asked to report back. "On three, tell me your answer to problem number three."

3. *Reinforce.* Students repeat a key term or a strong answer from a peer. "Can anyone tell me what this part of the expression is called? Yes, Trayvon, that's the exponent. Class, what's this part of the expression called? [Exponent!]"

4. *Review.* Students answer multiple questions pertaining to a body of previously mastered information: "OK, let's review cell structure and organelles. You can use your diagrams if you wish. Now, tell me, these make proteins and can often be found floating in cytoplasm. One, two! [Ribosomes!] OK, and these are known as the cell's power producers. One, two! [Mitochondria!]." Being able to access knowledge quickly is what allows students to make unexpected connections.

5. *Solve.* The teacher asks students to solve a problem and call out the answer in unison. "Class, see if you can find 40 percent of eighty. Take five seconds to get it in your

head. One, two! [Twenty-four!]." The challenge in having a group of people solve a problem in real time and call out the answer is that there must be a single, clear answer and a strong likelihood that all students will know it.

In-Cues

To be effective in any form, *Call and Response* should be universal—that is, all students should respond. To ensure this is the case, use a specific signal, verbal ("Class!" "Everybody!" "One, two …") or nonverbal (for example, a finger point), to indicate that students should respond. Such a signal, called an *in-cue*, allows everyone to answer on cue, and lets you hold responses when you want to call on a student. This is critically important. Every student should know whether a question you've asked is

- Rhetorical: "Is forty-two divided by seven going to be five?"

- About to be directed to a single student: "Forty-two divided by seven is what, Shane?"

- Awaiting a volunteer: "Who can tell me what forty-two divided by seven is?"

- Asked in anticipation of full-class *Call and Response*: "Class, forty-two divided by seven is …"

If students don't know how to quickly and reliably differentiate your expectations, you will lose the ability to intentionally use any of these techniques at your sole discretion. Instead, it will fall to each member of the class to infer which type of question he or she thinks is (or would like to be) applicable. For students to participate enthusiastically in *Call and Response,* they must confidently know when to sing out without fear that they will be the only one singing. So use a reliable and consistent signal and make 100 percent participation the rule.

Because a good in-cue is important, it's worth spending a little more time on the topic. There are a number of specific kinds of in-cues I've seen champion teachers use.

Count-Based In-Cues

Count-based in-cues are highly effective in that they can be cut short if students are not fully attentive or on task in the lead-up to the *Call and Response*. In other words, a count of "One two, ready, you!" can occasionally be cut off by the teacher ("One two … no, I don't have everyone") to show students they're not ready while still maintaining the anticipation of the fun that's to come. You can also speed up your counts or slow them down as necessary to set the pace you desire.

Group Prompt

Using a collective term for the whole class helps foster group identity, and these prompts remind students of your expectation. Saying "Everybody" or "Class" reminds students that you expect universal participation and, should you fail to get it, allows you to repeat the sequence by merely repeating the word with slightly greater emphasis: "*Every*body."

Nonverbal Gesture

A third kind of in-cue is a nonverbal gesture: a point, a hand dropped from shoulder height, a looping motion with the finger. These have the advantage of speed and don't require you to interrupt the flow of the lesson. They can also be challenging, in that the tone has to be just right or they can seem schoolmarmish.

Shift in Tone and Volume

A fourth kind of in-cue employs a shift in tone and volume. The teacher increases volume in the last few words of a sentence and inflects her tone to imply a question; students recognize this as a prompt and respond crisply. This is the most efficient form of *Call and Response*; in the long run, it's often the easiest to use—it's seamless, fast, and natural—but in the short run, it's the hardest to learn to do well. If you don't feel immediately confident and comfortable with *Call and Response,* consider beginning, as many teachers do, by mastering a simpler cue.

Call and Response 2.0

Over the past few years, my team and I have observed teachers using *Call and Response* in a variety of new ways and settings. Here are four especially effective ways to adapt and apply this technique.

Stretching the Response

Let's say you're a third-grade science teacher doing a lesson on states of matter. You want your students to remember key concepts such as "a solid always keeps its shape," so you do some *Call and Response* to help them remember those key points. It might sound like this:

"A solid always keeps its … [students via *Call and Response*: shape!]"

Remembering that "shape" doesn't provide much context, you'd do better to stretch the response out a little and add a little more verbiage each time—for example:

- A solid always keeps its … [shape!]
- Good, scholars. A solid … [always keeps its shape!]

- Good. Can you give me the whole thing, scholars? A … [solid always keeps its shape!]

- Good. What does a solid always do? [It keeps its shape!]

A related way to make *Call and Response* more rigorous is to add greater complexity to the response phrase, especially in terms of vocabulary and syntax. I recently watched an outstanding kindergarten teacher. Her little ones were learning to read bar graphs. She used *Call and Response* to help reinforce the definition of *data*. "Another word for data is?" she asked, the class calling "information" in response. The kids responded on cue, crisply and with great energy. They were engaged and focused. They knew that another word for data was information.

It's worth asking, though, about the accuracy and rigor of the definition. Was "information" really another word for data? And could kindergarteners master a more rigorous multiword definition? Could they remember that data is "information expressed in numbers," for example? Although I realize there can be nonnumerical data, this is kindergarten, and that's not the point. The point is, her students would have a better definition of data, as well as familiarity with and repeated experience using more advanced forms of language.

Consider *tragedy,* for example, a term chronically misused. It is forever showing up in news stories being treated as synonymous with really, really sad. But the technical definition of tragedy is specifically when someone great (or in some parts great) is brought down through his or her own flaws, especially excessive pride or hubris. Imagine the power of your ninth graders memorizing a definition for *tragedy*:

Teacher: *Tragedy,* class?
Class: The downfall of a hero by virtue of a fatal flaw, especially hubris!

In addition to knowing a really good definition of tragedy, the class would, after five or ten iterations spread across a week or so, have the words *downfall, fatal flaw,* and *hubris* forever in their useful vocabulary, not to mention familiarity with the phrase *by virtue of.* Now think of all the rigorous definitions, packed with advanced syntax and vocabulary, you could help students enter into their permanent vocabulary.

Call and Response with Vocabulary

Call and Response is also an outstanding tool for teaching and reinforcing vocabulary. It can help students to develop familiarity with words by using them and to grow comfortable with their pronunciation. When students are more comfortable saying a word, they are both more likely to use it and more likely to attend to it while reading.

If you wanted to use *Call and Response* to practice vocabulary words, you might adapt it to put particular emphasis on pronunciation—slowing down, enunciating carefully, even drawing students' attention to your mouth so that they can see how you vocalize a word. "E-PIFF-uh-nee" you might say slowly before asking students to respond several times with similarly careful enunciation.

Then, when you provided a definition, you might use another adaptation, a *Call and Response* reverse. "An epiphany is a sudden realization." You might then call "Epiphany," to which students would respond, "a sudden realization," after which you might reverse the two, calling "sudden realization" and having students respond "epiphany." This would cause students to practice both the definition and the word's pronunciation. You could drop this in very quickly—just after encountering a vocabulary word in your reading, say—to cause students to attend to it and remember it better with just a few seconds' investment.

Call and Response with Reading

In a recent lesson, Eric Snider of Brooklyn was reading an article describing the characteristics of science fiction with his students. He began reading aloud with the expectation that his students would follow along, reading on their own at their seats. But of course Eric did not want to just assume that his students were reading along with him; he wanted to check. To do so, he used a "*Call and Response* spot check."

"Some key facts to be mindful of," he began, reading, "Most science fiction writers create believable …" The next word was "worlds," but Eric didn't read it aloud. Instead he signaled to his students, most of whom chimed in "worlds!" This demonstrated that they were indeed following along. Eric, however, was concerned. "That was about 80 percent [of us]," he noted, walking to the overhead projector on which he was displaying the text. "We are right here," he continued, pointing to the place in the text where he was reading. He then began again. "Most science fiction writers create believable worlds with familiar elements," he read, continuing past the point of the original spot check. "Science fiction often contains advanced …" Here he signaled again, whereupon all of his students chimed in: "technologies." Having used *Call and Response* to check, he pushed forward, knowing that all students were reading with him.

Call and Response Culture Building

One of my favorite uses for *Call and Response* is to reinforce a great answer from a student. I've often observed Troy Prep's David Javsicas using this to excellent effect. When a student makes a great insight about a book the class is reading—for example, observing that in a particular passage, Holden Caulfield's behavior is "self-absorbed"—David might pause and then say, "Interesting. Micah says that Holden is what?" To which the whole class would respond, "self-absorbed!" David would then follow up in some manner, perhaps saying, "Well, do you agree?" with the brief punctuation of the remark showing the student that David thought her idea was important enough to ask the whole class to repeat it. Plus, his actions ensured that everybody heard and attended to the worthwhile comment he wished to discuss further. Because insights such as Micah's often contain strong vocabulary, David's approach is also a great way to reinforce strong usage.

Want More? Clip 35 and Clip 36. Want more *Call and Response*? Check out Janelle Austin in clip 35 and Jennifer Trapp in clip 36.

BREAK IT DOWN

When a student makes an error, provide just enough help to allow her to "solve" as much of the original problem as she can.

Break It Down is a powerful teaching tool, but it can be difficult to use because it is primarily a reactive strategy. You use it at one of the most challenging moments in teaching: immediately after an incorrect or insufficient answer.

How to respond effectively and efficiently to wrong answers is one of teaching's ongoing challenges. Just repeating the question isn't likely to help, but what do you do instead? Many teachers, on hearing a wrong answer, seek to *Break It Down*. Their goal is to ask a question or present new information that will help the student answer correctly while still doing as much of the thinking as possible. In simplest terms, they want to provide the smallest viable hint, helping the student use what he or she *does* know to get the correct answer.

Smallest Viable Hint

A teacher never really knows what knowledge a given student has, nor exactly how big the gap is between what the student knows and what he needs to know to succeed. Because the ideal is to cause a student to apply what he knows to the greatest degree possible, it's often best to try to provide the smallest (successful) hint possible.

Providing a minimal hint gets at the tension in *Break It Down*. Whereas one goal is to break things down to the least degree possible, another is to do it quickly, thus managing time and pace. Meticulously adding a thin slice of knowledge to each previous hint would be the perfect means of causing students to do the greatest amount of cognitive work, but would likely derail instruction in a series of exercises that destroyed your pacing and led to rapid frustration on your students' part. Sometimes, in the face of a wrong answer, you'll have to move on to something else. So while your long-term goal is to maximize the cognitive work students do and battle their fear that perhaps they can't, you'll also have to balance those long-term goals with practical short-term realities. The good news is that the more you use *Break it Down*, the better (and faster) your students will get at their half of the equation.

Given the importance of striking a balance, it's worth thinking about some of the different ways that information can be broken down, even in the case of a simple example like a student struggling to read the word *nature*, and what effect they might have. Merely rewriting the word on the board, for example, a very minimal hint, might prove effective. Whispering to the student "long *a*" would be a bigger hint, but would still provide a rule the student could apply. Starting the word for the student ("Nay … ") would do much more of the cognitive work, but would be more likely to yield instant success. I illustrate this challenge in "How *Break It Down* Works."

How *Break It Down* Works

You are reading *White Fang* and ask, "Where is the story set?"

A student replies, "In the North." This is not sufficient to be considered correct, so you must use your follow-up questions to bridge the gap.

Your first goal is to get the student to the correct answer.

Your second goal is to keep your *Break It Down* rigorous by providing the smallest viable cue.

Take a look at the figure on the next page. If you can provide a cue like A that makes the student fill in most of the gap, your classroom will be more rigorous than if you use a cue like C. Both are more challenging than D, which solves the problem without any *Break It Down* (by giving the answer or having another student give the answer). Again, you want the smallest cue that will work in consideration of pacing, timing, rigor, and so on.

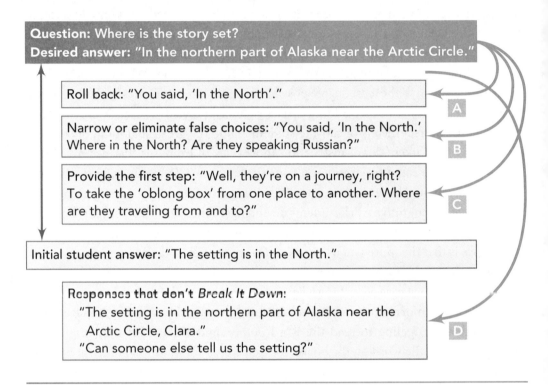

Question: Where is the story set?
Desired answer: "In the northern part of Alaska near the Arctic Circle."

Roll back: "You said, 'In the North'." ⟶ A

Narrow or eliminate false choices: "You said, 'In the North.' Where in the North? Are they speaking Russian?" ⟶ B

Provide the first step: "Well, they're on a journey, right? To take the 'oblong box' from one place to another. Where are they traveling from and to?" ⟶ C

Initial student answer: "The setting is in the North."

Responses that don't *Break It Down*:
"The setting is in the northern part of Alaska near the Arctic Circle, Clara."
"Can someone else tell us the setting?" ⟶ D

Planning for *Break It Down*

Break It Down is a complex and challenging technique. You're seeking to assess the gap between what the student knows and mastery, but you're guessing at what he or she really knows, as a wrong answer often reveals less knowledge than a student actually has.

You prepare for *Break It Down* by regularly doing a bit of it before class begins. For example, you might identify potential trouble spots in an upcoming lesson—the places where you think errors are likely to emerge. Then perhaps draft some wrong answers you think you might get. And then, most important, you draft a couple of hints you might use if those errors occur. You might use a template like the one on the next page.

Before you hyperventilate—"Is he kidding? I've got five classes a day and three preps and usually 150 papers to grade, and I just lost my planning period. And now I'm supposed to do *this??*"—this sort of thing is to me a planning *exercise*. If you can do it regularly, fantastic, but if you do it only occasionally, it can still help you. Whether you are right or wrong in the errors you predict and the resulting hints, you will get better

Break It Down Planning for [Date]

Question:			
Wrong Answer #1		Wrong Answer #2	
BID Hint #1	BID Hint #2	BID Hint #1	BID Hint #2

and better at anticipating the kinds of things that students get wrong and the responses that help. You do an exercise like this, in other words, as part of a long-term investment in your own understanding.

As you plan to *Break It Down*—or even when you use the technique without planning—there are benefits to building your "range," the types of prompts you're comfortable using. We all tend to be creatures of habit; over time, our hints become predictable. Using a variety of ways to offer hints to students can help you connect with more kinds of thinkers, as well as provide a wider and more flexible array of help.

Provide an Example

If you got a blank stare when you asked for the definition of a prime number, you might say, "Seven is one" or "Seven is one, and so is eleven." If you wanted to *Break It Down* further, you could cue: "Seven is one, but eight is not." You could then potentially take it a step further by observing, "Eight's factors include two and four." You can also provide additional examples if the question stumping the student was originally based on a category. For example, a student in Jaimie Brillante's fifth-grade writing class struggled to identify the part of speech of the word *owner*. Jaimie cued: "Well, *owner* would logically be the same part of speech as other words that end in *-er. Dancer, swimmer, singer.* What are those?" she asked. "They're people," the student replied. Jaimie prompted, "And people have to be ... ," as the student chimed in, "Nouns!"

Provide Context

Another student in Jaimie Brillante's class was stumped when asked to name the part of speech of the word *ancient*. "I hope nobody ever calls *me* ancient," cued Jaimie. Nothing. "Maybe in, like 2080, you could call me ancient, but that would be the only time it was acceptable." "Oh yeah, it's very old," the student successfully recalled. It's important to note that Jaimie is using this approach with a vocabulary word she knows the student learned but is having trouble remembering. This strategy would be far less effective if Jaimie did not know whether the student knew anything at all about the word.

Provide a Rule

In Christy Huelskamp's sixth-grade reading class at Williamsburg Collegiate in Brooklyn, a student guessed incorrectly that *indiscriminate* was a verb when used in the sentence, "James was an indiscriminate reader; he would pick up any book from the library and read it cover to cover." Christy replied with a rule: "A verb is an action or a state of being. Is 'indiscriminate' an action?" The student quickly recognized that it was modifying a noun. "It's an adjective," she said.

Provide the Missing (or First) Step

When a student in her fifth-grade math class was unable to explain what was wrong with writing the number fifteen sixths, Kelli Ragin cued: "Well, what do we always do when the numerator is larger than the denominator?" Instantly the student caught on. "Oh, we need to make a mixed number. So I divide six into fifteen."

Roll Back

Sometimes it's sufficient to repeat a student's answer back to him or her. Many of us instantly recognize our errors when they're played back for us, as if on tape. If a student in Kelli Ragin's class had proposed reducing an improper fraction to a mixed number by multiplying the numerator and denominator, Kelli might merely repeat that back to her: "You said that I would multiply six times fifteen to reduce." The degree of emphasis she places on the word *multiply* would be key in determining how much of the gap between answer and mastery Kelli was breaking down. (Emphasis on *multiply* makes the hint much bigger.) Regardless, hearing your own error in another's words is often revealing.

Eliminate False Choices

When Jaimie Brillante's student struggled to recognize that *owner* was a noun, Jaimie could have eliminated some false choices as follows: "Well, let's go through some of the options. If it were a verb, it would be an action. Can you or I owner? Well, what about an adjective? Is it telling me what kind or how many of some noun?"

Fighting Rigor Collapse

Watching video recently with the Uncommon Schools Teach Like a Champion Team, my colleague John Costello coined a useful term, *rigor collapse*. It refers to what happens when you ask a hard question that kids can't answer and you progressively *Break It Down* until the big question is a little question, but one that now lacks the rigor of the original.

Scaling down the question gradually and cautiously so that students do as much of the cognitive work as they are capable of is generally a good thing, but the question is, how do you achieve that outcome without having a class consisting of simple, or even simplistic, questions?

Our discussion arose from a video of a sixth-grade reading classroom. The class was reading *The Outsiders,* and the teacher had asked students about the following exchange between Cherry, a "Soc" (that is, someone in a higher socioeconomic class) and Pony Boy, a "Greaser" (of a lower socioeconomic class):

> "You read a lot, don't you Pony Boy?" Cherry asked.
> I was startled. "Yeah. Why?"
> She kind of shrugged. "I could just tell. I'll bet you watch sunsets, too.
> I used to watch sunsets, before I got so busy. I miss it."

The teacher asked what Cherry meant by "before I got so busy." Cherry was the sort of person who was likely "busy" doing things like schoolwork and after-school activities, the sorts of things on her side of the class divide, whereas Pony Boy was not. They could have been kindred spirits—watchers of sunsets—but class and caste expectations (at least partly) put them in different places.

The kids didn't get this. When asked, students postulated that the sorts of things Cherry was doing included "going shopping and hanging out with friends." Because hanging out with friends was what Pony Boy would do, the teacher tried to break the complexity down a bit. "Can anyone connect this to the phrase, 'the rat race'?" (They had discussed earlier Pony Boy's use of the term to disparage trying to succeed and cross the class divide.) Again students struggled to make the connection. So the teacher tried to break down the misunderstanding even further, trying to get the students to recognize the differences in how the two characters spent their time. Who was more likely to take music lessons? she asked. Cherry or Pony Boy? Why? Pony Boy didn't have parents to supervise him. If this was one sort of thing she might be doing when she was "busy," what were some others?

The good news is that the teacher uncovered and addressed the fundamental misunderstanding among her class, but the result was also that a rigorous, metaphorical conversation with implications about socioeconomic class had been replaced by a literal one. The sequence ended with a small and narrow inference about who was more likely to take music lessons and never got back to implications about character or class: rigor collapse.

Break It Down is better if, after necessarily winnowing the questions, teachers end the sequence by going broad again to make sense of the answer students gave. In the *Outsiders* example, imagine the teacher saying something like, "Good; now connect that to one of the themes we've discussed from the book," or "Good; now connect that to our essential question, 'How does class affect most people's lives in ways they don't see?'"

If *Breaking It Down* takes a broad question and narrows it—imagine the bottom of a wine glass, tapering at its stem to a tiny point—the last move in the sequence should be like the base of the wine glass: a sudden rewidening to connect the narrow to a broader point.

PEPPER

Use *Pepper* as a fast-paced, vocal review to build energy and actively engage your class.

For decades, baseball players have warmed up for games and practices by playing a game called Pepper. In a group of four or five players, one holds a bat, and the rest stand in a ring in front of the batter, a few yards away, gloves at the ready. One player tosses the ball to the batter. Without stopping to catch it, the batter taps it back; the nearest player fields it and, again without stopping, tosses it back to the batter, who hits the toss back to another player. The game is fast, providing dozens of opportunities to practice fielding and hitting skills in a short period of time, in a fast-paced and energetic environment. It doesn't propose to teach new skills or game strategy, and it picks up the energy level before a game, so players tend to love it.

Pepper, the teaching technique by the same name, also uses fast-paced, group-oriented activities to review familiar information and foundational skills. A teacher tosses questions to a group of students quickly, and they answer back. The teacher usually does not slow down to engage or discuss an answer; if it's right, she simply asks another student a new question. If it's wrong, she asks the same question of another student (though sometimes the same student), and always keeps moving. That's *Pepper*: a fast-paced, unpredictable review of fundamentals with lots of chances for participation in rapid succession.

Pepper is a great warm-up activity. Many teachers include it as part of a daily oral drill at the outset of class. It is also effective as an upbeat interlude to change the pace and bring energy to the class. It's perfect for wrapping up a lesson or filling in a stray ten minutes inside or outside the classroom with productive, engaging fun. Because *Pepper* is sometimes confused with *Cold Call*, let's look at some of the ways *Pepper* is different.

First, although *Pepper* often involves *Cold Call*, it doesn't have to. With *Pepper*, you can take hands if you prefer, calling on volunteers quickly and energetically. Most typically, I see the game start out with *Cold Call*, but transition into a version of *Pepper* that involves almost all students volunteering.

Second, *Pepper* almost always asks quick fundamental questions, often as review. This is different from *Cold Call*, which can involve questions of any type at any level. You'd be fine *Cold Calling* a student to discuss the primary causes of the Civil War, but less likely to cover that material in a game of *Pepper*. Because *Pepper* is often a means for review, teachers move from unit to unit within the game. They'll ask questions about properties of quadrilaterals for two or three minutes and then move on to a series of questions about coordinate geometry. They often do this even if the topics are not entirely related. In a social studies class, you could spend a few minutes on map skills followed by a few minutes on the original colonies.

Third, *Pepper* is a game. Thus classroom *Pepper* uses indicators that underscore for your class that they are playing a game. In some cases, this might mean that you ask all students to stand up, or you might call on students in a unique way—something you might not do outside the game. In *Pepper*, time is compressed, and the game has a clear beginning and end.

Lastly, a trademark of *Pepper* is its unpredictability: where each question goes, nobody knows. Many teachers take this a step further and use devices to engineer the randomization, most frequently using Popsicle sticks labeled with each student's name pulled at random out of a can, for example, but also including other variations, such as random number generation on a laptop. In such a system, teachers are in most cases relying on apparently random assignment of participation—but it doesn't have to actually be random. Only you know whose name is really on a Popsicle stick or a sheet of paper when you pick it, so you can easily pick John's stick but call out Susan's name if you so choose.

Want More? Clip 37.   Want more *Pepper*? Check out Art Worrell in clip 37.

CONCLUSION

If one of the goals of teaching is to cause students to carry more and more of the classroom's cognitive load, questioning is a critical tool in that process. But it is by no means the only way to increase ratio. In Chapter Eight, we'll look at the ways in which rigorous writing can cause students to do more of the most rigorous kinds of thinking that occur in classrooms.

Reflection and Practice

1. Many of the teachers I work with think that of all the techniques in this book, *Cold Call* is the one with the greatest and fastest capacity to shift the culture of their classroom. Why do you think they feel so strongly about it?

2. Take a lesson plan for a class you're getting ready to teach, and mark it up by identifying three places where it would be beneficial to use *Cold Call*. Script your questions and write them into your lesson plan. Make some notes about which students you'll *Cold Call*.

3. Take that same lesson plan and mark it up to add two short sessions of *Call and Response*. Again, script your questions. Try to ask questions at all five levels, and note the in-cue you'll use.

4. Make a short list of what you want your students to do or think about when you use *Wait Time*. Write yourself two or three five-second scripts that you can practice and use while teaching to reinforce effective academic behaviors and discipline yourself to wait.

USEFUL TOOLS   **FIND THESE TOOLS AT WWW.TEACHLIKEACHAMPION.COM/YOURLIBRARY**

Sharpen-up phrases for *Call and Response*. Draw from this bank of phrases the next time you need to prompt students to "sharpen up" a *Call and Response* that doesn't go as planned.

***Wait Time*: handy solutions for the challenges of self-discipline.** Use these twenty narrative phrases to build momentum and get more students to do the work during your *Wait Time*.

Making _Wait Time_ work in your classroom requires two types of self-discipline. First, there's _teacher_ self-discipline. You _know_ you're supposed to wait a few seconds before you take an answer, but it's hard. Your mind is on a thousand things, so it's difficult to remember. And even when you do, you're often down to ten minutes and have a lot of ground to cover before the end of class. You think you're waiting, but under time pressure what feels slow is actually fast. Here are a few practical actions that teachers have told us they take to discipline themselves to slow down:

- <u>Pick a spot.</u> Choose a sunny patch by the windows on the other side of the room. Make yourself walk there slowly before you take an answer.
- <u>Choose a daily number.</u> Pick a number between five and ten and count to that number after every question during a given lesson. Having a distinctive number for that lesson may help you remember.
- <u>Silently answer.</u> In your head, say what an ideal student's answer would be. Not only does this slow you down, but a quick review of what you're shooting for helps you hold out for an "all the way right" answer.
- <u>Punctuate with a smile.</u> Scan the room, smile warmly, and scan back the other way. The smile communicates your calm and intentionality to your students, and this can make you feel more confident in waiting.
- <u>Run an internal narration.</u> "Narrating hands" is useful for disciplining yourself. If you want to make sure to give real think time, you could practice narrating hands silently to yourself.
- <u>Perform the slow repeat.</u> Repeat your question, very slowly, either quietly aloud or just to yourself.
- <u>Call your shot.</u> Hold yourself accountable by saying it aloud—something like, "I'm going to take an answer in eight seconds, but not before."

Students also struggle with self-discipline. Their hands shoot up in the first second of _Wait Time_ and wave in the air when they're supposed to be thinking. Or you say, "I want you to go back to the text," but their hands are up anyway. Sometimes their hands are up even before you've finished asking the question!

- <u>Hands down.</u> If students' hands are down, they're more likely to keep thinking. Wave them off with a hands-down gesture, or gently say, "No hands yet."
- <u>"It's not that easy."</u> Use language to remind students that if they aren't using the time you provide, they're probably not thinking rigorously enough. "I'm confident that this is a question that will take you more than a second to think through. Take your time."

- Set a challenge. Give students "additional" tasks during think time. "If you've got a piece of evidence to cite, go back now and see if you can find at least one more. I want you to find several."
- Offer an incentive. Kids often put their hands up quickly because they especially want to be called on. Turn the tables on them by saying, "I'm going to call on someone who seems like they've really taken their time."
- Forewarn. Be transparent. "The question I am about to ask requires reflection. I don't want to see any hands until I give you the signal."

Chapter 8

Building Ratio Through Writing

Technique 37: Everybody Writes.   Prepare your students to engage rigorously by giving them the chance to reflect in writing before you ask them to discuss.

Technique 38: Art of the Sentence.   Ask students to synthesize a complex idea in a single, well-crafted sentence. The discipline of having to make one sentence do all the work pushes students to use new syntactical forms.

Technique 39: Show Call.   Create a strong incentive to complete writing with quality and thoughtfulness by publicly showcasing and revising student writing—regardless of who volunteers to share.

Technique 40: Build Stamina.   Gradually increase writing time to develop in your students the habit of writing productively, and the ability to do it for sustained periods of time.

Technique 41: Front the Writing.   Arrange lessons so that writing comes earlier in the process to ensure that students think rigorously in writing.

Building Ratio Through Writing

The amount and quality of writing students do in your classroom are two of the most important determinants of their academic success. Quite possibly, they are together the single most important thing, so one of the simplest and most powerful shifts you can make is to increase the amount of writing—especially high-quality writing—your students do. Why ask, "Who can tell me what Jonas has just realized about what it means to be *released*?" and have one or two students answer, when you could say, "Please tell me what Jonas has just realized about what it means to be *released*. One minute to write your best thoughts in your notes packet. Go!" and have every student answer and every student battle to frame the thought in precise syntax? In fact, the informal definition of a sentence that teachers often use is "a complete thought." By having students write more, we cause them to push their ideas from vague notion (developing idea) to complete thought, and to practice developing complete thoughts is to practice perhaps the core task of thinking.

Increasing the amount of writing in your class raises important questions, however, from the practical (How do I know they're using their writing time well? How do I make them actually write?) to the philosophical (Where in the sequence of learning is writing most valuable? How can I build a process-oriented culture of revision into my writing?). For that reason, using intentional approaches to writing is a critical topic for any teacher to think about. This chapter looks at techniques that can help you use writing for maximum effect on both participation ratio and think ratio.

EVERYBODY WRITES

Prepare your students to engage rigorously by giving them the chance to reflect in writing before you ask them to discuss.

I once watched a rigorous tenth-grade reading lesson at the highly successful Boston Collegiate High School. The teacher led her students through a discussion of Tim O'Brien's narratively complex short story, "The Man I Killed," from his book *The Things They Carried*. In the story, the narrator describes his inability to talk to others about killing an enemy combatant during the Vietnam War. In one of the culminating moments of the lesson, the teacher asked students, "Why would someone write a story about not being able to talk about what he did, and in so doing, talk about it? Why would he talk about not being able to talk about something?"

I was struck by two things: first, by how lucky the students were to be in a classroom with a teacher who asked rigorous and challenging questions about a demanding text; second, by the students' response, which was silence. They looked somewhat blankly at the teacher, and she, in the end, stepped in and gave them a very nice summary of what a college prep answer might sound like. It was a useful analysis, but the ratio was low. The purpose had been to hold a discussion, yet said discussion never emerged. Why?

Watching the students as they struggled, I thought about the paradox of their earnest confusion. No one looked bored or glanced longingly out the window. They wanted to answer, some of them craning forward as if to await some insight. Then they averted their eyes in hopes that the teacher wouldn't call on them. It was a watershed moment: the teacher asked exactly the kind of question that pushes students beyond their current conception of literature, the kind of question that exemplified true college preparatory expectations, the kind of question every teacher should ask, and she was rewarded with a great silence descending.

Was there any way around such a paradox? I asked myself what it would take for me to have been able to answer the question. Probably I would have needed a minute to think and, more important, to write down my thoughts and wrestle them into words. Perhaps a *Turn and Talk* (technique 43) would have helped, but, more likely, a question like this would take some silence, some reflection, some hashing out ideas in private. With time to reflect in writing, I'd have the best chance of being ready to participate—ideally, at some level of depth—because my ideas would be better and I would be more confident in them. Having written down my ideas, I'd be better able to listen to my peers in subsequent discussion and build off of their thinking.

Like Joan Didion, I often have to write to know what I think. In college, writing papers articulating the limits of my understanding, I sometimes did not truly grasp what I was trying to say until I had fought the idea into sentences, there on the page staring back at me in all their clarity or lack thereof. Only when the paper was written would my ideas have coalesced into coherent form. This makes me wonder how much better my participation in discussions might have been if they had come *after* I wrote the paper, a fact I recognized when one of my professors required us to write a short written reflection as our entry ticket to each class. In that class, everybody wrote first, and the conversation started where it ended in other classes. Another professor described a "notion" as a beginning thought, something two steps shy of an idea. Like many other students, I spent a lot of time talking about notions in college. I'd argue that it's in the writing that something like ideas—clear conceptions, coherently described—begin to emerge.

One way to make writing effective in your classroom, then, is to use it before discussions to give students the benefit of more writing, to foster a more rigorous discussion, and to help them answer questions—such as the one about Tim O'Brien's story—that stretch them to their limits. This is the rationale behind **Everybody Writes**, a technique in which teachers ask all students to prepare for more ambitious thinking and discussion by reflecting in writing for a short interval.

Ironically, our actions as teachers often tacitly assume that the first idea generated or the first student to raise a hand will yield the most productive discussion. When we ask a question and call on a student whose hand goes up within two or three seconds, what we get is the first and fastest answer, not necessarily the best or most thoughtful. Some students require time to generate worthy ideas or to feel confident enough in their ideas to share them. One benefit of *Everybody Writes*, then, is that ideas get better when students are allowed a few moments of reflection, and this is the case even (or especially) for those students whose hands tend to shoot up first. Allowing students time to write before you ask them to discuss builds participation ratio and think ratio, enabling all students — slow, reflective types included — to participate, and pushing students toward more rigorous thinking.

Here are some other benefits of *Everybody Writes*:

- Because you can review student ideas in advance by reading over shoulders, you're able to select effective responses to begin your discussion. Nikki Bridges, the principal at Leadership Prep Ocean Hill, calls this "Hunt and Gather." In a note to her teachers, she offered this simple and useful guidance: "Circulate and look for three scholars who have exemplary responses. Put a star on their papers. These are the scholars who will share during the closing."

- Every idea that gets shared in discussion is in effect a second draft, a 2.0 thought of higher quality than what would otherwise be shared off the top of a student's mind.

- It allows you to *Cold Call* students simply and naturally, because you know that everyone is prepared with thoughts. You can simply ask, "What did you write about, Ariel?" to kick things off.

- It enables you to give every student, not just those who can get their hands up fast, the chance to be part of the conversation.

- Processing thoughts in writing refines them, challenging students intellectually, engaging them, and improving the quality of their ideas and their writing.

- You set standards or steer students in a direction you think especially fruitful. For example, you could advise them to write a sentence defining the vocabulary word *imperceptible* and ask them to ensure that their sentence makes it clear that *imperceptible* is different from *invisible*. Or you could ask students to describe what the Capulets think of the Montagues in *Romeo and Juliet* and then push them to understand the intensity of the hatred by asking them to write their answer in the words a member of the family would use.

- Students remember significantly more of what they are learning if they write it down.

With all these advantages to writing, it's worth looking for every opportunity to have your students write before you discuss — or at least before key discussions — not just to improve the quality of those conversations but to improve the quality of student writing. More and more writing, especially writing with a distinct and immediate purpose—using writing to engage your peers just a minute or two afterwards, and being successful at doing that (feeling you have something to say, coming off feeling smart)—is a great positive reinforcement for students who may not understand the "why" behind writing. It helps them, and they see the benefit immediately; therefore, they like it and want to do more of it.

A final thought: the more you use writing, the better (and more efficient) your students get at using it. The first time you try it, it may take students a bit of time to get started; the quality may be only so-so. But by the time they are answering reflection prompt number 87, as Jessica Bracey's students at North Star Academy were in a recent lesson (which you can see on clip 23), they will be very good and very efficient at it. Practicing something important eighty-six times will have that effect. This was certainly evident in Jessica's class: not only was the postwriting discussion of high quality, but it began with almost every hand shooting into the air. Some students' energy in raising their hands nearly lifted their desks off the ground.

ART OF THE SENTENCE

Ask students to synthesize a complex idea in a single, well-crafted sentence. The discipline of having to make one sentence do all the work pushes students to use new syntactical forms.

38

When we teach writing, we spend significant time on vocabulary and word choice. We spend even more on paragraph formation: "Write a topic sentence, with three supporting sentences and a transition to link one paragraph to the next." But the sentences within the paragraphs our students write aren't always what they could be. They often rely on a simple, repetitious format, and take on a wooden quality that strains to capture complex ideas: "I think X. I think Y. I think Z."

Consider the difference between a mundane sequence of sentences such as "Jonas thinks A. Jonas tries to do B. Jonas says C" and something like this: "Bothered by thoughts of A, Jonas tries to do B, hiding his plans to do C from his parents." There aren't any fancy words in the latter sentence. What it has going for it is adept use of grammatical forms. Including a subordinate clause starting with the phrase "bothered by" and a participial phrase, it connects a series of thoughts, expressing the complexity of their relationship to one another in nuanced syntactical structures—and it does so in a single sentence. Learning to write sentences like that is learning not only to write effectively but also to develop and refine ideas by expressing their relationships through the structures of language. It is the key to great paragraphs and great essays, and is arguably far more central to rigorous writing (and thinking) than the admonition to have three sentences with supporting details from the text. One definition of a sentence, I noted previously, is "a complete thought," and helping students learn how to write increasingly complex, subtle, and nuanced sentences is teaching them to develop increasingly complex, subtle, and nuanced thoughts.

To use **Art of the Sentence**, then, you ask students to synthesize a complex idea, summarize a reading, or distill a discussion in a *single, well-crafted sentence*. Just one. The discipline of having to make one sentence do all the work pushes students to use new grammatical forms. It teaches the art not just of writing but of *sentence writing*, which is the (often missing) foundation of written expression. Asked to write (and ideally revise!) just one sentence, students can't rely on facile iterations of "I think B" and "I think C" to get an idea across. With the crutch of limitless space and time removed, they are forced by scarcity to push their writing, to let necessity give birth to invention.

Sentence Starters and Sentence Parameters

It's worth taking a moment to think about how students are likely to progress from writing "Jonas thinks A. Jonas thinks B" to writing "Bothered by thoughts of A, Jonas tries to do B," and so forth. After all, more practice writing simple wooden sentences will only get students better at writing simple wooden sentences. To use *Art of the Sentence* to maximum effect, then, you may find it powerful to use a rich variety of "sentence starters." Consider the difference between these two *Art of the Sentence* prompts from a science class:

- Summarize the data from this graph in one complete, well-written sentence.
- Summarize the data from this graph in one complete well-written sentence that begins with the phrase "Over time … "

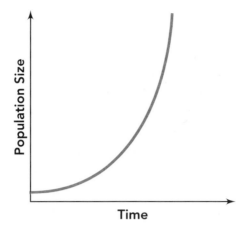

At first glance, the second prompt may appear to be easier to respond to because it contains scaffolding, but in many ways the opposite is true. The second sentence causes students to practice using a new (and useful) phrase that pushes them into new syntactical territory, territory they now have to write their way out of. Without being pushed and stretched in such ways, students aren't likely to expand their repertoire of syntactical forms very much. Now, imagine the different sorts of phrases with which you could ask students to begin a sentence:

- "Growing exponentially, … "
- "Not just increasing, but … "
- "The curve that expresses the function … "
- "The relationship between … "
- "In the long run, … "
- "When the line approaches vertical, … "

Each of these has a different effect on student writing and thinking, pushing them not only into new syntax but potentially into new thinking.

Another approach champion teachers use to guide the sentences their students write is *sentence parameters*. These range from asking students to use a specific word or phrase ("Be sure to use the phrase 'stock character' in your answer") to causing them to yoke together multiple ideas ("Explain in one well-crafted sentence what Swift says we should do with children *and* how you know he is being satiric"). Depending on what you teach, you might choose specific prompts to emphasize aspects of thinking in your discipline:

"Looking beneath the surface" for an art teacher; "Using the word *ambiguous*" for an English teacher; "To test this hypothesis" in science. Alternatively, naming a specific grammatical form to use can make writing instruction more applied and useful: "Write a sentence using a subordinate clause with the word *despite*," "Write a sentence beginning with a participial phrase," or, to familiarize students with a mode of academic discourse, "Use the second person or the pronoun *one,* as in 'One notices.'"

Not surprisingly, sentence starters or parameters work best when employed in a coordinated and systematic way, progressively over a period of several months to develop student writing and thinking. Troy Prep seventh-grade reading teacher David Javsicas set out to do this, with a goal of working toward more complex and challenging sentence-writing exercises over time. What follows are some examples of how David did that. The first few come from his class's reading of *Lord of the Flies*. David is concentrating on incrementally building up students' conception of what a good sentence looks like and how it works. He doesn't throw students into the deep end, but builds up to mastery step-by-step over the course of several months. By the end, he is pushing students to include multiple complex ideas in their sentences.

January 3

How did Ralph's actions lead to a "violent swing"? What did he do, and what was the effect of his actions? Use the following format:

Because Ralph _____, _____.

Ralph's action(s) – cause main effect(s) of Ralph's action(s)

January 11

What did Ralph do to make Jack's taunt "powerless"? Start your sentence with "Despite Jack's … "

January 24

In one beautiful sentence, explain the most important development in this section of the text.

The following last example occurs about six weeks later, in a lesson on *The Curious Incident of the Dog in the Night-Time*. It shows the progression from capturing one idea to relating multiple ideas in a single sentence.

March 12

Describe in one sentence how Christopher's father was feeling *and* how Christopher's response to the situation is different from his father's.

One ideal place to use *Art of the Sentence* is at the end of a lesson, given that part of its purpose is to help students synthesize and summarize. Imagine a school where every lesson in every subject ended with students writing (and revising!) a single, artfully crafted sentence capturing with nuance and sophistication the most important or challenging idea from that lesson. *Art of the Sentence*, in short, can do great service as an *Exit Ticket* or as the next day's *Do Now*. Imagine: you wrap up the lesson by having everyone distill a key idea in writing; the next day, students get their sentences back with individualized guidance ("Revise to use the phrase *in spite of*" or "Rewrite clarifying what the pronoun 'it' refers to") or with a challenge ("Great! Now see if you can use the word *anabolic*").

I want to return briefly to the comparison of an *Art of the Sentence* prompt that uses a sentence parameter and one that does not. I noted that the prompt with a parameter may surprisingly be more rigorous. This is often true, but of course not always. Sometimes an open-ended prompt such as "Describe Christopher's reaction in one artfully crafted sentence" is ideal, especially for students who have developed increasing fluidity with sentence structures. The best results are likely to come, I suspect, from asking students to write a balance of sentences both with and without parameters.

A final note: although some of the most powerful sentences one can write are short and sweet, an unintended consequence of using sentences parameters can be the tacit reinforcement of *long* sentences. One parameter you might occasionally consider is a limit on words: "In a sentence of six or fewer words ... "

See It in Action: Clip 39

In clip 39, you can watch eleventh-grade English teacher Rachel Coffin using *Art of the Sentence* to help her students develop their writing and thinking. You'll see Rachel first allow her students to draft rough ideas as they develop sophisticated thesis statements in response to a passage of Virginia Woolf's. Then she asks them to revise using a sentence starter: "Although Woolf mentions the gender inequalities present within a time of war, ... " She *Cold Calls* a few students to hear their examples and then asks them to rewrite yet again, using sentence parameters (in this case, a batch of strong verbs, such as *urges, encourages, prompts,* and *sways*). Notice also how much value Rachel's preparation and planning—her impeccably organized slides and handouts—place on the craft of writing.

SHOW CALL

Create a strong incentive to complete writing with quality and thought-fulness by publicly showcasing and revising student writing—regardless of who volunteers to share.

Imagine that you've just taught a lesson on a rigorous text, a challenging concept, or an especially thorny problem. Things appear to be going really well. Asked to explain, your students explain; pushed to expand their ideas under questioning, they elaborate with insight. You step back and let a bit of discussion bloom, and the result is lively and well informed. Near the end of the lesson, you ask students to write a brief paragraph in response to the discussion. Pencils scribble energetically. You collect the writing and wait eagerly for the bell, whereupon you set to reading. The results are devastating. The same students who argued passionately and cited evidence were clearly replaced by imposters who filled page after page with half-formed, hastily constructed thoughts supported by the barest reasoning. How could this have happened?

There are a variety of potential reasons for the meltdown. One is that writing is harder than speaking for most people. A speaker's gestures and tone can supply compensatory meaning in lieu of actual precision of words, for example, but a writer has no such aids. But another critical issue is a lack of incentive for producing quality written work. There's often not much accountability for the time students spend practicing their writ-ten expression. We often manage students' verbal lives much more intently than their written work, and we often assign writing without knowing whether it is done sloppily or well. We say, "Write a paragraph response" in the midst of class, but students need to write a lot more than we can collect and grade; if they're not going to turn it in, what's the incentive to do their very best work, especially given what hard work writing is?

One way to solve this problem is through **Show Call**, an adaptation of *Cold Call*. After a typical round of student writing ("Take five minutes to write a paragraph comparing the descriptions of the road in the first two paragraphs of *Tuck Everlasting*"), you might say, "Great! Let's see what kinds of ideas you've been working on, and how we can make them better" and then walk over to the desk of a student, take his paper, and project it to the class via a document camera. You've just made a *Cold Call* of his *written* work. Ideally, you'd make it positive, often celebrating the strengths of work you *Show Call*. If you were to *Show Call* predictably, students in the class would feel a strong incentive to complete all writing with quality and thoughtfulness. You would have implemented a system that builds accountability for written work, allowing you to assign more writing than you can grade while better assuring its quality. You could use this system to regularly show off top-quality student work and show the class what they could and should aspire to.

Although *Show Call* is incredibly powerful as an accountability tool for writing, it has a second aspect that's just as important. Imagine if, after *Show Calling* Martina's paper on the first two paragraphs of *Tuck Everlasting,* you went a step further and asked the class to analyze and revise Martina's paper, suggesting specific revisions and edits. Because they'd be asked to comment on work that was visible to all, they wouldn't have to make comments based on the gauzy threads of memory or vague recollections of what the text said. For example, a typical "editing" exchange (without *Show Call*) might involve Martina reading her answer aloud, followed by a conversation a little like this:

Teacher: Let's give Martina some feedback. What was effective about her answer?
Student: She had really good details.
Teacher: Good. What was good about her details?
Student: Um, I don't remember exactly; I just remember they were really good.

Socializing students to revise and edit their work is necessary to teaching them to write and think, but quality revision requires text that those who are editing and revising can examine and discuss. *Show Call* provides that key piece, enabling a teacher to ask for precise, actionable analysis. She can ask students what was good about the details and to point out the exact spot in the text where they occur. She can show exactly why exemplars are worthy of attention, and be specific about how to revise and improve. She could take "I like Martina's thesis sentence" and turn it into "I like Martina's thesis sentence, especially her use of a strong verb like 'devour'" or "I like Martina's thesis sentence, but it would be even better if she put it in the active voice. Who can show us how to do that?" or "Great, now let's all go through our sentences, check the ones that are in the active voice, and revise any that are in the passive voice." *That* is editing. Mutually trying to recall details of a text you heard read aloud is not.

See It in Action: Clip 41

You can see an example of a teacher using *Show Call* in clip 41 of Paul Powell at Troy Prep Middle School in upstate New York. At the start of Paul's *Show Call,* he calls his class to attention with a countdown as he makes his way over to a student named Kayla. At the end of his count, he discreetly takes Kayla's work. You might think this would be a stressful event, but he announces that he'll be "showing off" student work. Placing Kayla's paper under the document camera, he methodically reviews each step, praising it with sincerity and enthusiasm (for example, "Beautiful formula. Boom! If you can do that every time, you're going to get every point for this *and* the answer"). When he asks, "Who can identify the one little thing we could improve in her work?" Kayla's hand is the first (and straightest) in the air. The clip ends with Paul asking students to double-check their work to make sure it looks as good as Kayla's by placing a check mark next to each step and adding or revising anything that they missed. He's made Kayla proud and made her work better, he's normalized the process of "good to great," and sent a very clear message about accountability for written work.

Three Questions for Your *Show Call*

Show Call can help you achieve different purposes, and your answers to each question will inform the way you use it in the classroom. Here are three key questions you'll want to ask yourself when you *Show Call.*

1. **What kind of work do you want to *Show Call*?** Sometimes the student you choose to *Show Call* can be selected at random, but more often you'll want to choose intentionally. Teachers who do this tend to choose work for three reasons: because the work is exemplary, because it demonstrates a common error, or because it has a good balance of strengths and weaknesses.

   Show Calling exemplary work exposes students to the best work that's being done in their midst so that they can calibrate their own expectations accordingly. A bit of analysis can also help demonstrate *how* to achieve such success (for example, "Look at these dynamic and unusual verbs: 'slithered,' 'hissed,' 'shivered.' Your verbs are what makes your writing sing"). Given that it celebrates success, this approach to *Show Call* is unmistakably positive. In many classrooms where teachers *Show Call* regularly, students plead to have their work selected.

Show Calling a student whose work contains a common error is also useful because it allows you to address key teaching points efficiently and productively. I observed Maggie Johnson do this in a lesson at Troy Prep. She noticed that multiple students were attempting to restate the question in short responses as she had asked them to do, but were doing so in a stilted, ungrammatical manner, so Maggie approached a student who had struggled with this issue, whispering "Do you mind if I share your work so we can revise it a little bit?" and then called the class together. "Mel has been so gracious as to offer to let us revise his answer to make it even stronger, because this is something that I saw a couple of us do. So give him two claps," she said, as he handed her his work. "I want you to tell me what you think we can change to help him make it stronger, especially how we can improve his 'restate the question.'" She then used student suggestions to make edits to Mel's work and *show* what the improved version would look like. Next Maggie *Show Called* another student's work with a similar error and asked students what they would do. This time she asked them to check their own papers and revise their topic sentences accordingly.

Show Calling a student whose work is a good balance of strengths and weaknesses allows you to build a culture of "good to great." Each time you put up work, you call out both its strengths and ways to improve it. Over time, the message becomes "When work is good, we revise to make it better. Always."

2. **When do you want to *Show Call*?** When in the sequence of writing to *Show Call* is another key question. The most straightforward approach is to *Show Call* students after a bout of writing is complete. However, if you asked students to revise their own papers afterwards, you could follow that step with a subsequent *Show Call*. That is, if you said, "Go back and revise your thesis statement now," as Maggie Johnson did, you might then *Show Call* a student to examine the revisions he or she made, studying how effective they were and also now holding students accountable for both the initial writing *and* the task of revising.

A third approach is to *Show Call* while students are in the middle of a block of writing. For example, you might do this during a day when they are drafting essays for a longer block of time. Breaking up a longer stretch of writing with a look at the work of some classmates is an ideal way to insert some mileposts, make your pacing stronger (see Chapter Six), and provide students with ideas they can use right away. I recently observed John Huber of Achievement First Brooklyn High School assign students several minutes of group work during which they discussed and took notes on a topic. Midway through the group-work session, he called students' attention to the front of the room. "Take a look at the board for a second," he said. "Here are some top-quality notes I saw," displaying a series of papers demonstrating different effective ways students had been taking notes during the activity. "You don't need to take down the entire quote if that's taking you too long," he noted. "Brianna just wrote down a quick phrase from the quote to save her some time," he said as he displayed one paper. "Candace is writing down the qualities so that when she comes in to seminar tomorrow, she knows where she can find [information] to agree or disagree with people," he noted as he showed another paper before sending his students back into the activity.

3. **How many students do you want to *Show Call*?** A last question to think about: Do you want to *Show Call* just one student, perhaps diving fairly deep and looking at the totality of his or her work? Or maybe it makes more sense to *Show Call* multiple students, as John Huber did, to look horizontally at the ways multiple students attacked an issue in their writing—how three people used their quotations, began their conclusions, or made their arguments, for example.

Accountable Revision

One of the keys to using *Show Call* effectively is to emphasize *accountable revision*. If the purpose of *Show Call* is to help students make their writing better, then what happens *after* the *Show Call* is critical. Ideally you would have students revise written work *right away* based on the insights they gain through discussion about it—if not always, then as often as possible. This holds students accountable for actively listening, maximizes the value of feedback, and *normalizes revision* as something that is always a part of writing.

As a primer, here are a few ways that I've seen champion teachers emphasize accountable revision in their classrooms:

- **"Check or change."** When reviewing work, ask students to "check or change"—that is, to mark correct answers with a check or to write in corrections when they're wrong. Doing so ensures that there is no case in which students would *not* lift their pencils: they are either fixing their topic sentence or checking off that they wrote in the active voice, revising their fractions or affirming that they solved them correctly.

Passivity or impassivity is impossible, and this helps you hold students accountable for doing their part.

- **Offline rewrite.** After *Show Calling* student A's work, provide feedback, ask the class to revise, and then *Show Call* student Z's work to see if he or she applied the feedback as well. Doing so ensures that everyone is accountable for applying the feedback, not just the person whose work was *Show Called*. It also gives students the time and space they need to make thoughtful revisions. This can be especially helpful for students who need additional processing time before they can effectively apply feedback.

- **"Live edit" *Show Call*.** Ask students to fix their mistakes "live" while their papers are being projected. I first observed this ingenious twist to *Show Call* while sitting in on a lesson led by Bridget McElduff. She started by reviewing a problem on the board, then *Show Called* a student who got it wrong. There was a simple error. Students diagnosed it, and she had them walk the student through the solution. As they narrated, she projected his paper from his desk, and he corrected his own error "live." There was much praise for his willingness to share his mistake and his success in fixing it. The process not only made the solution to the problem visible but also made the principle of success in school—not being afraid to learn from mistakes—visible.

On Revising Writing

During the accountable revision phase of your *Show Call*, you'll want to steer students to look for specific things in their peers' writing. All revision tasks are not created equal, however. Here are some hints to help you make revisions as productive as possible.

Judy Hochman, developer of the Hochman Writing Program, which has been profiled several times for the dramatic results it has produced in a variety of schools, has observed that it is important to distinguish *editing*, which is fixing basic errors like capitalization, punctuation, and spelling, from *revising*, which is the task of improving writing—specifically by revising structure or word choice. As Hochman has pointed out, if you let students choose, they will generally edit, primarily because it is easier to add a missing capital letter than to revise a sentence so as to use a subordinating conjunction, say. In fact, many teachers, too, will choose editing over revising for this reason. But of course the real work is in revision.

One high-value task Hochman suggests is to ask students to add an appositive phrase to a sentence that lacks substance. In a lesson at New Dorp High School in Staten Island, a teacher began revising the sentence "Gandhi had an impact." The teacher first asked her students to use a *Turn and Talk* to write four good appositives to describe Gandhi. Students then inserted the best appositives into the sentence so that it read, for example, "Gandhi, a pacifist and important leader, had an impact." After the teacher asked her students to add a few more clarifications, the students came up with sentences like these: "Gandhi, a pacifist and important leader in India, had a strong impact on society." And the best part was not so much that her students had made this sentence markedly better, it was that they were learning how to use a replicable device, the addition of an appositive phrase, to improve any sentence they might write. That's the power of a good revision task: it teaches a replicable skill.

With thanks to Judy Hochman for the insights that inform some of these suggestions, here are a few more high-value revision tasks:

1. Take a look at Ivan's work here. I want you to find two places where more specific technical vocabulary could make his work even better.

2. Take a look at Ivan's work here. I want you to find at least one place where he could replace a direct quotation with a partial or full paraphrase. Be ready to show us how he could write into or out of the quotation.

3. Take a look at Ivan's work here. I want you to find his two best, most dynamic verbs and then find two verbs you could upgrade to make his writing stronger.

4. Take a look at Ivan's work here. I want you to use a subordinating conjunction to add crucial information.

5. Take a look at Ivan's work here. I want you to add a phrase beginning with "but," "because," or "so" to improve this sentence.

6. Take a look at Ivan's work here. I want you to take these two sentences and combine them to show how the ideas connect and make your writing more fluid.

During the *Show Call*: Two Key Moments

There are two especially important moments to manage during a *Show Call*: the take, the moment when you take a student's paper off his or her desk with the intent to project it; and the reveal, the moment when you show the work to the class. What you say and how you frame what you are doing are especially important at these points of inflection.

The Take

You would think that the "take," or the act of picking up students' work for a *Show Call*, could be a potential source of tension, but the best teachers make a take nearly seamless. One of the keys is to remain unemotional. Students often mirror a teacher's affect, so if you exude a casual *Emotional Constancy* (technique 61) when you perform it, students are far more likely to respond in kind.

One way to signal this is to perform the take without saying anything—an "unnarrated take." This tends to suggest that a take is part of the daily routine, hardly worthy of comment (though you'll probably want to explain what you're doing beforehand the first time you do it).

Another way champion teachers finesse their take is to frame it positively. "I'm looking for some really interesting work to share," you might say, to emphasize that being *Show Called* is a good thing, an honor. Or you could be more private and say this directly to your student: "Your work is really interesting. I'd love to share it with the class." You might do more such framing early on in your use, transitioning later to more unnarrated takes.

Some teachers use an "ask" with the take—a moment when they inquire whether the student is all right with having her paper taken. To keep an ask genuine and inviting, it can help to add some warmth with a smile or even some positive words of affirmation. To enhance privacy, it can also help to crouch down and put yourself at eye level with the student. This can help keep the *Show Call* feeling positive and can even strengthen a student's trust in the teacher.

It's up to you whether you want to give students the right to say no when you ask, but for most teachers, it's more of a courtesy than a real option. Either they don't ask or they might phrase their ask so that it would be hard to say no. That said, if a student were to object, you might respond with, "Well, let's see how it goes. I really think it will be worthwhile" or "OK, how about if I keep you anonymous?" or "Why don't I start, and if you get uncomfortable, you can signal me with this sign" (remember: it's a derivative of *Cold Call*!).

The Reveal

The way you "reveal" written work to the class frames the way students interpret it and sets the tone for the rest of the *Show Call*. One factor to consider is whether you want to name the student whose work you show. Naming a student can help you make *Show Call* feel like a reward, but anonymity can be effective as well, especially if it makes you and your students more comfortable being constructively and positively critical in the revision stage.

Another important part of the reveal is whether and how the work is read. You could have students read it silently, but often you or a student may want to read part of it aloud. Reading written work with expression, careful attention, and appreciation is one of the best and most sincere ways to show how much you value and appreciate it. It also unlocks much of the meaning and expression in the words.

A last factor in the reveal is whether you want to tell students what they should look for ("Let's look to see if Martina has used active, dynamic verbs. What do you think?") or use a nondirective reveal ("Here's what Martina wrote. What do you think?") A directive reveal can help you be more efficient and focused, ensuring a tight, productive discussion on what's most important. Giving students more latitude via a nondirective reveal can allow students to simulate the editing process more closely and to identify issues they consider relevant. Noting what students observe unprompted can also be a useful source of data.

Low-Tech *Show Call*

No document camera in your classroom? So be it. While you're remonstrating with district higher-ups to provide the single most useful (and pretty cheap) piece of technology in the classroom, here are four ways to do a low-tech *Show Call*:

1. *Show Call* a piece of writing from yesterday's class or last night's homework by collecting it and making a transparency for use with the 1980s version of high-tech—the overhead projector. There's probably one sitting in a closet somewhere.

2. If there's no overhead projector, you can always simply copy the student work (last night's homework or yesterday's in-class writing) and ask students to edit at their desks.

3. Ask students to work on "slates"—mini whiteboards students can write on at their desks. Select one and show it to the class as your *Show Call*.

4. Transcribe a crucial sentence from one student's work on the board and "live-edit" it with the class.

Want More? Clip 42. Want more *Show Call*? Check out Katie McNickle in clip 42.

BUILD STAMINA

Gradually increase writing time to develop in your students the habit of writing productively, and the ability to do it for sustained periods of time.

40

When students write answers to your questions, one of the big benefits is that everyone answers the question—and answers it with a significant degree of depth and rigor. When you say, "Take six minutes to explain what the Constitution's Establishment Clause was and why the framers included it in the First Amendment," every one of your students must try to answer, thinking about the Establishment Clause for six sustained minutes with pencils scratching away.

At least it's supposed to work that way. The benefits depend on student *stamina,* a term I use as a proxy for students' ability to start writing when you say go, sustain their writing throughout the allotted time, and write with intentionality and diligence all the way through to the end. If students make a habit of spending much of their "writing" time staring at their paper or starting to write only to erase, brush off the paper, erase and brush again, and so on, then the benefit is lost. The goal is to **Build Stamina**—to develop in your students the habit of writing productively, and the ability to do it for sustained periods of time.

Lauren Latto was at work *Building Stamina* in a recent lesson in her ELA classroom in Brooklyn, increasing her students' capacity to write reflectively for sustained periods, even though they were already able to write steadily and without much interruption for eight full minutes during the lesson in question. The focus was on the finale to *Romeo and Juliet,* and before they began writing, Lauren called on students to read the three different prompts they could choose from. Although it's also important for students to be able to write about one specific topic (it often makes for a better discussion if they have!), choice can be positive as well, especially when the goal is to motivate all students to write and to sustain their energy while you are teaching them to write for increasing durations. In Lauren's prompts there was something to interest everyone, and a student who'd written himself or herself out on one prompt could always go on to another. There was no excuse for sitting idly.

As she set her students to writing, Lauren headed off potential excuses that might be used to stop writing: she asked students, in advance, to recall what they should do if they felt as though they'd finished or were stuck. By doing so, Lauren ensured that students understood the expectation that they would write "wire to wire" — from when she said go until she said stop, with pencils always moving — the full eight minutes. Four minutes into the writing, Lauren spotted a student who was no longer writing, and used a minimally invasive *positive group correction* ("All pens should still be moving"). To help students manage their time, she then let them know they had four minutes left. She also *Circulated* steadily to gently remind students to keep writing, usually with just her tacit reinforcement — a light touch on a desk, a slowing of her gait as she passed — and no words. In some cases, she glanced over students' shoulders and read briefly — nodding, perhaps, to show that the product of their labors was important to her. Finally, the beeper sounded with her students still hard at the task.

Lauren signaled for students to stop. She noted that they'd run out of time and would have to hold their discussion until another day. But before she introduced the homework, she mentioned how excited she was to read what they wrote — a double whammy that both established her appreciation and added a layer of accountability by making it explicit that she would be reading their work.

A subtle but critical point might be easy to miss in this moment. Typically, when we run out of time in our classrooms, we drop what comes last — the independent work. It's worth reflecting on this. We run out of time a *lot.* Ask yourself: When was the last time everything went exactly as you planned, and you had just as much time as you anticipated in the waning moments of your lesson? Sometimes the last portion ends up shorter than we anticipated; sometimes it gets cut off entirely. And that truncated portion is almost always where we plan the writing; compounded over the course of a year, this lost writing time is hugely important. One effective response to this problem is to intersperse writing prompts steadily throughout your classes so that whether your students write or not is not predicated on a bet that the timings will work out. Of course, there will always be a bit of a tendency, for utterly logical and sound reasons, to put a chunk of writing at or near the end of class, so it's worthwhile to note Lauren's decision: short of time, she decides to skip the discussion and do the writing instead, rather than vice versa. If something is going to get squeezed out of a lesson, it's not going to be the time for students to write.

So how do you make your students able to write steadily for eight solid minutes, as Lauren's do? Here are some thoughts on implementing *Build Stamina*.

Practice Success

Chances are, your students will struggle to write wire to wire if you ask eight nonstop minutes of them the first time around. Build up their stamina for writing just as you would build stamina for running or swimming: start small and scale up. Ask for a minute the first time. Then a minute-and-a-half. Then two. Try to take the long view. The most important thing is to have students practice being successful at writing steadily through a block of time when asked to, not only because seeing themselves succeed convinces students that they can, but because it makes a habit of writing steadily through the time allotted whenever asked. The idea is that when you say go, they write straight through because they can't imagine anything else!

Pencils Moving

Start with the expectation that the students' pencils should be moving the whole time. This is useful because it's visible and therefore clear and easy to manage on your end. Strive to reinforce it with consistent language ("I need to see all pencils moving") and nonverbal reminders. If necessary, you could use a marking system where you put pluses or minuses on student papers as they met or failed to meet these expectations. I would tend to wait on such a system until I knew I needed it, however.

You can eliminate one significant distraction by outlawing erasers during writing when you are working on stamina. Erasing is easier than writing: it doesn't require students to create or develop any ideas, but it can be made incredibly time consuming when necessary. Students can exactingly, laboriously, tediously erase every last bit of graphite from their page, for example, before going on to engage your questions about Shakespeare. A colleague of mine calls this the "slow play": Write the opening of the first sentence repeating the question. Add a word. Nope, erase. Add again. Look inquisitive. Nope, erase. Time's up!

One very fair objection to *Build Stamina* and "pencils moving" in particular is that when writers whose skills are fully developed put pen to paper, they regularly stop to think and reflect. I agree, and recognizing this helps clarify the purpose of *Build Stamina* and the application of pencils moving. The purpose of the technique is to develop students' ability to write steadily and productively for significant stretches, but this does not imply that you need to be working on that goal or enforcing the pencils moving rule every time students write. You want to do enough of it to show your students that they can write for ten minutes without stopping and to build their capacity to do so—sometimes even at the expense of greater reflectiveness—so long as you also invest at other times in writing wherein your primary concern is quality and reflectiveness.

In short, you will want to use both types of prompts to develop both skills in writing. So, for example, I might encourage a teacher I was working with to use an *Art of the Sentence* prompt in just about every lesson and a stamina-based prompt every couple of days, perhaps, possibly more often at the outset of the year when she was training students to sustain their writing. Once she'd established her students' stamina, she could then remove most explicit stamina-building exercises until she needed them again. As with so many other classroom systems, just because you can ask students to do something (in this case, write without stopping) doesn't mean you always must.

Prime the Pump

Another way to make sure students hit the ground running is to make sure they have some decent ideas to work from, making it all but impossible to fall back on "I can't think of anything." Before you say go, say something like "OK, guys, let's hear three things you might write about" or ask students to do a lightning-quick brainstorm. Alternatively, you could read a few lines from the text students are writing about or some quotations about the topic or show some images related to it. Then very quickly say, "Now that you've got some ideas, you may begin. Go."

Valorize Student Writing

Motivate students to want to write by using *Precise Praise* (technique 59) for specific elements of their writing that you want to see other students replicate. Or, even more powerfully, read writing aloud. I still remember the day when my seventh-grade teacher read my journal entry to the class in a slow and reflective cadence. He didn't say a thing afterwards. The way he read it—lingering over words, nodding at a certain sentence—spoke volumes about what he thought about it. Writing is meant to be read, and in publicly putting student work to this purpose, you stress its value. You can do this by reading student work yourself—little pieces of it or whole compositions, informal work or polished, for the quality of the final product or of the edits that improved it, for word choice or sentence structure or imagery. You can read it orally or use *Show Call*. And, of course, you can ask students to read their own work—or another student's—aloud. In so doing, you make students want to write by making writing seem like the most valuable thing on Earth.

See It in Action: Clip 40

Watch Lauren Latto work on building her students' stamina in clip 40. Notice how she sets clear expectations, anticipates issues that might interrupt writing, coaches students gently along, and establishes an accountability loop at the end: "I can't wait to read them." Notice also that pressed for time in her lesson, Lauren chooses to drop the discussion and do the writing exercise—wisely, I think, but in contrast to what often happens in classrooms.

FRONT THE WRITING

Arrange lessons so that writing comes earlier in the process to ensure that students think rigorously in writing.

41

In many classes, writing serves as a capstone—to a discussion, a demonstration, a lab, a presentation, or some other part of the lesson. As I've mentioned, it's right and good and logical that writing come at the end of a topic in your lesson or of the lesson itself, as writing is an ideal tool for synthesizing and processing ideas—quite possibly the best. But there are also potential blind spots in a cycle where the writing is the last step, and it's important to understand them and design opportunities to **Front the Writing**—that is, to arrange the lesson so that the writing comes earlier in the process.

Consider, first, two common sequences—let's call them RDW (read-discuss-write) and ADW (activity-discuss-write) for short. You might do RDW if you were reading the Shirley Jackson classic "The Lottery," a story that ends with a bit of shocking ambiguity. Students—most of them, at least—suddenly realize that the lottery in question is much different from what they had assumed. Recognition comes suddenly in the last sentence, and the narration has a bit of subtlety to it (a stunning event related in an offhand manner and never named explicitly), so it's easy to miss or underestimate. You might finish the last paragraph and ask, as a discussion starter, "So tell me, what does the final line of the story mean when it says 'and then they were upon her'? Who did what to whom, exactly, and why?" A discussion might ensue, with students first making conjecture of varying degrees of accuracy. Eventually they'd bring evidence to the scene as the details of the story's climax were revealed. There would surely be some dropped jaws, and you might then use the opportunity to ask your students to write about the story.

As your students put pencil to paper, they'd be drawing on two key sources of information: what they took from reading the story themselves and what their classmates said in discussion. Ideally, a student would take his or her initial understanding from reading the story and add some nuance and additional detail gleaned from discussion, but it doesn't always work that way. It especially doesn't work that way for your weakest students, with the weakest readers particularly at risk.

In many cases, students are able to use their recollection of the discussion to write, potentially crowding out the need to learn from other sources of knowledge, such as reading. Essentially, they are able to use the comments other students make during discussion to compensate for things they did not learn directly from reading or your presentation or the lab experiment or some other activity. We might call this "piggy-backing." Because writing is "the coin of the realm"—the standard currency in which ideas are exchanged in school and in life thereafter—it's important (and rigorous) to use a final writing exercise to assess how much your students know or to allow them to process and synthesize ideas. But you (and they) could easily get a false positive—an erroneous indication of greater mastery than really exists—as a result of piggybacking. In fact, you can get a false positive from discussion as well, as some colleagues at a school I work with recently found. They were doing a unit in which students read a Shakespeare play and strove to have a college-level discussion about it. In this case, the discussion was a combination of online and in-class, a fact that had the unanticipated benefit of allowing teachers to go back to it and analyze it later. As the discussion unfolded, they thought their Shakespeare unit was a triumph. The discussion was rich and, thanks to the accountability of the "chat" structure, they could easily track who participated how many times, and every student added his or her insights.

As a capstone, students were asked to put their insights into writing. The papers they had to write asked them to analyze a passage from the play, and they were a stunning disappointment. Where had the trenchant insight and deep analysis of the discussion gone? My colleagues now realized the value of the transcript they possessed and went back and reviewed it. What they found was that the discussion was indeed full of outstanding ideas, but that, time and time again, those ideas were broached by just two students, with the rest of the class piggybacking on their breakthroughs. Most of the class was great at discussing a unique and powerful insight once it was made, but only two girls were consistently able to generate those underlying insights. They were able to discern the germ of core conflicts and themes in Shakespeare's Elizabethan verbiage and to distill, explain, and modernize it for their peers. Once they laid it clear, others were able to jump in. "Oh, it's about loyalty?! I can speak to that!"

It's good in some ways that the ideas of these two scholars permeated the room. But it also created a massive false positive for the teachers—it indicated that the students had greater and broader mastery of reading Shakespeare than they actually did. In fact, let's be honest and take this argument a step further. There are times in almost every teacher's class when students who haven't done the reading at all have successfully faked it by using the discussion that comes after as their primary source of information. In fact, I hereby acknowledge that, in the course of my own studies, I did this on occasion, despite the fine and worthy teachers with whom I was studying.

Writing based on other people's ideas is useful, but it can crowd out the important (and explicitly Common Core–aligned) skill of direct writing—writing directly from a text or after some other learning experience. It's worth taking a minute to reflect on how important being able to analyze and draw conclusions from primary sources is in our educational and professional lives.

As students advance in their educational careers, they will increasingly find themselves in situations where they must make sense of a text on their own—with no group of thirty colleagues with whom to distill and discuss first. In fact, as they mature, this is how they will probably add value at work—by being the equivalent of those two girls in the Shakespeare classroom, the ones who can generate ideas directly from the initial experience. It is certainly how they will write papers in college. Reading something, making sense of it entirely on their own, and writing about it are also what they'll have to do on the SAT to get to college at all. For you to accurately assess students' ability to generate and reflect on ideas with independence, writing has to happen "up front" before activities that can allow for piggybacking.

One of the simplest ways to add rigor to the writing your students do is to shift the cycle from RDW or ADW to read-write-discuss (RWD) or activity-write-discuss (AWD). You might do this by finishing a demonstration and asking students to write for five minutes to distill their key thoughts before discussing. You still get the benefit of an exchange of ideas at the end, but not before everyone practices thinking deeply and autonomously: What did I just see? What did it mean? How can I make sense of it? Even beyond the unique power and rigor of "putting it into writing," this is a powerful process. A block of writing disciplines students to engage in reflective thinking.

If stage one of *Front the Writing* is substituting RWD for RDW, stage two can solve yet another endemic challenge of teaching: helping students make the most of discussion. Think (or maybe write!) for a minute about this question: What is it that we want students to do, cognitively, during the part of discussion when they are listening to their peers? We want them to listen, of course, but what else? We often tacitly (or explicitly) ask them to decide whether they agree or disagree with the speaker, but this is a bit of an oversimplification of the sort of intellectual life we aspire to for our students. I rarely hear a comment and simply think, "I agree" or "I disagree." I think, "Hmmm, that version of events is interesting, and I find part A really thought provoking, but I think part B ignores some of the evidence" or "I had never thought of it that way, but how does that perspective reconcile itself with event X?"

As my colleague J. T. Leaird once wisely pointed out, asking students to spend their listening time in discussion focused on whether they agree or disagree can foment a highly unproductive situation: a discussion full of students with arms crossed saying, "Well, that's just what I think," perhaps a little louder the second time around. It's not usually very productive when students are focused on proving that their original opinion was just right and "winning" the discussion, rather than, say, listening for information that might cause them to change their original thought, even ever so slightly, to develop a more nuanced and flexible opinion that moderates and modulates their initial reaction in light of the perspective of others. Surely we are exasperated when, in our lives outside of school, we come across people who want to win discussions instead of hear others out in the assumption that they might learn something. We should be careful about building those types of students in our schools.

Next question, then: How can we socialize students to think of discussion as a tool to revise and amend their original opinions in light of the points made by others?

One effective way is to ask them to write an opinion or analysis and then listen to the discussion *with the understanding that the next step will be to revise their opinion or analysis* in the most tangible and accountable way: in writing. That is, moving to activity-write-discuss-revise or read-write-discuss-revise is even more rigorous than moving to read- or activity-write-discuss because it locks down this process: during a discussion, what students are doing, intellectually, is tracking ideas they will use to revise their opinion afterward. This approach not only provides lots of practice revising—a skill at least as important as writing an initial idea—but also causes students to engage in the discussion with a more rigorous and flexible mindset: What can I learn here, and how will I apply it to my idea? This mindset is not just theoretical—someone tells me I ought to be doing that. In practice, as a student, I am caused to have to practice doing it, ideally over and over again, with the result being my getting very good at coming up with an initial opinion, writing it down to formulate it into words, engaging in an exchange with peers in which I harvest ideas that I can weave into my own thinking, and then revising my initial opinion in writing—locking down the changes in my thinking in specific, visible words and syntax. If students could do that every day, I suspect they would be able to do great things.

See It in Action: Clip 38

Watch Gillian Cartwright *Front the Writing* in her lesson in clip 38. You'll notice that her students write in response to August Wilson's "Fences" for eighteen minutes (talk about stamina!), completing four entries in their Lit Logs about elements in the play they found "worthy of analysis." This leads to a series of Socratic discussions in which the students demonstrate their preparation and the autonomy of their thinking, with each student having his or her own reading of the play to support him or her in discussion. The autonomy Gillian offers her students starts with preparation through writing.

CONCLUSION

Writing is truly one of the most valuable skills students will learn over the course of their education. It's something that will follow them—or lead them—into their lives beyond your classroom, we hope into college and professional lives. It requires depth of thought and deliberate word choice even beyond that required by verbal responses. How we treat writing in our classrooms—by ensuring it happens regularly, by prioritizing it over other activities, and by not settling for poor quality—implicitly communicates its importance to students, and is one very effective way of shifting both the think ratio and the participation ratio more and more onto student desks.

Beyond questioning and writing, engaging in respectful and intelligent discourse with colleagues and peers is not only a way to increase ratio but also an important part of becoming an active citizen and human being. In Chapter Nine, we'll look at ways champion teachers increase the rigor in their classrooms with productive discussion.

Reflection and Practice

1. Take a lesson plan for a class you're getting ready to teach, and mark it up by identifying a place where all of your students will write an answer to your question before discussion. Be sure to consider where they will write and what the expectations will be. (Will you collect their work? Are complete sentences required?)

2. Pick a portion of your lesson plan to insert an *Art of the Sentence* moment. Consider

   a. Your lesson objective and question

   b. The level of scaffolding you will provide for students

   c. Whether you will focus more on participation ratio or think ratio

   d. What an exemplar *Art of the Sentence* response would look like and how you would support revision

3. Now plan a *Show Call* to review and revise your students' *Art of the Sentence* writing.

   a. What type of work will you *Show Call*: an exemplar? an example of a common error? a "good to great" case study?

   b. How will you narrate the take and the reveal?

   c. What will students look for in the *Show Call* analysis, and how will students revise their own work afterwards?

***Art of the Sentence* analysis.** Check out the *Art of the Sentence* prompts that seventh-grade reading teacher David Javsicas uses over the course of several weeks. Be sure to consider the different prompts this teacher uses and ask yourself how you might apply and adapt them.

Planning your *Show Call*: questions to consider. Before you implement your next *Show Call*, use the guiding questions and sample the technique in all its varieties.

***Build Stamina* scenarios and phrases.** Keep those pencils moving with this bank of writing stamina prompts.

Building Ratio Through Discussion

Technique 42: Habits of Discussion. Make your discussions more productive and enjoyable by normalizing a set of ground rules or "habits" that allow discussion to be more efficiently cohesive and connected.

Technique 43: Turn and Talk. Encourage students to better formulate their thoughts by including short, contained pair discussions — but make sure to design them for maximum efficiency and accountability.

Technique 44: Batch Process. Give more ownership and autonomy to students — particularly when your goal is a discussion — by allowing for student discussion without teacher mediation, for short periods of time or for longer, more formal sequences.

Building Ratio Through Discussion

Ratio, as you'll recall, is the process of making sure there's a mental workout in the classroom and that it belongs to students. The goal is for students to be constantly on their toes, answering questions, drawing on or developing their knowledge base, and refining their ideas. There are two discrete parts of ratio: *participation ratio* and *think ratio*. The first is a measure of how many students participate and how often. The second refers to the rigor and depth of thinking implicit in that participation. In a champion classroom, you need both: full and energetic participation from everyone, and work that is rigorous and demanding. In Chapters Seven and Eight, I considered the first two paths teachers can take to increase ratio: questioning and writing. In this chapter, I'll examine techniques for increasing ratio through *discussion*.

Of the three ratio chapters, I put discussion last in part because I suspect that when most teachers imagine a classroom with high ratio, they imagine discussion above all other things. On the basis of my own observation and analysis of classrooms, I'd agree that well-executed and strategic discussion is a critical part of a high-ratio classroom. But I also think it's important to recognize that discussion is not the only way to achieve high ratio, and that writing, in particular, can be an especially strong tool for causing all students to do lots of the most rigorous work. In general, great classrooms employ balance in lieu of either-or choices—the power is in the equilibrium between writing, questioning, and discussion rather than in the choice of one. But *if I had to choose just one,* which I admittedly do not, I would choose writing. Hammering an idea into precise words and syntax and then linking it to evidence and situating it within a broader argument are, for me, the most rigorous work in schooling.

Why mention that here, in the chapter on discussion? Because writing works in synergy with discussion much of the time; to write is to develop ideas with precision and specificity, but not necessarily to share in other people's thoughts. So hearing and discussing the differences among classmates after a bout of writing, and writing after a discussion to distill and come to grips with the range of opinions expressed, are critical ways in which the two approaches work together to create rigor and balance.

In another way, the three paths to ratio, discussion, writing, and questioning, also compete. Minutes in a classroom are finite, and there is always opportunity cost to any activity. To choose one is to choose not to do another, so the question for you as a teacher is not just whether the activity you choose in your classroom is "good" but whether it's "best"—for that moment, that group of students, and that lesson. But competition—for time in the classroom, in this case—can also raise standards. Once you can execute the alternatives to discussion with rigor and engagement—once you are not reliant on discussion as your only tool to get students to participate—the standards for the quality of your discussions increase. When other aspects of your classroom are functioning more effectively, discussion has to be rigorous and of high quality to justify itself. Although much of the time our discussion meets this high standard, there are also times when it clearly does not. This chapter is a reflection on *better* discussion, based on the subtle differences in how it is executed in the very best classrooms when compared to the perfectly good.

WHAT IS (AND ISN'T) A DISCUSSION?

So what exactly is a discussion? What differentiates it from, say, a group of people restating their opinions to one another? Imagine for a moment that we're sitting with a group of people, and the topic of an upcoming election comes up. You say, "I'm voting for Peter. He's smart." I say, "I'm voting for Sasha. She's trustworthy." Then our friend Jill joins in. "I'm not voting," she says. "I never vote."

This series of comments does not really qualify as a discussion—at least not in the fullest sense. Instead, it exemplifies what's often missing in many classrooms when we call disconnected verbal interactions a "discussion." My comment, "I'm voting for Sasha. She's trustworthy," is a good example of what I'm talking about. It makes no reference to what you had said just before I spoke. If I'd said something like, "Yeah, I agree, but smart people are as likely to cheat as others, so I prefer someone who's really honest like Sasha," I would be making implicit reference to your comment and situating mine in relation to it. I would be using the syntax of my comment to weave our thoughts together in a cohesive way.

Jill's comment was similar to mine. It didn't do anything to help us, the other participants, understand her comment in relation to ours. When she said, "I'm not voting," was she changing the subject abruptly? Excusing herself from the conversation on the grounds that she didn't have much to say on the topic? Trying to be dismissive of elections? Implying that she didn't vote because of the trust issue I'd mentioned? A bit of framing—"Yeah, integrity is what I care about, too. But I'm not voting because I'm not sure I can trust the people I vote for"—could have helped us to see those connections and knit our comments together. As it was, our comments were vaguely related, but not really a discussion so much as a series of atomized comments loosely grouped around an idea.

Conversations in the classroom are often similar. A discussion is supposed to be *a mutual endeavor by a group of people to develop, refine, or contextualize an idea or set of ideas,* and that's different from what sometimes gets called a discussion—a series of loosely related comments occurring in the same room. What I see in the most successful classrooms is a commitment to connecting and relating ideas and opinions. A discussion that's worth its own opportunity cost will feature comments that are designed to be consistently useful to others, not just interesting to those who made them, and that acknowledge the speaker's understanding of and interest in what was previously said.

Consider two moments from Rue Ratray's English class at Edward Brooke Charter School, during a discussion of Lois Lowry's novel *The Giver.*

A student, Cici, was asked to reflect on the singsong tone of Jonas's father's words as he commits a heinous act, the ramifications of which he may not understand. "He uses the word 'shrimp,'" she offered. "He's talking to the baby kind of like in a baby voice." Rue went directly to another student and allowed him to comment.

"I thought that he didn't have sympathy," the student began.

"Wait," Rue stepped in. "Do you agree or disagree?"

"I agree with Cici … " the student offered.

"What'd she say?" Rue prompted. The student then reverted to addressing the whole class.

"Cici said that Jonas's father was acting normal. I agree. He acts like this every day. The father didn't have any specific feelings or understanding for what he'd done."

A few minutes later, in the midst of discussion about the larger social forces at work in the book, a student commented that Jonas was "just not willing to accept or agree with the ideas of the government." Rue went straight to another student, Khalid, without making any comment himself, and Khalid shifted the subject.

"Carol and I talked about how we liked this phrase that … "

"Wait a minute, Khalid," Rue enjoined. "What do you think about what Sofia said?"

Sometimes during a discussion, we perceive our role to be to steer the *content* of what students are talking about. We say things like, "Did any one notice the father's use of the word 'shrimp'?" But Rue here played a different role: steering the *structure* of the discussion to ensure the responsiveness and connectedness among participants. Twice he directed students back to the previous speaker's idea, asking them to relate their comment to it and/or asking for a brief summary of the preceding comment. Rue was teaching students to turn what would otherwise be a series of atomized comments into a discussion, and (eventually) to learn to do so out of habit.

In the remainder of this chapter, I'll explore three techniques that can help you build the intentionality that leads to a sustained focus during discussion:

- *Habits of Discussion*
- *Turn and Talk*
- *Batch Process*

Let's start with the most foundational technique of the chapter: *Habits of Discussion*.

HABITS OF DISCUSSION

Make your discussions more productive and enjoyable by normalizing a set of ground rules or "habits" that allow discussion to be more efficiently cohesive and connected.

The productivity of a discussion is usually the result of specific actions that participants take. People who make a conversation effective not only listen carefully, for example, but also *show* they are listening carefully by occasionally offering, as Rue Ratray's students were learning to do, brief summaries of other participants' comments or by making a specific effort to connect the point they're making to what someone else said.

A skilled conversationalist might use these in our discussion about the upcoming election: "Yeah, that's interesting," they might say, validating the previous comment and showing that they are building off of it. "I see Sasha in a similar light, Karen. She's got a lot of Peter's intelligence, but trustworthiness, too." The person who makes a comment like this is connecting and relating ideas, working the spaces in between. Not just, "Well, Sasha is trustworthy," but a comment that refers back to earlier ideas and strives for the mutuality that makes for a discussion. The subtext of the earlier comment, for example, might be something like, "I agree with you that intelligence is important, Jamila, but Sasha's smart, and her trustworthiness is pretty exceptional." It even uses the name of the person it's directed to—a fact that both clarifies and shows respect.

Generally, of course, people don't think to themselves, "Hey, I think I'll validate and build off her point now." Most positive discussion-building actions are habits—used as a matter of course once they've been learned. Of course, some people never learn them. We know this is true because we've all had "discussions" in our lives outside the classroom with that person whose purpose in conversation appears to be to batter you with his opinions and "insights." None of the comments you or anyone else has made seems to cause the slightest variation in the pace or direction of the bombardment. He is talking at you, not with you.

Good discussion skills, in short, are not "naturally occurring." To reliably have great discussions in your classroom, it's necessary to instill them deliberately. Doing so is a technique I call **Habits of Discussion**. Practicing such habits are well worth it, and the return on the investment in teaching students how to discuss is immense.

Within the technique, there are four parts:

- Discussion fundamentals: voice, tracking, names
- Follow-on, and follow-on prompting
- Sentence starters
- Managing the meta

1. Discussion Fundamentals: Voice, Tracking, Names

Simple as it sounds, disciplined discussion starts with speaking loud enough to be heard, with speakers and listeners showing their engagement by looking at one another, maybe not every single second, but generally and with consistency. Doing so demonstrates that a student is listening to his or her peer and sends a message that the classroom is a community where we listen to each other and build off of each other's ideas. It helps students discipline themselves to "lock in" on the person they're listening to and helps them "hear more." By looking at the person talking, a listener picks up gestures and facial expressions that add meaning to the words themselves.

Finally, an often overlooked detail that improves discussions is the practice of expecting (and reminding) students to use one another's names. I often see great teachers reinforce this expectation in class, either verbally—"Great; turn to Janelle and tell her that"—or nonverbally (as Yasmin Vargas does in clip 43, which the authors of *Great Habits, Great Readers* use in Uncommon Schools' reading trainings), with a brief point of the finger or eyes reminding students to look at the person they're responding to.

2. Follow-on, and Follow-on Prompting

Any true discussion starts with listening, and although participants' looking at one another, speaking audibly, and using names are necessary preconditions, they aren't enough to actually ensure that listening occurs. Socializing students to listen involves a combination of accountability and inspiration. An adaptation of the "follow-on" from the *Cold Call* technique (technique 33) can help. In a follow-on, the teacher consistently asks one student to respond to something another student has said, whether or not the second student has volunteered to do so. Something as simple as, "Skylar, do you agree with Markus?" (asked in good faith and not as a "gotcha"; see *Cold Call* for more details) establishes the expectation that Skylar must always be listening well enough to be able to offer a reasonable response, even if only to say that he's not sure about a particular point. Expecting Skylar to be able to respond reinforces peer-to-peer listening and, important, reinforces that listening is an expectation no matter who is speaking—it is a courtesy not merely reserved for the teacher.

Follow-on *prompting* is another means of setting an "always listening, always ready" expectation during discussions. Instead of asking a directive question like, "Skylar, do you agree with Markus?" follow-on prompting is nondirective, with the result that it disrupts the thread of the conversation less and avoids steering the second student's response, which in some cases is part of the purpose of discussion. A teacher who's using follow-on prompting might keep his students on their toes and listening to one another by using fast follow-on prompts five or six times per class—enough to be predictably unpredictable without breaking the flow of students responding directly to one another via *Cold Call*. Here is just one example of how Patrick Pastore does this in his reading classes:

Patrick:	What's Jonas afraid of? Kesia?
Kesia:	He's afraid of pain.
Patrick:	Develop, David.
David:	He doesn't really know what pain is, how far it can go.
Patrick:	Add on, Carlton.
Carlton:	Well, on page 63 he's talking about …

Through this approach, Patrick holds his students accountable for listening carefully to their peers and adds nondirective prompts like "Develop" and "Evidence" to cause them to practice responding with little intervention from him. These are critical habits teachers promote to help build a culture of peer listening and discussion. Over time, follow-ons can be a strong and reliable enough habit to function without the support of *Cold Call*.

3. Sentence Starters

I mentioned earlier that participants who make discussions effective will often tacitly reference preceding ideas in their own comments, offering a bit of implicit context for them. They do this via syntactical structures embedded within the grammar of their sentences, and typically begin comments with phrases like these:

"I understand why you'd say that, but … "

"I was just thinking of something similar, that … "

"And then there was another example of that … "

"The thing that doesn't take into account is … "

"I want to build on what you said … "

In each of these examples—whether the new speaker is agreeing with the first speaker, disagreeing with her, or somewhere in between—the comment begins by framing the relationship between the present comment and the previous one, ideally in some respectful way. These frames shape the way people interact. Teaching students to use frames like this to weave their comments together with those around them is the core of the *Habits of Discussion* technique. This is usually accomplished through the use of *sentence starters*—short phrases that socialize students to use, and ultimately adapt, sentence frames that facilitate building off of someone else's idea. The result is that students talk (and later write) in a more cohesive manner.

Start by posting them on your wall and spending a few days asking students to practice using some basic ones, saying things like, "Great; can you use a sentence starter to frame that response and talk directly to Aleisha?" or "Today I'm just going to evaluate your discussion on how well you use our sentence starters to build off of one another." Over time, you'd add more to the list, but the list itself would become less critical as using the sentence starters and adaptations of them become a habit.

The simplest sentence starters are "I agree because …" or "I disagree because …" These are useful, especially, for getting students started responding to one another. They cause students to reference previous comments and situate theirs within the debate in a simple and direct way.

As many of the teachers I know have developed their use of sentence starters over time, they've pushed to get beyond "agree" or "disagree" pretty quickly. As ELA teacher turned principal J. T. Leaird explained to me, they're useful for getting kids started talking to one another because agreeing or disagreeing is so natural and intuitive, but sentence starters don't just reflect how students think during discussions; they shape it, too—in this case tending to socialize students to take sides, to focus on "winning" the discussion, to dig in their heels and try to prove their original comment was right. The best discussions are less about proving oneself right than they are about finding nuanced common ground. Some other examples of effective sentence starters include

"There's another piece of evidence of that …"

"There's some evidence that might contradict that …"

"I'd like to build on _____'s idea …"

"I understand, and I would like to add …"

"That makes sense because …"

"There's another example of what _____ is talking about …"

"Another way you might interpret that is …"

"I think it's more complex than what you're saying, _____, because …"

A list like this one can help students recall and select useful ways to put their own comment in context and is ideal as a reminder to post on your classroom wall.

Lastly, nonverbals can be critical to building up the habit of using sentence starters. Maggie Johnson, a reading teacher at Troy Prep Middle School, developed different hand signals that her students use when they want to develop someone else's idea as opposed to making a new comment. When they want to make a new point during a discussion, they raise their hand in the usual fashion. When they want to "add on," develop, or respond to the previous point, they raise two fingers. This allows Maggie to shape the direction of the discussion even without participating in it. She can decide whether it's more valuable to stick with the present point or move on to a new one, and she can move in that direction merely by choosing whom she calls on to go next. In fact, keeping a discussion focused on a point of importance or value is one of the most important things for a teacher to attend to during discussion, which brings us to the next point in *Habits of Discussion*.

4. Managing the Meta

In a recent lesson, Williamsburg Collegiate history teacher Ryan Miller's students were examining primary source documents about President Teddy Roosevelt's intervention in Panama. One student commented that Roosevelt's claims that the United States was not involved were an effort to hide the government's true intentions. The format of class here was a Socratic discussion in which Ryan allowed students to respond directly to one another, while he often stepped back for significant amounts of time. Whereas Ryan was less likely to step in on a point of content (for example, "That's not what the document says; let's read that again"), he was, like Rue Ratray at the beginning of this chapter, very willing to step in to shape the dynamics of the discussion and to keep the discussion disciplined. That's what he did in this case. The subsequent student's comment broached a brand-new topic, so Ryan said, "That's interesting, but I'd like to hear someone respond to Sara's comment before we move on to another one." This is what I call *managing the meta*. Ryan recognized that the power was in developing and expanding ideas through a series of connected comments. That sometimes requires keeping a discussion "inside the box."

The Case for Inside the Box

We tend to valorize "thinking outside the box": it smacks of creativity, cognitive leaps, and the raw stuff of insight. In classroom discussion, however, keeping it *inside* the box—staying focused on a specific topic; maintaining steady, deep reflection on all sides of an idea—is often more valuable. Of course, the two aren't mutually exclusive, but there is a certain tension between them. Students sometimes reach for comments that are broad afield rather than deep, reflective, and analytical because they believe that's how "outside the box" happens. We sometimes even encourage their doing so. Still, if we don't teach students how to keep insights on topic, we are guaranteed great leaps sideways, occasionally at the expense of forward progress. Let me give you an example.

I recently spent some time observing classes in a school near me, and one of the things that struck me was the way the discussions differed among classrooms. In some classes, students made relevant and insightful contributions that advanced the shared understanding of the topic. In others, comments were interesting to the student who made them, but not as useful or thought-provoking to others. They were arcane and solipsistic—smart, perhaps, but so self-absorbed that it was hard to say. The curious thing is that I was observing the same group of students in different rooms! I started to wonder, "Why were they focused and alert to their peers' perspective in one class and the opposite in another?"

In one classroom, discussion was characterized by students' making sudden, often absurd connections to trivial events. "What is fairness?" the teacher asked. One student answered with an obscure quotation from a science fiction novel. Another replied that it was like pizza. Soon it was one sudden, veering shift to a new idea after another. They were certainly outside the box—in a highly unproductive manner. In a few minutes, I realized why it was happening. During the discussion, the teacher consistently offered seemingly random associations with the text. The text was, at one point, like "that commercial on TV." Then it was like that song you all know. It was like that Xbox game. He called these text-to-text connections, but they weren't. They were obscure, private, and trivial comparisons, and their effect was not to cast the text in a new and revealing light but to distract the class from any sustained reflection on it. Students mirrored his actions. Further, when they referred to something arcane or comprehensible only to them (a book no one else in the room had read), which they seemed to relish doing, he never brought them back or helped them think about how useful their comments were to others. I once had a professor who would respond to some comments, "How does that relate to what we were just talking about?" His doing so helped us see very quickly that class discussion was not just about us and our desire to talk about what thoughts were on our minds, but about the mutual goal of developing shared insight on a topic.

The power of framing expectations about discussion was evident in the math class many of the same students had been in earlier in the day. It was their first day studying rate of change, and their teacher had just observed that time was almost always an independent variable when it appeared in a rate-of-change problem. "It's going to be your independent variable 99 percent of the time," he said, and clarified briefly. He asked students if they had any questions. Several ensued in which students reflected on how certain rate-of-change problems would be represented on a line graph. Then a student asked for an example of a situation in which time could be the dependent variable, and the teacher said, "To think of an example, I'd have to come up with something pretty obscure. Maybe we'll do that later, but for now let's just assume it's going to be the independent variable."

Despite his hint, another student raised her hand and began brainstorming "what ifs"—wondering aloud how time might become a dependent variable. It was great that she was asking herself this question, and although many teachers might have encouraged it, her comment was in some ways a flight of fancy, a peripheral issue, not the most important and not as relevant to others in the room. The teacher was trying to help the class come to a collective understanding of rate of change at a conceptual level, not to digress into an area he'd just indicated was not worth the time. His response, I thought, was brilliant: "You're thinking outside the box. But I want us to focus on thinking inside the box right now, on really understanding rate of change, what it is and how it works. So let's stay there right now." Although many teachers might be reluctant to circumscribe discussion in this way, his doing so was immensely productive.

He acknowledged something positive about her answer ("thinking outside the box" is positive), but also made it clear that there was a right and wrong time for a digression and that this was the wrong time. He provided her with information to help her understand why her response was less valuable right then. Essentially, he said, "Here's what we're doing as a group right now. That's something you should pay attention to when you speak up—what the group is trying to do and why." Then he smiled genuinely and sincerely to show that it was fine to make that mistake, and went back to talking about rate of change. Many teachers, I think, would have engaged the question briefly so as not to make the student "feel bad," thus distracting the class. In truth, part of a teacher's responsibility is to teach students when and how to participate productively in a discussion.

In short, you manage the meta when, through feedback and modeling, you guide students in the dynamics of building conversation, specifically how to have the kind of conversation that's most productive in a given setting. Rather than assuming they know how to make a discussion valuable, you invest in teaching them as they struggle forward. Perhaps there are times when you want *more* outside the box. If that's the case, you might use meta comments like "I'm hearing us stick too much with one idea. I want to see us bring in a wide variety of connections." Either way, managing the meta relies on two key tools: modeling the kind of participation you want in a discussion and providing constant supportive feedback on how to engage your peers in a meaningful, connected, and mutually productive way.

Want More? Clip 43. Want more *Habits of Discussion*? Check out Yasmin Vargas in clip 43, which the authors of *Great Habits, Great Readers* use in Uncommon Schools' reading trainings. Notice how she subtly reminds her students—they don't need much help!—to look at and respond to one another. The result is a rich discussion that's beneficial to all.

TURN AND TALK

Encourage students to better formulate their thoughts by including short, contained pair discussions—but make sure to design them for maximum efficiency and accountability.

A common tool used in thousands of classrooms is the short, contained pair discussion called **Turn and Talk**. It is a common practice, but the details of execution particular to champion classrooms can help ensure that when you use it, the result is efficient, accountable, and rigorous.

In a typical *Turn and Talk,* a teacher might say, "That was a fascinating chapter. Now I want you to think about how Jonas has changed by the end of it. Turn and talk to a neighbor about that." Ideally, everyone participates in the ensuing conversation, rehearses his own nascent ideas, listens carefully to his partner's, and, from this fusion, emerges a minute later energized and with better formed ideas. Sometimes it actually happens that way. Often, teachers don't actually know what students discuss when they participate. They could be talking about anything. They could be silly; they could be off task. One student could do all the talking while the other doesn't talk at all. Or they could be on topic but have a discussion that's banal and superfluous. Other times, the information and ideas that pass between students are wrong—misinformation that doesn't go corrected. Sometimes the teacher gets distracted by a student or a pair that's struggling, and the conversations in the rest of the room steadily peter out and students sit idly.

In short, there's a wide gulf between executing and succeeding.

Tools for Efficiency and Accountability

The first step to bridging that gulf is ensuring *efficiency* and *accountability*—students' feeling responsible for doing quality work to the best of their ability. Once you've done that, you can begin to design the activity for maximum rigor.

Setting Pairs

When you say, "Take one minute to discuss the most important factor in Grant's victory at Vicksburg," you cannot afford for your students to respond by turning to look for a partner, languidly attempting some eye contact, and then tacitly but halfheartedly agreeing to discuss. Who partners with whom should be prearranged so that pairings are unmistakable and conversations can begin without further action or discussion. Generally, partners should be pairs who are sitting side by side, and should commonly remain partners for the duration of a lesson. You may want to do some light arranging in advance if you're planning to use *Turn and Talk* in a lesson, ensuring that everyone knows who his or her partner is without asking—for example, by making sure that desks are set up in pairs and no one is sitting solo. If a student is absent, move another student up into his or her desk. Better to do it beforehand than have your *Turn and Talk* devolve into a "Turn, Look Next to You, Get Up and Walk Back a Few Rows, Disrupting Other Pairs as You Go, Greet a Friend with Nod and Smile and Only Then Start to Talk." The transitions need to be smooth, precise, and almost invisibly efficient, or the cost of the activity is not going to be worth the value you get from it. Generally speaking, the *Turn and Talk* will work only as well as the most disruptive pair, so it's important to have exactly zero disruptive pairs.

The In-Cue

If you asked a group of people (students, but often adults, too) to "turn and talk," their first thought might be to look around the room and see if other people were doing it. They might be somewhere between careful and skeptical. It would be embarrassing to earnestly turn to a neighbor and boldly opine about Grant at Vicksburg, only to have your partner stare impassively back and say nothing. And even if their first thought was more positive, they might spend time determining whom they'd talk to or who in a pair would talk first. And just to make sure they weren't the only one talking, they might wait it out a few seconds until it was clear others had started, just to be sure. Why risk it?

If students look around and don't see others participating, they won't perceive the activity to be sincere and rigorous—just obligatory. There's a bit of game theory afoot, a classroom permutation of the Prisoner's Dilemma: each student needs reassurance that everyone else is going to participate fully or else *he* won't participate fully, and if everyone takes a wait-and-see approach, you lose. Someone has to jump in first, so it's important to find a way to cause participants to start right away and pretty much in unison. That's the job of your in-cue.

I watched Rue Ratray of Edward Brooke Charter School do this in one of his lessons recently. Students were reading an interview with Lois Lowry about her famous youth novel, *The Giver,* and came upon a sentence that required close reading. "I agree with Nijah," Rue said. "We do need to break down the phrase 'Rejecting the authority and wisdom of the governing body.' What does *that* mean?" he asked the class, head tilted slightly in apparent befuddlement. He paused for a few seconds to let the question (and the idea that the sentence just might have stumped the teacher) sink in. Then: "Turn and talk to your partner. Go!"

As he said this the class snapped to life, the entire room engaging in energetic conversation exactly on cue. The phrase Rue used, "Turn and talk to your partner. Go!" was central to this success. It was familiar to Rue's students. He'd been using it steadily for weeks, if not every time he dispatched them to *Turn and Talk,* then at least with enough frequency that it had become a predictable stimulus to students, it was familiar, and it always resulted in all parties quickly and energetically engaging in a discussion. A good prompt is, like Rue's, familiar, consistent, and fast, and often includes a strategic bit of *Brighten Lines,* such as the word "Go!" (see technique 28) to cause students to snap to energetic discussion all at once.

It doesn't hurt when the teacher shows strong interest in the discussion topic, as Rue did, or causes *students* to show their interest. I recently saw Maggie Johnson of Troy Prep do this. Coming to the end of a chapter of *To Kill a Mockingbird,* she asked her students for an interpretation of Atticus's actions, with enthusiasm in her voice and a quizzical look on her face. Eight or ten hands went up. She paused. "Ooh, a lot of you know," she said, "but turn and talk to your partner for one minute first. Go!" Having publicly expressed their knowledge of and desire to talk about Maggie's question and primed by her clever use of suspense, the students snapped into discussion.

Now, not every champion teacher uses an in-cue that, like Maggie's and Rue's, includes the phrase "turn and talk." I watched Eric Snider of Achievement First Bushwick Middle School use a more unusual version of the in-cue. The class was reading Ray Bradbury. During a tense scene, Eric looked at his students. "What is David, the son, feeling worried about?" he asked, pausing briefly and then adding, "Long hair to short hair." That phrase was their prompt to *Turn and Talk.* It meant that the member of each pair with longer hair would start the conversation. Other times when Eric used the in-cue, he would say, "Short hair to long hair," to reverse whose turn came first and ensure balance in participation, but the *Turn and Talk* was implicit. I've seen different versions of Eric's idea to designate the two halves of each pair — for example, "Window to wall" (and "Wall to window") to designate students to start according to which side of the room they're sitting on. Although these in-cues seem different from Maggie's and Rue's, they share the same characteristics: fast, consistent, concise, offered with a bit of energy. In fact, one benefit of "Long hair to short hair" or "Window to wall" is that it establishes *managed turns*. This means that no time is wasted deciding who goes first, and it ensures balance in the cognitive work: kids who tend to be quieter get to carry as much of the discussion as kids who are more willing (and sometimes too willing) to talk.

In addition to sometimes designating who starts the conversation, you may at times wish to designate when speakers change turns, to ensure that both people get a chance to talk. You could do this with a verbal designation halfway through the allotted time ("Switch"), or even a nonverbal like clapping. For most champion teachers, managing turns is something they choose sometimes to do and sometimes not, especially as students grow more adept at managing turns on their own. Still, a certain amount of managing turns ensures healthy balance within your *Turn and Talks*; it's worth teaching your signal and using it occasionally so you have it at your disposal when you need it.

The Out-Cue

If an in-cue is important, you're probably thinking that an out-cue must be as well. When you end a *Turn and Talk,* your primary goal is efficiency. You want to wrap things up quickly and cleanly, so you don't waste time and so that the energy and ideas from the *Turn and Talk* flow seamlessly into whatever activity comes next. You definitely don't want to stand at the front of the room saying, "OK guys. Bring it back. Bring it back, please. Guys, I need you back."

You want students returning their attention to you quickly and automatically. But you also want to show respect for student conversations so that you don't cut them off too abruptly. For that reason, a good out-cue often includes a short countdown during which students can "wrap up their thoughts." I recently observed Amy Parsons of Leadership Prep Bedford Stuyvesant using the out-cue "Bring it back in three, in two, in one. Thank you" and then without delay asking students to share the details of their discussion. It was mutually understood that students could wrap up their conversations and thus still be talking during the countdown, so long as they were ready at the end. The key principles here are pretty straightforward: use a consistent, familiar prompt that's the same almost every time so that students learn to react to it automatically; be concise; and make the end prompt imply a defined amount of time for students to finish their thoughts—a countdown like Amy's or, as I noticed Eric Snider using, a series of snaps after which students have four seconds to finish their thought and come to "quiet."

See It in Action: Clip 44

In clip 44, you can see Rue Ratray using a variety of methods to keep his *Turn and Talks* engaging for his students. They're discussing *The Giver,* and in the first *Turn and Talk* he executes, he places two versions of a key sentence from the text on the board: one that's as it was written in the book, another that's slightly rewritten for a different tone. He asks the class to compare the two, giving them a long stretch of *Wait Time* during which you can hear the gasps of insight before he sends them to a crisp *Turn and Talk*. The connection here is obvious but easily overlooked: Rue's students snapped to it because they have lots they want to say, and they have lots to say because he asked them a rigorous and engaging question and then gave them significant time to develop an opinion before the *Turn and Talk* began.

In the second *Turn and Talk* in the clip, he takes another approach, asking students to explain the meaning of a challenging sentence. Students raise their hands, expressing their desire to respond to his question, but Rue then quickly asks them to put their hands down and *Turn and Talk* instead, channeling their energy into the pair activity first.

Crest of the Wave

Two general rules of thumb can help you to manage time (and timing) during *Turn and Talks*. The first, *crest of the wave,* relates to the observation that a *Turn and Talk* is almost always a preliminary activity. It's rarely the capstone to work on a topic, but rather a midpoint where ideas are rehearsed and developed and students are engaged before those ideas get harvested, refined, and developed. If you are transitioning from a *Turn and Talk* to an activity that allows for better synthesis, such as whole-class discussion or independent writing, you want students to still be actively wrestling with ideas and eager to take them forward, rather than feeling "done" with an idea as the *Turn and Talk* ends. If it goes on too long and students have talked through all of their ideas, running out of things to say as the clock keeps ticking, it will sap energy and cause students to

Figure 9.1 Crest of the Wave. Time your out-cue so that the *Turn and Talk* ends at the crest of interest and energy, not as it peters out.

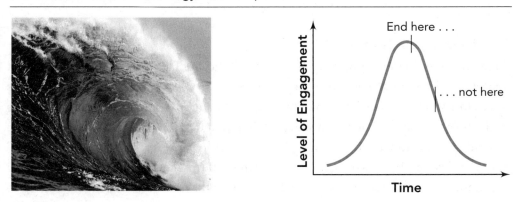

perceive *Turn and Talk* as an activity in which there's not much urgency to discuss things because there's more than enough time. An incentive to only partially engage can infect behavior in all *Turn and Talks*.

If you were to graph the level of energy during a *Turn and Talk*, then, it might look like a normal curve with a fat tail at the end. Ideally you would end it at its maximum point, when ideas were bursting and students eager to get to next steps, before the long slope downward. That's the crest of the wave. (See Figure 9.1.)

Precise Time Limits

The second general rule is to be precise with time. Imagine you're a student and are participating in a *Turn and Talk*, but you don't know how long it's going to last. Forty-five seconds? Two minutes? Fifteen minutes? Not knowing this basic information can make it hard for you to gauge how much to say. Do you need to get the basic idea out and stop so that the other person can broach an idea? Is your conversation about deep analysis? Should you ask your partner a thoughtful question? Your informing participants of the time parameters helps them manage their comments and their conversations to make the best use of time. Saying things like "Turn and talk to your neighbor for the next forty-five seconds" or "Two-and-a-half minutes to discuss the role of setting. Go" provides guidance; further, your use of specific and odd increments shows that your time allocation is careful, specific, and intentional. It tells students that time and its careful use matter to you, so they should matter to them. If you use a stopwatch to track those time allocations, it also helps you keep yourself accountable for moving the lesson forward and not losing track of time while checking in with a stuck or highly engaged pair, say. And, over time, it will help you make smarter and more specific time allocations for *Turn and Talks*.

Engagement You Can See

Another powerful tool for making *Turn and Talks* accountable is asking for engagement you can see. One teacher at a workshop modeled a *Turn and Talk* on Langston Hughes's "Harlem [A Dream Deferred]" like this: "One minute to discuss the imagery you see in the poem. Turn … ," she then said, pausing for a moment and using a nonverbal to remind students to face one another, "and talk." The pause between the words "turn" and "talk" was perhaps two seconds, but during that time she made a point of scanning the room to show that she was looking for evidence that everyone had indeed turned to his or her partner and was ready to participate. By making students' engagement visible, she could better manage their participation.

There are other ways I've seen great teachers connect observable student actions to active and engaged participation in the *Turn and Talk* task. One teacher asks her students to turn "knee to knee" so she can see that they're engaged. Another asks students to complete a task such as "summarizing key points from your partner's ideas." This not only causes students to listen better but also enables a teacher to see if they are taking notes and participating.

Although I might be inclined to use note taking or writing during a *Turn and Talk* throughout the year, other forms of engagement you can see are especially useful for initially teaching and reinforcing participation during *Turn and Talk*. As with so many other aspects of classroom life, with *Turn and Talks,* as students become more skilled, scaffolds generally can be pulled away over time.

See It in Action: Clip 45

In clip 45, seventh-grade reading teacher Eric Snider of Achievement First Bushwick Middle School prompts his students to answer the following comprehension questions in pairs: "Where is the Bittering family from? How'd they get to Mars?" He then follows the *Turn and Talk* with a whole-class share-out of their answers.

In the clip, Eric is stressing participation ratio—maximizing student engagement and interest in a very challenging text so that he can read it closely with sustained energy. As he does that, you'll notice

- **Standardized in-cue.** Eric uses a quick and simple prompt ("Long hair to short hair") to initiate the *Turn and Talk*. His in-cue language also is a form of managing turns by identifying who should speak first. This helps him maximize the amount of time students can spend talking and thinking.

- **Engagement you can see.** During the *Turn and Talk*, Eric also *Circulates* and scans the class for signs of engagement. When Eric notices that a student is slow to comply, he uses a nonverbal gesture to redirect him. In doing so, he also signals to the rest of the class that he cares and notices whether or not they discuss the question.

- **Crest of the wave.** Eric doesn't wait until the conversation sputters to an end, but instead interrupts them at what seems to be the peak or "crest" of their engagement level. In doing so, he ensures that students will have some insights to share and some insights to gain during the whole-class conversation.

- *Turn and Talk* **nonverbals.** Eric uses a quick nonverbal gesture (moving his hand from left to right) to prompt students to face each other. He then snaps to signal the close of the *Turn and Talk* and bring the students' attention back to him. These gestures allow him to facilitate the pair conversations with strong economy of language.

- **Other techniques.** Eric exits his *Turn and Talk* with a *Call and Response* and a *Cold Call*. His use of both techniques keeps students on their toes, improves the pacing of the lesson, and maintains a high energy level.

Here are some additional thoughts on processing your *Turn and Talk* to maximize accountability and focus:

1. Use *Cold Call* (technique 33) positively and even transparently to emphasize for students that everyone must be ready to talk about some insight he or she gleaned from the activity. You might say, "One minute to discuss with your partner the imagery you see in the poem. I'll *Cold Call* a few of you coming out of the *Turn and Talk*, so be ready with those great insights. Go!"

2. Make your *Turn and Talk* a "Turn and Task," wherein the partners or each partner is asked to write—cite three important details, solve a problem, list useful words to describe the scene. You might thus tweak the previous example to make it, "One

minute to list in rank order the three images you think are most important in the poem. I'll ask a few of you to share your best image, so be ready. Go!" Now you can monitor students' thinking more clearly during the duration of the *Turn and Talk*. It also gives you a nice change-up to add variety if you use *Turn and Talk* frequently.

3. Try a "partner share" where participants debriefing the *Turn and Talk* are asked to discuss what their partner said. This increases accountability for listening and supports attentiveness to peers' ideas.

Design for Rigor

Recently I watched a lesson from a middle school science class. The topic of the lesson was friction, and the teacher asked his students to *Turn and Talk* to discuss ways friction might affect what happened during a basketball game. The teacher's in-cue was crisp, and he had established a culture of positive accountability, so students buzzed into action, sharing their energy, their excitement, and, as it turned out afterwards, a great deal of misinformation. When the teacher asked students to share the ideas they'd discussed in pairs, three out of four shared ideas that misapplied or misunderstood how friction worked. There are times, in other words, when even with efficient and accountable systems, *Turn and Talks* can be predominated by the spread of low-quality ideas—or erroneous ones. In the class I watched, the teacher stumbled on this fact through the good fortune of hearing answers that revealed the problems, and the wise decision to process the *Turn and Talk* through a broader, teacher-led discussion afterwards. But let's pause here to consider all of the *Turn and Talks* where misinformation has blithely and earnestly been spread among participating students who did not know that what they were hearing (or saying and driving into memory) was dead wrong, all without the teacher's being aware of it. Some certainly are not that way, but some surely are. And, for the most part, the *Turn and Talk* itself makes it all but impossible to determine which is happening in your classroom at a given time.

Turn and Talk, then, is an outstanding activity for building participation ratio and *initiating* think ratio. It can allow students to rehearse ideas and refine their thinking, inscribing it in memory and preparing them for discussion. It can allow students to listen to the ideas of classmates and compare them to their own. That's a lot of upside. But *Turn and Talk* is also a time when students can engage at the most simplistic level or when they can inscribe, apply, and instill into memory flawed information and ideas. And whether this is happening in any given *Turn and Talk* is very difficult to track. That doesn't mean you shouldn't use *Turn and Talk*—just that you should use it in a way that considers the challenges. The best way to do that is to pair your *Turn and Talk* with a subsequent activity that allows you to reinforce rigor and check for understanding.

Another way to think about *Turn and Talk* is as a prelude, a catalyst to some other activity: a whole-class discussion, a written synthesis, a charting and comparison of ideas generated. The *Turn and Talk*'s purpose is generative—let's get a lot of ideas going, figure out what makes sense, and why. After a *Turn and Talk,* it's important to take the ideas that were generated and analyze them in a public way, editing, revising, and prioritizing them so that students see what was good, what was better, and possibly what was wrong. Consider also asking for some further processing, ideally in writing, to ensure that rigor and clarity emerge from the investment you've made.

After *Turn and Talk:* Pushing for Greater Rigor

Here, then, are four key "after" activities to make sure that *Turn and Talk* brings rigor and high standards to your classroom.

Whole-Class Analysis

Teach students that the first idea is not always the best idea, that developing a strong answer often requires going back through your initial thoughts and considering them in light of further criteria or analysis. This might sound like "Let's look at some of the ideas we came up with and see which ones make the most sense" or "Let's try to use what we know about friction to test a few of our ideas and see if they were accurate." Or you could try something like "Let's put a couple of these on the board and list the evidence that seems to support (or not support) some of our ideas."

Whole-Class Discussion

Use *Turn and Talk* as the starting point for a deeper whole-class discussion that builds on and stretches students' initial thinking. This might sound like "Let's build on the thinking we've started ... ," possibly with a coda like "As we talk, feel free to add to what you already wrote down." Or you might try, "Now let's try to put our ideas together to come up with a few 'best' examples." Or, finally, you could just acknowledge that the initial *Turn and Talk* was a warm-up: "Now that we've started to discuss some ideas, let's take a look at the sentence together and see if we can make sense of what it means."

Whole-Class Note Taking

Follow up the *Turn and Talk* by processing those initial thoughts—by having students share, improve, and prioritize the contents of their collective "pair" discussions. The expectation here is that they take what they talked about in their *Turn and Talk*, develop it by listening and comparing to what others took from the discussion, and track a wide array of thoughts on the topic, not just their own. This might sound like "Add two sentences to the bullets on page 3" or "Now let's look at the passage and circle all the evidence we found as a group. Make sure to take notes on your sheet so you've got all of our class's ideas in your notes."

Whole-Class Guided Discussion, Then Written Processing

Wrap up pair and whole-group discussion by having students synthesize the most important insights into writing, perhaps in a single, well-crafted sentence (see technique 38, *Art of the Sentence*). For example, following a whole-class discussion about states of matter and phase change, you might say: "OK, everyone take ninety seconds to explain what sublimation is and how it might work. Begin your sentence with the phrase, 'Ordinarily, a solid …' Go." Another example: "To close, I'm going to ask you to describe the tension between the two sisters in this chapter in a single, well-written sentence that starts with the word 'Despite.'" Or you could make the writing a shared endeavor: "Now let's see if we can write a paragraph together that describes what the evidence in this passage suggests about who is really in charge."

Another option would be to flip things on their head to make your *Turn and Talk* into an error analysis portion. That is, you could take an answer and ask, "Is that correct? If so, could it be better yet? If not, why? Thirty seconds. In pairs. Go." Of course, you still have the whole class analyze after the *Turn and Talk,* but you set the tone for reflection on quality and correctness.

Each of these four approaches or adaptations (or combinations of them) can help you make sure that your *Turn and Talk* is a productive tool that leads to a lesson of the highest standards.

See It in Action: Clip 46

In clip 46, Laura Fern, an instructional leader at North Star's Vailsburg Elementary, executes a *Turn and Talk* on the carpet with her students. The students are working on identifying types of "show, not tell" language in a piece of writing. As you watch it, consider the following question: What does Laura say and do to make the *Turn and Talk* efficient and rigorous?

To ensure efficiency, Laura:

- <u>Uses consistent cues.</u> Laura has taught her scholars that the words "Turn and talk" is the signal to turn immediately to their partner and begin talking, and a silent five-second countdown means that they need to wrap up their conversation and turn back. Note how she starts with the phrase "On my signal" so that it's a crisp start.

- <u>Uses nonverbal gestures.</u> Laura uses a quick clap that the scholars echo if she needs their attention in the middle of the *Turn and Talk,* and a nonverbal to lower the volume of their conversations. The cues and nonverbal gestures allow Laura to transition the class in and out of the *Turn and Talk* with strong economy of language and a sense of urgency.

- <u>Avoids paraphrasing answers.</u> Laura doesn't repeat or paraphrase each of her students' answers. This holds students accountable for actively listening to each other and gives Laura more time to build on and stretch her students' thinking.

- <u>Engages in "batch calling."</u> Laura reduces the transaction costs of calling on different students by taking three hands in advance (more on this technique later). Because students know who is sharing and when, Laura is able to facilitate each share-out with greater efficiency.

To boost rigor, Laura uses:

- <u>Strong questioning.</u> Laura begins this sequence with a substantive question that has multiple correct answers. The question requires students to provide evidence from the text and, with follow-up, explain their evidence: "What examples of 'Show, Not Tell' did you hear?" "And what type of 'Show, Not Tell' is that, Kyana?"

- *Circulate.* Laura listens in on several student conversations, pausing to push more thorough expression of an idea—"How, Sydney?"

- <u>Hunting and gathering.</u> Laura deliberately listens for high-quality answers and gathers them to be shared out efficiently with the whole class.

- <u>Visual scaffolds.</u> The poster on the board identifying different types of "Show, Not Tell" supports students in applying the types (and the concepts they represent) to the text they just heard.

BATCH PROCESS

Give more ownership and autonomy to students — particularly when your goal is a discussion — by allowing for student discussion without teacher mediation for short periods of time or for longer, more formal sequences.

There are times when, as a teacher, you need to constantly guide discussion, prompting and steering after just about every student comment to ensure rigor, focus, and mastery. Sometimes, though, it's better not to mediate every comment — to give more ownership and autonomy to students — particularly when your goal is a discussion. **Batch Process** is a technique in which you allow for student discussion without teacher mediation, for short periods of time or for longer, more formal sequences.

In its simplest form, *Batch Process* means allowing short strings (batches) of student-to-student conversation. You might think of it as playing volleyball instead of tennis. Three, four, or perhaps five kids might get to offer an insight or give their opinion before you step in to comment and steer. Your job would be simply to call on the next student to speak but not offer any further commentary. In its more complex forms, you might intentionally step back from discussion entirely, allowing students to manage both the process and content of their discussion for a defined period of time. Many teachers call this a Socratic discussion, a Socratic seminar, or sometimes a fishbowl.

To cultivate either type of peer-to-peer conversation, a bit of discretion and a bit of transparency are likely to help. On discretion: some teachers are drawn to activities like a Socratic discussion or a fishbowl seminar right away. Their feeling is that activities in which you put all the kids around a table, stand in the background, and say, "Go, now discuss" are the most rigorous, and that perhaps reasons for this have to do with your own absence. My observations have led me to be a bit more cautious about Socratic seminars. Yes, they can be beneficial; they're important practice for college, for example. And done well, they can build a culture of intellectualism. There's nothing quite like students seeing themselves engage in learning and the life of the mind without the teacher present to insist on it.

However, peer-to-peer conversations can be unproductive without the most informed person in the room steering them away from banal moments and pushing the level of discussion to higher levels. Plus, whether the conversations are rigorous or not, they are always logistically challenging. They take a long time to set up, often involve several rounds to make sure all students participate, and require activities for the rest of the class to do while some are discussing. (In general, unmediated discussions by more than a dozen people rarely work well, whether those people are students or not, so successfully conducting a Socratic discussion with twenty-five students at once is a long shot.) Due to these factors, most of the highly effective teachers I know who conduct these large-scale activities do so as an infrequent event: the capstone on a unit about the Civil War, say, perhaps once a month or twice a semester.

In many cases, the sort of *Batch Processing* that's most effective at building students' participation thinking habits is also easier to implement: small amounts of daily practice. Many of the best teachers I've observed do *Batch Processing* as a less formal activity for just a few minutes per day. In one school, all teachers are asked to take one minute during every lesson and say, "OK, it's your turn. You're going to talk to each other about this. Go." In many ways, a small amount of practice every day is much more productive and easier to orchestrate, and has a much lower transaction cost than a great, big activity.

Champion teacher Ryan Miller believes that this simpler, more consistent application of student-to-student discussion is the real driver of thinking skills. In his class, there are a few basic ground rules. The first: "Two minutes, on the clock, every day." This means that in every lesson, Ryan asks a really rigorous question, sets a clock for two minutes, and then steps back and lets the kids play volleyball—talk and respond directly to one another with little mediation or intervention from him. He finds two minutes to be plenty. It's actually quite a lot of time for a discussion, and it brings out the best ideas without letting the question or process linger for too long. It also honors the time he needs to do and teach other things. By putting it on the clock, he holds himself accountable, and by doing it every day, he makes it a habit, with students getting better over time.

Some other points Ryan made about his daily *Batch Process:* he's always disciplined about making the conversation connect to the central idea of the lesson. To help with this, before starting the daily practice, he trained his students on *Habits of Discussion*. This includes skills in how to respond to one another and build off of each other's ideas. Ryan never hesitates to interrupt to manage the meta—to shape students' actions in discussing—but does so far less often for content issues. The idea is that he has fifty-eight more minutes in class to help his scholars see the facts and interpretations of history the way he believes they should. They're therefore allowed to wrestle with intellectual ideas with varying degrees of success during the two-minute *Batch Process*. Still, they aren't allowed to discuss in an undisciplined manner, make off-task comments, stray from the topic, or not develop the previous idea. For those things, Ryan said, he steps in and refocuses the discussion.

Question Delegation

To boost think ratio, *question delegation* allows students to determine the topic and decide what's important to discuss. For example, Gillian Cartwright of Uncommon High School in Brooklyn asked her students to read a long section of *Fences* by August Wilson and then identify specific passages from the text that they thought were "worthy of analysis." Cartwright's students read and took notes for eight minutes, noting key points that they thought fit that criterion. Then they discussed, with Cartwright starting by asking, "So what did you think was worthy of analysis?" and students answering, "This scene was worthy of analysis because … "

Another productive tool that facilitates question delegation is having students write discussion questions. For example, you could ask students to submit a rigorous discussion question in advance, perhaps as homework; then you would select a few that were especially rigorous or insightful to offer to the class: "OK, let's take a minute to discuss some of your questions. One of you wanted to discuss Troy's anger and whether it was changing in a permanent way." You could also have students frame discussion questions as part of a *Do Now*. This would cause students to be thinking about the discussion they'd have later as they were participating throughout class. Your selection of questions would, over time, intimate to students a great deal about what a quality question looks like, even while giving them the autonomy to write them themselves.

Why is question delegation important? Because students are used to having questions, assignments, and paper topics given to them. But most of the time in college, and often in high school, students must not only decide what to say about a topic but also, even before the rigorous analysis begins, decide what is "worthy of analysis." Doing that well is often half the paper, one could argue. Deciding what's worth talking about is an important skill to practice. Question delegation lets students do that in a strategic, defined, and efficient manner.

CONCLUSION

Although I have divided the topic of ratio into three chapters—questioning, writing, and discussion—it would be a mistake to think of the three as discrete entities, functioning in their own little silos independent of one another. Each brings its own unique benefits in boosting think and participation ratio, and the three work together in a larger synergy, increasing the overall rigor of student work and shifting cognitive load from the teacher's desk to the students'. Whereas this part of the book looked at the various ways champion teachers work to shift that load, Part Four looks at how to build the behavioral and cultural foundation that supports and enables real academic work.

Reflection and Practice

1. Thinking in terms of think ratio and participation ratio, what are some of the successes and challenges you have experienced (or anticipate experiencing) using *Turn and Talk*? How might you amplify successes and minimize challenges?

2. Identify two behaviors you want students to do while in the *Turn and Talk*. Draft what you will say when you model and describe the behaviors. Script your in-cue and out-cue language and signals, and select a tool to help students generate ideas before talking.

3. Choose one of the questions (or create a new one) from your lesson script that you would like to use as a *Turn and Talk*. Indicate whether the purpose of your *Turn and Talk* is to boost participation ratio or think ratio. Also plan a number of ways you will extend students' thinking after the *Turn and Talk*.

USEFUL TOOLS

FIND THESE TOOLS AT WWW.TEACHLIKEACHAMPION.COM/YOURLIBRARY

Habits of Discussion **sentence starters.** Use these proven sentence starters to prepare students for productive, scholarly, and disciplined discussions that promote active listening and shape thinking.

Turn and Talk **planning guide.** Use our *Turn and Talk* planning guide to keep them as efficient, accountable, and rigorous as possible.

- "I agree because ... " / "I disagree because ... "

- "I understand why you'd say that, but ... "

- "Yes, I was just thinking of something similar, that ... "

- "And then there was another example of that ... "

- "The thing that doesn't take into account is ... "

- "There's another piece of evidence of that ... "

- "There's some evidence that might contradict that ... "

- "I'd like to build on _____'s idea ... "

- "I understand, and I would like to add ... "

- "That makes sense because ... "

- "There's another example of what _____ is talking about ... "

- "Another way you might interpret that is ... "

- "I think it's more complex than what you're saying, _____, because ... "

Part 4

Five Principles of Classroom Culture

THE TECHNIQUES IN CHAPTERS TEN THROUGH TWELVE FOCUS ON BUILDING classroom culture—making your room a place where students work hard, model strong character, are polite and attentive, and strive to do their best. Therefore, it's worth taking a few pages to reflect on classroom culture more broadly.

Cultures are complex, and a classroom culture that sustains and drives excellence requires a variety of types of interactions. To help you promote such a culture, I've identified five principles that, if well balanced, can ensure a culture that's healthy and strong. The words I've chosen to describe the principles are familiar ones, but their familiarity belies the fact that they are often confused or lumped together. Keeping their differences in mind and reflecting on each separately can help you understand your classroom and why its culture is thriving—or how to make it better.

DISCIPLINE

Most people use the word *discipline* as a verb, one that's synonymous with punishment: "I had to discipline that student." I prefer to use it as Ronald Morrish does in his excellent book *With All Due Respect*: as a noun that refers to the process of teaching someone the right way to do something: "I taught my students to have discipline." This sense of the word is also captured in the meaning of *self-discipline* and in the form of the word that refers to a body of ideas or a method of thinking (as an academic discipline). This reminds us that at the core of this definition of discipline is teaching—teaching students the right and successful way to do things.

> ### The Five Principles of Classroom Culture
>
> Discipline
>
> Management
>
> Control
>
> Influence
>
> Engagement

Ironically, many teachers forget this element, even though it's closely aligned to how they define their job. They expect to teach the content, but not necessarily the habits of being a successful student and community member. They set up systems of reward and consequence to hold students accountable. They assume that students know *how* to do the things teachers want or ask them to do. They say, "Pay attention," for example, but don't think to teach their students: "When I ask you to pay attention, I am asking you to sit up straight and show your engagement by looking at the person who's talking, and taking notes on what we write on the overhead." Too often, teachers overlook this step and assume that their students have inferred a knowledge of the right way to do things in previous classrooms or in their lives outside of school. As my colleague Doug McCurry wisely put it, "If students aren't doing what you asked, the most likely explanation is that you haven't taught them how."

Teaching with discipline implies a front-end investment in teaching your students how to be students, and that requires a fair amount of planning. How will your students sit, line up, enter the classroom, and take notes? How will they disagree respectfully? It also means investing in a whole lot of practice. The results of emphasizing and investing in discipline can be stunning, however; it turns out that there are a lot of kids on the margins of classroom culture who want to do what's expected of them. They're just waiting to be taught.

Most of Chapter Ten (among other parts of this book), then, is really about discipline, about starting with a vision of what "doing right" looks like and then practicing it so that it becomes a matter of habit.

MANAGEMENT

Management, by contrast, is the process of reinforcing behavior through the use of consequences and rewards. What we typically call "disciplining" is often really management: giving consequences. Some teachers see this as the whole game, with what at first may appear to be significant justification.

Effective classrooms need management systems. But because management is the element of school culture that yields the most visible short-term results, it's easy to fail to recognize its particular reliance on the other four elements, and its limitations without them. Although management makes operating an achievement-focused classroom more direct and efficient, it cannot sustain itself without the other four elements of positive culture. Without them, management, even in the best systems, ultimately suffers from diminishing marginal returns: the more you use it, the less effective it is. The most common way to undercut and erode management systems is to overuse deductions, laying on consequence after consequence until they appear meaningless and students have nothing left to play for.

Slightly less common but equally critical is the nonstrategic use of rewards. We call this "throwing dollars." When a teacher throws dollars, he rewards students for doing what merely meets expectations. Answer a question—get a "scholar dollar." Follow a direction—earn a token. This approach suggests that the behaviors were not the teacher's expectation, but were, in his mind, exceptional; ironically, this undercuts expectations. It cheapens praise and lowers standards—not only for the teacher in question but for everyone who shares the management system with him.

When schools or teachers overrely on management, a death spiral ensues: students become desensitized to consequences and Machiavellian about rewards; more of each is required to achieve the same or lesser effect; students become increasingly insensitive to the larger doses, and the larger doses signal to students either the desperation of their teacher or that they are problem kids, not successful kids; and the currency of management becomes less rational and more negative.

Strong management is not only a positive part of an effective classroom culture but also a necessary part. To succeed, however, it must operate in combination with the other four elements, or it will soon become ineffective. You must teach students how to do things right before you establish consequences for doing them wrong, for example. To truly succeed, you must be able to control students—that is, get them to do things regardless of consequence, and inspire and engage them in positive work. You also are building relationships with students that are nontransactional; they don't involve rewards or consequences, and they demonstrate that you care enough to know your students as individuals.

Much of the design and implementation of management systems is beyond the scope of this book, but the technique *Art of the Consequence* addresses it directly, and techniques addressing tone—*Firm Calm Finesse* also in Chapter Eleven and *Warm/Strict* in Chapter Twelve—all relate to interactions involving classroom management.

CONTROL

Control is your capacity to cause someone to choose to do what you ask, regardless of consequences. It's a dirty word to some people. There has to be something wrong with controlling someone else. It's undemocratic, they think, and coercive. The intention to control another person seems especially reprehensible in a teacher, because teaching is to help people think for themselves. However, a bit of context should make it clear that all of us exert control over other people's actions and that we do it because it's the right thing to do, especially for teachers. In many cases, benign, enlightened control is a very good thing: a teacher reliably gets students to ask why and how questions when reading history; to be suspicious of claims not supported by evidence; and to work hard, value learning, and respect their peers.

In fact, my definition of control does not imply a lack of agency in the people you cause to do what you ask. They still choose. Controlling merely involves asking in a way that makes them more likely to agree to do it. No choices are entirely neutral. Looking someone in the eye and speaking firmly is clearly exerting control—but so is saying please and showing that you appreciate her willingness to do something she may not want to. (Shouting, ironically, almost always is *not*.)

The biggest paradox about control is that it is more than a necessary evil. It often supports freedom. I know this as a parent. I can give my children the freedom to run ahead of me on a sidewalk and explore on their own only if I have successfully taught them the rules for crossing the street (that is, if I have "disciplined" them to know how to stop at the curb). But I also must know for certain that if they neared a driveway with a car unexpectedly backing out and I called to them to stop, they would stop, instantly and without fail. I must have control, or I cannot be effective in protecting my children or in affording them opportunities to grow. The more I have the power to exercise responsible control, the more freedom I can give my children (or my students) — ideally in ways that truly matter.

Teachers who have strong control succeed because they understand the power of language and relationships: they ask firmly and confidently, but also with civility, and often kindly. They express their faith in students' ability to meet expectations. They replace vague commands like "calm down" with specific and useful ones like "Please return to your seat and begin writing in your journal." These actions evince clarity, purposefulness, resolve, and caring. If you can get students to reliably do what you have asked, and if the things you've asked help them to succeed, then you are doing your job. If you can do this consistently, you can save your consequences for when you need them most. Getting comfortable with the need to exert benign control is part of a teacher's preparation for success. Many of the techniques in this book support control. *Strong Voice, What to Do,* and *Radar/Be Seen Looking* are some of the more straightforward ones. But so are the things you do to build trust and relationships with students. People whom students mistrust rarely exert effective control over the long run.

INFLUENCE

Ideally, all teachers connect to their students and inspire them to want achievement and success for themselves. Inspiring students to believe, to want to succeed for intrinsic reasons, is influencing them. Influence is the next step beyond control. If control gets them to do things you suggest, then influence gets them to want to internalize the things you suggest. Although less visible than getting kids to *behave*, getting them to *believe*—to want to behave positively—is necessary to long-term success and to a healthy classroom culture. Belief, as the history of every powerful idea from democracy to the tenets of any religious faith demonstrates, is a powerful and lasting motivator. If influence is the process of instilling belief, maximizing it should be an intentional goal of every teacher's classroom culture.

The power of influence can often remain hidden, however. A classroom with discipline, management, and control may initially appear successful, and the need for influence may not at first demand the teacher's attention. In the end, however, a teacher cannot sustain order unless the students believe, and you must begin moving them from "behave" to "believe" before you realize you need to do so—from day one, in fact. It's fairly common to see a teacher achieve orderliness for the first few weeks of the year, only to experience a backlash and lose his students, often for the duration of the year. The reason for this, often, is a failure to leverage influence to help students believe in and trust that the classroom culture was designed primarily for their own benefit. Control will not endure without influence.

Aspects of influence appear throughout the book, sometimes in obvious places, such as the chapter on building relationships and trust, but also in some unexpected places, such as in the emphasis on "purpose over power" in *Firm Calm Finesse*.

ENGAGEMENT

One of the most common reasons for poor classroom culture is an insipid lesson. The human mind is a powerful thing, and when it does not encounter stimuli to challenge and fascinate it, it will soon find something else to challenge and fascinate it. Great teachers always seek to give students plenty to say yes to, plenty to get involved in, plenty to lose themselves in. They get students busily engaged in important, interesting, and challenging work.

When children go to school in an environment where culture is poor and behavioral expectations are low, one of the first things they lose is what I call "real science"—that is, science with beakers, test tubes, Bunsen burners, and microscopes. Sadly, when behavior isn't reliable, adults take those things away—how can you leave glassware in a classroom where students won't follow directions? But please remember that as you build a healthy culture, students must get real science back; adults must return to them their microscopes and Bunsen burners. When students are engaged in the worlds those tools unlock, they become vested in learning and see the benefits of the bargain they have struck through their positive behavior. Great and rigorous lessons are standard fare in a classroom with outstanding culture.

Thinking about these five principles can be a useful diagnostic tool. It can help you take action to right your culture based on what's working and what needs more attention. If you're a leader, it can serve the same purpose—helping you help teachers make their culture positive. This is especially powerful because people often think of classroom culture as a single thing, which of course it isn't. It's complex, and trying to do more of the same is not always the way to ensure that it thrives. In the following chapters, we'll look at the ways in which the five principles come together in champion classrooms.

Chapter 10

Systems and Routines

Technique 45: Threshold.   Meet your students at the door, setting expectations before they enter the classroom.

Technique 46: Strong Start.   Design and establish an efficient routine for students to enter the classroom and begin class.

Technique 47: STAR/SLANT.   Teach students key baseline behaviors for learning, such as sitting up in class and tracking the speaker, by using a memorable acronym such as STAR or SLANT.

Technique 48: Engineer Efficiency.   Teach students the simplest and fastest procedure for executing key classroom tasks, then practice so that executing the procedure becomes a routine.

Technique 49: Strategic Investment: From Procedure to Routine.   Turn procedures into routines by rehearsing and reinforcing until excellence becomes habitual. Routinizing a key procedure requires clear expectations, consistency, and, most important, patience. Even so, it's almost always worth it.

Technique 50: Do It Again.   Give students more practice when they're not up to speed—not just doing something again, but doing it better, striving to do their best.

Chapter 10

Systems and Routines

I wish everyone could have seen Sam DeLuke and Meghan Hurley's second-grade classroom at Troy Prep Elementary School on the day I visited last fall. When I first walked in, I found Sam sitting in one corner, listening in on five students rigorously discussing a chapter book. As I inched closer, I overheard students making sophisticated statements like "I think you missed one piece of evidence, Zariah" and "I agree with David's point and want to develop it" (see technique 42, *Habits of Discussion*). In another corner, Meghan read a book about ants aloud to an audience of ten wide-eyed students who hung on every word. In the center of the room, a group of six sat silently, engrossed in the pages of independent reading books, while another six students had hunkered down to draft paragraphs explaining the theme of a story they read the day before.

A few minutes later, Sam said go, and with no further prompting, ten students stood and walked to Meghan's corner exactly on cue and with pin-drop silence. Others, who did not transition, kept working away. Meghan resumed instruction, but soon after glanced over and noticed that one independent worker was off task. She gently redirected her with a familiar nonverbal signal. Later, Sam realized that several students didn't have books they'd need for the next activity. Still working with a reading group, with a subtle gesture and without ever interrupting her instruction, she prompted a scholar to distribute books to his peers.

Students in Meghan and Sam's class worked in an atmosphere of autonomy and freedom — the room almost seemed to run itself. Paradoxically, this freedom and autonomy were the products of demonstrable structure and clear expectations. The moments when a single prompt initiated a perfectly orchestrated transition were not in contrast to the moments when students worked at their desks with complete independence; they allowed them, fostered them, and made them productive.

Sam and Meghan had invested heavily in their *procedures,* which provide students with explicit guidance on how to execute such recurring tasks as working independently, transitioning between small groups, and answering questions in class. During the first few weeks of the year, they relied on constant practice and a management system to reinforce their expectations. If you'd seen them then, you might not have understood where it was all leading — Why all the structure? Why all the "just so" with every little piece? Aren't they being a little obsessive with the rules for lining up and moving? But over time, each of those "just so" pieces took its place within a system, a network of smaller procedures that allowed Sam and Meghan to teach students productive and ultimately independent behavior. Over time, these procedures became automatic, or *routine* — students could, for the most part, execute them on their own. From that point, Sam and Meghan's role was to initiate and then lightly manage the familiar routines. They could afford to grant their students autonomy because students knew how to manage their autonomy productively and because teachers could initiate it, correct it, or rein it in with a single word or gesture.

Talking About Systems and Routines

Discussing systems and routines can benefit from a bit of terminology. Here are some definitions of key terms:

- <u>Procedure:</u> the design a teacher establishes for the way she and her students will efficiently and productively execute a recurring task or action in the classroom

- <u>System:</u> a network of related procedures that help teachers accomplish end goals: help students maintain an organized binder, manage behavior, move materials, participate successfully in a discussion, and so on

- **Routine:** a procedure or system that has become automatic, which students do either without much oversight, without intentional cognition (in other words, as a habit), and/or of their own volition and without teacher prompting (for example, note taking while reading)

My goal in this chapter is to pull back the curtain a bit and reveal the ways in which teachers like Sam and Meghan use structure—specifically, a systematic approach to discipline—to create rigorous, joyful, and orderly classrooms that grant students real independence. To start this process, we'll look closely at three classic routines: *Threshold, Strong Start,* and *STAR/SLANT.* Afterward, we'll explore the "how" behind installing, reinforcing, and maintaining systems and routines so that you can set up students for success in your classroom and beyond.

THRESHOLD

Meet your students at the door, setting expectations before they enter the classroom.

45

With students, first impressions matter, not just on the first day of school, but every day. This is why champion teachers are thoughtful and strategic about how they manage their first interaction with each student. How you choose to greet each student as he or she crosses the threshold of your doorway helps establish expectations and sets the tone for the rest of class. With culture, getting it right and keeping it right are much easier than fixing it once it goes wrong. **Threshold** ensures that you make a habit of getting it right at the start of each day.

Ideally, you would find a way to greet your students by standing in the physical threshold of the classroom—astride the door, taking the opportunity to remind students where they are (they are with you now, and no matter what the expectations elsewhere, you will always expect their best), how you feel toward them (caring, warm, but also with a hint that strictness can emerge as needed), and what you will expect of them (excellence, scholarship, and effort). During this routine, each student who enters shakes your hand, looks you in the eye, and offers a civil and cordial greeting, and vice versa.

You can use the greeting to engage students briefly and build rapport: "Loved your homework, David"; "Nice game last night, Shayna"; "Looking for great things from you today, Mr. Williams!"; "Your hair looks great, Shanice!" You won't have time to say something like this to every student, but you can pick a few each day, over time connecting with each student and reminding them all that you know them as individuals. You can also build rapport while reinforcing expectations for *Threshold* by warmly acknowledging students with strong greetings: "Nice strong shake, Jamal." "I love the enthusiasm, Terry."

You can also welcome the procession of students through the doorway with a description of what's to come and a reminder of what's expected: "We have a quiz today. Better use that *Do Now* to get ready." You should also use *Threshold* to set expectations by correcting weak handshakes, untidy attire, apathetic or sarcastic greetings, or poor eye contact. Fortunately, this is easy to do because *Threshold* offers a built-in consequence. Get it wrong, and you go back in the line and try it again; when you meet the expectations of the room, you enter on good terms. Incidentally, this is another reason for using a handshake: it allows you to control access to the room. If a student walks past you with his or her head down or without a greeting, you can gently hold on to the student's hand until the student corrects his or her behavior.

When you stand at the doorway, position yourself to *see both sides* so that you can maintain visibility of the students who have already entered your classroom as well as those you're greeting. Once they enter, narrate a bit of positive behavior: "Thanks for getting *right* to work, A'Fonte"; "Good work, Jamila. Appreciate that homework on the corner of your desk." If you notice that several students in class are not meeting expectations, you can warmly remind them of what they should be doing: "Make sure those chairs are tucked in so that everyone can get by" or "Remember, we enter with 'voices off.'" Also remember to strike a balance between which sides you look at and when. Staring for too long at either side can lead to poor management of the other and can undermine the culture and tone you're trying to establish with *Threshold*.

Threshold will naturally take on a feel that corresponds to your own tone and style: it can be outgoing or quiet, warm or crisp. Regardless of the affect, *Threshold* should always accomplish two things: (1) help you establish a personal connection with your students through a brief individual check-in (ideally one in which you greet each student by name), and (2) reinforce your expectations for what students should do before and after they enter your classroom.

In a lesson that I've watched and rewatched perhaps a hundred times, Dacia Toll adds a bit of her own style to the greeting she offers each of her sixth-grade writing students one day early in the life of New Haven's now legendary Amistad Academy. "Good morning, Sisuelas," she says to one student as she shakes her hand. "Nice to see you again, Sandria." Her warm, convivial greeting underscores just how excited she is to see each of her students. When one student greets her with an informal, "Hey, what up?" she responds with warmth, "'What up' is not appropriate," gently holding his hand as he passes and directing him to the back of the line. A few seconds later, he greets her with a "Good morning" and, without retribution, she nods: "Good morning, Jabali."

Throughout this interaction, Dacia refrains from shaming or punishing the student for his behavior. Instead, she models the professionalism and civility that she expects everyone to show her during *Threshold*. In doing so, she not only preserves (and quite possibly, strengthens) her relationship with the student but also turns the interaction into an opportunity to implicitly teach him — and everyone else who's watching — the right way to enter the classroom.

When I observed him at North Star Academy in Newark several years ago, Jamey Verrilli added a few wrinkles of his own. As his students waited outside the classroom, he quizzed them on vocabulary words. "OK, *tilled*. Who would do tilling, and what kind of work was it?" The message this sent was powerful: every minute matters; we are in school even when we are not in class. After a brief preamble — "OK, gentlemen, when you come in, you need to set your desk with your homework at the top. Your *Do Now* today is going to require you to spell some of these words we've been studying. Clear?" — Jamey posted himself in the doorjamb. Like Dacia, he offered personal greetings as he shook each student's hand. He was warm but muscular, referring to students by their last names: "Good afternoon, Mr. Mumford. Good afternoon, Mr. Reeves." A young Mr. Early slouched a bit and glanced away. "Stand up straight and give me good grip," Jamey responded, and Mr. Early readily complied, seeming to appreciate Jamey's expectations for him. Two students later, young Mr. Smallwood approached, wearing a new pair of glasses. "Looking sharp, Mr. Smallwood!" Jamey boomed, breaking his general tone of formality with a burst of enthusiasm. Things were not going quite so swimmingly for Mr. Merrick, who had been talking. "Step out [of the room], please," Jamey said, as he sent him back to repeat his entrance until he got it right.

In Jamey's classroom, the mood was warm but industrious. All of the students were hard at work just a few seconds after hitting the door—even Mr. Merrick, who was soon settled, redirected, and ready for class, with *Threshold* setting expectations from the start.

If it's not possible for you to greet students at the door (either for school policy reasons or because you float to classrooms), invent another ritual to signify the start of something formal. For example, you might walk the rows briefly greeting students during the *Do Now*. Whether or not you have a doorway is beside the point. What matters is that you leverage the power of ritual to help students see, from the moment they enter your classroom, that it is different from the other places they go.

TECHNIQUE

46

STRONG START

Design and establish an efficient routine for students to enter the classroom and begin class.

For many busy teachers, the time students spend entering class and working on a *Do Now*—the time before the main lesson starts—can be a bit of an afterthought. Some use it to complete clerical tasks—stapling packets, organizing instructional materials, writing lesson objectives on the board, or even briefly collecting their thoughts. In their eyes, the opening minutes of class are ideal for preparing for a lesson that won't begin until they start delivering new content.

Of course there are times when they have to grab a minute to attend to some task, but champion teachers understand that every lesson begins *as soon as students walk through the door*. They intentionally design and reinforce a most efficient *right* way for students to enter the classroom, complete the *Do Now,* prepare their learning materials, and get to the heart of the lesson. I refer to the sequence of events from the moment students enter the room until the heart of the lesson begins as the **Strong Start**.

The success of a lesson hinges on *Strong Start* for three reasons:

- It sets the tone for everything that comes after. Classroom culture is not static from day to day. It is shaped by the opening minutes of a lesson—whether you intentionally engineer them or not. That's why champion teachers prepare to start their lessons on a high note by finding genuine opportunities to convey warmth and enthusiasm.

- From a pacing perspective, a strong, energetic start to your lesson builds momentum. It socializes students to work with discipline, urgency, and efficiency as soon as they walk through the door. Get off to a slow start, and you could find yourself spending the rest of your lesson fighting to rebuild momentum you lost and may never win back.

- *Strong Start* sets the table for mastery by efficiently previewing or reviewing high-quality content students need to master. *Strong Start* isn't just about tight procedures and efficiency. These conditions should be in service of the overarching goal: equipping students right off the bat with the academic tools they'll need to succeed.

If you stepped inside a champion teacher's classroom shortly after the bell rang, you would probably find that you could divide the routine students use to start the day into three parts: (1) Door to *Do Now*, (2) *Do Now*, and (3) Review Now.

Door to *Do Now*

The first component of *Strong Start* comprises how students get from the door to their *Do Now*. Unlike *Threshold*, which immediately precedes students' entry into the room and focuses on setting behavioral norms and expectations, Door to *Do Now* is about making a habit out of what's efficient, productive, and scholarly as students take their seats.

A typical arrangement might look something like this: as soon as students cross the threshold of the classroom door, they pick up a packet of materials from a small table just inside. In some cases, especially at the lower elementary grades, packets might already be at students' desks. A couple of key points maximize the effectiveness of the Door to *Do Now*:

- It's more efficient to have students pick up their packets from a table than it is for you to try to hand the packets to them at the door. The latter approach slows you down and forces you to multitask when your mind should be on setting expectations and building relationships.

- Students should know where to sit. Time spent milling around, looking for a seat, deciding where to sit, or talking about deciding where to sit ("Can I sit next to him?

Will he think I'm flirting?") is a waste of learning time and energy. Assign seats or allow students to sign up for regular seats.

- Whatever students need to do with homework (put it in a basket, place it on the front left corner of their desk, pass it to a proctor), they should do the same way every day without prompting. This lets you collect it seamlessly, and collecting it at the start of every class tacitly underscores its importance. Put your *Do Now* (the second part of this routine) in the same place every day: on the board, on an interactive handout, or in the packet. The objectives for the lesson, the agenda, and the homework for the coming evening should be on the board already, also in the same predictable place every day.

- Narrate (a little bit of) the positive to show appreciation for the productive behavior you see and build momentum toward compliance (for example, "Thanks for getting *right* to work, James," "Lindsay is already copying down today's objective," and the like). Discipline your narration so that it's pithy and precise, and quietly reinforces industrious behavior. Once the opening procedures become routine, use narration with diminished frequency. The goal is to get to a point where you need to say very little—if anything—to set your Door to *Do Now* routine in motion.

Do Now

As part of *Strong Start,* establishing the routine of the *Do Now* is invaluable. A *Do Now* enables you to maximize instructional time, build industrious habits, and make use of a discrete block of time when your students can practice and thus sustain and build their proficiency with skills they've already mastered. This issue—making sure students don't lose through disuse what they'd once mastered—is one of the hidden challenges of teaching.

My focus here is on how to make the greatest use of the *Do Now* after students have completed it. For more on the details of the what and how of the *Do Now* itself, check out the longer discussion of *Do Now* in Chapter Five.

Review Now

To make the most of every minute of Review Now, highly effective teachers carefully engineer the transition after students have completed independent work on the *Do Now* so that it's crisp, efficient, and often energetic. The goal is to come out of the *Do Now* as quickly and orderly as possible and with the kind of urgency that signals: *we've got a lot of important content to cover today, so let's get started.* Before we discuss the elements that make for an exemplar transition to Review Now, let's discuss an example of what it looks like in action.

In one example, Bridget McElduff, a fifth-grade math teacher from Troy Prep Middle School, circulates and observes while students complete the *Do Now*. She's using a timer to keep track of how long she's spent on the *Do Now* and starts to move to the front of the room as the last few seconds wind down. When the timer goes off, Bridget is already standing at the front of the room, smiling. She gives concise, observable directions: "Pencils down and tracking me in five … four … " The short countdown adds some productive urgency to her request, but gives students a bit of time to finish their last thought. Later in the year, she may not use the countdown as explicitly and will just rely on students to react quickly when they hear the timer go off, but for now she is explicitly building their skill and efficiency at coming to attention quickly. She swivels her head and scans the room with confidence and finesse as she gets to "one" on her countdown. When every student is with her, she asks them to celebrate their speedy completion of the *Do Now* with a Prop (described later in this chapter), and on her cue, students pound their desks once in unison with a loud "huhh!" Then Bridget moves swiftly into firing off a sequence of whispered questions—several of which are *Cold Calls*—to review the completed *Do Now*. Throughout the review, she keeps everyone accountable for tracking the discussion by requiring students to "check or change" their work. In other words, there's no reason not to pick up your pencil (either to correct or check off) at the end of each reviewed problem. Interestingly, she is also using a timer here. Even if she adds time when the four minutes she's allotted winds down, she wants to make sure she doesn't lose track of time and put herself in a bind for the rest of her lesson.

Although Bridget does a lot of things effectively in that sequence, we'll distill her transition into two replicable components:

- **Three … two … one … *Go!*** Bridget transitions students out of the *Do Now* with urgency and efficiency by *Working the Clock* and *Brightening Lines* between the *Do Now* and the Review Now. Her countdown signals to students that Bridget values Review Now time and thinks it is worth protecting. She then brightens the line between the *Do Now* and the Review Now by using the desk-pounding Prop. Her lightning-quick transition into asking questions makes the start of the Review Now pop crisply with energy.

- **Emphasis on accountable review.** Students might potentially disengage during the review of the *Do Now,* but Bridget alternates between taking hands and *Cold Calling* during Review Now to keep kids on their toes and actively tracking the discussion.

As she's reviewing answers with students, Bridget's timer goes off—she's used the time she allocated to reviewing and knows it's time to go on to the main lesson. She wraps up a last problem and, announcing that they have exciting things to do today, asks students to "flip the page" in their packets to the main part of the lesson. Thanks to her use of the *Double Plan* technique, everything she needs is right there in the packet, and she's able to start in on her main lesson just seconds after she's finished the Review Now.

Other strategies teachers use to make the most of Review Now include *Show Call* (technique 39) and *Show Me* (technique 5). The latter is especially helpful in using the Review Now as an opportunity to collect data on student mastery; the former can make the Review Now an opportunity to review student work and to study and learn from both student errors and exemplary work.

STAR/SLANT

Teach students key baseline behaviors for learning, such as sitting up in class and tracking the speaker, by using a memorable acronym such as STAR or SLANT.

Regardless of how great your lesson is, if students aren't alert, sitting up, and actively listening, teaching it will be like pouring water into a leaky bucket. Although many teachers practice lining up students for fire drills and making sure everyone knows the routine for finding the right bus at the end of the day, many neglect to teach behaviors that are more critical over the long run, those that help students concentrate, focus, and learn.

To maximize students' ability to pay attention, teachers in top-performing schools and classrooms commonly use sticky acronyms to teach students key baseline behaviors for learning. One popular variation is **STAR**:

Sit up

Track the speaker

Ask and answer questions like a scholar

Respect those around you

Another common alternative is **SLANT** (which originated in KIPP schools):

Sit up

Listen

Ask and answer questions

Nod your head

Track the speaker

One of the best aspects of these acronyms is that they serve as shorthand. Once you've taught students how to *STAR/SLANT,* all you ordinarily have to do is use the phrase, and students are able to use it to self-correct. Saying, "Back in *STAR/SLANT*" acknowledges that students were already in *STAR/SLANT.* Alternatively, you can opt for "Show me *STAR/SLANT*" or "Check your *STAR/SLANT,*" both of which sound even more positive, with a bit of challenge and the assumption that a small reminder of the expectations will cause students to self-correct.

The use of a consistent acronym is quick and efficient. Even better, *STAR/SLANT* can be broken apart when necessary. Teachers can remind their students about the *S* in *STAR/SLANT* or the *T.* In the best classrooms, the word is deeply embedded in the vocabulary of learning, as a noun ("Where's my *STAR/SLANT*?") and a verb ("Make sure to *STAR/SLANT* ").

Because *STAR/SLANT* is such a critical part of a high-performing classroom, you might also consider developing nonverbal signals that allow you to reinforce and correct without interrupting what you're otherwise doing. For instance, you might fold your hands in front of you to remind students to sit up straight, or point to your eyes with two fingers to prompt students to track you when you're speaking.

ENGINEER EFFICIENCY

Teach students the simplest and fastest procedure for executing key classroom tasks, then practice so that executing the procedure becomes a routine.

48

Whether they use the term or not, nearly all educators develop and teach students *procedures,* or set ways to complete such recurring tasks as filling out a header, marking up text, or turning in homework. One reason why procedures are so ubiquitous in classrooms is that, when designed well, they help teachers conserve their most precious nonrenewable resource: time. A second, slightly more hidden benefit is that when students know what to do without being told, teachers are freed to talk to them about other things. Still, as every teacher knows, all procedures are not created equal. Sometimes, a procedure that's supposed to make it easier and quicker for students to get the job done can actually make doing so more difficult. To avoid this pitfall, highly effective teachers design procedures that satisfy four criteria: Simplicity, Quick Is King, Little Narration Required, and Planned to the Detail.

- **Simplicity.** Teach students the simplest right way to complete a key classroom task. Although this point might seem obvious, it's natural for teachers to feel tempted to design elaborate, ornate procedures because teaching and executing them can be fun. Adding that extra sequence of *Call and Response* or holding students in a crisp line for an additional fifteen seconds can also be gratifying because it makes things feel orderly and confirms that you control your room. But in the end, these are perverse incentives. You want order so that you can get to learning. Period. So the simplest procedure is the best.

  If you're not sure whether or not you should add something to your procedure, ask yourself: Does it help my students accomplish the task? Will I want to require them to do this step every time they do this task for the rest of the year? Will the productivity I gain be greater than the cost in time? The answer will often be yes, but strive to make certain of that for each step, and trim the procedure down to a handful of actions. Then, breaking a procedure into a handful of specific, discrete steps makes it easier for both you and your students to commit it to memory.

- **Quick Is King.** Make the most of class time by showing students the fastest right way to do something. Even tightening your procedures by mere seconds can lead to big savings over the course of one school year. To get a sense of just how much time is at stake, let's say that your students completed ten tight transitions per day. Next, imagine that you pruned these transitions down by a minute apiece and sustained that pace for two hundred school days. Practically speaking, this would enable you to add back an entire *week's* worth of instructional time. That's one more week you could spend analyzing the themes in *Animal Farm,* teaching students how to dissect a frog, or helping students master the skill of adding fractions with unlike denominators. Looking at it the opposite way can give you a sense of just how much time inefficient procedures can steal from you and your students.

To challenge your students to get it right as quickly as possible and to discipline yourself to focus on speed, practice procedures against the clock, preferably with a stopwatch. Use the stopwatch to measure and celebrate progress while continuously challenging kids to execute the procedures a little faster. "We did this in sixteen seconds yesterday; let's shoot for twelve today!"

That said, keep in mind that you are shooting for the fastest possible "right version"; if your students go so fast that they get it wrong, it's better to have them go back, do it slower but just right, and then keep practicing. Once it's done correctly you can speed it up.

- **Little Narration Required.** When it comes to establishing a procedure, using fewer words to manage the execution is preferable. The goal is autonomy, and too many directions from you keeps students from internalizing how to do it on their own. Autonomy is also lost if students need you there to explain each detail.

  Further, providing too much verbal support (in the form of hints or reminders) cheapens the sense of satisfaction students get from successfully completing a procedure without your help. Saying less helps them feel more independent and take more ownership of it.

  Plan the phrases you want to use at each step to ensure their clarity and efficiency. Use them consistently and with as little other verbiage as possible. Over time, begin removing verbal reminders and only use nonverbals, which students can refer to only if they need them. As students prove ready, remove those reminders as well; only step in to reinforce the procedure if students show you they need it.

- **Planned to the Detail.** The teachers with the tightest procedures plan for what they *and* their students will do at every step. They plan each step in a procedure and then even walk through it themselves (or with peers) to make sure it works and there are no unexpected blind spots.

  And, as my team and I recently discovered after watching a video of outstanding routines in the classroom of North Star Academy ELA teacher Julia Goldenheim, these teachers plan their prompts. We visited Julia to ask more about her procedures, and she responded with this brilliant insight: "My biggest piece of advice would be to plan out the key phrases you will use every day with your procedures and practice them. This will ensure that you are clear with your language, especially at a time when *you* are learning the systems as well. They should be clear, efficient, and specific: 'Pass down your homework. Write it in your planner and file it away,' etc."

Recently, my team and I watched Laura Fern, a former first-grade teacher and now dean of curriculum at North Star Academy Vailsburg Elementary School, applying these principles during a tight transition between a phonics exercise and a reading activity. At first glance, her application of the Quick Is King criterion immediately jumped out at us. Within fifteen seconds of their phonics lesson, students managed to sing a song to mark the start of "story time," collect their books from underneath their chairs, flip to the correct page, and sit in *STAR* to await further instruction. Even better, students completed much of the transition without Laura's help.

After watching the transition a second time, we realized that her clip also illustrated the power of strong, detailed planning. For example, we noticed that she strategically placed students' books underneath their chairs so that they could easily find them. This eliminated the transaction cost of distributing a book to each student. In true Planned to the Detail fashion, Laura also planted a book beneath her chair so that she could pick it up as soon as her students were ready. Moreover, Laura used sticky notes (both in her copy of the book and theirs) to bookmark the page students would need to flip to, which instantly eliminated the transaction cost of finding the correct page. She also planted a timer within arm's reach, which meant that she wasted no time looking for it. She was ready to resume instruction at the drop of a hat.

Getting Beyond Behavior

It's not just tasks like moving to the carpet and passing in homework that respond well to routinizing in the classroom. Key recurring academic tasks are ideal as well. In fact, the more a behavior occurs and the more central it is to what you seek to accomplish in the classroom, the more responsive to routine it is. Think, for example, of the power of having a routine for making annotations or marking-up text. You tell your class, "Every time we read, we do so with pencils in hand—we underline key details, circle vocabulary words, and summarize important scenes in the margin," or something along the same lines. You practice that until students can use the system with near-automaticity. Then for the rest of the year you can simply say, as Rue Ratray of Edward Brooke Charter School in East Boston did in a lesson I recently watched, "Take five minutes to read and annotate this passage. Go." One of your key academic tasks ensues without further explanation or discussion. The same principle applies for text analysis, math, or any number of academic tasks. And, of course, a virtuous cycle is in play here. Once you have a system, it's easier to enact—the transaction cost for starting goes down; the efficiency goes up—so the better and better students get at it. You increase the rate of improvement at core tasks by systematizing them.

In math you might use a "mad minute" to reinforce automaticity with fundamental skills, for example; or consider the power of a routine for text analysis in language arts: "When I give you an excerpt from a text we're reading and ask you to 'analyze it,' you'll do four things: (1) identify the characters who are present and the setting, (2) explain the passage's place in the plot of the novel, (3) describe how the scene exemplifies or challenges a key theme from the book, and (4) compare the scene to another from the same book or another we've read as a class this year." If your students could do that in five minutes, you could practice it as part of the Do Now (another routine!) or seamlessly drop text analysis practice into your lesson several days a week. Systematizing any activity lowers its transaction cost and increases the efficiency of its output, and that's critically important when you know what your core academic exercises are.

STRATEGIC INVESTMENT: FROM PROCEDURE TO ROUTINE

49

Turn procedures into routines by rehearsing and reinforcing until excellence becomes habitual. Routinizing a key procedure requires clear expectations, consistency, and, most important, patience. Even so, it's almost always worth it.

The process of turning a procedure into a routine begins with a strong rollout and with ongoing reinforcement that gradually wanes as excellence becomes habitual—but never goes away entirely. Champion teachers understand the importance of this process, which is why they make a **Strategic Investment** in laying the groundwork for effective procedures from the start. They understand that routinizing a key procedure requires clear expectations, consistency, and, most important, diligence. Paradoxically, teachers who bypass this process end up having to spend even more time teaching students how to do things the right way, or reacting to the fact that students don't appear to know the right way to do certain things. The longer teachers wait to make this investment, the more entrenched students' bad habits get, and the more difficult it becomes to change course. Ultimately, the moral of the story is that when it comes to procedures, you need to teach them well up front, or plan to teach them all year long.

Although the process of routinizing a procedure might seem daunting and mysterious, it can be summed up in four concrete stages: Number the Steps, Model and Describe, Pretend Practice, and Transfer Ownership.

Number the Steps

In order to make excellence habitual, students need to know what it looks like. Once you've determined what the "right way" to do something is, you then need to distill it into a form that students can process and internalize. One way teachers do this is by chunking the procedure into a small number of discrete steps and then numbering them. For example, let's say you were teaching your third graders how to transition from their desks to the carpet. You could say something like, "When I say 'one,' please stand and push in your chairs. When I say 'two,' please turn to face the door. When I say 'three,' please follow your line leader to the place to line up." Once you've done that, you merely have to call the number for the appropriate step to cue it. Interestingly, by calling the number (or not), you control the pace of the transition — slowing it down to ensure success and accountability, speeding it up when students are ready. Once students have mastered the procedure, you'll be able to discard the numbers altogether and say, "When I say go, please line up."

If you're teaching students how to transition from one location to another, it can also help to use a method called *point-to-point movement*. The idea is to identify a location or an action and then prompt students to move to that point and stop (for example, "Please stop at the corner of the hallway"). Parsing the transition into steps provides you with clear starting and stopping points, allowing you to control the pace with more precision. If you don't establish clear end points, releasing students to practice a new transition can lead to a mass of confusion, shoving, and squabbling that's difficult to stop, let alone manage.

Model and Describe

One of the most effective and efficient ways to teach students how to complete a procedure is to describe it and show them what it looks like. Doing both gives students a visual road map that they can follow and establishes a common language around the procedure. Later, when you want to tighten it up, you can refer back to this language and feel confident that students know what you're talking about.

When teaching students, it's essential that you model *and* describe. Modeling the procedure without describing it can leave students confused about what they should take away from what you're demonstrating. And at best, it would take you much longer to sufficiently describe a procedure in words without modeling it.

A recent example illustrates how powerful Model and Describe is as a teaching tool. On the first day of school, I watched as Juliana Worrell masterfully modeled and described how students should raise their hands to answer questions. Following is the text from her first-day rollout of a procedure she (and other teachers in her building) refer to as "vertical hands":

> If you have something to say, you raise what we call a "vertical hand." This is what a vertical hand looks like. [She holds her right arm straight up and then points to her arm with her left hand for emphasis.] I'm not waving it in the air. I'm not holding it over my head. It is straight up and down. I'm going to put my hand down, and then I'm going to show you again. [She models vertical hand again.] Sharp!

During this rollout, Juliana does three things particularly well:

- First, she tags the procedure with the sticky name "vertical hands" and repeats that name several times to help the young students remember it. She then shows students exactly what it looks like and carefully describes it as she *Circulates* past each row to give them a closer look (for example, "It goes straight up and down. It is right next to my ear").

- Second, she deftly anticipates and then models "pain points," or common mistakes students will make when raising their hands ("I'm not waving it in the air. I'm not holding it over my head"). This makes the differences between correct and incorrect more visible to students.

- Finally, she again models an exemplar vertical hand. In doing so, she inscribes her vision of success in students' minds before she sends them off to practice their vertical hands.

Pretend Practice

To truly master procedures, students need lots of practice as well as timely feedback on their execution. Far too often, teachers don't ask students to practice before releasing them to execute procedures on their own. This sets up students for failure because they'll rarely complete a new procedure the right way on their first try. And if you ask them to practice but don't provide feedback, students will likely practice (and get better at) doing it wrong.

We often see teachers with the most effective procedures using Pretend Practice—that is, distorting practice deliberately in ways that make it less realistic but more focused and effective at building skills.

Here are some ways you might see Pretend Practice:

1. *Isolated step.* Sometimes teachers will choose just one small aspect of a procedure and practice it over and over or at half speed to make sure their students get it. Only then will they speed it up to real time or link it to the steps before and after it.

2. *Strategically simplified.* Sometimes a teacher will remove a distraction to make practice more effective—for example, by practicing a transition without books the first few times ("Imagine you're carrying your books") or by practicing the process for putting materials away in art class without the actual supplies the first few times. That way students can lock in on the steps with simplicity and without pencils and crayons rolling around on the floor.

3. *Faux errors.* Other times, a teacher will ask students to deliberately make a common error to role-play how to respond. "What do you do if you go to the left if everyone is going to the right? Let's try it and work it out."

Transfer Ownership

Once students are able to complete a procedure in the right way, the best teachers pass off the baton of responsibility to them. Doing so gives students a greater sense of accomplishment, independence, and ownership over classroom structures.

See It in Action: Clip 47

To give you a sense of what a classroom can look and sound like once a teacher has begun transferring ownership of routines over to students, I'll walk you through a scene from Stephen Chiger's high school English classroom (clip 47). The scene begins with Stephen greeting students as they cross the threshold of his doorway and enter class. Before they step inside, each student knows to give Stephen a firm, cordial, and professional handshake and greeting. This step has been routinized, and happens without reminder. Once they've entered, students walk silently to their seats, get out their homework, place it on their desks, and start the *Do Now* while a "binder helper" passes their binders out to each of them. Halfway through his *Threshold*, Stephen thinks he hears a sound and leans into the classroom to listen. He realizes that he doesn't hear chatting, and says aloud, "I thought I heard whispering, but I don't." It's clear that students have internalized his expectation for silence during the entry routine, but it helps that he's reinforcing his attentiveness to those expectations for students who are about to enter the room.

After Stephen greets the last student, he enters his room to find everyone working silently and industriously on his or her *Do Now*. He responds by thanking students for "knowing as always what to do." The culture is rigorous and scholarly, and students seem to quietly relish the autonomy Stephen gives them. The scene ends with Stephen checking in with students to prepare them for the next phase of the lesson.

From this brief snapshot, we can get a sense of just how powerful the culture of autonomy is in Stephen's classroom, as well as some insight into a bit of the "how" that makes it possible. Namely, we see traces of one of the most effective ways to transfer ownership onto students: delegating roles. In the scene I just described, we see that one student was assigned the role of "binder helper." This freed up Stephen to check in with individual students and set other parts of the lesson in motion. The student is so eager to perform well in this role that she approaches Stephen once she realizes that a binder is missing. It's almost as if she perceives increased responsibility as a reward.

Recently, we taped a lesson to watch Maggie Johnson's eighth-grade English class at Troy Preparatory Middle School and uncovered a hidden gem in the first few seconds of the video.

"Pencils down when you hear the beep," she said, referring to the timer that's about to go off and signifies the end of independent work. "No countdown today." In fact, there would be no countdown as part of Maggie's routine for the rest of the year, she later told them. Maggie was transitioning her kids from one highly effective system to another—replacing a teacher-narrated countdown with a simpler, faster, and more mature system wherein her students come to attention on their own at the beep. Maggie's countdown system was very effective, and sometimes it's the things that go well in our classes that we hold on to hardest—sometimes for a fraction too long, or that's the risk at least. In Maggie's case, despite the effective system already in place, she realized either that as eighth graders, her students were ready for a bit more autonomy and self-management, or that eliminating the countdown would be faster and less disruptive to the work they were doing, or both.

In short, what we were observing in Maggie's class was a transfer of ownership. In effect, Maggie was saying, "You've proven you can master this part of being scholars on your own, so now I give you more autonomy. You 'own' the rate at which you earn more freedom to self-manage." This can be a powerful trade, especially when students understand that the autonomy is earned via mastery and follow-though.

A caveat is important here: some teachers assume that because earned autonomy is an effective form of transferred ownership, they would do well to transfer ownership at the outset with a tacit bargain: "I'm going to give you a lot of autonomy, but I want you to show me that you understand how to use it, or I'll take it away." This is usually less effective. Unless you've started with discipline—teaching and establishing what routines should look like—students won't know what you mean by "how to use it" and will likely struggle. Your choice will then be to remove the autonomy you initially offered—potentially messaging that the systems you now establish are a punishment rather than "how we do things," and undertaking a more difficult installation (taking away freedom is harder than giving it)—or to fail to rein in the freedoms when students struggle, which means poor systems and routines for the year. Earning autonomy will help students value and understand it.

See It In Action: Clip 48

Doug McCurry models tight transitions in clip 48. I discuss this clip in the Introduction to the book as well because of the incredible return on Doug's invested time in teaching his students to pass out papers. What's equally powerful about the clip is the students' response. Far from being annoyed and frustrated by being asked to pass papers back and forth to achieve a faster time, they love the challenge and are literally on the edge of their seats. Much of the key to accomplishing this alchemy is Doug's *Positive Framing* (technique 58), specifically his constant use of challenge.

Better Late Than Never: Tips for Resetting Procedures and Routines

Procedures are best installed and routinized at the beginning of the year, but there are always times when a new procedure or system (that is, a set of related procedures) needs to be installed midyear. Behavior has begun to slip, or morale to wane. You realize several months into the year that there's something you wish you'd routinized from the outset. Perhaps you've even arrived new, midyear and in the wake of a teacher without systems, and have been asked to rebuild the culture. A classroom "reset," which often involves rolling out brand-new systems and reintroducing or modifying old ones, can be a necessity. Before you reset, consider these tips to ensure that it goes as smoothly as possible:

- <u>Invent a "news peg."</u> Connect the reset to an inspiring, headline-grabbing goal (for example, "We have only 68 days left until we take our comprehensive exams. We need to be ready!").

- <u>Reset after an extended break.</u> Take advantage of these periods away from class; they provide you with a natural excuse to reintroduce old procedures or to make a clean break from the past.

- <u>Be transparent.</u> Briefly explain *why* you're hitting the reset button. If you don't, you risk confusing students and losing their buy-in. "Sometimes when we do things over and over, we get a little sloppy with our execution. It's normal for everyone, but it's causing us to lose important learning time that you need to get ready for college. We're going to think back to when I taught you X at the beginning of the year—we'll review what we need to do and practice doing it not just well but perfectly."

- <u>Let students Model and Describe.</u> Reward outstanding students with an opportunity to model a procedure that you want to reintroduce. This is a great way to reward excellence, boost engagement during modeling, and increase student buy-in.

- <u>Follow up with *Precise Praise*.</u> Acknowledge progress, and praise students who exceed your expectations. If students pick up the procedures with less practice than they did at the beginning of the year, recognize their growth. This shows students that your reset isn't a punishment or indictment, but rather an expression of your belief in their ability to meet your high expectations.

Props

Props are a form of public praise for students who demonstrate excellence or exemplify virtues. If you can consistently enable classmates to deliver resounding praise to one another in two seconds flat, you can build a culture that valorizes achievement and effort without sacrificing order or time on task. As students come to relish the culture of Props, you might even teach them a wide variety of them (see the end of the chapter for a list of suggestions) and let a student nominate Props for a classmate who did a great job.

The key is to invest the time at the outset to teach students to give Props the right way: crisply, quickly, and enthusiastically, just as you would with any routine. Ensuring that you teach your students to deliver Props that meet the following criteria will go a long way to ensuring your success:

- **Quick.** You should be able to cue a Prop in one second. Similarly, the Prop itself should be fast because you don't have time to waste and because there's nothing less energizing than an exhortation that starts strong but peters out. If it's not sharp, reinforce with *Do It Again* (technique 50, later in this chapter) and make sure to get it right.

- **Visceral.** Props are often powerful when they rely on movement and sound, especially percussive sound. Props that don't use much in the way of words are less likely to get tiresome; their half-life is longer because there's no phrase to wear out. A quick "Oh, yeah," is fine, but something like "On the way to college!" is likely to get old (and show its age) quickly. Furthermore, there's something fun and muscular about the thunder of group percussion.

- **Universal.** When you give Props, everybody joins in. It's up to you to set and enforce this expectation.

- **Enthusiastic.** The tone is energetic and lively. It should be a break—brief and fun—from hard work. Resist the temptation to make it too grown-up; it doesn't have to narrate values and express a mission-aligned personal credo. If it's a little bit of silly, it will reinforce moments when students have already demonstrated those things. Props are the exclamation point, not the sentence.

- **Evolving.** Let your students suggest and develop ideas for Props. They will constantly renew the systems with fresh and funky ideas and will participate more vigorously because they have helped invent them. And if students are forever thinking of new ones, Props will never get tired, boring, or obligatory.

Want More? Clip 49 and Clip 50. Want more examples of strong procedures? Watch Nikki Bowen (clip 49) and Lauren Moyle (clip 50). In clip 49, originally published in *Great Habits, Great Readers: A Practical Guide for Reading in the Light of Common Core* by Paul Bambrick-Santoyo, Aja Settles, and Juliana Worrell, Nikki works through procedures with her students until these become second nature. Meanwhile, Lauren's class transitions from desks to floor by singing a song.

DO IT AGAIN

Give students more practice when they're not up to speed—not just doing something again, but doing it better, striving to do their best.

50

Getting lots of practice is critical to building procedures and routines into productive classrooms systems, so giving students more practice is the perfect response to a situation where they show they're not yet fully up to speed performing a task. When there is an established expectation—a way that things are supposed to be done—doing it again and doing it right or better or perfectly is often the most powerful response. That's the idea behind **Do It Again**. By having students strive to do it one more time perfectly, you leverage the power of repetition and practice to build strong culture and discipline.

Of course, *Do It Again* is also a more versatile tool, helpful, as so many teachers know, in a variety of situations—as a simple and low-impact "consequence" for nonproductive behavior, as a tool for inculcating a culture of "always better," as a way to always stress the possibility of doing something better, and so on.

Why? *Do It Again* is especially effective because

- *It shortens the feedback loop.* Behavioral science has shown that the shorter the time lag between an action and a response, the more effective the response will be in changing the behavior. Let's say you have a clear expectation for entering the classroom, and a group of students comes in from recess in a disorderly way. Having the group stay in for recess three hours later is less likely to change their behavior than is a lesser response that occurs right away. If the reaction comes immediately after, while the original action is fresh in the students' minds, the two will be more clearly associated in their memory. In the three-hours-later scenario, they will be more likely to think "She kept me in for recess." In the moment, they are more likely to recall and reflect on how they entered the classroom. *Doing It Again* shortens the feedback loop in comparison to almost any other consequence.

- *It sets a standard of excellence, not just compliance. Do It Again* is appropriate not just for times when students do something poorly; it's ideal for times when students do something "just fine" when the goal is excellence. Saying, "That was good, but I want great" or "In this class, we're going to strive to do everything world class; let's see if we can use a bit more expression when we read" enables a teacher to set a standard of excellence, where good can always be better and better can always shoot for best. This can drive your classroom culture by replacing acceptable with excellent, first in the small things and then in all things.

- *There is no administrative follow-up.* If you are using *Do It Again* as a consequence — that is, for behavior that is below standard — it happily requires no data entry, no parent phone calls, no briefing for administrators. The consequence is over as soon as the goal is reached. In the life of a busy teacher, that's a blessing. And because it requires no detention policy or schoolwide rewards system, *Do It Again* is almost completely freestanding. It can be used in any classroom.

- *It promotes group culture and accountability.* Although individuals can easily be asked to *Do It Again*, the technique is also effective as a response to a group. One or two students talk while everyone is lining up, and they all try it again. This holds the group accountable in a reasonable, nonpunitive way for the behavior of all of its individuals. It builds incentives for individuals to behave positively because it makes them accountable to their peers as well as their teacher. As an aside, there are times when it feels wrong to hold groups too accountable for individuals who try to co-opt their purposes. Suffice it to say that because you *can* leverage group accountability does not mean you should in every situation.

- *It ends with success.* The last thing you remember of an event often shapes your perception of it more broadly. *Do It Again* ends not with punishment or failure but with success. The last thing students do in a sequence is to do an activity the right way. This helps engrain the perception and memory of what right looks like. It also helps build muscle memory. Students build the habit of doing it right, over and over.

- *It is reusable. Do It Again* can be reused. You can *Do It Again* and then do it another time if necessary. And you can do the same thing again ten minutes later. Within reason, it doesn't lose its legs. You don't need to keep inventing new consequences. You can be positive in administering the third iteration: "I still think we can do this even better. Let's give it one more shot!" Add a stopwatch to some routines, and the challenge of *Do It Again* (and do it better) only gets more powerful.

Given these advantages, it's no wonder that champion teachers use *Do It Again* so often. However, it's important to execute the technique well. *Do It Again* should be positive whenever possible, with a keen focus on getting better and, in a great class-room, informed by a constant narrative of "good, better, best." That is, "just doing it" gets replaced by doing it well. In fact, one colleague suggested that a better name for this technique is *Do It Better,* as *better* captures the idea that doing things over again to be as good as you can be is what school is about. The goal is not mere compliance but excellence, even in the little things.

Do It Again can be an effective tool for managing affect. Sometimes people's attitudes change from the outside in. Asking a low-energy class to repeat something with enthu-siasm (especially, and critically, while modeling those attributes yourself) can start to be a self-fulfilling prophecy. *Do It Again* is a great opportunity to challenge students positively to show you their best. Saying, "Oooh, let's line up again and prove why we're the best reading group in the school" is often better than saying, "Class, that was very sloppy. We're going to do it again until we get it exactly right," even if the purpose in both cases is to *Do It Again* until you get it exactly right.

Lastly, teachers sometimes think they need to wait until an entire routine or activity is done before asking the class to try it again. In fact, you should have students go back and try it again as soon as you know that the level of execution will not meet the standard you set for it. Don't wait for the routine to end. Again, this will better connect the stimulus to the response. Let's say students are lining up for lunch, and the drill is to stand up quietly, push in their chairs, turn to face the door, and then follow the table leader to the door. If students forget to push in their chairs, have them sit back down and try it again right then. This saves time and reinforces instant accountability.

Putting It All Together

In a lesson that's a classic in my estimation, Suzanne Vera (then of Leadership Prep Bedford Stuyvesant) demonstrated *Do It Again* at its most inspiring in her kindergarten art class. She was investing in discipline by teaching her students the right way to do things and then practicing those procedures at the beginning of the year. Her method, which was to simplify the procedure the first few times her students did it, was designed to ensure that they practiced successfully. Suzanne had cleverly arranged to practice first without materials ("Pretend you're drawing!") that might distract her students and get in the way the first few times she taught a procedure.

Suzanne's tone was positive, and this underscored her words to them: "That was good, but it could be great," before she asked them to try a step in the procedure again. She also gave her students specific feedback about how to be better by describing the solution and not the problem: "You need to be looking at me"; "Remember that you turn your neck if you can't see me." This feedback is a great example of the *Positive Framing* skill "live in the now" (technique 58).

Some teachers might assume that students would naturally grouse about having to do basic tasks over and over again to get better at them. As it happens, students are more often quite happy practicing and getting better, especially when the practice is framed positively, because they enjoy being successful and getting better at things. Lastly, Suzanne's use of a stopwatch made an implicit challenge to kids that she is set up to make explicit in the future: "Yesterday we cleaned up in twelve seconds; let's see if we can do it in ten today!"

Want More? Clip 51.   In the first half of clip 51, watch Sarah Ott of Leadership Prep Ocean Hill teach her kindergarteners how to do classroom tasks, such as coming together on her signal, via two upbeat *Do It Agains*. It's hard to imagine not wanting to do your best in Sarah's classroom.

CONCLUSION

It may seem counterintuitive to say that structure and discipline can give rise to freedom and autonomy, but the fact of the matter is that the more natural and routinized your classroom systems become, the less they feel like restrictions. The rules of the road aren't restrictions on your freedom as a driver, per se; rather, they are the guidelines put in place such that drivers can safely and freely move from place to place. They're there so that nobody runs into each other (or at least not often) and the flow of traffic is smooth. Of course, when someone drives too quickly, rolls through a stop sign, or regularly flouts the generally accepted rules of the road in some other way, there are usually consequences. In Chapter Eleven, we'll look at the kinds of behavioral expectations and remedial strategies that help keep champion classrooms between the lines.

Reflection and Practice

1. Script the steps and expectations for the five most critical routines in your classroom.

2. Make a poster outlining everything your students need to have to be prepared at the beginning of class. Post it on your wall. Practice referring students to it (nonverbally perhaps) before class begins.

3. Make a list of some of the most common requests students make while you are teaching. Determine an appropriate nonverbal signal they can give you to make each request and return to *STAR/SLANT*. Make a poster with the acronym you use spelled out. Practice pointing at the poster and asking students to return to their seat if they do not ask for and receive your nonverbal approval. (You'll want them to practice recognizing a nonverbal indicating that they should wait, which you should sometimes use if the request comes during key instructional time.)

FIND THESE TOOLS AT WWW.TEACHLIKEACHAMPION.COM/YOURLIBRARY **USEFUL TOOLS**

What teachers systematize. Looking to revamp or introduce new systems into your classroom? Check out this list of processes teachers often "systematize" to keep their classrooms running smoothly and efficiently.

Six ideas for Props. Borrow or adapt from this list of tried-and-true classroom Props to add joy to any lesson.

A gallery of classroom images. Browse a gallery of classroom photos and see if you can identify the systems these teachers use to keep their classrooms humming with efficiency and productivity.

WHAT TEACHERS SYSTEMATIZE

To spark your thinking, here is a quick list of things that teachers commonly "systematize." As you read the list, consider: What would you add to this list? Which of these might you consider systematizing?

- *Habits of Discussion* (see technique 42 to learn more)

- Moving materials

- Helping students maintain an organized binder

- Moving students from one activity or location to another

- Asking questions

- Answering questions

- Using the classroom library

- Note taking

- Reviewing/grading completed work

- Shared reading

- *Turn and Talk* (or, more generally, group work)

- Correcting a teacher's errors

- Independent work/reflection

- Managing behavior

- Text markup/reading interactively

SIX IDEAS FOR PROPS

Here are six ideas for Props (most of them stolen from great teachers, who themselves borrowed them or invented them with the help of students):

- *The Hitter.* You say, "Let's give Clarice a Hitter." Your kids pretend to toss a ball and swing a bat at it. They shield their eyes as if to glimpse its distant flight. Then they mimic crowd noise suitable for a home run for some fraction of a full second.

- *The Lawnmower.* You say, "Let's give Jason a Lawnmower." Your kids reach down to pull the cord to start the mower, and yank upward twice. They make engine sounds, grip the imaginary handles, and smile for some fraction of a full second.

- *The Roller Coaster.* You say, "Oh, man, that answer deserves a Roller Coaster." Your kids put their open hands in front of them pointing upward at forty-five degrees, palms down. They "chug, chug, chug" (three times only) with their hands, mimicking a roller coaster slugging its way up the last steep hill. Then they shout "woo, woo, woo" three times as their hands mimic a coaster speeding over three steep hills after the big drop.

- *Hot Pepper.* You say, "An answer like that deserves a Hot Pepper." Your kids hold up an imaginary hot pepper, dangling it above their mouths. They take a bite and make a sizzle sound "tssssss" for exactly one second.

- *Two Snaps, Two Stomps.* You say, "Two Snaps, Two Stomps for Jimmie P!" Your kids deliver two snaps and two thundering stomps that end perfectly on cue. (You can vary the sounds to include snaps, claps, stomps, desk slaps, and even an "Oh, yeah!")

Chapter 11

High Behavioral Expectations

100%, Part 1. Technique 51: Radar/Be Seen Looking. Prevent nonproductive behavior by developing your ability to see it when it happens and by subtly reminding students that you are looking.

100%, Part 2. Technique 52: Make Compliance Visible. Ensure that students follow through on a request in an immediate and visible way by setting a standard that's more demanding than marginal compliance. Be judicious in what you ask for, specifically because it will uphold the standard of compliance.

100%, Part 3. Technique 53: Least Invasive Intervention. Maximize teaching time and minimize "drama" by using the subtlest and least invasive tactic possible to correct off-task students.

100%, Part 4. Technique 54: Firm Calm Finesse. Take steps to get compliance without conflict by establishing an environment of purpose and respect and by maintaining your own poise.

100%, Part 5. Technique 55: Art of the Consequence. Ensure that consequences, when needed, are more effective by making them quick, incremental, consistent, and depersonalized. It also helps to make a bounce-back statement, showing students that they can quickly get back in the game.

Technique 56: Strong Voice. Affirm your authority through intentional verbal and non-verbal habits, especially at moments when you need control.

Technique 57: What to Do. Use specific, concrete, sequential, and observable directions to tell students what to do, as opposed to what not to do.

High Behavioral Expectations

There's something paradoxical about classrooms like Erin Michels's, where the focus always seems to be on learning in its most rigorous forms. On a recent morning, Erin asked her fourth graders to figure out the area of a complex, irregular polygon, not in "square units" as most fourth-grade teachers would, but in "triangulous" units. She called on a student, Jared, for the answer, and when he gave the correct answer, she pressed him for more: "Go ahead, Jared. Tell us how you figured this out."

His classmates watched attentively as he sought to describe his thinking process in words. "I figured it out because at first I had to try and ..." He paused to reflect and self-correct. "First I had to trace around the whole entire shape."

"What were you tracing?" Erin interjected. "Use that mathematical language, Jared."

"The perimeter of the shape," Jared clarified, as Erin encouraged him with a nod. His classmates followed him with their eyes, and no noise broke the spell of his thought. "And then after I traced the perimeter of the shape, I removed the shape and started counting each square unit," he continued.

Listening carefully, Erin asked for clarification: "Each *square* unit?" she asked.

"I mean each triangulous unit," Jared corrected, "and I kept going until I found thirty triangulous units."

The interaction demonstrates several strengths that are typical of a classroom with a culture of high academic expectations. The ratio is high, and Jared's thinking is sustained and rigorous, with Erin merely prompting him occasionally. Jared is asked not only to arrive at an answer but also to *Stretch It* and explain his answer using technical vocabulary. He reflects on and refines his own thinking as he goes. The problem is rigorous and complex, and it pushes students to develop a fuller conception of what area is.

Erin's classroom is, in short, the kind of place people imagine themselves working when they enter this profession. No one I am aware of enters this work because they love to tell students to pay attention or sit down or stop calling out. Most of us would love to leave all that behind and ride off in the direction of "why" and "how" and "Can you use more precise language to describe that phenomenon?"

However, none of those moments of academic rigor happen without a foundation of behavioral expectations. Jared's reflections in math class start, for example, with reliable and universal attentiveness. Erin can ask Jared a question and not fear that his classmates will shout out the answer or, worse, make some banal, distracting, "funny" comment as Jared takes the time to think. Only in such a space are Jared's elaboration and self-correction possible. Only in such a space can a teacher like Erin listen carefully to Jared's answer without the distractions of inattentive students eroding her capacity to prompt him just so ("Each *square* unit?").

Further, Jared's explanation is enlightening not just to him but to his classmates. In Erin's class, Jared's classmates' heads move from Jared to Erin as if at a tennis match. They are attentive. When asked to write and reflect on the math, they spring into vigorous action. They are 100 percent ensconced in the previously unimagined world of area expressed in triangulous units.

 Want More? Clip 52. Want more? Check out Erin Michels in clip 52, in which she demonstrates a number of high behavioral expectations.

Students rely on teachers to create such environments if they are to aspire to academic greatness. Nonetheless, many observers misunderstand these environments of undisturbed inquiry and think that they occur naturally or that the ability to enforce silence means driving out student voices. It's folly to think that left to their own devices, a room full of people (almost *any* room full of people) will behave as Erin's class does, or will support learning in the most productive way. Classrooms like Erin's are achieved through meticulous attention to building the behavioral environment, step-by-step.

Ends and means are easily confused. Because effective classroom culture is nearly invisible for stretches of time, some people will not see the work that goes into it; they will see teachers who don't talk to their students much about behavior, and believe that the answer is not to talk about behavior much with your students. The result is paradoxical: if you try to ignore behavior, you will end up talking about little else, whereas if you are intentional and consistent about behavioral culture to start, distractions will ultimately fade into the background as you talk about history, art, literature, math, and science. What you see in Erin's classrooms is not "better kids" who miraculously behave, or the magic of "more engaging teaching" to eliminate all of the challenges of society, poverty, and learning. What you see is meticulous intentionality in its dormant state.

You must be able to establish order to have a learning-intensive classroom. Some readers might assume that by this statement I am referring only to inner-city classrooms, but I am referring here to all classrooms for all students. A friend recently observed classes at one of New York City's elite prep schools and described many outstanding classrooms. He also described several classrooms where students threw paper wads at one another and mocked their classmates as they answered the teacher's questions. All students deserve to go to school in classrooms with a positive, orderly and efficient culture that respects and defends the primacy of the academic learning. Although my own focus is primarily on schools serving students of the greatest need, for whom disruption of teaching is the theft of an opportunity not easily replaced, the more time I spend looking at classrooms beyond those where I primarily work, the more I am convinced that this is a universal issue.

There is another side to the challenge of understanding the role of order in an effective classroom, however, and it is the flip side of the coin. Order for order's sake, high behavioral expectations without real and rigorous academics, is an empty vessel. I am stating this at the outset of this chapter because the changes that occur when a teacher brings order to his or her classroom can be so powerful that they can cause one to lose focus on this point. If you have lived with disorder and then suddenly find your students sitting silently and attentively, the temptation can be to keep them sitting silently when they should be interacting. Once you teach students to line up in an orderly way, the temptation can be to line them up and keep them in lines. An orderly room must be orderly *to allow academic rigor to thrive*. Students must be silent *so that a classmate may speak in a climate of respect*. They must line up quickly *so that they can get where they need to go for maximum learning*. And as I often tell skeptics of high behavioral expectations, just because a teacher *can* cause her classroom to be pin-drop quiet does not mean she always must. It gives her an option she can exercise at will, not an obligation. In fact, it gives her the sure knowledge that she can allow her students a bit *more* freedom because she knows she can quickly rein them back in if things get too messy. So both reminders are necessary: that there is no academic rigor without high behavioral expectations, and that order is the means, not the end. You can see the connection between order and academics clearly in this photo of Ashley Hinton's classroom (Figure 11.1.)

Later in this chapter, you'll see two videos of Ashley's skillful behavior management and the orderly productive environment she builds. In this photo, however, her students are sitting *on* their desks, joyfully reading Harry Potter aloud. Her ability to establish control allows her to let kids do things like this because (1) the kids know what's expected of them, and (2) Ashley knows that if things get a little carried away, she can bring back order quickly, easily, and painlessly. It's *because* of her rock-solid classroom culture that she can get all crazy with her Harry Potter.

The goal, of course, is to establish behavioral expectations as efficiently and simply as possible and to maintain it with as little disruption to learning as you can. Although they may seem less important than the topics in more "academic" chapters, the methods by

Figure 11.1   Ashley Hinton's Classroom

which order is efficiently established and positive culture is built are worthy of deep and often sustained study. The techniques can be technical and nuanced, and their results can be magical. Watching champion teachers work with finesse, skill, craft, passion, and diligence even though the topic is often dismissed or given secondary importance inspires me to share their knowledge and wisdom with you.

100%—A CYCLE OF TECHNIQUES

Great teachers ensure that they have 100 percent of students with them for the teaching and learning; their expectation is 100 percent of students, 100 percent of the time, 100 percent of the way. Great classroom managers generally step in to address distractions earlier than other teachers, allowing their interventions to be almost imperceptible. The recipe implicit in their success is simple and powerful: catch it early and fix it noninvasively, without breaking the thread of instruction. The 100% Cycle describes the skills required to execute that recipe; they are classic examples of little things with big muscles.

The 100% Cycle

100%, Part 1. Technique 51: Radar/Be Seen Looking

100%, Part 2. Technique 52: Make Compliance Visible

100%, Part 3. Technique 53: Least Invasive Intervention

100%, Part 4. Technique 54: Firm Calm Finesse

100%, Part 5. Technique 55: Art of the Consequence

In addition to the 100% Cycle, *Strong Voice* and *What to Do* can also help you set clear expectations for appropriate behavior in your classroom.

100%, PART 1: RADAR/BE SEEN LOOKING

Prevent nonproductive behavior by developing your ability to see it when it happens and by subtly reminding students that you are looking.

51

The first step to preventing nonproductive behavior is to consistently see it when it happens. I call the skill of reliably seeing what's happening in your classroom **Radar**.

As students, we all knew the teachers who reliably saw what we were up to as soon as we started doing it. We talked about the "eyes in the back of their head," for example, and toed the line. Others were not so observant, and this often emboldened us to behave less well. Not only was there a lack of accountability in those classrooms, but there was often tacit peer pressure to see how much we could get away with. When everyone knew you *could*, there was tacit pressure to *do*. A slippery slope develops quickly, so good teachers need to see what's happening in their classroom. Taking time to develop and improve *Radar*, then, is time well spent.

Radar's foundation: the Swivel. If you watch teachers like Patrick Pastore or Rachel King, you'll see them scanning their classrooms regularly, disciplining themselves to look as a matter of habit. And when they look, they scan across the entire room. You'll notice how every few minutes and after key directions, great teachers take the time to scan the room. It takes only a second or two, but it is an act of self-discipline, made habit,

Figure 11.2 Typical Positioning

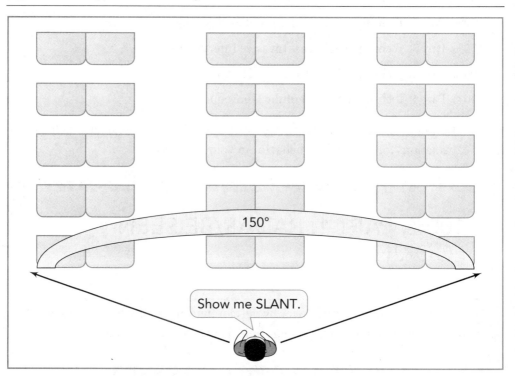

that defends against blind spots. Looking consistently and intentionally is the first step to seeing.

You also might notice something about *where teachers like Patrick and Rachel stand when they observe*—in the corner of the room. This is beneficial in several ways. First, moving off to the side helps them see the room from a new perspective. A bit of defamiliarization may help them see it more clearly.

But their post in the corner is useful for an even more compelling reason. Imagine you're Patrick and you want to scan your classroom from the front of the room (see Figure 11.2).

To see the room, you have to scan a field of about 150 degrees. That's a lot to see. But if you merely walk to the corner of your room, you can see the whole room by scanning a visual field of just 80 degrees (Figure 11.3).

What Patrick is trying to see is now much simpler to observe. Of course he sees better from there. In fact, we find this position so helpful that we've named it "Pastore's Perch."

Figure 11.3 Pastore's Perch

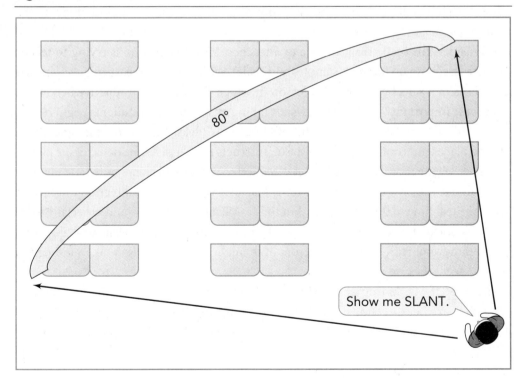

See It in Action: Clip 53 and Clip 54

In clip 53 of Rachel King, you'll notice Rachel moving to Pastore's Perch at exactly the moment she wants to monitor her class most closely. While there, she needs to make only the tiniest of dance moves (discussed later in "*Be Seen Looking* Dance Moves")—a bit of the Tiptoes—to show that she's watching carefully. You can see Patrick Pastore moving to his perch to see his room better—and the beneficial results—in clip 54.

Be Seen Looking

Think again about being a student. When we recognized that a teacher had *Radar*, we thought we were super-smart for figuring it out. In retrospect, we weren't half as clever as we thought—the teacher had probably taken steps to *help* us figure it out. She had shown us that she was a good and careful observer. A slow, simple nod or a tilt of the head might say, "I see the rubber band, Doug Lemov, and you will put it back in your desk now." This skill, too, has a name: **Be Seen Looking**. It's the yin to *Radar*'s yang. One is seeing well, and the other is contriving ways to subtly remind students that you see.

Consider this scene from the life of a teacher, Ms. Mason, who is trying to teach a science lesson involving rock samples and scales, with students measuring weight, size, and mass in a series of steps. It's a lesson in which 100 percent productive behavior is especially important—if the samples start falling off of tables and students begin playing with scales, the entire lesson could fall apart quickly. "Please find the rock sample labeled #1 and place it in front of you," Ms. Mason instructs her class. As she does so, she glances down, using the moment just after her direction to double-check her notes and glance at her watch to see how she's doing for time. Just after you've given a direction might seem like the ideal time to do such things, but to Ms. Mason's students—and especially to her most skeptical or distractible students—she has communicated that she probably won't know if they put rock sample #1 in front of them, because she doesn't take a moment to look to see if they do so.

Imagine if Ms. Mason changed her approach ever so slightly, so that immediately after she gave her directions, she briefly looked up and scanned the room, left to right, taking just a second or two in all. Let's even say she scanned with a bit of intentionality, looking to see if everyone jumped to it, and making sure to double back with her eyes very quickly to check her blind spots. If she did this consistently, just a few seconds each time she gave a direction, she would discipline herself to look for follow-through among her students and would be able to reinforce it. *Then* she could take a moment to look down at her notes.

Champion teachers use different versions of this sort of thing over and over again. They look carefully and find ways to show students they are looking throughout a lesson, but without taking any time away from the lesson.

Be Seen Looking Dance Moves

Over time, my team has given humorous names to various unspoken pantomimes teachers do to ensure that their students see them looking. They include the Swivel I described earlier, but also several subtle iterations that cleverly communicate awareness of keen observation back to students. Here are a number of these "dance moves":

The Invisible Column: Wherein a teacher moves her head slightly to the side after giving a direction as if she's trying to look around something (an invisible column) to make sure her students are doing as they should.

The Tiptoes: Wherein a teacher stands for a moment on her tiptoes while looking out at the room, as if she's just making doubly sure everything is okay in some hard-to-see spot in the room.

The Sprinkler: Wherein a teacher starts her Swivel across the classroom, but at one point, snaps back a few degrees in the direction she'd just scanned to intimate, kabuki style, "Oh, I think I just saw something I shouldn't ha—No. Everything is okay." It makes your scan a bit less predictable, which is generally good.

The Disco Finger: Wherein a teacher traces the track of her gaze in a Swivel with her finger outstretched, pointer style, like one of the killer disco moves you haven't dusted off in a decade or two. It intimates, "Let me just check all of these places" and makes the Swivel obvious to those who are least likely to notice it.

The Politician: Wherein a teacher channels aspiring office holders who walk onstage before a big speech, and points in recognition to all of her apparent friends and supporters in the audience—one over here, one over there. As a teacher, you send a similar upbeat message of "I see you all out there" when you gesture briefly to the folks in the audience who are similarly demonstrating that they are with you.

The QB: Wherein a teacher makes like an NFL quarterback (QB) who, crouching behind the center, gazes quickly at the defense. Just because he's low doesn't mean he's not going to scan. Similarly, as champion teachers crouch to confer with a scholar, they flash their eyes briefly across the room, to make sure they see the field.

Whereas not looking for follow-through after we give a direction can suggest that we don't notice or don't care whether students follow through on our directions, doing the reverse—showing that we care that they do what we asked—is actually a very strong incentive for most students.

See It in Action: Clip 55

Watch Michael Rubino in clip 55. He's doing *Pepper* with his students (see technique 36), and when he asks a question, he scans the room with a quick Swivel as a matter of habit after every question. At this point, he probably barely even notices he's doing it. The scan is nearly automatic, and it takes perhaps a fraction of a second each time—much, much quicker than having to mop up a distraction after it breaks out.

The last time Michael looks around the room, he cranes his neck a bit, as if he's trying to see carefully around a hand. It's an Invisible Column, and in a fraction of a second, his gesture intimates that he is looking carefully and double-checking that everything is just as it should be. In fact, you could say the purpose is as much to *Be Seen Looking* as it is to see better.

A final thought: although *Radar* and *Be Seen Looking* are a constant part of the repertoire of champion teachers, their subtlety is also a reminder of how noninvasive the technique can be. It can work, and someone watching you can hardly even notice it's there.

100%, PART 2: MAKE COMPLIANCE VISIBLE

Ensure that students follow through on a request in an immediate and visible way by setting a standard that's more demanding than marginal compliance. Be judicious in what you ask for, specifically because it will uphold the standard of compliance.

As a rule of thumb, the more visible the action you ask students to execute, the easier it is for you to see what students do, and the more that students implicitly recognize that you can clearly see what they do. This makes them more likely to do what you've asked and makes it easier for you to hold them accountable. Some of the most clever teachers I've watched have a way of making "observable directions" fun and tactile, increasing both the incentive to follow through and their ability to manage.

Getting Control: The Visible Reset

Drawing on *Radar* and *Be Seen Looking*, the idea of a *visible reset* comes from principal David McBride. While working with a teacher who struggled to keep kids focused, David asked the teacher to script three points into his lesson when he would bring his students, intentionally and fully, back to orderliness. At least three times a lesson, they'd be at 100 percent.

What David asked him to do was

- Give an observable direction.

- Use *Radar* (that is, scan intentionally and strategically to see whether it's done).

- Stand in Pastore's Perch while scanning.

- Narrate the follow-through of at least two students who've done right away what the teacher has asked. Fix or improve at least one student if things are at all rocky, to set higher expectations.

The visible reset worked pretty well. In some cases, though, the teacher continued to struggle, and didn't always see off-task behaviors, so David upped the ante. "I want you to substitute 'Pencils down and eyes on me' for 'Eyes on me' when you give your direction, and then I want you to look for that as you scan." The results were dramatic. Students putting their pencils down were ten times more visible to the teacher than was mere eye contact, making it much easier to respond accordingly with accurate affirmation or correction.

Not only that, but students sensed the increased accountability implicit in the new directions. It was clearer to them that it would be more apparent whether they followed through. Eliminating this gray area immediately brought opportunistic noncompliers into the fold. Not only that, but when students complied, it was more obvious to their classmates. This increased the normality of compliance.

A visible reset can be an immense and immediate help. Recognize that follow-through is easier to manage and monitor when directions ask students to do something visible. If you can see it, you can manage it. So, for example, you might *Make Compliance Visible* by asking for

"Pencils in the tray" instead of "Pencils down"

"Books open in front of you" instead of "Books out"

"I want to see your pencils moving" instead of "You should be writing"

By the way, students are exhibiting "marginal compliance" when they do the minimum possible to comply with your request. When they do this, they are implicitly asking, "Is this enough?" or "Will you settle for that?" *Make Compliance Visible* sometimes has the effect of also making these sorts of implicit questions more visible. You ask for "scholarly hands," meaning hands raised straight and all the way up, and a student raises a hand partially: Is this OK? These moments are worth anticipating and enforcing. If you don't enforce marginal compliance, you risk undercutting the veracity of your expectations more broadly. Be judicious in what you ask for, especially because you know you will have to uphold that standard — and then uphold it.

 Want More? Clip 56 and Clip 57. Want more *Make Compliance Visible*? Check out Amy Youngman in clip 56 and Ashley Hinton in clip 57.

100%, PART 3: LEAST INVASIVE INTERVENTION

Maximize teaching time and minimize "drama" by using the subtlest and least invasive tactic possible to correct off-task students.

53

The goal of *100%* is to get attentiveness and compliance *so that you can teach,* but, ironically, constant, time-consuming interventions often intended to ensure compliance can make it all but impossible to teach. When instruction comes to a halt, whether for a student disruption or a teacher correction, often *no one* is on task because, for a time, there is no task. Worse, interruptions often result in students finding something else to pay attention to during the hiatus, meaning that more students are off task when instruction finally restarts. Because it's impossible to eschew correction entirely, and lengthy interruptions do their own damage, the trick is to use the **Least Invasive Intervention** to fix the problem, then get back to work.

Let's say I am teaching, but Roberta has flopped her head down on her desk and, eyes closed, is either asleep or feigning sleep. I am keenly aware of the importance of fixing the situation. Not only is it counterproductive for Roberta to be allowed to sleep through class, but her behavior is eminently public. It's a statement to other students: "I'm outta here; I've got no interest in this, and I can check out any time I like." If I allow the behavior, I will soon have a classroom where, when it suits them, some portion of my students flop their heads down in silent, damning judgment of school or society or adults or my teaching. And I will have a classroom where there is tacit pressure to assume this posture because others do it.

Let's say that, knowing I need to make a correction, I stop my lesson on the Great Depression and address Roberta: "Roberta, what we're studying today is critically important. It's important for you to know, it will help you when you get to college, and it's my expectation that you pick your head up and stay with us." Even in the best-case scenario—Roberta raising her head without further dissent and getting back to work — my interaction took several seconds, and, during that time, a couple of things probably happened. First, there was no further discussion of the Great Depression. It's not just that learning stopped; engagement stopped, and sharp minds are now looking for a substitute. Students who might have been interested in the lesson now look out the window, take out their cell phones, or speak quietly to a peer. They do just as you or I would, waiting somewhere — at a train station, in a store — for delays to work their way out.

So now I've got other fires to fight. "Jamila, there are no cell phones allowed in this class," I say. "Carlos, my expectations for Roberta are also true for you. I need you paying attention." Each time I stop to correct one student, I risk losing another. I am now in a death spiral and may never catch up.

Another possibility is that students join in and opportunistically pour fuel on my interaction with Roberta. "Yeah, Roberta, there's no *sleeping* in class! Where do you think this is!?" Now in the hands of droll and clever students, my intervention has become a counterproductive exercise in faux outrage, which — fun as it is — is now more likely to crop up at the next opportunity. Or perhaps Roberta's classmates just stare at her and shake their heads. Even this rewards her with attention — for the moment, we all wonder about what's going on with Roberta, and perhaps this makes her likely to persist. Roberta's actions seem to present an untenable paradox: I know I have to fix off-task behavior, but how do I keep from making it worse? Is it better just to let well enough alone and hope for the best?

What about behavioral champions? Would they intervene with Roberta? Almost assuredly. But they would make the correction as invisibly as possible and, perhaps more important, they would make the correction *while still teaching*. They would put a premium on privacy. They would be calm and steady. But most of all, they would be as fast as possible in order to keep the thread of instruction alive for the other twenty-nine students in the classroom. And therein lies the secret: if you can manage to correct non-invasively, you are likely to be able to set and reinforce expectations successfully and consistently.

Six Interventions

In watching champion classroom managers over and over, we've made a list of six useful interventions, ranked in order of invasiveness from least to most. The goal, generally speaking, is to be as near to the top of this list as possible as often as possible.

Nonverbal Intervention

First on the list is a *nonverbal intervention*. I observed this in action in a recent lesson of Ashley Hinton's. As Ashley taught her students to write descriptive paragraphs, she constantly made micro corrections with either (1) a hand gesture or (2) intentional modeling of the corrective action she expected students to take. As she did this, she never stopped the thread of her engaging teaching; distracted students were corrected at no cost to the lesson.

See It in Action: Clip 58

In clip 58, you can watch Ashley Hinton correct off-task behavior almost exclusively with nonverbals. First, you'll see that Ashley catches behavior early. Fixing things while they're small makes the solution small and simple as well. Second, because the solution is small and simple, Ashley can stay positive in her tone as she makes her corrections.

In addition, Ashley *Circulates* (technique 24) constantly while she makes her corrections. She's always on the move, so when she approaches a student to give a bit more of a tone of accountability to her corrections, it's not especially obvious to other students that she's using proximity to a specific classmate. Her constant movement masks any single specific corrective measure. Her gestures are consistent—she focuses on just two or three expectations that she wants to see—and, of course, she keeps teaching.

It's important to remember that a nonverbal intervention is not inherently noninvasive. To be noninvasive, you have to keep teaching and keep moving and embed corrections in the larger flow of class. I was recently watching a teacher struggling to use nonverbals to address behavior in her classroom. The reason? She failed to continue teaching while making nonverbal corrections. She broke off her discussion of the novel her class was reading, for example, and walked two rows to her left as the class watched her intently. She stopped and made a dramatic *SLANT* gesture to a student and stared at him waiting for him to comply. At this point, with no instruction going on, everyone was staring at her and the student in question, despite the entire interaction's being nonverbal, and her intervention was not successful.

Lastly, nonverbals work best when they are consistent and limited in scope. To begin using nonverbals, I might choose the one or two most common low-level distractions in my classrooms and develop a consistent nonverbal for each. If there are only a few signals, you can use them and your students can process them without distracting any of you from the content of the lesson. For her part, Ashley Hinton chose to use gestures to remind her students to track the speaker with their eyes, to put their hands down when a classmate was talking, and to sit attentively in *STAR* (see technique 47).

Positive Group Correction

Slightly more invasive but still with a very small footprint is *positive group correction*—a quick, verbal reminder offered to the entire group, advising them to take a specific action. Like a nonverbal intervention, a positive group correction is ideal for catching off-task behavior early. ("I need to see everyone's eyes on me" isn't a great response when someone's swinging a chair in the air.) The concept "positive" comes from the fact that this intervention always describes the solution (a positive) rather than the problem (a negative). "Group" refers to the fact that it's targeted to the entire class as opposed to specific students. Because the goal is to be noninvasive, this form of correction tends to be very short and preserves economy of language. "Check your SLANT" is a classic. Three words, about a second, and back to teaching. If you need to boost the level of accountability with specific students, you might do that nonverbally at the same time; that is, you might say, "I need to see everyone writing," while you briefly fix an individual student who needs a bit more support with some eye contact and perhaps a slight nod of your head. The idea is that, in speaking to the group, it also corrects those students whom you might not see.

Of course, while you can establish nonverbal accountability for individuals, you keep noncompliers off the public stage. Saying a student's name usually causes people to look at him, and sometimes that is exactly what a noncompliant student wants. If you make the effort to show that you are trying to solve something—with a targeted nonverbal, for instance—but don't "call a student out," the result is usually positive.

See It in Action: Clip 59

Watch Alexandra Bronson in a recent lesson of hers. "Oooh, check your SLANT," Alex intoned to her class. Presumably there was a specific student or two about whom she was concerned, but her whole class reacted by resetting to their most productive learning position. They all made a quick self-assessment and took small steps to make sure it wasn't they who were slouching. This reminds me of how powerful the word *check* is—as in "check your SLANT." It asks students to choose to correct themselves. This is an ideal way for a correction to happen and can always be followed with a more explicit "I need to see tracking eyes" if students don't choose to check themselves.

Anonymous Individual Correction

The next intervention features anonymity right in the name: *anonymous individual correction*. An anonymous individual correction is similar to a positive group correction in that it describes the solution; however, it makes it explicit that there are people (as yet anonymous) who have not yet met expectations. You might combine it with a positive group correction to make it sound like this: "Track me, please [positive group correction]. I need two more sets of eyes [anonymous individual correction]."

As with the positive group correction, you can supplement an anonymous individual correction with nonverbals, especially eye contact and a quick nod, to establish directly and privately whom you are expecting to fix the situation fast. The combination of verbal group accountability and nonverbal individual accountability can be especially effective.

See It in Action: Clip 60

You can watch two examples of an anonymous individual correction that are both outstanding but also very different. Bob Zimmerli uses his at a break in class, as he is about to give homework. It's more of a full stop, and about as high in terms of transaction cost as you'll see in an anonymous individual correction. It's early in the year, and Bob is clearly trying to build a habit of follow-through. He makes absolutely sure that students understand that an anonymous individual correction means "fixing it."

Laura Brandt, by contrast, uses two anonymous individual corrections in the midst of a rich discussion, a comparison between religious freedom in Syria and religious freedom during the Puritan era. Both are lightning fast, and she is careful to keep the discussion moving apace. Laura also uses a nonverbal to support her anonymous individual correction, reminding a student to track the speaker. In the end, there was a lovely bit of symmetry: the girl Laura corrected ended the sequence with a beautiful and meritorious answer.

Private Individual Correction (PIC)

The next level of intervention is a *private individual correction*. When you have to name names, you can still make use of privacy. And when you need to take more time with a student, you can make it less invasive by asking the class to work independently, or by making your intervention at a time when it's easy to be offstage.

In the case of our head flopper, Roberta, for example, you could give your class a quick task—"Check in with your partner to make sure you have strong definitions for our key terms, and we'll pick the discussion back up in thirty seconds. Go"—at which point you might crouch down and speak to Roberta using a voice that preserves as much privacy as possible: "Roberta, what we're studying today is critically important. It's important for you to know; it will help you when you get to college. Let me see you with your head up, joining the discussion and tracking it in your notes." Here, with your voice dropped to show you are not trying to make something public out of it, the intervention is likely to be more effective, especially if you are careful to describe the solution, not the problem (see technique 57, *What to Do*) and to emphasize purpose ("This is important for you to learn") over power ("When I ask someone to sit up, I expect to see them do it"). If you need to return, it's probably time for a consequence. Again you want to do this privately: "Roberta, we need you with us so you can learn. I'm going to have to [move your card to yellow, take two scholar dollars, ask you to come in and practice at recess]. Now please show me your best."

See It in Action: Clip 61

In clip 61, Jaimie Brillante of Rochester Prep demonstrates the private individual correction. Notice how she makes her intervention an exercise in purpose, not in power: the reason Jaimie's talking to her student is that she wasn't able to answer correctly. The goal is for the student to succeed academically (purpose), not merely to kowtow to Jaimie's authority. Notice how Jaimie first assigns a "task for the class" to give other students something to attend to. The last thing she wants is a lot of Nosey Parkers peering over her shoulder when she has this conversation. She even gets tissues for another student to make her approach less obvious and her interaction thus more private. Finally, notice the calm, firm, nonjudgmental tone. Jaimie is careful to tell her students how to solve the problem.

Private Individual Precise Praise (PIPP)

We call a private individual correction a PIC for short, and its new partner is the PIPP, or private individual precise praise. When you use PIPP, you walk over to a student, just as you would when you make a PIC, but whisper positive feedback instead of criticism. If students come to expect that a private intervention could be either positive or corrective, they will be more open to you as you approach them. You also earn trust for your criticism by balancing it with praise. Most of all, you build a defense against the sort of eavesdropping that students do when they are curious about or take delight in the misfortune of others. In other words, if the content is unpredictable—sometimes positive, sometimes corrective or constructive—the urgent need to listen for the juicy bits of discipline disappears. Frankly, the idea that you might approach Roberta and say, "I thought that answer was outstanding. Keep up the good work" is not terribly intriguing to eavesdroppers. Such comments create a bit more privacy when you need to tell Roberta to sit up.

Lightning-Quick Public Correction

It would be great if you could make every correction quickly and privately, but we all know that a complex place like a classroom just doesn't work like that. You will be forced, at times, to make corrections of individual students during public moments. In those cases, your goals should be to limit the amount of time a student is "onstage" for something negative, to focus on telling the student what to do right rather what he or she did wrong, and then to normalize the positive behavior of the majority of the class by directing attention to something more productive. This is called a *lightning-quick public correction,* and it might sound something like "Quentin, I need your pencil moving . . . just like those sharp-looking scholars in my back row!" or "Quentin, I need your pencil moving . . . just like Josefina. And like Malichai." In rare cases, you may wish to emphasize your attentiveness to Quentin's accountability by adapting the sequence: "Quentin, I need your pencil moving. Looking sharp, back row! Thank you, Quentin. Much better."

Think for a moment about how the rest of the class reacts to your correction. They are working, and they hear Quentin's name. Probably, before they even hear the rest of your sentence, several of them look at Quentin to see why you've spoken to him. This ironically may provide Quentin with a perverse incentive. It may be that he likes having everyone in class look at him more than he dislikes any negative consequences of this outcome. In such cases, it's much better to direct attention to something that causes the rest of the class to see the normality of positive behavior in your room. For a lightning-quick public correction, you want your off-task student to be onstage for as short a time as possible, and the sequence to end with a productive example.

Notice the importance of speed and the practical utility of the correction. Merely saying Quentin's name doesn't provide Quentin with any guidance about how to meet your expectations. Too much gray area doesn't help your student and allows him to pretend he doesn't know what steps to take.

See It in Action: Clip 62

In Jason Armstrong's clip, he makes two corrections of students who are off task, and both are essentially public. He's standing in front of the class when he makes them, but they *feel* like private individual corrections because he whispers them. Essentially, he gets the benefits of privacy—he messages "I am trying to do this without calling too much attention to you"—by creating the illusion of privacy. We call this a *whisper correction*.

Even if you are standing in front of a classroom with twenty-six pairs of eyes on you, you can create many of the benefits of a private correction merely by dropping your voice to a whisper or, in fact, a stage whisper. Whispered, "Roberta, I need you sitting up" is for her benefit alone, even if pretty much everyone in the class hears it.

Common Misperceptions

One common misperception about the levels of intervention is that they represent a process or a formula: "Teachers will always progress methodically through each level, trying all six types of correction in sequence before giving a consequence." Although the goal is to be as close to the top of the list as possible, great classroom managers maintain fidelity to what works. Sometimes they go straight to the sixth level or straight to a consequence, sometimes back and forth among the levels; and occasionally they use several interventions with an off-task student. In fact, using levels 1 to 6 implies that students are making (or appear likely to be making) a good-faith effort to comply with expectations when reminded. Behavior that is deliberate has earned a consequence.

Another common misperception is that ignoring misbehavior—or addressing it by praising students who are behaving—is the least invasive form of intervention. In fact, ignoring misbehavior is the *most* invasive form of intervention, because the behavior becomes more likely to persist and expand. The goal is to address behavior quickly, while its manifestation is still minimal and the required response still small.

Want More? Clip 63. Want more *Least Invasive Intervention*? Check out how Lucy Boyd uses a variety of different nonverbal interventions in this clip.

100%, PART 4: FIRM CALM FINESSE

Take steps to get compliance without conflict by establishing an environment of purpose and respect and by maintaining your own poise.

54

Great classroom managers are steady at the helm. They may show passion when discussing history or science, but when they ask a student to sit down or get to work, they are calm and composed. They act as if they couldn't imagine a universe in which students wouldn't follow through, and this, lo and behold, causes students to follow through. These teachers do their work with finesse, and generally take steps to get compliance without conflict. Here are seven general rules for teaching with **Firm Calm Finesse.**

Catch It Early

Sometimes we want to believe that a problem, left alone, will cure itself. Most often, it persists or gets worse because we've sent the message that we'll tolerate it for a while. Eventually, we have to step in with a bigger fix, in part because the behavior has gotten more bold or disruptive, and in part because we are starting to get frustrated. Here's a rule of thumb I've used that teachers have often found helpful for self-reflection: if you're mad, you've waited too long. It's usually better to fix something with a tiny adjustment very early than to make a bigger intervention later. You're far more likely to correct positively and with a smile when your corrections feel like tiny adjustments to you as well as to your students.

Value Purpose over Power

The reason you correct behaviors in the classroom is that doing so leads to achievement and self-discipline for the students surrounding an off-task scholar, as well as for the scholar in question. Strive to make your language constantly stress that the goal is helping students learn and succeed, not reinforcing your power as the king or queen of room 315. Statements like "When I ask you to sit up, I want to see you sitting up" are best avoided. "I need to see you sitting like a scholar" makes the point subtly and without a lot of fuss and extraneous verbiage. Keep corrections tight and crisp, but try to remind students (and yourself) that your high expectations are, in the end, about the students, not you.

Remember That "Thank You" Is the Strongest Phrase

Saying thank you after a student follows a direction is one of the most subtly powerful things you can do, for two reasons. First, when society is in decay, "please" and "thank you" are the first things to go. It's useful to signal that civility and thus society are fully intact in your classroom by modeling "please" and "thank you" constantly, especially when students might see evidence of fraying. In other words, when you see Maya making a disruption during your science lesson, you want to say, "Hands to yourself, please, Maya" or, even better, something more specific like "Hands folded in front of you, please, Maya." Then, when Maya folds her hands, you can say, in a low and slightly muted tone: "Thank you."

Second, "thank you" reinforces expectations and normalizes compliance in the subtlest way possible. You would only say thank you because Maya followed your direction. Therefore, "thank you" subtly reminds everyone else in the class that Maya did just that. The interaction ended with your reinforcing expectations successfully. It has the secret and subtle effect of normalizing compliance.

Use Universal Language

Look for chances to remind students that expectations are universal and not personal. Although "I need you with me" is fine, "We need you with us" is better. It suggests that learning is a team sport, and subtly says that the rest of the class is also meeting the expectations I am asking you to adhere to. Saying something like "Let me see you looking like a Blue Jay" if that's your class mascot, or "Like a Lincoln Prep scholar" or even just "Like a scholar" also reinforces that expectations are group and not personal criteria. Expectations are part of being here—not a reflection of personal feelings about you.

Show Your Bright Face

Your bright face is your teaching smile — or at least your age-appropriate, default expression of "I like this work, I like the people here, and I'm pretty confident that I'm in charge." You can see Patrick Pastore's bright face when he looks up to scan his class most days. He starts with a smile, not a scowl. His bright, pleasant face is confident. His plan, it says, is to trust but verify. This is very different from a teacher whose scowl says (1) I'm not happy here, (2) I'm worried about compliance, or even (3) I'm waiting for noncompliance because I'm sure it's going to happen. That is a self-fulfilling prophecy for sure.

To underscore, your bright face does not have to be a huge, fake, beaming smile. It's just a pleasant face, a confident "it's good to be here, and I have a plan" face that exudes a degree of positivity and confidence that matches your style and the age group of your students. With kindergarteners, it might really be an irrepressible smile. With high schoolers, it might be a bit more subdued.

Deploy Your Confirmation Glance

Trust, and demonstrating trust, are among the most important things you can communicate in building a relationship with others. Showing trust is self-fulfilling — if you signal that you trust, students will follow through when you make a request.

There are times when it's critical to ask and then look or walk away. Here, a confirmation glance is the verification tool used just after you signal trust: walk (or look) away and then glance back. Sometimes a student needs just a bit of space to pull it together and decide he or she wants to do the right thing, and a confirmation glance can provide it. It's best to start small with the length of the delay before a confirmation glance, and then get a bit longer with time. Sometimes teachers use it explicitly with students, as in "I'm going to walk away, and when I look back I am going to see you with your pencil in your hand writing your response." Of course, you will need to follow up decisively if your confirmation glance reveals lack of follow-through, but using it can intimate a potent, calm, self-assuredness to your class.

Stay Steady at the Helm

Generally, when you manage behavior, you want to remain calm and steady. As I discuss in technique 61, *Emotional Constancy,* inserting emotion into the process distracts students from reflecting on or adjusting their own behavior. Stay calm and steady. Don't suggest to students that their behavior can get a rise out of you. Keep them focused on what they need to do.

For difficult behavioral situations that may "set you off," practice with students in advance, while they are calm, and have them imagine that they'd done that behavior. Then, in the moment that it occurs for real, you can remind students—and yourself— "I can see that you're upset. But we practiced how you'd handle this. Let me see you do that now."

Want More? Clip 64. Want more *Firm Calm Finesse*? Check out Channa Comer in clip 64.

100%, PART 5: ART OF THE CONSEQUENCE

55

Ensure that consequences, when needed, are more effective by making them quick, incremental, consistent, and depersonalized. It also helps to make a bounce-back statement, showing students that they can quickly get back in the game.

Consequences are notoriously tricky. As I'm sure nearly every teacher can attest, consequences do not always have the intended effect. Who hasn't given a consequence that, instead of fixing a behavior, actually made it worse? As my team and I set out to learn from great teachers, we discovered classrooms where consequences had the intended effect not just some of the time but nearly all of the time, and these observations inform what I have dubbed **Art of the Consequence**.

Principles of the Effective Consequence

Consequences, used properly, are not merely punishments with a sanitized name. Their purpose is to efficiently reinforce sound decision making—to use situations in which mistakes are made so that students can learn from them. Their goal should be to develop and teach, and this goal can and should be evident in how you employ them. The following sections describe a few principles of effective consequences.

Quick

An immediate consequence is more closely associated with the action that caused it. If the goal is to shape behavior rather than to punish it, try to give a consequence right away. Ironically, giving a smaller consequence in the moment (for example, "Scholars, go back to the door and come into this classroom like scholars") will often be more effective than a larger consequence later ("Gentlemen, I will see you here after school"). Quick consequences also reduce the amount of time a student's behavior remains onstage. This latter benefit removes students' incentive to engage in attention-seeking behavior and minimizes the odds of escalating behavior.

Incremental

Designing consequences so that they can be allocated in strategic increments lets students learn from mistakes at manageable cost. Small mistake, small consequence works really well for students, and it's better for you as well. If your consequences are all massive and heartbreaking to give to the students you love, you will hesitate and either not use them or make the situation more visible. Plan out a series of consequences that start small and scale up in severity. The first response should be a disincentive, not a life-altering event. As Doug McCurry of Achievement First says, "Save your nuclear bombs for nuclear moments."

One example of a system like this is the one Emilie Tarraf uses at Leadership Prep Ocean Hill. We've all seen an elementary school student flop down and weep over a color change. But in Emilie's system, four checks result in a color change (green to yellow or yellow to red). This enables her to address small behaviors consistently and to distribute checks without hesitation, without having to immediately resort to a card color change (which can be a big deal to young kids).

A student who loses all of his or her privileges has no incentive to stay in the game. Another benefit of small, scaled consequences is that they enable you to escalate strategically to respond to significant behavior, but also offer students a clear and feasible way back.

Consistent

Responses should be predictable in students' minds: "If I do X, Y will happen." If they aren't sure what will happen, then they have an incentive to "test" and see. Consistently using the same language or approach reduces the transaction costs involved with giving consequences, and also makes them more legible to students (for example, "Darryl, hands, check" or "Michael, tracking, two dollars"). Students won't have to worry about trying to decipher your consequences, and you won't have to spend time and energy brainstorming responses. If you and your students shift activities or move to different areas of the room, your management system should follow. Whether you're teaching from desks or the carpet, stick with the system and approach that students know and understand. Otherwise, students will quickly learn when and where they can test the limits.

Depersonalized

Avoid personalizing consequences by keeping them as private as possible (with a whisper, during a one-on-one interaction, with a nonverbal gesture, and the like) and by judging actions instead of people. Maintaining privacy shows consideration to the student, which can go a long way to preserve your relationship with him or her. It also keeps behavior offstage, which reduces the likelihood of attention-seeking behavior or a public standoff that benefits no one.

Finally, strive to remember that emotions distract students from reflecting on the behavior(s) that resulted in a consequence. Maintain a neutral facial expression and steady tone of voice when you deliver the consequence, and then continue teaching with warmth and enthusiasm.

Principles of Delivering a Consequence

In addition to exuding *Emotional Constancy,* creating the illusion of privacy, and making sure consequences are focused on purpose, not power, teachers who give consequences that reliably change behavior for the better follow the principles described in the next sections.

Tag the Behavior

Tagging the behavior is an important way to help students internalize the connection between their choices, actions, and consequences. Identifying the nonproductive behavior—very quickly and simply—can be the first step toward helping students learn how to self-manage.

When you tag behavior, strive for consistency. One tried-and-true approach is to name the student, identify the behavior, and list the consequence (for example, "Michael.

Talking. Two dollars."). Whatever language you choose to use, make sure the student knows which behavior resulted in a consequence and how he or she can fix it. Doing so makes it easier for you to clearly and efficiently communicate your expectations, makes the consequence more legible for students, and helps them internalize which behaviors they should strive to replicate and which they should avoid.

Finally, tagging the behavior in the same way every time reduces the likelihood of pushback, because it makes consequences appear more systematic. When you give consequences in the same way to everyone, students are more likely to realize that you're not trying to antagonize them but just holding them accountable in the same way you would anyone else.

Want More? Clip 51. Want to see more *Art of the Consequence*? In the second half of clip 51, you can watch Sarah Ott give two "checks" (a small consequence equal to one-third of a "color change") in her kindergarten classroom. Notice how she calmly and steadily names the student, tags the behavior, and keeps moving. Watch carefully, or you might miss it! Many teachers think of *Do It Again* as a very small consequence. You can see Sarah use *Do It Again* here, keeping it positive while she does so.

Use a Bounce-Back Statement

It's probably safe to say that every teacher has encountered a student who shuts down once he or she receives a consequence, or who only halfheartedly complies with your requests. In that instant, some students feel as though the whole world is against them, including you, so they convince themselves that they should cut their losses and stop trying. Your goal is to suggest otherwise and nudge them forward into a productive direction. One way is by delivering a "bounce-back" statement that shows students that success is still within their grasp. For example, you might say something like "Two dollars. Pick up your pencil; get back to writing like I know you can." When you use bounce-back statements routinely, you socialize students to persist in the face of emotional duress, which is a life skill that will benefit them long after they leave your classroom.

Maintain the Pace

Responding to behavior by lecturing or giving a speech disengages the rest of the class and increases the likelihood of other fires sprouting up. Here are a couple tips for maintaining the pace when emotions run high and you have to give a consequence:

- Describe what students *should be doing* as opposed to what they *are not doing* ("Michael, I need your eyes" is better than "Michael, for the last time, stop getting distracted!").

- Use the least amount of verbiage you can ("That's two bucks. I need you tracking," rather than "You just earned a two-buck deduction because you chose to draw cartoons when you were supposed to be listening to my lecture. You should know better . . .," and so forth). Doing so maximizes instructional time and minimizes the amount of time students are left onstage.

See It in Action: Clip 65

Watch sixth-grade math teacher Ana O'Neil deliver two consequences with grace and calm. Both consequences involve "catching it early"—giving a small consequence (a very small scholar-dollar deduction of two dollars) early on to help reset a student. "Two bucks; I need you tracking," Ana whispers to the first student, having moved near him and "squared up"—both to make sure he understood and to allow her to whisper gently and privately. Ana's second student is across the room—no proximity here—but again her easy warmth ("Two bucks, kiddo") and the speed with which she gets back to work help to keep this interaction a molehill, not a mountain.

Get Back on Track

When it comes to consequences, the goal is to get in, get out, and *move on* with the business of teaching. Teachers who are able to get *all* students back on track after a consequence remember to show that it's over.

What you focus on after you give a consequence speaks volumes to students about what you value. If you want them to get back on track with the lesson, resume instruction with warmth and energy. Find an opportunity to talk to students in a calm, relaxed manner to show that the interaction is over. You can even go a step further by getting the student who received a consequence positively back into the flow of class by asking a question or acknowledging his or her work. Doing so models forgiveness and shows students that you still value them and want them to be successful.

The Million-Dollar Question: Consequence or Correction?

One of the trickiest aspects of managing a classroom is deciding when to give a consequence rather than a correction. The question is tough, in part because teachers must decide on a case-by-case basis. That being said, we have identified some helpful rules of thumb:

- **Persistence and repetition.** When students *persistently* engage in off-task behavior that they know they shouldn't, you should err on the side of a consequence. This is especially true when students continue in spite of your correction(s). If instead the behavior appears to be a good-faith error caused by distraction or misunderstanding, err on the side of correction.

- **Degree of disruption.** If a student's behavior doesn't disrupt others' learning, then it's probably better to give a correction. In contrast, if the student's behavior distracts others, give a consequence.

- **Motivation.** If a student is clearly testing your expectations, give a consequence. Tolerating willful defiance corrodes your authority in the eyes of the student as well as the rest of the class.

- **And, not or.** You could also give a correction *and* a consequence. If you do, it's better to give a correction before the consequence, because it allows the student time to reflect. Correcting first also communicates confidence because it shows others that you don't need a consequence to achieve compliance. Conversely, if you lead with a consequence, you are a lot likelier to provoke an emotional response or student shutdown.

See It in Action: Clip 66

One of our favorite examples of how to give a consequence is shown in this clip of Bridget McElduff's fifth-grade math classroom.

At the start of this lesson, Bridget asks Precious to read the directions for the next assignment. When Precious struggles to read the word "examine," a student sitting at the far end of the room begins snickering. Bridget responds by warmly reassuring Precious and helping her through the pronunciation as she makes her way to where the laughing student sits. The following is an outline of just some of the many principles that Bridget exemplifies in this *Art of the Consequence* moment:

- <u>Illusion of privacy.</u> Bridget leans in close to the student and gives him a whispered correction and consequence, showing the student warmth and consideration, preserving the student's privacy, and avoiding the possibility of humiliating either or both students involved in this incident.

- *Emotional Constancy* <u>and bounce-back statement.</u> In delivering a consequence in a way that assumes the best, Bridget shows the student that she has faith in his ability to fix his behavior and models the compassion that she'd like him to show his classmates.

- <u>Tagging the behavior.</u> Note the way Bridger comments on actions as opposed to judging traits ("Laughing is ten dollars" as opposed to "How *dare* you laugh at her?!").

- <u>Purpose, not power.</u> Bridget frames the consequence in terms of the cultural norms of the class, helping the student understand *why* his actions were inappropriate as well as how to show compassion to his peers in the future.

- <u>Maintaining the pace.</u> Bridget gets in, gets out, and gets back to teaching the rest of her class.

- <u>And, not or.</u> Bridget knows she can't afford to leverage a correction *or* a consequence, so she chooses to leverage both tools. In doing so, she maintains a strong classroom culture and preserves the integrity of her relationship with both students.

56

STRONG VOICE

Affirm your authority through intentional verbal and nonverbal habits, especially at moments when you need control.

Some teachers have "it": they enter the middle school lunch room at 12:15 and are instantly able to "command the room." Potentially inflammatory situations resolve themselves in low tones rather than blowing up into raised voices and tense standoffs.

It's hard to say exactly what "it" is and why some teachers have it. Much of it is surely intangible — a manifestation of the unique power of individuals to earn respect and credibility, build relationships, and exude confidence and poise. Happily, though, if you talk to "it" teachers, they just as often profess no great gift for the interpersonal. Sometimes it's a matter of doing a few simple things calmly and with confidence.

The Six Principles of *Strong Voice*

After watching hour after hour of footage of "it" teachers, my team and I were able to distill some of the skills that are so effective in commanding a room that yearns toward entropy — six of them, specifically. Mastering these skills may not make you the "it" teacher, but having a **Strong Voice** will surely get you a lot closer.

Use a Formal Register

Register is the word I'll use to describe the tenor of a conversation, encompassing eye contact, body position, gestures, facial expression, and rhythm of language. Delivering an important message in a casual register can ultimately undercut the formality of the message. Telling a student "I need you to sit up" while you lean casually against a wall with your hands in your pockets, generally suggests discretion for the listener: "Sit up if you feel like it" is what the casual register says. If it contradicts the words the teacher is using, it's likely to win out.

A formal register, it turns out, bespeaks the importance of the message and causes a purposeful attentiveness in the listener. Champion teachers tend to use the formal register for the great majority of the statements in which they seek control. Watch them in action, and you'll see them standing straight and symmetrically, choosing words carefully, holding their eyes steady. If they make a hand gesture, it's controlled and simple. A formal register is the wrapping that makes *Strong Voice* especially effective.

Although champion classroom managers address expectations and behavior most often using the formal register, their teaching — the moment when they're talking academic content — is not as consistent. Some are casual; some are more formal. Still, when they "drop into" their no-nonsense voice, there's a distinctive change that helps to ensure attentiveness in students.

An urgent register should be spared for urgent situations. An overuse of urgency can be like crying wolf. Further, using an urgent register when a situation isn't really urgent makes you seem panicky and nervous. Being calm and steady when others are nervous is often the sign of people who have "it."

In short, do the joyful and academic part of teaching in whatever balance of casual and formal that's "you." When you need to get a response in a difficult situation, drop noticeably into formal register, but save your urgent register for the truly urgent—maybe once a year.

Square Up/Stand Still

Many times when we give a direction, we communicate to listeners that the direction is an afterthought because we appear to be doing something else while we give it. The message: something else is foremost in my mind relative to this direction. If you are passing out papers while you direct students, you suggest that your directions aren't that important. If you stop moving, you show that there is nothing more important than the direction you just gave. When you want directions followed, don't engage in other tasks at the same time. It may even help to strike a formal pose.

Exude Quiet Power

When you get nervous or sense that your control may be slipping away, your first instinct is often to talk louder and faster. When you get loud and talk fast, you show that you are nervous, scared, and out of control. You make your anxiety visible and send a message that students can control you and your emotions by making you anxious and upset. When you get loud, you also make the room louder and thus make it easier for students to successfully talk under their breath. Even though doing so runs against all your instincts, become slower and quieter when you want control. Drop your voice and make students strain to listen. Exude poise and calm.

Use Economy of Language

Fewer words are stronger than more. Demonstrating economy of language shows that you are prepared and know your purpose in speaking. When you need your directions followed, use the words that best focus students on what is most important, and no more. Don't dilute urgent issues with topics that can wait. Avoid initiating distractions and using excess words. When you need to be all business, be clear and crisp. Then stop talking.

To be clear, I am not suggesting that you need to use economy of language when you are discussing anaerobic respiration or the last chapter of *Lord of the Flies*—just when you're discussing behavior and when there are potential distractions.

Do Not Talk Over

If what you're saying is truly worth attention, then every student has the right and the responsibility to hear it. When you need them to listen, your words must be far and away the most important in the room, so make a habit of showing that they matter. Before beginning, wait until there is no other talking or rustling. By ensuring that your voice never competes for attention, you will demonstrate to students that their decision to listen isn't situational. Moreover, controlling who has the floor is the mark of your authority and a necessity to your teaching. If you have to repeat ten instructions per day at half a minute per instruction, you will waste two full days of school per child over the course of the year. You cannot afford to talk over students.

In some cases, you may need to stop in order to start—that is, start a sentence and break it off to show that you will not go on until you have full attention. Using this method, the *self-interrupt,* makes the fact that you are stopping obvious. A champion teacher would likely execute his self-interrupt in the middle of a word, as in "Sixth grade, I need y—" This makes the break more striking and calls more attention to it.

Adding some formal posture to your self-interrupt makes it stronger. Right after you break, move to a more formal posture and hold it, still, for a second or two. If you are in the middle of a movement, you also might consider freezing and holding your pose for a second. To up the listening ante, another smart move is to drop your voice a little lower right after your self-interrupt.

See It in Action: Clip 67

One of my favorite clips in this book is an example of Christy Lundy using the self-interrupt. The situation is one just about every teacher has faced, and Christy handles it about perfectly. In the light circle, you'll see two students kicking each other under the table as Christy teaches. (I've watched the video a hundred times, and I still don't know who started it.) When Christy calls on her scholar, she doesn't get the answer to her question about the book, but an attempt to move the discussion to the topic of kicking.

"Three, two, one," Christy responds, giving her scholar a few seconds—but not much more—to process the emotion of it all before telling her that the time is not right (and in choosing the phrase "inappropriate time," she is not ruling out a potential time to discuss). To take it up a notch higher, Christy tells her scholar, "You need to answer my question." The last message she wants to send is that students can get out of doing work by creating a trivial distraction. Christy has dropped into her quiet power voice a bit, and when she comes out of it, her voice practically sings. The message: there is joy when we talk about books, and not as much when we talk about distractions.

Do Not Engage

When you are discussing behavior with students, avoid engaging in other topics until you have satisfactorily resolved the topic you initiated. Of all the situations in which a student might try to change topics, the moment in which you ask her to take accountability for her actions is among the most likely. Refusing to engage establishes a tone of focused accountability in your classroom. Students can't change the topic. They need to act first and explain later. It also means that the issue of who is bugging whom is more easily delayed until a time when instruction is not taking place. Here's one example:

Teacher: James, you are talking. Please move your card to yellow.
James: It wasn't me!
Teacher: Please move your card to yellow.
James: Shanice was talking! Not me!
Teacher: I asked you to move your card. Please get up and move your card to yellow.

It may be reasonable for the teacher to discuss who was talking with James, but the expectation needs to be that the latter conversation doesn't happen until James has first done what his teacher asked. Until he has obeyed the initial request, there is no other conversation.

It is critical not to engage when students call out answers. No matter how fascinating the comment or how needed the right answer, if you engage when it is called out, you will erode your ability to control future conversations in your classroom. No matter how intriguing the answer, it's better in the long run to remind students of what to do—"In this class, we raise our hands when we want to speak"—without engaging the answer.

 Want More? Clip 68 and Clip 69. Want more *Strong Voice*? Check out Jessica Merrill-Brown in clip 68 and Mike Taubman in clip 69.

WHAT TO DO

Use specific, concrete, sequential, and observable directions to tell students what to do, as opposed to what not to do.

57

There are three potential causes of off-task behavior by students. The first is defiance. Students can be off task because they simply don't want to do what you've asked and don't care if you feel otherwise. The second is incompetence. I use that word in a non-judgmental sense merely to refer to those times when students don't yet have the skill to do a task reliably. Finally, there's opportunism. Students see a gray area and lack of clarity about what's supposed to be happening, so they take advantage of it to act on the most convenient or enjoyable interpretation of the situation.

What to Do is a profoundly simple technique, involving giving directions in a format that clearly describes what you want in concrete terms—as opposed to giving instructions in vague and confusing terms, or telling students what *not* to do. In schools, we may issue a lot of vague, inefficient, and unclear commands, even without realizing it: "Don't get distracted." "Stop that." "That behavior was inappropriate." They force students to guess at what you want them to do. This gray area leaves the door open to inaccurate interpretations, making it harder for students to do as you've asked, both now and in the future.

You need to be able to distinguish incompetence from defiance by making commands specific enough that they can't be deliberately misinterpreted, and helpful enough that they explain away any gray areas. If I ask John to pay attention, sit up, or get on task, and he doesn't, it's crucial that I know whether he cannot or will not. If he cannot, the problem is incompetence. If he will not, the problem is defiance. How I respond depends entirely on what the root of the problem is.

If the issue is incompetence, I must teach John. If I punish him for not complying when he is unable to do so, the consequence will seem unjust and may erode my relationship with him. Consequences may appear random and disconnected from his actions. Learned helplessness—the process of giving up because you believe your own choices and actions are irrelevant—generally results from a perception that consequences are random. If the issue is defiance, my obligation is to provide a consequence. Unless I act clearly and decisively in the face of a challenge to my authority, John will establish a precedent of impunity. If I respond to defiance with teaching, I am just as bad off as I am if I respond to incompetence with punishment.

Confusing incompetence and defiance has damaging consequences, and this is why making the distinction reliably and consistently has such far-reaching ramifications for your classroom. By giving concrete, specific, observable, and sequential directions, you can make the distinction consistently and fairly—responding by teaching when you should teach and exerting your authority when you must.

What to Do not only can make a big difference in your students' follow-through but also can improve your relationships with them. It socializes us as teachers to reflect on the quality of our directions before we proceed with other (and potentially more forceful) behavior management approaches.

Four Characteristics of *What to Do*

Differentiating consistently between defiance and incompetence will have a pervasive effect on your classroom culture, as well as on your relationships with students. *What to Do* directions should have the following four characteristics:

- **Specific.** Effective directions outline manageable and precise actions that students can take. For example, instead of advising a student to "pay attention," I might advise him to put his pencil on his desk or keep his eyes on me. It is easy to remember, solution oriented, and hard to misunderstand.

- **Concrete.** Effective directions involve, when possible, clear, actionable tasks that students know how to execute. If I tell my student to put his feet under his desk rather than to "stop fooling around," I have given a tangible direction that I am sure he knows how to follow. Concrete directions require no prior knowledge, and this eliminates the sort of gray area wherein a student might plausibly claim not to know how.

- **Sequential.** Effective directions should describe a sequence of concrete, specific actions. In the case of my student who needs help paying attention, I might advise him, "John, put your feet under your desk, put your pencil down, and put your eyes on me." In some cases, I might add, "When I write it on the board, that means you write it in your notes."

- **Observable.** It is hard for me to monitor a student's degree of paying attention accurately. In contrast, it is easy for me to monitor whether his legs are under his desk. If I follow up a lack of follow-through with a consequence, my student might protest, "But I *was* paying attention." It is much harder for him to say, "But my legs *are* under my desk" when they aren't. I can clearly see whether they are, and he also knows perfectly well that I can see whether he has complied. All of this makes him more likely to follow through.

What to Do 2.0

As with our other techniques, great teachers have mastered *What to Do* and applied it in a variety of ways. In this section, I'll pay it forward by sharing some of the most effective applications by teachers over the past four years.

Consistent *What to Do*

Use the same direction in the same words over time to make it a habit (for example, always say "pencils in the tray" and perhaps, over time, "trays," as opposed to "pencils in your trays," "pencils in their homes," "pencils down," "put your pencils down," and so on). Standardizing the language of your directions allows you to effectively and efficiently prompt students to complete specific tasks without the need for more description or explanation. This frees you up to focus on your lesson, and makes it easier for students to do what you've asked.

Adding a Gesture

Understanding and compliance increase if you add a nonverbal gesture, especially one that resembles what you want students to do (for example, folding your hands to signal that you want kids in "learner's position"). Even if students do not comply the first time, make sure to deliver your nonverbal gestures with *Emotional Constancy* (technique 61), keeping students focused on your directions rather than on your emotional response to noncompliance. It can help to deliver nonverbal gestures with a neutral facial expression or to add warmth with a smile.

What to Do with Checking for Understanding

One barrier to student compliance arises when adults give directions that aren't as clear as they thought they were. To account for this, you can check that students understand your directions before releasing them to move forward autonomously. Ask students to tell you whether or not they understood your directions or, even better, ask students to show you they understand your directions by asking them to rehearse what you've asked them to do. You might say, "Point to where you're going to put your binder. Good. Go."

Simplified *What to Do*

If a student does not respond appropriately to your *What to Do* direction, simplify it, either by removing words, requesting an even more concrete action, or reducing the number of steps you've asked the student to follow-through on. For example, you say to a student, "Stand up at your desk and track the door," and she doesn't do it, so you say, "Stand up at your desk." She still doesn't do it, so you say, "Push your chair back. Good. Now stand up. Thank you." Breaking down directions makes it easier to teach and reinforce your expectations for how students should complete a task.

What to Do Out Front

Giving a *What to Do* direction in advance of a cue to begin a routine behavior is a great way to build facility and autonomy in that routine. For example, saying, *before the timer goes off,* "When you hear the timer, please have pencils in your trays and be ready to review" gives a clear reminder of the expectation before the behavior is required. It allows students to execute on their own—they're moving from following directions to remembering the expectation. This will help you install the routine going forward.

Assuming the Best

Whenever the root cause of a student's noncompliance is unclear, assume the best by showing students that you believe they are making a good-faith effort and will comply once they understand what you're asking them to do. For example, if I ask students to get into learner's position and they do not, I might say, "Hmmm, I must not have been clear enough. When I said 'learner's position,' I also meant 'with voices off.'" This shows students that I am confident in my authority and believe that they can and will do what I've asked.

CONCLUSION

Over the course of this chapter, we've scrutinized the ways a number of champion teachers foster an engaging, productive, and positive classroom culture. Although the routes to such a culture—and the ultimate shape of such a culture—are as varied as the teachers who strive to build them, what champion classrooms all have in common is

100 percent compliance. That is to say, when students are in champion classrooms, they understand that the classroom is a place where engaging discussion, rigorous thinking, and serious writing take place, not some of the time, not most of the time, but *all of the time.*

Of course, there is more to building a productive classroom culture than behavioral expectations. After all, the teacher–student relationship is still a relationship. Like all good, supportive, and trusting relationships, this one is also built on a foundation of trust. In Chapter Twelve, we'll look at techniques champion teachers use to foster a trusting environment.

Reflection and Practice

1. For each of the common off-task behaviors listed here, write down and practice with a friend or in front of a mirror a nonverbal intervention you could use to correct it while you were teaching:

   - Student slouched in his chair

   - Student with her head down on her desk, eyes up

   - Student with her head down on her desk, eyes hidden

   - Student gesturing distractingly to another student

   - Student persistently looking under his desk for an unidentified something

2. For each of the off-task behaviors in question 1, script a positive group correction and an anonymous individual correction to address them.

3. Make a list of at least five positive student behaviors you could reinforce with nonverbal interventions. Plan a signal for each.

4. Revise the following statements using *What to Do* to make them specific, concrete, observable, and sequential:

   - "Class, you should be writing this down!"

   - "Tyson, stop fooling around."

   - "Don't get distracted, Avery."

   - "Are you paying attention, Dontae?"

   - "I'd like to get started, please, class."

***What to Do/Strong Voice* case study rewrites.** In this useful tool, you'll find descriptions of common behavior management situations. It's a great exercise to rewrite these to make sure your *What to Do* directions are specific, concrete, sequential, observable, and delivered with strong economy of language. Also included is an example of what an effective rewrite might look like.

Building Character and Trust

Technique 58: Positive Framing.   Guide students to do better work while motivating and inspiring them by using a positive tone to deliver constructive feedback.

Technique 59: Precise Praise.   Make your positive reinforcement strategic. Differentiate between acknowledgment and praise.

Technique 60: Warm/Strict.   Be both warm and strict at the same time to send a message of high expectations, caring, and respect.

Technique 61: Emotional Constancy.   Manage your emotions to consistently promote student learning and achievement.

Technique 62: Joy Factor.   Celebrate the work of learning as you go.

Chapter 12

Building Character and Trust

The meaning of a message changes subtly, drastically, and sometimes completely, depending on the setting and tone of its delivery. In a school, the challenge of effective communication is exacerbated by the sheer number and complexity of settings in which you are required to communicate, not to mention the range of topics you must cover.

Your conversation with Steven at the close of school on Wednesday, one of hundreds you will hold this week, may be conducted, depending on the details, in private, in quasi-private (overheard by others), or in public. If there is an audience, it may be large or small, and made up of foes, allies, authorities, or admired peers (of yours *or* of Steven's). Your purpose may be to correct, praise, inquire, or instruct. You may be referencing previous conversations, explicit or implicitly. You may be trying to prepare Steven for future conversations. You may be seeking to change his perception of himself, of you, of schoolwork, of education, of his peers, of certain values, of who he can be. You may be attempting to do this with humor, warmth, sternness, subtlety, or bluntness. Steven (and you) may be angry, elated, upset, impassive, defensive, motivated, or grateful. You may be late for class. You — or Steven — may urgently need to use the bathroom.

In this conversation, you may affect Steven's actions today, tomorrow, or next year. You may change his perceptions of you or of school. You will assuredly (and without realizing it) change your perceptions of your work: Are you successful? Are you changing lives? Are you respected? Is it worth it? Should you just get your real estate license?

In short, the conversation with Steven, like all others, is a high-wire act. You will need some rules, not just for the words you use but for the tone they strike in talking to Steven.

POSITIVE FRAMING

Guide students to do better work while motivating and inspiring them by using a positive tone to deliver constructive feedback.

People are motivated by the positive far more than by the negative. Seeking success and happiness will spur stronger action than seeking to avoid punishment. The power of the positive should influence the way you teach. It doesn't mean that you shouldn't be meticulous about responding to off-task or nonconstructive behavior. For example, you still need to fix and improve behavior, and you need to do so consistently and with clear and firm consequences when necessary, but your interventions will be far more effective if they are framed positively — if they remind the person you're talking to that you want her to be successful and that you believe in and trust her intentions (unless she gives you explicit cause to think otherwise). **Positive Framing**, then, is about framing your interactions — particularly corrections of the academic and behavioral variety — so that they reinforce this larger picture of faith and trust, even while you remind students of a better course of action.

One common but significant misinterpretation of *Positive Framing* is that it means you should avoiding making corrections and instead talk only about positive behavior. I sometimes call this "circum-narration": David is off task, and instead of telling David to be on task in a way that's positive, the teacher narrates a circle around David, praising all of the students in that circle for their "positive" behavior. Such an approach risks giving positive reinforcement to mediocre behavior when it happens to occur in convenient proximity to negative behavior, and this causes more mediocre behavior by making students think that what was so-so was praiseworthy. Or, if students realize that your praise of convenient mediocrity isn't sincere, it makes your praise disingenuous. Further, it suggests that you're afraid to address David's behavior head-on, and David may choose to test that theory.

It's much better, in short, to address David directly but positively: "David, show me your best!" or "David, check yourself to make sure you're sitting up."

When teachers develop the capacity to make corrections in a positive way, it allows them to address academic and behavioral missteps consistently, without hesitation and without fear of creating a negative tone to their classroom. Using *Positive Framing* allows you to give more critical feedback, keep culture strong, and just maybe signal that making mistakes and learning from them are positive.

Use *Positive Framing* to correct and guide behavior by following the six rules described in the next sections.

Live in the Now

In public — that is, in front of your class or while your lesson is under way — avoid harping on what students can no longer fix. Talk about what should or even must happen next. If necessary, you can do this firmly and forcefully (see technique 57, *What to Do*), but you should focus corrective interactions on the things students should do to succeed from this point forward. There's a time and place for processing what went wrong; but the right time is not when your lesson hangs in the balance. Give instructions describing the next move on the path to success. Say, "Show me SLANT!" not "You weren't SLANTing." Say, "Keana, I need your eyes forward," not "Keana, stop looking back at Tanya."

Assume the Best

We often assume intentionality behind a mistake. Our words imply that you did it on purpose or, worse, you were selfish, deliberately disrespectful, or lazy. Especially clear examples might be "Stop trying to disrupt class!" "Why won't you use the feedback I gave you on your first draft?" or "Just a minute, class; some people seem to think they don't have to push in their chairs when we line up." Such statements attribute ill intention to what could be the result of distraction, lack of practice, or genuine misunderstanding. What if the student was trying to use your feedback, or just plain forgot about the chair?

Unless you have clear evidence that a behavior was intentional, it's better to assume that your students have tried (and will try) to do as you've asked.

To assume the best, then, you might consider using the word *forgot,* as in "Just a minute; a couple of us seem to have forgotten to push in their chairs. Let's try that again." With the benefit of the doubt, your scholars can focus their energy on doing the task right instead of feeling defensive. Further, this approach builds trust, showing your students that you assume they want to do well and believe they can—it's just a matter of nailing some details. Finally, it asserts your faith in your own authority: you struggle to imagine a universe in which students would deliberately be off task in your room. If you show you are constantly on the vigilant watch for the first indications of a wave of disrespect you're convinced is going to come sooner or later, it can suggest that you expect to be disrespected, that you're just waiting for it to happen; this can become a self-fulfilling prophecy. So assuming the best not only builds your relationships but also shows your faith in your own control. You act as though you could barely imagine a universe in which, if a student didn't do what you asked, there wasn't some simple and obvious explanation.

Confused is another good assume-the-best word, as in "Just a minute; some people appear to be confused about the directions, so let me give them again." Another approach is to assume that the error is your own: "Just a minute, class; I must not have been clear: I want you to find every verb in the paragraph working silently on your own. Do that now." This last one is especially useful. It draws students' attention more directly to your belief that only your own lack of clarity would mean lack of instant follow-through by your focused and diligent charges. And of course, it also forces you to contemplate that, in fact, you may not have been all that clear.

Another nice way to assume the best is to use phrases that express minor struggles as "sins of enthusiasm." When you label something a sin of enthusiasm, you suggest that there was a positive intention for a behavior that merely went awry. In a behavioral situation, this might sound like, "Gentlemen, I appreciate your enthusiasm to get to math class, but we need to walk to the door. Let me see you go back and do it the right way." In an academic setting, it might sound like, "I appreciate that you are trying to build complex and expressive sentences, but this one might have a little too much in it for clarity."

Of course you need to be careful not to overuse the assume-the-best approach, and to use it only when motivation is unclear. If a student is clearly exhibiting a case of ill intention—is challenging or testing you, is clearly being disrespectful—don't pretend. In such cases, address the behavior directly with something more substantive, such as a consequence or perhaps a private individual correction. Your direct and decisive action will stand out more if students commonly hear you assuming the best. Even in the toughest cases, however — say, a student has done something very wrong with clear intention — there is often a place for a bit of assuming the best. You might be careful to let your words judge a specific behavior ("That was dishonest") rather than a person ("You are dishonest"). Perhaps even say, "That was dishonest, and I know that's not who you are." A person is always more and better than the moments in which he or she errs, and our language choices give us the opportunity to show in those moments that we still see the best in the people around us.

Allow Plausible Anonymity

You can often allow students the opportunity to strive to reach your expectations in plausible anonymity as long as they are making a good-faith effort. This would mean, as I discuss in Chapter Eleven, beginning by correcting them without using their names when possible. If a few students struggle to follow your directions, consider making your first correction something like "Check yourself to make sure you've done exactly what I've asked." In most cases, this will yield results faster than calling out laggards, unless the laggards are deliberately flouting your authority. Saying to your class, "Wait a minute, Morehouse (or "Tigers" or "fifth grade" or just "guys"), I hear calling out. I need to see you quiet and ready to go!" is better than lecturing the callers-out in front of the class.

As with assuming the best, you can still administer many consequences while preserving anonymity: "Some people didn't manage to follow directions the whole way, so let's try that again." When there is no good-faith effort by students, it may no longer be possible to maintain anonymity, but naming names shouldn't be your first move. Also, it's important to remember both that you can deliver consequences anonymously and that doing so stresses shared responsibility among your students. Some students weren't doing their job, and we all own the consequence.

Narrate the Positive and Build Momentum

Compare the statements two teachers recently made in their respective classrooms:

Teacher 1: *(stopping before giving a direction)* I need three people. Thank you for fixing that, David. Now we're almost ready. Ah, now we're there, so let's get started.

Teacher 2: *(same setting)* I need two people paying attention at this table. Some people don't appear to be listening. *This* table also has some students who are not paying attention to my directions. I'll wait, gentlemen, and if I have to give detentions, I will. If you're going to waste my time, I can waste yours.

In the first teacher's classroom, things appear to be moving in the right direction because the teacher narrates the evidence of his own command, of students doing as they're asked, of things getting better. He calls his students' attention to this fact, thereby normalizing it. He doesn't praise when students do what he asks, but merely acknowledges or describes. He wants them to know he sees it, but he also doesn't want to confuse doing what's expected with doing "great." If I am sitting in this classroom and seek, as most students do, to be normal, I now sense the normality of positive, on-task behavior and will likely choose to do the same.

The second teacher is telling a different story. Things are going wrong and getting worse. He's doing his best to call our attention to the normality of his being ignored and the fact that this generally occurs without consequence. The second teacher is narrating the negative, broadcasting his anxieties and making them even more visible and prominent in shaping students' view of what happens in his classroom. In a sense he's creating a self-fulfilling prophecy: he narrates negative behavior into being.

The first teacher is exemplifying the basic principle of *narrating the positive*. Help students to see the normality of positive and constructive behavior when it happens. Use it after a direction and catch positive responses early as they begin to break out, and assume there will be more of them. Reinforce lightly; too much praise makes you seem surprised. Just describing what you see, without much value judgment added to it ("Marcus is ready to go"), or offering a sincere thank you ("Thanks, Jasmine") is sufficient.

Consider the same two teachers yet again:

Teacher 1: *(after giving a direction for students to draft a thesis statement)* I see those pencils moving *(a pause here to let students work)*. Those ideas are rolling out *(delivered in a stage whisper)*. *(a few seconds later)* Nice. Marcus, Roberto, can't wait to read 'em!

Teacher 2: *(same setting)* Not everyone has begun yet. Do you need me to help you think of a topic, D'Andre? Let me remind you, class, that this is not an optional activity.

In the first class, the teacher is not only narrating the positive but also building momentum — causing students to look forward in anticipation to the next event in class. In the second class, there's only a sense of stultifying lack of action. Perception is often reality, and not only is this teacher narrating the negative, but the droning and carping only distract students from where they're going. Even a correction like "I need to see all those pencils moving. We've got work to do and paragraphs to write" establishes a bit of momentum.

Narrating the positive, though useful, is also extremely vulnerable to misapplication, so here are a couple of key rules:

- Narrate the positive only when there are positives; do not narrate mediocrity.
- Use it as a tool to motivate group behavior as students are deciding whether to work to meet expectations, not as a way to correct individual students after they clearly have not met expectations.

If you narrate positive on-task behavior *during* a countdown, for example, you are describing behavior that has exceeded expectations. You gave students ten seconds to get their binders out and be ready to take notes, but Jabari is ready at five seconds. It's fine to call that out. It's very different to call out Jabari for having his binder out after your countdown has ended. At that point it seems as though you are using Jabari's compliance to plead with others who have not followed through in the time you allotted.

Another common misapplication would be this: You're ready to discuss *Tuck Everlasting*, but Susan is off task, giggling and trying to get Martina's attention. You would not be using positive framing or narrating the positive effectively if you circum-narrated a "praise circle" around Susan: "I see Danni is ready to go. And Elisa. Alexis has her book out." In this case, I recommend that you address Susan directly but positively: "Susan, show me your best, with your notebook out. We've got lots to do." If you use the praise circle, students will be pretty aware of what you're doing and are likely to see your positive reinforcement as contrived and disingenuous. And they're likely to think you're afraid to just address Susan. In fact, Susan may think that as well. And with that your intervention has become highly counterproductive.

Challenge!

Kids love to be challenged, to prove they can do things, to compete, to win. So challenge them: exhort them to prove what they can do by building competition into the day.

Students can be challenged as individuals or, usually better, as groups, and those groups can compete in various ways:

- Against other groups within the class
- Against other groups outside the class (another homeroom)
- Against an impersonal foe (the clock; the test, to prove they're better than it is; their age—"That was acceptable work for seventh graders, but I want to see if we can kick it up to eighth-grade quality")
- Against an abstract standard ("I want to see whether you guys have what it takes!")

Here are some examples to get you started. I'm sure you'll find it fun to think of more:

- "You guys have been doing a great job this week. Let's see if you can take it up a notch."
- "I love the tracking I see. I wonder what happens when I move back here."
- "Let's see if we can write for ten minutes straight without stopping. Ready?!"
- "Ms. Austin said she didn't think you guys could knock out your math tables faster than her class. Let's show 'em what we've got."

Talk Expectations and Aspirations

When you ask students to do something differently or better, you are helping them become the people they wish to be or to achieve enough to have their choice of dreams. You can use the moments where you ask for better to remind them of this. When you ask your students to revise their thesis paragraphs, tell them you want them to write as though "they're in college already" or "that with one more draft, they'll be on their way to college." If they're fourth graders, ask them to try to look as sharp as fifth graders. Or tell them you want to do one more draft of their work and have them "really use the words of a scientist [or historian, and so on] this time around." Tell them you want them to listen to each other like senators and members of Congress. Although it's nice that you're proud of them (and it's certainly wonderful to tell them that), the goal in the end is not for them to please you but for them to leave you behind on a long journey toward a more distant and more important goal. It's useful if your framing connects them to that goal.

See It in Action: Clip 70

In clip 70, Janelle Austin of Rochester Prep demonstrates *Positive Framing*. Notice how effectively she kicks off class by narrating the positive ("Ooooh, look at all those hands") and then narrating it a second time but mixing in a challenge ("I love the track I'm seeing right now. I wonder what happens if I move around the room").

A few moments later, Janelle again narrates the positive—"I see hands up that are ready to read!"—this time mixing in some expectations and aspirations by describing the motivation behind the hands (they want to read) to make it explicit to all students. Notice the response from her students in terms of additional hands that go up.

Later Janelle again narrates the positive ("I really like the enthusiasm that I'm seeing. This column right here is really grabbing hold to it"), this time combining elements of the previous two examples, making the mental state behind a raised hand explicit ("enthusiasm") and throwing down an implicit challenge to the rest of the class by identifying a group that's particularly strong ("This column right here").

Although this clip shows perhaps a dozen examples of *Positive Framing* (it's a montage of short moments from Janelle's class over about half an hour), it is important to note that too much of a good thing can cheapen it. To use a cooking analogy, it's often best to sprinkle in *Positive Framing* regularly, but in small amounts throughout a lesson, rather than dump in a quart all at once. Think "Salt to taste."

PRECISE PRAISE

Make your positive reinforcement strategic. Differentiate between acknowledgment and praise.

59

Whereas *Positive Framing* focuses on how you make constructive or critical feedback feel motivating, caring, and purposeful to the recipient, **Precise Praise** is about managing positive feedback to maximize its focus, benefit, and credibility. As the examples in the table here suggest, positive tone is important with praise, too. Positive feedback can be destructive if the tone is sarcastic, for example.

	Positive Tone	Negative Tone
Corrective Content Response to an insufficient sentence	*Positive Framing* "Good start. Let me see you write it one more time using the words of a scientist!"	Criticism (often nagging or deflating) "You still haven't used the technical terminology."
Positive Content Response to a worthy sentence	*Precise Praise* "Nice. Not only did you use 'mitosis,' but you said the cells divide 'via' mitosis."	Sarcasm "Hey, look. You *can* use scientific vocabulary when you want to."

Avoiding sarcasm is important, but there's a lot more to getting the most out of positive reinforcement than that. Although it might seem like the simplest thing in the world, positive reinforcement helps students more if it's intentional, and you must constantly defend against the potential for it to become empty or disingenuous through overuse. In the end, positive reinforcement is one of the most powerful tools in every classroom, and there's a lot more to it than merely heeding even the oft-repeated advice to praise three times as often as you criticize. To get the most out of positive reinforcement, try these rules of thumb for *Precise Praise.*

Reinforce Actions, Not Traits

Positive reinforcement is clearly about an action that has just occurred: a student does something well, and you tell her she's done a nice job. At its best, positive reinforcement is also about the future. You don't just want a student to feel good about having done something correctly, you want to help her understand how to succeed again the next time. Even more deeply, you want to reinforce a way of thinking about learning that embraces struggle and adversity — relishes it even. Carol Dweck's seminal research on this topic, discussed in her book *Mindset,* has shown that in the long run, people who have a growth mindset far outpace those with a fixed mindset.[1] Her research suggests that the difference is one of the strongest predictors of success. People with a fixed mindset see intelligence and skill as something static. You're smart, or you're not. You're good at something, or you're not. People with a growth mindset see intelligence and skill as fluid. You work hard, and you get better. Smart isn't what you are; it's what you do.

Individuals with a fixed mindset see a challenge and think, "Oh, no. This is going to be difficult." Individuals with a growth mindset see a challenge and think, "Oh, boy. This is going to be difficult."

Dweck finds that praise is central to the development of mindset. If students are praised for traits ("You're smart"), they become risk averse: they worry that if they fail, they won't be smart anymore. If students are praised for actions ("You worked hard, and look!"), they become risk tolerant because they understand that the things within their control — their actions — determine results.[2] It's critical then to praise actions, not traits, and further to carefully identify actions that students can replicate. You are praising them in part to help them see the inside of the success machine: the more actionable the thing you reinforce, the more students can replicate their success. "Go back and look at your draft, Maria. See those cross-outs and rewrites? That's why your final draft is so strong."

Offer Objective-Aligned Praise

Of course, praising (or positively reinforcing) actions means calling out things like hard work and diligence, but some of the best teachers I've observed align their praise to learning objectives. Suppose students are working on including strong transitions in their writing. As you *Circulate* (technique 24) and observe, you specifically reinforce those who have used transitions or, better, those who have gone back and added to or revised their transitions to make them better. Perhaps you even use a *Show Call* (technique 39) to show off their work. "Scholars, look up here. This is Melanie's paper. Look at this paragraph. She included a solid transition, but then she went back and revised it to make it capture the contrast between the paragraphs more clearly. Now her paper really holds together. That's how you do it. Great work, Melanie." Now not only does Melanie know what was behind her success, not only does she understand that success is determined directly by her own actions, but the rest of the class sees it, too.

Differentiate Acknowledgment from Praise

Acknowledgment is what you often use when a student meets your expectations. Praise is what you use when a student exceeds expectations. An acknowledgment merely describes a productive behavior or perhaps thanks a student for doing it, without adding a value judgment and with a modulated tone. Praise adds judgment words like "great" or "fantastic" or the kind of enthusiastic tone which implies that such words might apply. "Thanks for being ready, Marcus" is an acknowledgment; "Fantastic insight, Marcus" is praise. "Marcus is ready" is acknowledgment; "Great job, Marcus" is praise. Distinguishing the two is important, as reversing some of the examples will demonstrate. If I tell Marcus it's fantastic that he's ready for class, I suggest that this is more than I expect from my students. Ironically, in praising this behavior I tell my students that my standards are pretty low and that perhaps I am a bit surprised that Marcus met my expectations. Perhaps they aren't expectations after all. Either way, praising students for merely meeting expectations may reduce the degree to which they do so over the long run. It also makes your praise seem "cheap." When Marcus writes a powerful response to a piece of literature and you call it "fantastic," you will be describing it in a manner on par with how you described coming to class on time, and this may perversely diminish his accomplishment. In the long run, a teacher who continually praises what's expected risks trivializing both the praise and the things she really wishes to label "great," eroding the ability to give meaningful verbal rewards and to identify behavior that is truly worthy of notice. In short, save your praise for when it is truly earned and use acknowledgment freely to reinforce expectations.

Modulate and Vary Your Delivery

Because teachers most often give reinforcement, positive and negative, in a public setting (that is, in a room with twenty-five other people in it), it's critical to be attentive to the degree to which a statement engages others in the room—Is it loud or quiet, public or private? Do others overhear it?

Generally, privacy is beneficial with critical feedback. As I discuss in Chapter Eleven, among other places, whispered or nonverbal reminders assume the best about students: they allow them to self-correct without being called out in public. The private individual correction discussed in technique 53, *Least Invasive Intervention,* is a classic example of this. But what about the reverse? Should praise therefore be loud? Turns out it's not quite that simple. Positive reinforcement works best when it is genuine and memorable. To make it memorable, you'll want it to stand out a bit, keeping its format a bit unpredictable.

A bit of public praise can be powerful—you stop the class to read Shanice's sentence aloud and say to the class, "Now that is how a strong, active verb can give muscles to a sentence!" People can't replicate it if they don't know about it, so that's one clear benefit to public praise. In addition, the fact that you thought Shanice's work was so good that everybody should hear will make your words memorable to her—but they will stand out more if *all* praise isn't public. Part of what's powerful about the public delivery is that it's a bit unexpected, so it can also be powerful to walk up to Shanice and whisper, "Now that is a strong, active verb. It sounds like you wrote this for a college paper." In fact, you capture the greatest benefit by delivering positive reinforcement using an unpredictable variety of settings and volumes.

Among the benefits of private praise is that it often sounds especially genuine to the listener because, implicitly, it *is* private and therefore only about her, as opposed to public praise, which is also about those who hear it and your desire for them to observe and possibly replicate what the student you're praising has done. The power of pulling Shanice aside as she enters the classroom and saying, "I just wanted to tell you that I graded the exams last night, and yours was really outstanding," may be equal to or even greater than your public recognition of her work. When a teacher takes a moment to speak to a student privately, she intimates that what she is going to say to that student is very, very important, and this raises the question: What could be so important? To find that it is a response to your excellent work is both powerful and unexpected for a student.

One further benefit of private praise is that it creates uncertainty and additional privacy around all private interactions, and this is immensely productive. If all of my private and quiet conversations with students were critical (that is, they were all private individual corrections), students might become defensive upon my approach. Further, other students might be motivated to eavesdrop, knowing that listening in might provide them with the juicy details of a classmate's misfortune. Most people can't help but be curious about such things. If, however, my approaching or leaning down to speak quietly with a student is just as likely to be an example of private individual precise praise (PIPP, also discussed in Chapter Eleven), then students will consider the approach with balanced equanimity, and their classmates will have no incentive to eavesdrop. Either message is thus heard more openly by the intended recipient and ignored by those for whom it's not intended.

That said, there are also benefits to loud praise and praise that's semiprivate—that is, deliberately intended to be overheard by others. Praise always walks the line between the benefit of allowing others to overhear what's praiseworthy and thus encouraging them to seek to emulate it, and the benefit of the genuine sincerity of its just being about the recipient. In terms of how to balance these benefits, my sense is that both are more powerful if they aren't entirely predictable and that although socializing and influencing others through praise are beneficial, they're less critical than the long-term benefit of maintaining the credibility and genuineness of praise. I would skew toward privacy a bit more for the most substantive feedback.

Want More? Clips 71, 72, and 73.
Want more *Precise Praise*? Check out Hilary Lewis in clip 71, David Javsicas in clip 72, and Steven Chiger in clip 73.

WARM/STRICT

Be both warm and strict at the same time to send a message of high expectations, caring, and respect.

We're socialized to believe that warmth and strictness are opposites: if you're more of one, it means being less of the other. I don't know where this false conception comes from, but if you choose to believe in it, it will undercut your teaching. The fact is that the degree to which you are warm has no bearing on the degree to which you are strict, and vice versa. You should be neither only warm nor only strict. In fact, as the **Warm/Strict** technique shows, you must be both. You should be caring, funny, warm, concerned, and nurturing—but also strict, by the book, relentless, and sometimes inflexible. Consider the difference between "I care about you, but you still must serve the consequence for being late" and "Because I care about you, you must serve the consequence for being late."

In fact, you should seek not only to be both warm and strict but often to be both *at exactly the same time*. When you are clear, consistent, and firm while being positive, enthusiastic, caring, and thoughtful, you send the message to students that having high expectations is part of caring for and respecting someone. This is a very powerful message. You can make your *Warm/Strict* especially effective in these ways:

- *Explain to students why you're doing what you're doing* (see *Explain Everything*), and how it is designed to help them: "Priya, we don't do that in this classroom because it keeps us from making the most of our learning time." (*Explain Everything* is highlighted in the first edition of this book. The technique helps students understand how what you and they are doing in the classroom will advance them academically. For more information, visit www.teachlikeachampion.com/yourlibrary.)

- *Distinguish between behavior and people.* Say "Your behavior is inconsiderate" rather than "You're inconsiderate."

- *Demonstrate that consequences are temporary*. Show a student that when he has dealt with the consequences of a mistake, it is immediately in the past. Smile and greet him naturally to show that he is starting over with a clean slate. Tell a student, regarding her consequence, "After you're done, I can't wait to have you come back and show us your best." Once you've given a consequence, your next job is to forgive. Remember that you use a consequence so that you won't have to hold the grudge. Get over it quickly.

- *Use warm nonverbal behavior*. Put your arm on a student's shoulder and kindly tell him that you're sorry, but he'll have to redo the homework. You just know he's capable of better. Bend down to a third grader's eye level and explain to her firmly that she won't be allowed to talk to her classmates that way.

In balanced proportions, warm (being positive, enthusiastic, caring, and thoughtful) and strict (being clear, consistent, firm, and unrelenting) together in combination can even help students internalize apparent contradictions and overcome what Jim Collins rightly called, in his seminal book *Built to Last,* "the tyranny of the 'or.'"[3] It reminds students that many of the either-or choices in their lives are false constructs: "I can be hip *and* successful; I can have fun *and* work hard; I can be happy *and* say no to self-indulgence."

EMOTIONAL CONSTANCY

Manage your emotions to consistently promote student learning and achievement.

School is a sort of social laboratory for students; it often is the place where the majority of their interactions with broader society occur, and in it, they experiment with decisions about who they are and what their relationship will be to the people and institutions around them. Our goal as teachers is to do as much as we can to help those experiments turn out successfully, but also to remember the nature of experiments. We want the result to be "Ah, I like it when I work hard and engage fully in learning." But even an experiment that ends perfectly contains some trial and error. A theory is developed ("Perhaps I don't need to do my homework every day"), tested, and evaluated ("OK, I think it is better when I do my homework"). Few long-term experiments proceed without such theory testing. (Think back briefly to your own youth if you wish to document this.)

What that means is that students need to be able to figure out how to interact, and even to make mistakes, without being judged too heavily and without seeing you explode. There may be consequences for some of the trial and error—this is one way, in fact, that consequences are useful, as they allow us to act early and at limited cost to check an experiment gone awry. But if our job is to provide feedback that helps students learn, then maintaining **Emotional Constancy**—lessening the intensity of strong emotion, especially frustration and disappointment—is a key part of that job. This may be contrary to expectations. Some teachers tend to think that strong emotions help them deliver such messages more powerfully: raise your voice, and people will hear you better. But it's worth thinking about the downside of expressing feelings in the classroom. Generally speaking, strong negative emotions by teachers only intensify emotions among students. A student behaves poorly and takes a bit of an attitude; the teacher bristles back; the student reacts to the rising emotion by talking back more strongly, and a small mistake becomes larger. Or a student makes a mistake and a teacher snaps angrily at him while giving a consequence; part of him thinks, *Why is she yelling at me? Does she yell at me more than she yells at others?* He has these thoughts instead of reflecting on the connection between his actions and the consequence. The teacher's emotions insert another variable into the equation and distract him from his own behavior.

Here are some tips for maintaining your *Emotional Constancy*:

- **Walk slowly** as you approach a situation where you have to intervene in behavior. This can give you a few precious seconds to compose yourself and choose your words carefully. It also signals to students that you are calm and composed.

- **Criticize behaviors rather than people.** "That behavior is rude" is a statement about a temporary situation. It's also a statement that, with a bit of tweaking, would allow you to show that you don't think that it's typical of a given student: "It's unlike you to behave rudely. Please fix it immediately." This is better than making a permanent statement about a student: "You are rude." If your goal is trust, it can be a long way back from too many statements of that kind.

- **Take your relationship out of it.** Telling a student you feel disappointed or betrayed by his or her actions, or personalizing your response—for example, "I thought

I could trust you"—makes the interaction about you rather than about a student learning productive and socially responsible behavior. Framing things impersonally diffuses emotion, focuses the conversation on expectations, and allows you to avoid showing students that they can make you upset by taking certain actions—there will be times when that's what they want.

- **Avoid globalizing.** Saying "you always" do X or asking "why are you always doing" Y makes the conversation about events that are no longer within a student's control—and that he or she may not even remember. This makes the issue seem bigger and less focused on a specific action, and can make your correction feel like a "gotcha."

Wrong Answers: Don't Chasten; Don't Excuse

It's also important to think about *Emotional Constancy* in response to academic, not just behavioral, interactions. Strive to avoid chastening wrong answers—for example, "No, we already talked about this. You have to flip the sign, Ruben." And do not make excuses for students who get answers wrong: "Oh, that's OK, Charlise. That was a really hard one." In fact, if wrong answers are truly a normal and healthy part of the learning process, they don't need much narration at all.

It's better, in fact, to avoid spending a lot of time talking about wrongness and get down to the work of fixing errors as quickly as possible. Although many teachers feel obligated to name every answer as right or wrong, spending time making that judgment is usually a step you can skip entirely before getting to work. For example, you could respond to a wrong answer by a student named Noah by saying, "Let's try that again, Noah. What's the first thing we have to do?" or even, "What's the first thing we have to do in solving this kind of problem, Noah?" This second situation is particularly interesting because it remains ambiguous to Noah and his classmates whether the answer was right or wrong as they start reworking the problem. There's a bit of suspense, and they will have to figure it out for themselves. If you do choose to name an answer as wrong, do so quickly and simply ("Not quite") and keep moving. Because getting it wrong is normal in your classroom, you don't have to feel bad about it. In fact, if all students are getting all questions right, the work you're giving them isn't hard enough.

Right Answers: Don't Flatter; Don't Fuss

Praising right answers can have one of two perverse effects on students. As I've mentioned, if you make too much of a fuss, you suggest to students—unless it's patently obvious that an answer really is exceptional—that you're surprised that they got the answer right. And whereas praising students for being "smart" perversely incentivizes them not to take risks, praising students for working hard motivates them to take risks and take on challenges.

Thus, in most cases when a student gets an answer correct, acknowledge that the student has done the work correctly or has worked hard; then move on: "That's right, Noah. Nice work." By not making too big a deal of either right or wrong answers, champion teachers show their students that they expect both. Of course, there will be times when you want to sprinkle in stronger praise ("Such an insightful answer, Carla. Awesome"). Just do so carefully, so that such praise isn't diluted by overuse.

JOY FACTOR

Celebrate the work of learning as you go.

The finest teachers offer up their work with generous servings of energy, passion, enthusiasm, fun, and humor—not necessarily as the antidote to hard work but because those are some of the primary ways that hard work gets done. It turns out that finding joy in the work of learning—the **Joy Factor**—is a key driver of not just a happy classroom but a high-achieving classroom. People work harder when they enjoy working on something—not perhaps in every minute of every day, but when their work is punctuated regularly by moments of exultation and joy. The joy can take a surprisingly wide array of forms, given the diversity of teachers who employ it, and the diversity of moments in which they use it. Joy exists for students in all the forms it exists for adults: loud or quiet, as individuals or as parts of groups small or large. The common theme is for teachers to find a way to let their own genuine version of joy shine through. *Joy Factor* moments can, but need not, involve singing or dancing. For some, quiet passion is the most common form; for others, it's humor; still others prefer high-energy antics.

Of course, *Joy Factor* moments are not ends in themselves. Good *Joy Factor* in the classroom has to be "the servant"—that is, its purpose is to support the day's objective. It should also be something you can quickly turn on and off. There is nothing worse than a *Joy Factor* that ends with a lecture because students couldn't handle the fun without coming off the rails (or more precisely, because the teacher didn't teach the kids how to have fun without coming off the rails). A champion teacher recognizes that his job is not only to share joy but also to teach students to manage the joy.

Here are five categories of *Joy Factor* activities that champion teachers use in their classrooms.

Fun and Games

These activities draw on kids' love for challenges, competition, and play. Examples include having students compete to see who can "roll their numbers" (do repeated addition) the fastest or who can put the midwestern states in alphabetical order by last letter the fastest. Bees (spelling, geography, math), content-based around-the-worlds, relay races, and Jeopardy also fit here. At one school, students play their teachers in math baseball: to hit a single, you have to solve the problem faster than the teacher who's covering first base.

Us (and Them)

Kids, like everybody else, take pleasure in belonging to a group. One of the key functions of cultures—those in the classroom and more broadly—is to make members feel they belong to an important "us," a vibrant and recognizable entity that only some people get to be part of. Through unique language, names, rituals, traditions, songs, and the like, cultures establish "us"-ness. In many cases, the more inscrutable these rituals are to outsiders, the better. The inscrutability reinforces the presence of the "them" that's necessary to any "us."

Champion teachers who use these activities develop markers to remind students that they are insiders in a vibrant culture. At Rochester Prep, for example, history teacher David McBride came up with nicknames for all of his students and used them to call on students in class or to greet them in the hallways. Being greeted with "Mornin', T-bone!" feels more special than being greeted with "Good morning, Taylor." After all, the people who make up nicknames for you are the people who care about you most.

If you've ever watched Chris Berman dish out his hilarious nicknames for athletes on ESPN's *Sportscenter* (Greg "Crocodile" Brock, Vincent "Ultimate" Brisby, Barry "Bananas" Foster), you get the gist of what McBride did, and you also know how fun and funny such a game can be. When you watch Berman, you listen for the nicknames because you're in on the gag. If you have to ask, "Is that guy's nickname really 'Personal'?!" you're not "us."

Developing secret signals and special words is related to this. Teachers hum a secret song—for example, "We're All in This Together"—without the words. The subtext is: *This is our song; we all know the words and why we're singing it; no one on the outside needs to (or can) understand this. We are an "us."* Some classrooms even have development myths: shared stories provided by the teacher to prove a point or teach a lesson—for example, a story about "my cousin Martha, who gives up when the going gets tough" gets referenced before each test: "Don't go pulling a Martha here."

Drama, Song, and Dance

Music, dramatic play, and movement raise spirits and also establish collective identity. This is why they exist within every identifiable ethnic or national culture on earth. The spirit lifting is all the more potent among the youthful, especially those who are chair bound. Acting things out and singing about them can be an exceptional way to remember information.

Drama, song, and dance also power up memory. My seventh-grade Spanish teacher taught us a hokey Spanish version of "Jingle Bells." As much as I would like to forget it, or keep it from occasionally rattling through my unconscious, I cannot. Sometimes I forget my own phone number, but I will always have her Spanish version of "Jingle Bells" imprinted in my memory. To learn a song about something—especially one that's a tad absurd or unusual or one you sing regularly—is, for many, to know it for life. The power of song or dance can be harnessed to instill and reinforce any specific knowledge or belief. Imagine if I had a song rattling through my head telling me when to use *ser* and *estar*, the two forms of the Spanish verb "to be," instead of "Jingle Bells." My Spanish would be forever improved (not to mention various awkward moments in my life avoided). To sing is to remember.

Humor

Laughter is one of the base conditions of happiness and fulfillment, making it a powerful tool for building an environment of happy and fulfilled students and teachers. A tool this powerful should be used. Although I can't give you much of a recipe, I can give you an example.

One champion teacher taught his kids a song for dozens of formulas in sixth-grade math. After they had made a habit of learning these, he told them he was working on a song to help them determine the circumference of a circle, but that what he had so far was too uncool to use. He sang a quick snippet of what he was working on: "$2\pi r$, my Lord" to the tune of "Kumbaya." His kids laughed, and he admonished them: "Don't tell anyone about that. There is no song for circumference. Is there a song for circumference? No, we've got no song for that!" Whenever studying circumference, he would ask the class: "Remind me, do we have a song for circumference?" After the class resoundingly answered, "No!" he would hum "Kumbaya" to himself, repeating a reliably funny inside joke that made it all but impossible not to remember the formula for circumference.

Suspense and Surprise

Routines are powerful drivers of efficiency and predictability. They also make occasional variations all the more fun, silly, surprising, and inspiring. If harnessed judiciously, the unexpected can be powerful. The two together make the classroom an adventure, no matter what the content.

An art teacher I know takes the samples she ordinarily shows her class—a landscape, a still life, a traditional carving—and puts them in a wrapped box like a present. She begins her lesson by saying, "I've got something in the mystery box that's really cool and exciting. I can't wait to show you because it's an example of what we're talking about today." Several times during a typical mini-lesson, she'll build the anticipation by walking over to the box and then "deciding" to wait, or by peeking in and hamming up her reaction: "Ouch, it *bit* me!" By the time she shows the kids what's in the box, they can hardly wait to see it. A math teacher does something similar with his number rolling songs: "Oh, man, you're gonna love the last verse. It's really funny. And if we keep working, we'll get to hear it soon."

A third-grade teacher occasionally hands out her vocabulary words in sealed envelopes, one to each child. "Don't open them yet," she'll whisper. "Not until I say." And by the time she does, there's little in the world each of those would trade for the opportunity to see what their word is.

Want More? Clips 74 and 75.   Want more *Joy Factor*? Check out Roberto de Leòn in clip 74 and Taylor Delhagen in clip 75.

CONCLUSION: THE SYNERGY OF THE FIVE PRINCIPLES

The techniques described in the last few chapters rely on all five principles of classroom culture—discipline, management, control, influence, and engagement—to varying degrees. Some require more of one than another, but because the synergy of the five makes each one stronger, an effective teacher ideally leverages all five. Teachers who use only one or two will ultimately struggle to build a vibrant classroom culture. A teacher who uses control but not discipline, for example, will produce students who never learn to do things on their own and always need firm directives to act. A classroom in which the teacher does not have control will overuse the consequences, accustom students to the consequences, and erode their effectiveness in his own and other classes. A teacher who engages and influences without control and management will build a vibrant but inefficient culture that allows some students to opt out of learning. And a teacher who doesn't discipline will not adequately prepare students to succeed once they leave the microcosm of their classroom, because they will not have had sufficient practice in or knowledge of how to sustain successful habits of scholarship.

Champion classrooms all find their own unique balance of the five principles. One doesn't work well without the others, and building a productive classroom culture involves finding the right mix for your style and your students.

Reflection and Practice

1. The following statements are negatively framed. Try rewriting them to make them positively framed.

   ◦ "We're not going to have another day like yesterday, are we, Jason?"

   ◦ "Just a minute, Jane. Absolutely no one is giving you their full attention except Noah and Beth."

   ◦ "I need the tapping to stop."

   ◦ "I've asked you twice to stop slouching, Jasmine!"

2. Consider what specific behavioral traits (hard work, listening to peers, checking or rereading their work, or reading carefully, for example) you most want students to demonstrate in your classroom. For each, write three or four scripts you might use to reinforce them using *Precise Praise*.

3. Make a list of the situations in which you are most vulnerable to losing your *Emotional Constancy*. Script a calm and poised comment you might make to the other people involved that also reminds you to remain constant.

4. Brainstorm ten ways you could bring more *Joy Factor* into your classroom. Use at least four of the types of joy described in the chapter.

Precise Praise planning tool. Use this handy template to plan praise that sets students up to succeed.

Positive Framing examples and nonexamples. Knowing what *Positive Framing* looks and sounds like is just as important as knowing what it doesn't. Refer to this list of examples and nonexamples to get clear on both.

LIVE IN THE NOW

Example: Show me your eyes, fifth grade.

Nonexample: Fifth grade, some of us are looking out the window.

Example: Third grade, Tina is describing the setting. Our eyes should be on the speaker.

ASSUME THE BEST

Example: Just a minute, fourth grade. A couple of people were so excited to write about Roald Dahl that they went ahead before I told them to start.

Nonexample: Fourth grade, none of us should be trying to sneak ahead of the rest of the class.

Example: A couple of people forgot our rules about tracking, Tina. Give them a second before you start.

Nonexample: Tina, please wait to answer until Jeffrey decides to join us.

ALLOW PLAUSIBLE ANONYMITY

Example: Fourth grade, check yourself to make sure you're in your best SLANT with your notes page in front of you.

Nonexample: Jason, I want to see you in SLANT with your notes page in front of you.

NARRATE THE POSITIVE/BUILD MOMENTUM

Example (narrating the positive): I see lots of hands. The left side of the room is really with it!

Example (narrating the positive + building momentum): I see five, six, seven hands. Now ten hands ready to start reading *Hatchet*!

Nonexample (narrating weaknesses): I'm seeing the same few hands. A lot of you are not participating, and it's going to show up in your participation grades.

CHALLENGE!

Example: You've got the idea, but let me hear you use the word *elusive* in your answer. Can you do it?!

Example: The sixth-grade girls are killing it, boys. Can you keep the pace?

TALK ASPIRATION

Example (to a fourth grader): Good, Juan. Now let me hear you make it a fifth-grade answer by using the word *product*.

Example: Can you answer that in the words of a scientist [historian/writer/musician]?

Example: When you get to college [or middle school or high school], your thesis statements are going to blow your professors away. Let's see if we can do this one more time so you guys really take the campus by storm.

The End Is Still the Beginning

Artists, athletes, musicians, surgeons, and performers of a thousand other varieties achieve greatness only by attending to the details of their technique. Their constant refinement of it perpetually renews their passion for the craft and allows them to seek the grail of better performance, expression that sings, the ability to make the greatest possible difference. This focus on technique and its constant refinement is also the path to excellence for teachers. It's the reason I wasn't 100 percent satisfied with the first edition of *Teach Like a Champion,* and it's the reason my team and I will keep growing and adapting.

When I suggest that teaching is an art, I mean that education is difficult, requires finesse and discretion in its application and craftsmanship, and takes careful and attentive development of technique to master it. That path is different for each teacher. The techniques developed by champion teachers and described in this book can belong to any teacher who embraces the concept of constant, attentive refinement of techniques. Only that approach, coupled, I hope, with at least some of the wisdom of the teachers whom I studied to write this book, will be sufficient to change the equation of opportunity in our schools and close the achievement gap at scale. Adapted, refined, improved, and, perhaps in a few cases, ignored because not everything in this book can be right for you, these techniques can transform your classroom.

A colleague of mine, Ben Markovitz, founder of New Orleans's Collegiate Academies, achieved exemplary first-year results with high school students who had not previously been successful. This school has made extensive and focused use of the techniques in this book, with dozens of staff meetings and training sessions. Yet when Ben was recently asked how he ensures that his teachers use this material, he observed that he doesn't. He manages his teachers for results and provides these techniques to get them there. They are free to use them or not. All of them do, with an energy and vigor I am humbled by, but Ben insists that the tools here are a means to results, not an end in themselves. I wholeheartedly agree with him. In fact, I would like that fact to distinguish this book from so many others: it starts with and is justified by the results it helps teachers achieve, not by its fealty to some ideological principle. The result to aim for is not the loyal adoption of these techniques for their own sake, but their application in the service of increased student achievement. Too many ideas, even good ones, go bad when they become an end and not a means.

The techniques I've written about were derived from observing outstanding teachers at work. But more exciting than that is the way this book has changed over the years as I have been writing it. During that time, it has evolved from an informal document within Uncommon Schools, to a more explicit guide to instruction that I shared with colleagues and offered trainings on, to the first version of *Teach Like a Champion*, to the older, wiser, and more thoughtful book you've now read. It has changed and evolved and gained the depth that I hope has made it worthy of your time. What gives this book its depth and focus is the unrelenting application of the ideas by remarkable teachers. What I first wrote was a skeleton of what is now in place; the techniques that appeared in it were described in insufficient terms and short aspirational paragraphs. Only when other teachers applied them, adapted them, and improved them (and let me videotape them in action) did the truly useful parts of this book emerge. With more and more application and adaptation, good techniques continue to evolve into better ones, and new ones emerge where they may have before gone unnoticed. In short, what's good here is good only because of the process of constantly refining and adapting techniques in the relentless and restless drive for excellence. That observation seems a fitting one with which to end.

Notes

Introduction

1. Jason Felch, "No Gold Stars for Excellent L.A. Teaching," *Los Angeles Times,* August 29, 2010, http://www.latimes.com/local/teachers-investigation/la-me-adv-good-teacher-20100828-story.html#page=1.

Chapter 2

1. Tim Heemsoth and Aiso Heinze, "The Impact of Incorrect Examples on Learning Fractions: A Field Experiment with 6th Grade Students," *Instructional Science,* December 2013, http://link.springer.com/article/10.1007%2Fs11251-013-9302-5#page-1.

Part 2

1. Renaissance Learning, *What Kids Are Reading: The Book-Reading Habits of Students in American Schools,* 2014, http://doc.renlearn.com/KMNet/R004101202GH426A.pdf, 31.

Chapter 3

1. Carol Dweck, *Mindset: The New Psychology of Success* (New York: Random House, 2006).

2. Basil Bernstein, *Class, Codes and Control. Volume 1: Theoretical Studies Towards a Sociology of Language* (New York: Routledge, 1971); Basil Bernstein (Ed.), *Class, Codes and Control. Volume 2: Applied Studies Towards a Sociology of Language* (New York: Routledge, 1973).

Chapter 7

1. Daniel T. Willingham, *Why Don't Students Like School* (San Francisco: Jossey-Bass, 2009); Daisy Christodoulou, *Seven Myths About Education* (New York: Routledge, 2014), 39; E. D. Hirsch Jr., *The Knowledge Deficit* (New York: Houghton Mifflin, 2006).

2. Christodoulou, *Seven Myths,* 39.

Chapter 12

1. Carol Dweck, *Mindset: The New Psychology of Success* (New York: Random House, 2006).

2. Ibid.

3. Jim Collins and Jerry I. Porra, *Built to Last: Successful Habits of Visionary Companies* (New York: HarperBusiness, 2004).

Index

Questioning *(continued)*
for self-report, 29–34; in Stretch It technique, 108–116; students' strategies in response to, 104–106; think versus participation ratio in, 239–244; in Turn and Talk technique, 335; wait time for, 31, 244–249. *See also specific techniques*
Quick Is King criterion, 362–363, 364

R

Radar/Be Seen Looking technique, 387–392
Ragin, K., 166, 167, 272
Rally killers, 219–220
Ratio: approaches to, 19; Cold Call technique and, 250–251, 254; content and, 242–244; definition of, 19, 234, 313; discussion to build, 311–339; examples of, 240; goal of, 240, 313; illustration of, 241; knowledge and, 19; questioning to build, 237–276; rigor and, 234–235, 242; think versus participation, 234–235, 240–244; video clips of, 241–242; writing to build, 279–308
Rationale, for lessons, 133
Ratray, R., 186, 187, 315, 317, 321, 326, 328, 365–366
Read-discuss-write sequence, 304
Reading: Begin with the End technique for, 134–137; Call and Response technique with, 267; hurdle rate for, 180–181; importance of, 171, 180–181; independent versus public, 171–172; "I/We/You" lessons in, 160; model program for, 180–181; Name the Steps technique for, 167–168; routines for, 364–365; of students' work by teachers, 185. *See also* Independent reading
Reading aloud: challenges of, 172–173; Control the Game technique for, 175–180; guidelines for, 175–179; importance of, 174–175; versus independent reading, 171–172; in Show Call technique, 298; of students' writing, 302–303; by teachers, 178–179
Read-write-discuss sequence, 306, 307
Real think time, 247–248
Recognition, 291, 292, 293
Reflection and idea generation (RIG): in Brighten Lines technique, 230; in Change the Pace technique, 205–206, 207; Everybody Writes technique for, 282–285; while writing, 302; before writing, 282–284
Register, 413
Reinforcing actions, not traits, 434–435

Reinforcing behaviors, 217; Call and Response technique for, 263; in Door to Do Now technique, 358
Reinforcing skills, 262–263
Reject Self-Report technique, 27; description of, 30–34; example of, 42–43; self-monitoring in, 32–34
Relay Graduate School of Education, xxii
Reliability, 37–39
Renaissance Learning, 84
Repeat Call and Response technique, 263
Repeating answers, 272
Repetition: Call and Response technique for, 263; consequences versus corrections and, 411; guidelines for, 189; importance of, 188; in "I/We/You" lessons, 159
Report Call and Response technique, 263
Research, 7
Restricted code, 120
Reteaching, 63–64
Reuler, M., 41, 55, 59–60, 144, 260–261
Reveals, 298
Review Call and Response technique, 263
Review Now technique, 358–360
Reviewing lessons: Call and Response technique for, 262–263; Do Now technique for, 162; Exit Ticket technique for, 191; Pepper technique for, 275; Strong Start technique for, 357, 358–360
Revising writing: versus editing writing, 295–296; examples of, 296; Show Call technique for, 290–299
Rewards, 344
Rhetorical questions, 30–32
Rickey, B., 132
Riffle, A., 224–225
RIG. *See* Reflection and idea generation
Right answers. *See* Correct answers
Right Is Right technique, 87, 103–107
Rigor. *See* Academic ethos
Rigor collapse, 272–274
Riordan, L., 192
Risk tolerant, 435
Risk-taking, 71–72
"The Road Not Taken" (Frost), 78–79
Rochester Prep, 400, 433
Roller Coaster, 379
Rollout speeches, 252
Rounding up, 101

How to Access the Video Contents

If you purchased a new copy of this book, you will find a unique single-use access code for the video clips inside the back cover. Go to www.teachlikeachampion.com/your library and click "Activate New PIN." Follow the instructions on the website for registration and access the video clips.

To find *Your Library* directly from www.teachlikeachampion.com, click *Resources*.

If you purchased an ebook version, or any other version, please go to www.teachlikea champion.com/yourlibrary and click on the link to answer a few verification questions. Once registered, you will receive an email with your access code and instructions for signing in.

CUSTOMER CARE

If you have trouble with your PIN, or any other issues related to the video contents access, contact Wiley Product Technical Support at http://support.wiley.com. You can also call the Wiley Product Technical Support phone number at 800-762-2974. Outside the United States, call 317-572-3994.

SYSTEM REQUIREMENTS

PC or Mac with a DVD drive running any operating system with an HTML-compatible web browser.

USING THE DVD WITH WINDOWS

To view the content on the DVD, follow these steps:

1. Insert the DVD into your computer's DVD drive.

2. Select Home.html from the list of files.

3. Read through the license agreement by clicking the License link near the top-right of the interface.

4. The interface appears. Simply select the material you want to view.

IN CASE OF TROUBLE

If you experience difficulty using the DVD, please follow these steps:

1. Make sure your hardware and systems configurations conform to the systems requirements noted under "System Requirements" above.

2. Review the installation procedure for your type of hardware and operating system. It is possible to reinstall the software if necessary.

CUSTOMER CARE

If you have trouble with the DVD, please call the Wiley Product Technical Support phone number at (800) 762-2974. Outside the United States, call 1(317) 572-3994. You can also contact Wiley Product Technical Support at http://support.wiley.com. John Wiley & Sons will provide technical support only for installation and other general quality control items. For technical support of the applications themselves, consult the program's vendor or author.

Before calling or writing, please have the following information available:

- Type of computer and operating system
- Any error messages displayed
- Complete description of the problem

It is best if you are sitting at your computer when making the call.

More Ways to Engage and Learn with Teach Like a Champion

COMPANION WEBSITE

We invite you to join the Teach Like a Champion community on our website, www.teachlikeachampion.com, to continue the conversation through Doug's blog, free downloadable resources, and our community forum.

TRAIN-THE-TRAINER WORKSHOPS

Uncommon School's train-the-trainer workshops prepare instructional leaders to deliver high-quality training on *Teach Like a Champion* and *Practice Perfect* techniques. Participants learn both the fundamentals and subtleties of *Teach Like a Champion* techniques through analysis of video clips, case studies, and live modeling, then apply their emerging understanding immediately in carefully designed practice.

PLUG AND PLAYS

Designed specifically for busy instructional leaders, Uncommon School's Plug and Plays provide all needed materials for two- to three-hour teacher training sessions on specific *Teach Like a Champion* techniques. Each Plug and Play provides leaders with ready-made PowerPoint presentations with embedded videos of the technique in action, facilitator notes, practice activities, and handouts. View a sample on teachlikeachampion.com.